Elias Nason

Songs for social and public worship

Elias Nason

Songs for social and public worship

ISBN/EAN: 9783337265250

Printed in Europe, USA, Canada, Australia, Japan

Cover: Foto ©Thomas Meinert / pixelio.de

More available books at **www.hansebooks.com**

SONGS

FOR

Social and Public Worship,

EDITED AND COMPILED BY A NEW ENGLAND PASTOR.

"IT IS GOOD TO SING PRAISES UNTO OUR GOD, FOR IT IS PLEASANT, AND PRAISE
IS COMELY."

BOSTON:

HENRY HOYT, No. 9 CORNHILL,

1863.

PREFACE.

This Manual of Sacred Song has been prepared with express reference to the wants of the people worshipping God, either in the Sanctuary, the Prayer and Conference Meeting, or at the Family Altar.

The Editor has had access to extensive materials in Poetry as in Music; and has endeavored to bring together into this single work the most valuable Hymns and Tunes of ancient and of modern times:—hymns rich in sentiment, as well as dignified in style;—music pleasing in melody, as well as correct in harmony;—such, indeed, as the people love to sing.

The Hymns will be found to cover the leading doctrines of Christianity, and to meet the various conditions of our Christian life and culture, and the different occasions, whether public, social, civil, private, sad or joyous, on which men meet to worship God. An unusual number of them, however, refer to Christ and his offices, and to the Holy Spirit as manifest in the work of missions, in revivals, and the extension of the Church. It is hoped, therefore, that the work will prove eminently devotional, inspiring and PRACTICAL.

New times develope new phases of religious experience; new plans, new fields of action; and these, in turn, demand new hymns, new music, new life, new beauty.

Good compilations in psalmody and hymnology are now before the churches; but the churches are advancing, and thus, are needing better ones; they CALL for them; and hence, this fresh effort to select the "best from the best," in order to meet this want so naturally, so deeply felt;—so earnestly expressed.

Much of the matter in this book, including Hymns as well as Tunes is copyright property, and is here printed by consent of the proprietors, without whose authority it cannot be published.

To such persons as have, by furnishing hymns or tunes, aided him, in his laborious undertaking, the Editor would tender his most cordial thanks; and would, also, express the hope that this new contribution to the music of the house of God may serve to bring many voices to ascribe still loftier praises to Immanuel's name below, and also help to swell

> "—— the hymn that rolls its tide
> Along the realms of upper day."

BOSTON, DEC. 1, 1862.

SONGS

FOR

SOCIAL AND PUBLIC WORSHIP.

HAMBURG. L. M. Dr. Lowell Mason.
From Gregorian Tone I.

Great God, we sing that mighty hand, By which sup-por-ted still we stand;

The opening year thy mer - cy shows; Let mer-cy crown it till it close.

2 By day, by night, at home, abroad;
Still are we guarded by our God ;
By His incessant bounty fed,
By His unerring counsel led.

3 With grateful hearts the past we own ;
The future all to us unknown,
We to Thy guardian care commit,
And, peaceful, leave before Thy feet.

4 In scenes exalted or depressed,
Thou art our Joy, and Thou our Rest ;
Thy goodness all our hopes shall raise,
Adored through all our changing days.

2

1 My God, my King, Thy various praise
Shall fill the remnant of my days;

Thy grace employ my humble tongue,
Till death and glory raise the song.

2 The wings of every hour shall bear
Some thankful tribute to Thine ear ;
And every setting sun shall see
New works of beauty done for Thee.

3 Let distant times and nations raise
The long succession of Thy praise,
And unborn ages make my song
The joy and labor of their tongue.

4 But who can speak Thy wondrous deeds ?
Thy greatness all our thoughts exceeds ;
Vast and unsearchable Thy ways ;
Vast and immortal be Thy praise.

DUKE STREET. L. M.

ALLEGRETTO.   J. HATTON.

O, for a sweet, in-spir-ing ray, To an-i-mate our fee-ble strains,

From the bright realms of endless day; The blissful realms where Jesus reigns.

2 There low before His glorious throne,
Adoring saints and angels fall ;
And, with delightful worship, own
His smile their bliss, their heaven, their all.

3 Immortal glories crown His head.
While tuneful hallelujahs rise,
And love, and joy, and triumph spread
Through all the assemblies of the skies.

4 He smiles, and seraphs tune their songs
To boundless rapture while they gaze ;
Ten thousand thousand joyful tongues
Resound His everlasting praise.

4

1 O THE immense, the amazing height,
The boundless grandeur of our God,
Who treads the worlds beneath His feet,
And sways the nations with His nod !

2 Let noise and flame confound the skies,
And drown the spacious realms below,
Yet will we sing the Thunderer's praise,
And send our loud hosannas through.

3 Celestial King ! Thy blazing power
Kindles our hearts to flaming joys ;
We shout to hear Thy thunders roar,
And echo to our Father's voice.

4 Thus shall the God our Saviour come,
And lightnings round His chariot play;
Ye lightnings, fly to make Him room !
Ye glorious storms, prepare His way !

5

1 JEHOVAH reigns ; He dwells in light,
Girded with majesty and might :
The world, created by His hands,
Still on its first foundation stands.

2 But ere this spacious world was made,
Or had its first foundations laid,
Thy throne eternal ages stood,
Thyself the ever-living God.

3 Like floods the angry nations rise,
And aim their rage against the skies ;
Vain floods, that aim their rage so high !
At Thy rebuke the billows die.

4 Forever shall Thy throne endure ;
Thy promise stands forever sure ;
And everlasting holiness
Becomes the dwellings of Thy grace.

6

1 HAIL to the Prince of life and peace,
Who holds the keys of death and hell ;
The spacious world unseen is His,
And sovereign power becomes Him
well.

2 In shame and torment once He died ;
But now He lives forevermore ;
Bow down, ye saints, around His seat,
And all ye angel bands adore.

3 So live forever, glorious Lord,
To crush Thy foes and guard Thy friends,
While all Thy chosen tribes rejoice
That Thy dominion never ends.

4 Forever reign, victorious King ;
Wide through the earth Thy name be
known ;
And call my longing soul to sing
Sublimer anthems near Thy Throne.

ESPRESSIVO.

Who shall ascend Thy heav'nly place, Great God, and dwell be-fore Thy face?

The man who minds re-li-gion now, And humbly walks with God below.

2 Whose hands are pure, whose heart is clean;
Whose lips still speak the thing they mean;
No slanders dwell upon his tongue;
He hates to do his neighbor wrong.

3 He loves his enemies, and prays
For those who curse him to his face;
And does to all men still the same
That he would hope or wish from them,

4 Yet when his holiest works are done,
His soul depends on grace alone:
This is the man Thy face shall see,
And dwell forever, Lord, with Thee.

8

1 KINDRED in Christ, for His dear sake,
A hearty welcome here receive;
May we together now partake
The joys which only He can give.

2 May He, by whose kind care we meet,
Send His good Spirit from above,
Make our communications sweet,
And cause our hearts to burn with love.

3 Forgotten be each worldly theme,
When Christians see each other thus;
We only wish to speak of Him
Who lived, and died, and reigns for us.

4 Thus, as the moments pass away,
We'll love, and wonder, and adore,
And hasten on the glorious day
When we shall meet to part no more.

9

1 WHAT was thy crime, my dearest Lord:
By earth, by heaven Thou hast been tried,
And guilty found of too much love ;—
Jesus, our Love, is crucified !

2 O break, O break hard heart of mine !
Thy weak self-love and guilty pride
His Pilate and his Judas were :—
Jesus, our Love, is crucified !

3 Come take thy stand beneath the cross,
And let the blood from out that side
Fall gently on thee, drop by drop :—
Jesus, our Love, is crucified !

4 A broken heart, a font of tears,—
Ask, and they will not be denied ;
A broken heart love's cradle is ;—
Jesus, our Love, is crucified !

10

1 O CHILDHOOD'S innocence ! The voice
Of thy deep wisdom is my choice !
Who hath thy love is truly wise
And precious in our Father's eyes.

2 Spirit of childhood ! loved of God,
By Jesus' spirit now bestowed ;
How often have I longed for thee ;
O Jesus, form thyself in me !

3 And help me to become a child
While yet on earth, meek, undefiled,
That I may find God always near,
And Paradise around me here.

11

1 Why should we start and fear to die ?
What timorous worms we mortals are!
Death is the gate of endless joy,
And yet we dread to enter there.

2 Jesus can make a dying bed,
Feel soft as downy pillows are,
While on his breast I lean my head,
And breathe my life out sweetly there.

MODERATO.   DR. LOWELL MASON.

Thus far the Lord has led me on; Thus far His pow'r prolongs my days;

And ev-'ry evening shall make known Some fresh me-mo-rial of his grace.

2 Much of my time has run to waste,
  And I perhaps am near my home ;
  But he forgives my follies past ;
  He gives me strength for days to come.

3 I lay my body down to sleep ;
  Peace is the pillow for my head ;
  While well-appointed angels keep
  Their watchful stations round my bed.

4 Thus, when the night of death shall come,
  My flesh shall rest beneath the ground, ·
  And wait Thy voice to rouse my tomb,
  With sweet salvation in the sound.

13

1 FAR from my thoughts, vain world! begone,
  Let my religious hours alone :
  Fain would mine eyes my Saviour see ;
  I wait a visit, Lord ! from Thee.

2 My heart grows warm with holy fire,
  And kindles with a pure desire ;
  Come, my dear Jesus ! from above,
  And feed my soul with heavenly love.

3 Blest Saviour ! what delicious fare—
  How sweet Thine entertainments are !
  Never did angels taste above
  Redeeming grace and dying love.

4 Hail, great Immanuel, all-divine !
  In Thee Thy Father's glories shine :
  Thou brightest, sweetest, fairest One,
  That eyes have seen or angels known ?

14

1 GOD in His earthly temple lays
  Foundations for His heavenly praise ;
  He likes the tents of Jacob well,
  But still in Zion loves to dwell.

2 His mercy visits every house
  That pays its night and morning vows ;
  But makes a more delightful stay
  Where churches meet to praise and pray.

3 When God makes up His last account
  Of natives in His holy mount,
  'Twill be an honor to appear
  As one new-born or nourished there.

15

1 WAIT, O my soul, thy Maker's will ;
  Tumultuous passions, all be still ;
  Nor let a murmuring thought arise ;
  His ways are just, His counsels wise.

2 He in the thickest darkness dwells,
  Performs His work, the cause conceals ;
  But, though His methods are unknown,
  Judgment and truth support His throne.

3 In heaven, and earth, and air, and seas,
  He executes His firm decrees ;
  And by His saints it stands confessed,
  That what He does is ever best.

4 Wait, then, my soul, submissive wait,
  Prostrate before His awful seat ;
  And 'mid the terrors of His rod,
  Trust in a wise and gracious God.

16

1 LORD, now we part in Thy blest name,
  In which we here together came ;
  Grant us our few remaining days
  To work Thy will and spread Thy praise.

DOLCE. THOS. HASTINGS.

From ev - ery stormy wind that blows, From ev - ery swelling tide of woes,

There is a calm, a sure re-treat; 'Tis found be-neath the mer - cy seat.

2 There is a place where Jesus sheds
  The oil of gladness on our heads,
  A place than all besides more sweet ;
  It is the blood-bought mercy-seat.

3 There is a scene where spirits blend,
  Where friend holds fellowship with friend,
  Though sundered far, by faith we meet
  Around one common mercy-seat.

4 There, there on eagle wings we soar,
  And sense and sin seem all no more ;
  And heaven comes down our souls to greet,
  And glory crowns the mercy-seat

5 Oh! let my hand forget her skill,
  My tongue be silent, cold and still,
  This bounding heart forget to beat,
  If I forget the mercy-seat.

18

1 RETURN, my roving heart, return,
  And chase these shadowy forms no more;
  Seek out some solitude to mourn,
  And thy forsaken God implore.

2 Wisdom and pleasure dwell at home ;
  Retired and silent seek them there ;
  True conquest is ourselves to o'ercome,
  True strength, to break the tempter's
    snare.

3 And Thou, my God, whose piercing eye
  Distinct surveys each deep recess,
  In these abstracted hours draw nigh,
  And with Thy presence fill the place.

4 Through all the mazes of my heart,
  My search let heavenly wisdom guide,
  And still its radiant beams impart,
  Till all be searched and purified.

5 Then with the visits of thy love,
  Do Thou mine inmost spirit cheer ;
  Till every grace shall join to prove
  That God has fix'd his dwelling here.

19

1 WHEN silent steal across my soul
  Remembrances of broken vows,
  And tears, almost beyond control,
  Flow, as my guilty spirit bows,—

2 'Tis then I've caught the Saviour's eye,
  Viewing with looks of injured love,
  A soul, for whom He deigned to die,
  Inconstant and ungrateful prove.

3 O, had he not so kindly glanced,
  My weeping soul in anguish cries,
  I could have borne that searching look,
  But now I yield ; my spirit dies.

4 No more on promises I'll rest,
  Nor resolutions vainly made,
  But leaning on my Saviour's breast,
  Implore His Spirit's gracious aid.

20

1 My soul before Thee prostrate lies ;
  To Thee, her Source, my spirit flies ;
  My wants I mourn, my chains I see ;
  O, let Thy presence set me free.

2 Lost and undone, for aid I cry ;
  In Thy death Saviour, let me die ; [pain,
  Grieved with Thy grief, pained with Thy
  Ne'er may I feel self-love again.

3 In life's short day, let me yet more
  Of Thy enlivening power implore ;
  My mind must deeper sink in Thee,
  My foot stand firm, from wandering free.

ALLEGRO.

Ex-alt-ed Prince of life, we own The roy-al honors of thy throne,

'Tis fixed by God's al-mighty hand, And seraphs bow at Thy command.

2 Exalted Saviour, we confess
The sovereign triumphs of thy grace,
Where beams of gentle radiance shine,
And temper majesty divine.

3 Wide Thy resistless sceptre sway,
Till all Thine enemies obey ;
Wide may Thy cross its virtues prove,
And conquer millions by its love.

22

1 GOD of the morning, at whose voice
The cheerful sun makes haste to rise,
And like a giant doth rejoice
To run his journey through the skies !

2 From the fair chambers of the east,
The circuit of his race begins,
And, without weariness or rest,
Round the whole earth he flies, and shines.

3 O, like the sun may I fulfil
The appointed duties of the day ;
With ready mind, and active will,
March on and keep my heavenly way.

23

1 ARISE, in all Thy splendor, Lord ;
Let power attend Thy gracious word ;
Unveil the beauties of Thy face,
And show the glories of Thy grace.

2 Send forth Thy messengers of peace ;
Make Satan's reign and empire cease ;
Let Thy salvation, Lord, be known,
That all the world Thy power may own.

1 Ye sons of men, with joy record
The various wonders of the Lord ;
And let His power and goodness sound
Through all your tribes, the earth around.

2 Let the high heavens your songs invite,
Those spacious fields of brilliant light,
Where sun, and moon, and planets roll,
And stars, that glow from pole to pole.

3 But O, that brighter world above,
Where lives and reigns Incarnate Love !
God's only Son, in flesh arrayed,
For man a bleeding victim made.

4 Thither, my soul, with rapture soar ;
There, in the land of praise, adore ;
This theme demands an angel's lay,
Demands an undeclining day.

25

1 THE starry firmament on high,
And all the glories of the sky,
Yet shine not to Thy praise, O Lord,
So brightly as Thy written word.

2 The hopes that holy word supplies,
Its truths divine and precepts wise,
In each a heavenly beam I see,
And every beam conducts to Thee·

3 Almighty Lord, the sun shall fail,
The moon forget her nightly tale,
And deepest silence hush on high
The radiant chorus of the sky.

4 But fixed for everlasting years,
Unmoved amid the wreck of spheres,
Thy word shall shine in cloudless day,
When heaven and earth have passed away

ALLEGRETTO. W. B. BRADBURY.

Fa-ther of mer-cies, God of love! O, hear a hum-ble suppliant's cry;

Bend from thy lof-ty seat a-bove, Thy throne of glorious maj-es-ty.

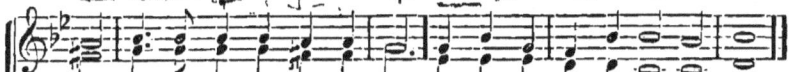

O, deign to hear my mournful voice, And bid my drooping heart re-joice.

2 I urge no merits of my own,
No worth to claim thy gracious smile :
No : when I bow before Thy throne,
Dare to converse with God awhile,
Thy name, blest Jesus, is my plea—
Dearest and sweetest name to me !

3 Father of mercies, God of love !
Then hear thy humble suppliant's cry ;
Bend from thy lofty seat above,
Thy throne of glorious majesty :
One pard'ning word can make me whole,
And soothe the anguish of my soul.

27

1 WEARY of wandering from my God,
And now made willing to return,
I hear, and bow beneath the rod ;
For Thee, not without hope, I mourn :
I have an Advocate above,
A Friend before the throne of love.

2 O Jesus, full of truth and grace !
More full of grace than I of sin ;
Yet once again I seek Thy face,
Open Thine arms and take me in ;
And freely my backslidings heal
And love the faithless sinner still.

3 Thou know'st the way to bring me back,
My fallen spirit to restore ;
Oh, for Thy truth and mercy's sake,
Forgive, and bid me sin no more !
The ruins of my soul repair,
And make my heart a house of prayer.

28

1 ETERNAL Father ! throned above,
Thou fountain of redeeming love !
Eternal Word ? who left Thy throne
For man's rebellion to atone ;
Eternal Spirit, who dost give
That grace whereby our spirits live:
Thou God of our salvation, be
Eternal praises paid to thee !

12

STACCATO.

VENUA.

My soul with sacred joy survey The glories of the lat-ter day; Its dawn al-

ready seems begun—Sure earnest of the rising sun, Sure earnest of the rising sun.

2 " Behold the way," ye heralds cry;
Spare not, but lift your voices high;
Convey the sound from shore to shore,
And bid the captive sigh no more.

3 " Behold the way to Zion's hill,
Where Israel's God delights to dwell;
He fixes there His lofty throne,
And calls the sacred place His own."

4 The north gives up; the south no more
Keeps back her consecrated store;
From east to west the message runs,
And either India yields her sons.

5 Auspicious dawn, thy rising ray
With joy I view, and hail the day;
Thou Sun, arise, supremely bright,
And shed abroad Thy holy light.

30

1 WHAT equal honors shall we bring
To thee, O Lord our God, the Lamb,
When all the notes that angels sing
Are far inferior to Thy name?

2 Worthy is He who once was slain,
The Prince of Peace, who groaned and
died;
Worthy to rise, and live and reign
At his almighty Father's side.

3 Blessings forever on the Lamb,
Who bore the curse for wretched men:
Let angels sound the sacred name,
And every creature say, Amen!

1 THE heavens declare thy glory, Lord;
In every star Thy wisdom shines;
But when our eyes behold Thy word,
We read Thy name in fairer lines.

2 The rolling sun, the changing light,
And nights and days, Thy power confess;
But the blest volume Thou hast writ
Reveals Thy justice and Thy grace.

3 Sun, moon, and stars convey Thy praise
Round the whole earth, and never stand;
So when Thy truth began its race,
It touched and glanced on every land.

4 Nor shall Thy spreading Gospel rest,
Till thro' the world Thy truth has run;
Till Christ has all the nation's blessed,
That see the light or feel the sun.

5. Great Sun of Righteousness, arise;
Bless the dark world with heavenly light;
Thy Gospel makes the simple wise;
Thy laws are pure, Thy judgments right.

32

1 AWAKE, arise, and hail the morn,
For unto us a Saviour 's born;
See how the angels wing their way,
To usher in the glorious day.

2 Hark ! what sweet music, what a song,
Sounds from the bright, celestial throng !
Sweet song, whose melting sounds impart
Joy to each raptured, listening heart.

3 Come, join the angels in the sky:
Glory to God, who reigns on high;
Let peace and love on earth abound,
While time revolves, and years roll round.

ERNAN. L. M.

PIACEVOLE.

DR. LOWELL MASON.

How blest the sacred tie that binds, In union sweet, ac - cord-ing minds!

How swift the heavenly course they run Whose hearts, whose hopes, whose faith are one.

33

2 To each the soul of each how dear!
What jealous love! what holy fear!
How doth the generous flame within
Refine from earth and cleanse from sin!

3 Their streaming eyes together flow
For human guilt and mortal woe;
Their ardent prayers together rise,
Like mingling flames in sacrifice.

4 Together oft they seek the place
Where God reveals His awful face;
How high, how strong their raptures swell,
There's none but kindred souls can tell.

5. Nor shall the glowing flame expire,
When nature droops her sickening fire;
Then shall they meet in realms above—
A heaven of joy because of love.

34

1 LORD, how secure and blest are they
Who feel the joys of pardon'd sin;
Should storms of wrath shake earth and sea,
Their minds have heavenly peace within.

2 The day glides swiftly o'er their heads,
Made up of innocence and love;
And soft and silent as the shades,
Their nightly minutes gently move.

3 Quick as their thoughts their joys come on,
But fly not half so swift away;
Their souls are ever bright as noon,
And calm as summer evenings be.

4 How oft they look to th' heavenly hills,
Where groves of living pleasure grow;
And longing hopes and cheerful smiles,
Sit undisturbed upon their brow.

5 They scorn to seek earth's golden toys,
But spend the day, and share the night,
In numb'ring o'er the richer joys
That heaven prepares for their delight.

35

1 WHAT various hindrances we meet
In coming to a mercy-seat;
Yet who that knows the worth of prayer,
But wishes to be often there.

2 Prayer makes the darken'd cloud withdraw;
Prayer climbs the ladder Jacob saw;
Gives exercise to faith and love;
Brings every blessing from above.

3 Restraining prayer we cease to fight;
Prayer keeps the Christian's armor bright;
And Satan trembles when he sees
The weakest saint upon his knees.

36

1 THOUGH I have grieved Thy Spirit, Lord,
Thy help and comfort still afford;
And let a wretch come near Thy throne
To plead the merits of Thy Son.

2 A broken heart, my God, my King,
Is all the sacrifice I bring;
Thou God of grace, wilt Thou despise
A broken heart for sacrifice?

3 My soul lies humbled in the dust,
And owns the dreadful sentence just:
Look down, O Lord, with pitying eye,
And save a soul condemned to die.

O hap-py day that fixed my choice On Thee, my Saviour and my God!
Well may this glowing heart re-joice And tell its raptures all a-broad.

Hap-py day, hap-py day, when Je-sus washed my sins a-way.

FINE.

Close with second strain.

He taught me how to watch and pray, And live re-joic-ing ev-ery day.

37

2 O happy bond, that seals my vows,
To Him who merits all my love!
Let cheerful anthems fill His house,
While to the sacred shrine I move.

3 'Tis done, the great transaction's done;
I am my Lord's, and He is mine;
He drew me, and I followed on,
Charmed to confess the voice divine.

4 Now rest, my long-divided heart;
Fixed on this blissful centre, rest;
With ashes who would grudge to part,
When called on angels' bread to feast?

5 High heaven, that heard the solemn vow,
That vow renewed shall daily hear,
Till in life's latest hour I bow,
And bless in death a bond so dear.

38

1 Our Lord is risen from the dead,
Our Jesus is gone up on high;
The pow'rs of hell are captive led—
Dragg'd to the portals of the sky.

2 There his triumphal chariot waits,
And angels chant the solemn lay:
"Lift up your heads, ye heav'nly gates!
Ye everlasting doors give way!"

3 Loose all your bars of massy light,
And wide unfold the radiant scene;
He claims those mansions as his right—
Receive the King of Glory in.

4 "Who is this King of Glory, who?"
The Lord, that all his foes o'ercame;
The world, sin, death, and hell o'erthrew,
And Jesus is the conqu'ror's name.

5 Lo! his triumphal chariot waits,
And angels chant the solemn lay;
"Lift up your heads, ye heav'nly gates!
Ye everlasting doors, give way!"

6 "Who is the King of Glory, who?"
The Lord of boundless pow'r possest;
The King of saints and angels too,
God over all, forever blest!

by Dr. Lowell Mason.

Moderato.

God is the re-fuge of His saints, When storms of sharp distress in-vade;

Ere we can of-fer our complaints, Be-hold Him present with His aid.

39

2 Let mountains from their seats be hurled,
Down to the deep and buried there;
Convulsions shake the solid world;
Our faith shall never yield to fear.

3 There is a stream, whose gentle flow
Supplies the city of our God; .
Life, love, and joy, still gliding through,
And watering our divine abode.

4. That sacred stream, thy holy word,
Our grief allays, our fear controls;
Sweet peace thy promises afford,
And give new strength to fainting souls.

40

1 Come, let our voices join to raise
A sacred song of solemn praise:
God is a sovereign King; rehearse
His honors in exalted verse.

2 Come, let our souls address the Lord,
Who framed our natures with his word:
He is our Shepherd, we the sheep
His mercy chose, his pastures keep.

3 Come, let us hear his voice to day;
The counsels of his love obey;
Nor let our hardened hearts renew
The sins,and plagues that Israel knew.

4 Seize the kind promise while it waits,
And march to Zion's heavenly gates;
Believe, and take the promised rest;
Obey, and be forever blest.

41

1 Here at thy cross, my dying God,
I lay my soul beneath Thy love,
Beneath the droppings of Thy blood,
Jesus! nor shall it e'er remove.

2 Should worlds conspire to drive me hence,
Moveless and firm this heart should lie:
Resolved, (for that's my last defense,)
If I must perish—here to die.

3 Yes, I'm secure beneath Thy blood,
And all my foes shall lose their aim:
Hosanna to my dying God:
And my best honors to His name.

42

1 From deep distress and troubled thoughts
To thee, my God, I raised my cries;
If Thou severely mark my faults,
No flesh can stand before thine eyes.

2 But Thou hast built Thy throne of grace,
Free to dispense Thy pardons there,
That sinners may approach Thy face,
And hope and love, as well as fear.

3 As the benighted pilgrims wait,
And long and wish for break of day,
So waits my soul before Thy gate:
When will my God His face display?

4 My trust is fixed upon Thy word,
Nor shall I trust Thy word in vain;
Let mourning souls address the Lord,
And find relief from all their pain.

Jesus, thy blood and righteousness My beauty are, my glorious dress;

'Mid flaming worlds in these arrayed, With joy shall I lift up my head.

2 When from the dust of death I rise,
To take my mansion in the skies,
E'en then shall this be all my plea :
" Jesus hath lived, and died for me."

3 Bold shall I stand in that great day;
For who aught to my charge will lay?
While, through Thy blood, absolved I am
From sin's tremendous curse and shame.

4 O, let the dead now hear Thy voice;
Bid, Lord, Thy banished ones rejoice;
Their beauty this, their glorious dress,
Jesus, the Lord, our Righteousness.

44

1 WHERE two or three, with sweet accord,
Obedient to their sovereign Lord,
Meet to recount his acts of grace,
And offer solemn prayer and praise,—

2 " There," says the Saviour, " will I be
Amid this little company;
To them unveil My smiling face,
And shed My glories round the place."

3 We meet at Thy command, dear Lord,
Relying on Thy faithful word;
Now send the Spirit from above,
And fill our hearts with heavenly love.

45

1 LORD, fill me with an humble fear;
My utter helplessness reveal;
Satan and sin are always near,—
Thee may I always nearer feel.

2 O that to Thee my constant mind
Might with an even flame aspire;
Pride in its earliest motions find,
And mark the risings of desire.

3 O that my tender soul might fly
The first abhorr'd approach of ill;
Quick as the apple of an eye,
The slightest touch of sin to feel.

4 Till thou anew my soul create,
Still may I strive, and watch, and pray
Humbly and confidently wait,
And long to see the perfect day.

46

1 To honor those who gave us birth,
To cheer their age, to feel their worth,
Is God's command to human kind,
And owned by every grateful mind.

2 Think of her toil, her anxious care,
Who formed thy lisping lips to prayer;
To win for God the yielding soul,
And all its ardent thoughts control.

3 Nor keep from memory's glad review
The fears which all the father knew,
The joy that marked his thankful gaze
As virtue crowned maturer days.

4 God of our life, each parent guard,
And death's sad hour, O, long retard;
Be theirs each joy that gilds the past,
And heaven our mutual home at last.

DOLCE.

W. B. BRADBURY.

Asleep in Je-sus! Blessed sleep! From which none ever wakes to weep;

A calm and un-dis-turbed re - pose, Un-brok-en by the dread of foes.

47

2 Asleep in Jesus ! Peaceful rest !
Whose waking is supremely blessed;
No fear, no woes, shall dim that hour
Which manifests the Saviour's power.

3 Asleep in Jesus! Time nor space
Debars this precious hiding place ;
On Indian plains or Laplaud's snows
Believers find the same repose.

4 Asleep in Jesus ! O, how sweet
To be for such a slumber meet!
With holy confidence to sing
That Death has lost his renomed sting.

5 Asleep in Jesus ! O, for me
May such a blissful refuge be;
Securely shall my ashes lie,
And wait the summons from on high.

48

1 O Thou that hear'st when sinners cry,
Though all my crimes before Thee lie,
Behold them not with angry look,
But blot their memory from Thy book.

2 Create my nature pure within,
And form my soul averse to sin;
Let Thy good spirit ne'er depart,
Nor hide Thy presence from my heart.

3 I cannot live without Thy light,
Cast out and banished from Thy sight;
Thine holy joys, my God, restore,
And guard me that I fall no more.

4 Though I have grieved Thy Spirit, Lord,
His help and comfort still afford,
And let a wretch come near Thy throne,
To plead the merits of Thy Son.

49

1 Sweet is the scene when Christians die,
When sinks a righteous soul to rest;
How mildly beams the closing eye,
How gently heaves the expiring breast !

2 So fades a summer cloud away,
So sinks the gale when storms are o'er,
So gently shuts the eye of day,
So dies a wave along the shore.

3 Triumphant smiles the victor's brow,
Fanned by some guardian angel's wing;
Where is, O grave, thy victory now,
And where, insidious death, thy sting ?

50

1 Dear Lord, and shall Thy Spirit rest
In such a wretched heart as mine ?
Unworthy dwelling ! glorious Guest !
Favor astonishing ! divine !

2 When sin prevails, and gloomy fear,
And hope almost expires in night,
Lord can Thy Spirit then be here,
Great Spring of comfort, life, and light?

3 Sure the best Comforter is nigh;
'Tis He sustains my fainting heart ;
Else would my hopes forever die,
And every cheering ray depart.

4 Let Thy kind Spirit in my heart
Forever dwell, O God of love,
And light and heavenly peace impart,
Sweet earnest of the joys above.

EFFINGHAM. L. M.

ALLEGRETTO.   ENGLISH.

At anchor, laid remote from home, Toiling I cry sweet Spi-rit come;

Ce-les-tial Breeze, no longer stay, But swell my sails and speed my way.

51

2 " Fain would I mount, fain would I glow,
   And loose my cable from below;
   But I can only spread my sail; [gale."
   Thou, Thou must breathe the auspicious

52

1 WHY sinks my weak, desponding mind?
   Why heaves my heart the anxious sigh?
   Can sovereign Goodness be unkind?
   Am I not safe if God is nigh?

2 He holds all nature in His hand;
   That gracious hand on which I live,
   Does life, and time, and death command,
   And has immortal joys to give.

3 Forgive my doubts, O gracious Lord,
   And ease the sorrows of my breast;
   Speak to my heart the healing word,
   That Thou art mine, and I am blest.

53

1 I spread my sins before the Lord,
   And all my secret faults confess;
   Thy gospel speaks a pardoning word,
   Thy Holy Spirit seals the grace.

2 How safe beneath Thy wings I lie,
   When days grow dark, and storms appear!
   And when I walk, Thy watchful eye
   Shall guide me safe from every snare.

54

1 O THOU, to whom in ancient time,
   The Psalmist's sacred harp was strung,
   Whom kings adored in songs sublime,
   And prophets praised with glowing
   tongue:—

2 Not now on Zion's height alone,
   The favored worshipper may dwell,
   Nor where, at sultry noon Thy Son,
   Sat weary by the patriarch's well.

3 From every place below the skies,
   The grateful song, the fervent prayer,
   The incense of the heart, may rise
   To heaven, and find acceptance there.

4 O Thou, to whom in ancient time,
   The holy prophet's harp was strung;
   To Thee, at last, in every clime,
   Shall temples rise, and praise be sung.

55

1 GOD of my life, through all my days
   My grateful powers shall sound thy praise;
   My song shall wake with opening light,
   And cheer the dark and silent night.

2 When anxious cares would break my rest,
   And griefs would tear my throbbing breast,
   Thy tuneful praises raised on high,
   Shall check the murmur and the sigh.

3 When death o'er nature shall prevail,
   And all the powers of language fail,
   Joy thro' my swimming eyes shall break,
   And mean the thanks I cannot speak.

4 But O, when that last conflict's o'er,
   And I am chain'd to earth no more,
   With what glad accents shall I rise
   To join the music of the skies.

Dr. Boyce

I know that my Redeemer lives; What comfort this sweet sentence gives!

He lives, he lives, who once was dead, He lives, my ev - er - liv - ing Head.

56

2 He lives, triumphant from the grave;
He lives, eternally to save;
He lives, all glorious in the sky;
He lives, exalted there on high.

3 He lives, to silence all my fears;
He lives, to stoop and wipe my tears;
He lives, to calm my troubled heart;
He lives, all blessings to impart.

4 He lives, and grants me daily breath;
He lives, and I shall conquer death;
He lives, my mansion to prepare;
He lives, to bring me safely there.

5 He lives; all glory to his name;
He lives, my Jesus still the same;
O, the sweet joy this sentence gives,
" I know that my Redeemer lives!"

57

1 GRANT the abundance of the sea
May be converted, Lord, to Thee,
And every sailor on the shore
Return to God, to roam no more.

2 The nations, then, with joy shall hail
The Bethel flag in every sail;
And every ship that plows the sea
A gospel messenger shall be.

3 Hasten, O Lord, that glorious day,
When seamen shall Thy word obey,
And safe from port to port be driven,
To point a ruined world to heaven.

58

1 ' TIS finished! So the Saviour cried,
And meekly bowed his head and died!
' Tis finished! yes, the race is run,
The battle fought, the victory won.

2 ' Tis finished! Let the joyful sound
Be heard thro' all the nations round:
' Tis finished! Let the echo fly,
Thro' heaven and hell, thro' earth and sky.

59

1 LORD, now we part in Thy blest name,
In which we here together came;
Grant us our few remaining days
To work Thy will, and spread Thy praise.

2 Teach us in life and death to bless
The Lord our Strength and Righteousness;
And grant us all to meet above;
Then shall we better sing Thy love.

60

1 WORTHY the Lamb of boundless sway,
In earth or heaven the Lord of all;
Let all the powers of earth obey,
And low before his foot-stool fall.

2 Higher, still higher, swell the strain;
Creation's voice, the note prolong;
Jesus, the Lamb, shall ever reign;
Let hallelujahs crown the song.

61

To Father, Son, and Holy Ghost,
The God whom heaven and earth adore,
Be glory as it was of old,
Is now, and shall be evermore.

My God, per-mit me not to be A stranger to my-self and Thee;

A-mid a thousand tho'ts I rove, For-get-ful of my high-est love.

2 Why should my passions mix with earth,
And thus'debase my heavenly birth?
Why should I cleave to things below,
And let my God, my Saviour go.

3 Call me away from flesh and sense;
One sovereign word can draw me thence;
I would obey the voice divine,
And all inferior joys resign.

4 Be earth, with all her scenes withdrawn;
Let noise and vanity be gone:
In secret silence of the mind
My heaven, and there my God, I find.

63

1 ALL scenes alike engaging prove
To souls impressed with sacred love!
Where'er they dwell they dwell with Thee,
In heaven, in earth, or on the sea.

2 To me remains nor place nor time;
My country is in every clime:
I can be calm and free from care
On any shore, since God is there.

3 While place we seek, or place we shun,
The soul finds happiness in none;
But with a God to guide my way,
'Tis equal joy to go or stay.

4 Could I be cast where Thou art not,
That were, indeed, a dreadful lot,
But regions none remote I call,
Secure of finding God in all.

64

1 When we, our wearied limbs to rest,
Sat down by proud Euphrates' stream,
We wept with doleful thoughts oppress'd,
And Zion was our mournful theme.

2 Our harps that when with joy we sung,
Were wont their tuneful thoughts to bear,
With silent strings neglected hung
On willow trees that withered there.

3 How shall we tune our voice to sing,
Or touch our harps with skillful hands?
Shall hymns of joy, to God our King,
Be sung by slaves in foreign lands?

4 O Salem! our once happy seat,
When I of thee forgetful prove,
Let then my trembling hand forget
The tuneful strings with art to move.

65

1 OH! from the world's vile slavery,
Almighty Saviour, set me free;
And as my treasure is above,
Be there my thoughts and there my love.

2 But oft, alas! too well I know,
My thoughts, my love are fixed below;
In every lifeless prayer I find
The heart unmoved, the absent mind.

3 Oh! what that frozen heart can move,
Which melts not at a Saviour's love?
What can that sluggish spirit raise,
Which will not sing the Saviour's praise?

4 Lord, draw my best affections hence,
Above this world of sin and sense;
Cause them to soar beyond the skies,
And rest not, till to Thee they rise.

ANIMATO. C. ZEUNER.

Ye Christian heralds, go proclaim Sal-va-tion in Im-man-uel's name;

To dis-tant climes the tidings bear, And plant the Rose of Sha-ron there.

66

2 He'll shield you with a wall of fire,
With flaming zeal your breasts inspire,
Bid raging winds their fury cease,
And hush the tempest into peace.

3 And when your labors all are o'er,
Then we shall meet to part no more;
Meet with the blood-bought throng, to fall,
And crown our Jesus Lord of all.

67

1 TRIUMPHANT Zion, lift thy head,
From dust, and darkness, and the dead;
Though humbled long, awake at length,
And gird thee with thy Saviour's strength.

2 Put all thy beauteous garments on,
And let thy various charms be known:
The world thy glories shall confess,
Decked in the robes of righteousness.

3 No more shall foes unclean invade,
And fill thy hallowed walls with dread;
No more shall hell's insulting host
Their victory and thy sorrows boast.

4 God from on high,.thy groans will hear;
His hands thy ruins shall repair;
Reared and adorned by love divine,
Thy towers and thy battlements shall shine.

68

1 AWAKE, our souls, away, our fears;
Let every trembling thought be gone;
Awake, and run the heavenly race,
And put a cheerful courage on.

2 True, 'tis a strait and thorny road,
And mortal spirits tire and faint;
But they forget the mighty God,
That feeds the strength of every saint.

3 The mighty God, whose matchless power
Is ever new and ever young,
And firm endures, while endless years
Their everlasting circles run.

4 From Thee, the overflowing Spring,
Our souls shall drink a fresh supply
While such as trust their native strength
Shall melt away, and droop and die.

5 Swift as an eagle cuts the air,
We mount aloft to Thine abode;
On wings of love our souls shall fly,
Nor tire amid the heavenly road.

69

1 O LORD of Hosts! Almighty King!
Behold the sacrifice we bring!
To every arm Thy strength impart,
Thy spirit shed through every heart.

2 Be Thou a pillared flame to show
The midnight snare, the silent foe;
And when the battle thunders loud,
Still guide us in its moving cloud.

3 God of all Nations! Sovereign Lord!
In thy dread name we draw the sword,
We lift the starry flag on high,
That fills with light our stormy sky.

4 From treason's rent, from murder's stain,
Guard Thou its folds till Peace shall reign:
Till fort and field, till shore and sea
Join our loud anthem, Praise to Thee!

OLIVE'S BROW. L. M.

Dolce.

Wм. B. Bradbury.

'Tis midnight, and, on Olive's brow, The star is dimm'd that late-ly shone;

'Tis midnight; in the garden, now, The suff'ring Saviour prays a - lone.

70

2 'Tis midnight; and from all removed,
The Saviour wrestles lone with fears;
E'en that disciple whom He loved
Heeds not his Master's grief and tears.

3 'Tis midnight; and, for others' guilt,
The Man of sorrows weeps in blood;
Yet He, who hath in anguish knelt,
Is not forsaken by His God.

4 'Tis midnight,—and from ether-plains
Is borne the song that angels know:
Unheard by mortals are the strains
That sweetly soothe the Saviour's woe.

71

1 At Thy command our dearest Lord,
Here we attend Thy dying feast;
Thy blood, like wine, adorns Thy board,
And Thine own flesh feeds every guest.

2 Our faith adores Thy bleeding love,
And trusts for life in One that died;
We hope for heavenly crowns above
From a Redeemer crucified.

3 Let the vain world pronounce it shame,
And fling their scandals on the cause;
We come to boast our Saviour's name,
And make our triumphs in His cross.

4 With joy we tell the scoffing age,
He that was dead has left His tomb;
He lives above their utmost rage,
And we are waiting till He come.

72

1 Come, gracious Spirit, heavenly Dove,
With light and comfort from above;
Be Thou our guardian, Thou our guide;
O'er every thought and step preside.

2 The light of truth to us display,
And make us know and choose Thy way;
Plant holy fear in ever heart,
That we from God may ne'er depart.

3 Lead us to holiness—the road
That we must take to dwell with God;
Lead us to Christ—the living Way,
Nor let us from His pastures stray.

73

1 Lord, am I Thine, entirely Thine,
Purchased and saved by blood divine?
With full consent Thine I would be,
And own Thy sovereign right in me.

2 Thee my new Master now I call,
And consecrate to Thee my all;
Lord, let me live and die to Thee,
Be Thine through all eternity.

74

1 No more, my God, I boast no more
Of all the duties I have done;
I quit the hopes I held before,
To trust the merits of Thy Son.

2 Now, for the love I bear His name,
What was my gain, I count my loss;
My former pride I call my shame,
And nail my glory to His cross.

3 Yes, and I must and will esteem
All things but loss for Jesus' sake;
Oh, may my soul be found in Him,
And of His righteousness partake!

MODERATO.   DR. LOWELL MASON.

Lord, let Thy goodness lead our land, Still saved by Thine al - mighty hand,

The tri - bute of its love to bring To Thee, our Saviour and our King.

75

2 Let every public temple raise
Triumphant songs of holy praise;
Let every peaceful, private home
A temple, Lord, to Thee become.

3 Still be it our supreme delight
To walk as in Thy glorious sight;
Still in Thy precepts and Thy fear,
Till life's last hour, to persevere.

76

1 O God, beneath Thy guiding hand,
Our exiled fathers crossed the sea;
And when they trod the wintry strand,
With prayer and psalm they worshipped
Thee.

2 Laws, freedom, truth, and faith in God,
Came with those exiles o'er the waves;
And where their pilgrim feet have trod,
The God they trusted guards their graves.

3 And here Thy name, O God of love,
Their children's children shall adore,
Till these eternal hills remove,
And spring adorns the earth no more.

77

1 Lord, visit Thy forsaken race;
Back to Thy fold the wand'rers bring; .
Teach them to seek Thy slighted grace,
And hail in Christ their promised King.

2 That veil of darkness rend in twain,
Which hides their Shiloh's glorious light;
That sever'd olive-branch again
Firm to its parent-stock unite.

3 Hail, glorious day—expected long! [pour;
When Jew and Greek one prayer shall
With eager foot one temple throng,—
With grateful praise one God adore.

78

1 Behold, the heathen waits to know
The joy the Gospel will bestow;
The exiled captive to receive
The freedom Jesus has to give.

2 Come, let us, with a grateful heart,
In this blest labor share a part;
Our prayers and suff'rings gladly bring
To aid the triumphs of our King.

3 Our hearts exult in songs of praise,
That we have seen these latter days,
When our Redeemer shall be known,
Where Satan long hath held his throne.

4 Where'er His hand hath spread the skies,
Sweet incense to His name shall rise;
And slave and freeman, Greek and Jew,
By sovereign grace be formed anew.

79

1 Assembled in our school once more,
O Lord, Thy blessing we implore;
We meet to read, and sing, and pray,
Be with us, then, through this Thy day.

2 Our fervent prayer to Thee ascends   .
For parents, teachers, foes and friends;
And when we in Thy house appear,
Help us to worship in Thy fear.

3 When we on earth shall meet no more,
May we above to glory soar,
And praise Thee in more lofty strains,
Where one eternal Sabbath reigns.

N. D. GOULD. 1833.

What tho' the wild waves rage around ? What tho' the waters o'er thee roll ?

Why should'st thou tremble at the sound? They touch not the im - mor - tal soul.

80

2 Silent and slow they glide away;
Steady and strong their current flows,—
Lost in eternity's wide sea,
The boundless gulf from whence it flows.

3 Great Source of wisdom, teach my heart
To know the price of every hour,
That time may bear me on to joys
Beyond its measure and its power.

81

1 THERE is none other name than Thine,
Jehovah Jesus! Name divine!
On which to rest for sins forgiven—
For peace with God, for hope of Heaven.

2 There is none other name than Thine,
When cares, and fears, and griefs, are mine,
That, with a gracious power, can heal
Each care, and fear, and grief I feel.

3 There is none other name than Thine,
When called my spirit to resign,
To bear me through that latest strife,
And ev'n in death to be my life.

82

1 THE Lord of life this table spread
With His own flesh and dying blood;
We on the rich provision feed,
And taste the wine, and bless our God.

2 Let sinful sweets be all forgot,
And earth grow less in our esteem,
Christ and His love fill every thought,
And faith and hope be fixed on Him.

3 While He is absent from our sight,
'Tis to prepare our souls a place,
That we may dwell in heavenly light,
And live forever near his face.

83

1 ALMIGHTY Maker of my frame,
Teach me the measure of my days;
Teach me to know how frail I am,
And spend the remnant to Thy praise.

2 My days are shorter than a span;
A little point my life appears;
How frail at best is dying man!
How vain are all his hopes and fears!

3 Vain his ambition, noise, and show;
Vain are the cares which rack his mind;
He heaps up treasures mixed with woe,
And dies, and leaves them all behind.

4 O, be a nobler portion mine;
My God, I bow before Thy throne;
Earth's fleeting treasures I resign,
And fix my hope on Thee alone.

84

1 WHEREFORE should man, frail child of clay,
Who, from the cradle to the shroud,
Lives but the insect of a day,
O, why should mortal man be proud?

2 His brightest visions just appear,
Then vanish, and no more are found;
The stateliest pile his pride can rear,
A breath may level with the ground.

3 By doubt perplexed, in error lost
With trembling step he seeks his way;
How vain of wisdom's gift the boast!
Of reason's lamp how faint the ray!

4 God of my life, Father divine,
Give me a meek and lowly mind;
In modest worth, O, let me shine,
And peace in humble virtue find.

MODERATO. THOS. TALLIS, 1650.

Glo - ry to Thee, my God, this night, For all the blessings of the light;

Keep me, O keep me, King of kings, Beneath Thine own al - migh - ty wings.

85

2 Forgive me, Lord, for Thy dear Son,
The ills that I this day have done;
That with the world, myself, and Thee,
I, ere I sleep, at peace may be.

3 Let my blest Guardian, while I sleep,
His watchful station near me keep;
My heart with love celestial fill,
And guard me from the approach of ill.

4 Teach me to live, that I may dread
The grave as little as my bed;
Teach me to die, that so I may
Rise glorious in the latter day.

86

1 Awake, my soul, and with the sun
Thy daily stage of duty run;
Shake off dull sloth, and joyful rise
To pay thy morning sacrifice.

2 Wake, and lift up thyself, my heart,
And with the angels bear thy part,
Who all night long unwearied sing
High praises to the eternal King.

3 Lord, I to Thee my vows renew;
Scatter my sins as morning dew;
Guard my first springs of thought and will,
And with Thyself my spirit fill.

4 Direct, control, suggest, this day,
All I design or do, or say,
That all my powers, with true delight,
In Thy sole glory may unite.

87

1 Great God, whose universal sway
The known and unknown worlds obey,
Now give the kingdom to Thy Son,
Extend His power, exalt His throne.

2 As rain on meadows newly mown,
So shall He send His influence down;
His grace on fainting souls distils,
Like heavenly dew on thirsty hills.

3 The heathen lands, that lie beneath
The shades of overspreading death,
Revive at His first dawning light,
And deserts blossom at the sight.

4 The saints shall flourish in His days,
Dressed in the robes of joy and praise;
Peace, like a river, from His throne
Shall flow to nations yet unknown.

88

1 Who can describe the joys that rise
Through all the courts of paradise,
To see a prodigal return,
To see an heir of glory born?

2 With joy the Father doth approve
The fruit of His eternal love;
The Son with joy looks down and sees
The purchase of His agonies.

3 The Spirit takes delight to view
The holy soul He formed anew;
And saints and angels join to sing
The growing empire of their King

LEGATO.   GERMAN.

My God, ac-cept my ear-ly vows, Like morning in-cense in Thy house;

And let my nightly worship rise, Sweet as the eve-ning sac-ri-fice.

89

2 Watch o'er my lips, and guard them, Lord,
From every rash and heedless word;
Nor let my feet incline to tread
The guilty path where sinners lead.

3 O, may the righteous, when I stray,
Smite and reprove my wandering way,
Their gentle words, like ointment shed.
Shall never bruise, but cheer my head.

4 When I behold them pressed with grief,
I'll cry to heaven for their relief;
And by my warm petitions prove
How much I prize their faithful love.

90

1 O HOLY, holy, holy Lord,
Bright in Thy deeds and in Thy name,
Forever be Thy name adored,
Thy glories let the world proclaim!

2 O Jesus Lamb, once crucified
To take our load of sins away,
Thine be the hymn that rolls the tide
Along the realms of upper day?

3 O Holy Spirit from above
In streams of light and glory given,
Thou source of extacy and love
Thy praises ring through earth and
heaven!

4 O God triune! to Thee we owe
Our every thought, our every song;
And ever may Thy praises flow
From saint and seraph's burning tongue!

91

1 MAY not the sovereign Lord on high
Dispense His favors as He will;
Choose some to life, while others die,
And yet be just and gracious still?

2 Shall man reply against the Lord,
And call His Maker's ways unjust,
The thunder of whose dreadful word
Can crush a thousand worlds to dust?

3 But, O my soul, if truth so bright
Should dazzle and confound thy sight,
Yet still His written will obey,
And wait the great decisive day.

4 Then shall He make His justice known,
And the whole world before His throne,
With joy or terror, shall confess
The glory of His righteousness.

92

1 Lo! God is here! let us adore,
And own how dreadful is this place!
Let all within us feel His power,
And silent bow before His face.

2 Lo, God is here! Him day and night
The united choirs of angels sing;
To Him, enthroned above all height,
Heaven's hosts their noblest praises
bring.

3 Being of beings! may our praise
Thy courts with grateful fragrance fill;
Still may we stand before Thy face;
Still hear and do Thy sovereign will.

From a theme by M. LUTHER.

DANIEL READ.

Broad is the road that leads to death, And thousands walk to-geth-er there;

But wisdom shows a narrow path, With here and there a tra-vel-ler.

93

2 " Deny thyself, and take thy cross,"
   Is the Redeemer's great command ;
   Nature must count her gold but dross,
   If she would gain this heavenly land.

3 Lord, let not all my hopes be vain;
   Create my heart entirely new—
   Which hypocrites could ne'er attain,
   Which false apostates never knew.

94

1 WITH broken heart and contrite sigh,
   A trembling sinner, Lord, I cry ;
   Thy pardoning grace is rich and free :
   O God, be merciful to me !

2 Far off I stand with tearful eyes,
   Nor dare uplift them to the skies;
   But Thou dost all my anguish see :
   O God, be merciful to me !

3 Nor alms, nor deeds that I have done,
   Can for a single sin atone;
   To Calvary alone I flee :
   O God, be merciful to me !

4 And when redeemed from sin and hell,
   With all the ransomed throng I dwell,
   My raptured song shall ever be,
   God has been merciful to me !

95

1 Snow pity, Lord, O Lord forgive;
   Let a repenting rebel live;
   Are not Thy mercies large and free?
   May not a sinner trust in Thee?

2 O, Wash my soul from every sin,
   And make my guilty conscience clean;
   Here on my heart the burden lies,
   And past offences pain mine eyes.

3 My lips with shame my sins confess,
   Against Thy laws against Thy grace;
   Lord, should Thy judgment grow severe,
   I am condemned, but Thou art clear.

4 Should sudden vengeance seize my breath,
   I must pronounce Thee just in death;
   And if my soul were sent to hell,
   Thy righteous law approves it well.

5 Yet save a trembling sinner, Lord,
   Whose hope still hovering round Thy word,
   Would light on some sweet promise there,
   Some sure support against despair.

96

1 THE day of wrath, that dreadful day,
   When heaven and earth shall pass away !
   What power shall be the sinner's stay ?
   How shall he meet that dreadful day ?

2 When, shrivelling like a parched scroll,
   The flaming heavens together roll;
   When louder yet, and yet more dread,
   Swells the high trump that wakes the dead

3 Oh! on that day, that wrathful day,
   When man to judgment wakes from clay,
   Be Thou the trembling sinner's stay,
   Though heaven and earth shall pass away

BRIGHTON. L. M. (6 lines.) Dr. Lowell Mason. English.

When gath'ring clouds around I view, And days are dark, and friends are few,

On Him I lean, who, not in vain, Ex-pe-rienced ev-'ry hu-man pain.

He sees my griefs, al-lays my fears, And counts, and treasures up my tears.

97

2 If aught should tempt my soul to stray
From heavenly wisdom's narrow way,
To fly the good I would pursue,
Or do the thing I would not do,
Still He who felt temptation's power,
Will guard me in that dangerous hour.

3 When, mourning, o'er some stone I bend,
Which covers all that was a friend,
And from his hand, his voice, his smile,
Divides me for a little while,
My Saviour marks the tears I shed,
For "Jesus wept" o'er Lazarus dead.

4 And, O, when I have safely passed
Through every conflict but the last,
Still, Lord, unchanging, watch beside
My dying bed, for Thou hast died;
Then point to realms of cloudless day,
And wipe the latest tear away.

98

1 The Lord my pasture shall prepare,
And feed me with a shepherd's care;
His presence shall my wants supply,
And guard me with a watchful eye;
My noonday walks He shall attend,
And all my midnight hours defend.

2 When in the sultry glebe I faint,
Or on the thirsty mountain pant,
To fertile vales and dewy meads
My weary, wandering steps He leads;
Where peaceful rivers, soft and slow,
Amid the verdant landscape flow.

3 Though in the paths of death I tread,
With gloomy horrors overspread,
My steadfast heart shall know no ill,
For Thou, O Lord, art with me still;
Thy friendly crook shall give me aid,
And guide me through the dreadful shade.

4 Though in a bare and rugged way,
Through devious, lonely wilds I stray,
Thy bounty shall my pains beguile;
The barren wilderness shall smile
With sudden greens and herbage crowned
And streams shall murmur all around.

99

1 At evening time let there be light:
Life's little day draws near its close;
Around me fall the shades of night,
The night of death, the grave's repose;
To crown my joys, to end my woes,
At evening time let there be light.

2 At evening time there shall be light,
For God hath spoken; it must be;
Fear, doubt, and anguish take their flight;
His glory now is risen on me;
Mine eyes shall His salvation see;
'Tis evening time, and there is light.

ANDANTE.

How sweetly flowed the gospel's sound From lips of gentle-ness and grace,

Where list'ning thousands gathered round, And joy and rev'rence filled the place.

100

2 From heaven He came, of heaven He spoke,
To heaven he led His followers' way;
Dark clouds of gloomy night He broke,
Unveiling an immortal day.

3 " Come, wanderers, to my Father's home;
Come, all ye weary ones, and rest."
Yes, sacred Teacher, we will come,
Obey Thee, love Thee, and be blest.

4 Decay, then, tenements of dust;
Pillars of earthly pride, decay;
A nobler mansion waits the just,
And Jesus has prepared the way.

101

1 ABIDE with us ; the evening shades
Begin already to prevail;
And, as the lingering twilight fades,
Dark clouds along the horizon sail.

2 Abide with us; and still unfold
Thy sacred, Thy prophetic lore;
What wondrous things of Jesus told !
Stranger, we thirst, we pant for more.

3 Abide with us; our hearts are cold;
We thought that Israel He'd restore;
But sweet the truths Thy lips have told,
And, Stranger, we complain no more.

4 Abide with us; amazed they cry,
As, suddenly, whilst breaking bread,
Their own lost Jesus meets their eye,
With radiant glory on His head !

102

1 WHEN power divine, in mortal form,
Hushed with a word the raging storm,
In soothing accents Jesus said—
" Lo ! it is I; be not afraid."

2 Blessed be the voice that breathes from
To every heart in sunder riven, [heaven
When love, and joy, and hope are fled—
" Lo ! it is I; be not afraid."

3 And when the last dread hour is come,
While shuddering nature waits her doom,
This voice shall call the pious dead—
Lo ! it is I; be not afraid."

103

1 O, WHERE is now that glowing love
That mark'd our union with the Lord ?
Our hearts were fix'd on things above,
Nor could the world a joy afford.

2 Where is the zeal that led us then
To make our Saviour's glory known;
That freed us from the fear of men,
And kept our eyes on Him alone ?

3 Where are the happy seasons spent
In fellowship with Him we loved ?
The sacred joy, the sweet content,
The blessedness that then we proved ?

4 Behold, again we turn to Thee,
O cast us not away, though vile !
No peace we have, no joy we see,
O Lord, our God, but in Thy smile.

WELLS. L. M.

ANDANTE.   ISRAEL HOLDRAYD.

Life is the time to serve the Lord, The time to insure the great reward;

And while the lamp holds out to burn, The vil - est sinner may return.

104

2 Life is the hour that God has given
  To escape from hell and fly to heaven—
  The day of grace,—and mortals may,
  Secure the blessings of the day.

3 The living know that they must die,
  But all the dead forgotten lie;
  Their memory and their sense are gone,
  Alike unknowing and unknown.

4 Then what my thoughts design to do,
  My hands, with all your might pursue;
  Since no device nor work is found,
  Nor faith, nor hope, beneath the ground.

5 There are no acts of pardon passed
  In the cold grave to which we haste;
  But darkness, death, and long despair
  Reign in eternal silence there.

105

1 WHILE life prolongs its precious light,
  Mercy is found and peace is given;
  But soon, ah, soon, approaching night
  Shall blot out every hope of heaven.

2 While God invites, how blessed the day!
  How sweet the gospel's charming sound!
  Come, sinners, haste, O, haste away,
  While yet a pardoning God He's found,

3 Soon, borne on time's most rapid wing,
  Shall death command you to the grave;
  Before His bar your spirits bring,
  And none be found to hear or save.

4 In that lone land of deep despair,
  No Sabbath's heavenly light shall rise;
  No God regard your bitter prayer,
  Nor Saviour call you to the skies.

106

1 O FOR a glance of heavenly day,
  To take this stubborn stone away,
  And thaw, with beams of love divine,
  This heart, this frozen heart of mine.

2 The rocks can rend; the earth can quake;
  The seas can roar; the mountains shake;
  Of feeling, all things show some sign,
  But this unfeeling heart of mine.

3 To hear the sorrows Thou hast felt,
  Dear Lord, an adamant would melt;
  But I can read each moving line,
  And nothing move this heart of mine.

4 But something yet can do the deed,
  And that dear something much I need;
  Thy Spirit can from dross refine,
  And move and melt this heart of mine.

107

1 How shall the sons of men appear,
  Great God, before Thine awful bar?
  How may the guilty hope to find
  Acceptance with the Eternal Mind !

2 Not vows, nor groans, nor broken cries,
  Not the most costly sacrifice,
  Not infant blood, profusely spilt,
  Will expiate a sinner's guilt.

3 Thy blood, dear Jesus, Thine alone,
  Hath sovereign virtue to atone;
  Here we will rest our only plea,
  When we approach, great God, to Thee.

MAZZINGHI.

Peace, troubled soul, whose plaintive moan Hath taught each scene the note of woe ;

Cease thy complaint, suppress thy groan, And let.... thy tears for - get to flow ;

Behold, the precious balm is found, To lull thy pain and heal thy wound.

108

2 Come, freely come, by sin oppressed;
　On Jesus cast thy weighty load;
In him thy refuge find, thy rest,
　Safe in the mercy of thy God;
Thy God's thy Saviour—glorious word!
Oh, hear, believe, and bless the Lord!

109

1 When adverse winds and waves arise,
And in my heart despondence sighs;
When life her throng of cares reveals,
And weakness o'er my spirit steals,
Grateful I hear the kind decree,
That "as my day, my strength shall be."

2 When, with sad footsteps, memory roves
'Mid smitten joys and buried loves,
When sleep my tearful pillow flies,
And dewy morning drinks my sighs,
Still to Thy promise, Lord! I flee,
That "as my day, my strength shall be."

3 One trial more must yet be past;
One pang—the keenest and the last;
And when, with brow convulsed and pale,
My feeble, quivering heart-strings fail,
Redeemer! grant my soul to see
That "as my day, my strength shall be."

110

1 Blessed who with generous pity glows,
Who learns to feel another's woes,
Bows to the poor man's want his ear,
And wipes the helpless orphan's tear:
In every want, in every woe,
Himself, Thy pity, Lord, shall know.

2 Thy love his life shall guard, Thy hand
Give to his lot the chosen land;
Nor leave him in the dreadful day,
To unrelenting foes a prey.
When languid with disease and pain,
Thou, Lord, his spirit shalt sustain.

111

1 Sweet is the last, the parting ray
　That ushers placid evening in,
When with the still, expiring day
　The Sabbath's peaceful hours begin;
How grateful to the anxious breast
The sacred hours of holy rest!

2 Oft as this peaceful hour shall come,
　Lord, raise my thoughts from heavenly things,
And bear them to my heavenly home,
　On faith and hope's celestial wings,
Till the last gleam of life decay
In one eternal Sabbath day.

ROTHWELL. L. M.

ANIMATO.   WM. TANSUR.

Kingdoms and thrones to God belong; Crown Him, ye nations, in your song; His wondrous

name and powers rehearse; His honors shall enrich your verse. His honors shall enrich your verse.

112

2 He guides our feet, He guards our way;
His morning smiles bless all the day;
He spreads the evening veil and keeps
The silent hours while Israel sleeps.

3 Israel, a name divinely blest,
May rise secure, securely rest;
Thy holy Guardian's wakeful eyes
Admit no slumber, nor surprise.

113

1 JEHOVAH reigns; let all the earth
In His just government rejoice;
Let all the isles, with sacred mirth,
In His applause unite their voice.

2 Darkness and clouds of awful shade
His dazzling glory shroud in state;
Justice and truth His guards are made,
And fixed by His pavilion wait.

3 Rejoice, ye righteous, in the Lord;
Memorials of His holiness
Deep in your faithful breasts record,
And with your thankful tongues confess.

114

1 ETERNAL Spirit, we confess
And sing the wonders of Thy grace:
Thy power conveys our blessings down,
From God the Father and the Son.

2 Enlightened by Thy heavenly ray,
Our shades and darkness turn to day;
Thine inward teachings make us know
Our danger and our refuge too.

3 Thy power and glory work within,
And break the chains of reigning sin;
Do our imperious lusts subdue,
And form our wretched hearts anew.

4 The troubled conscience knows Thy voice.
Thy cheering words awake our joys;
Thy words allay the stormy wind,
And calm the surges of the mind.

115

1 My soul, thy great Creator praise;
When clothed in His celestial rays,
He in full majesty appears,
And like a robe His glory wears.

2 The heavens are for His curtains spread,
The unfathomed deep He makes His bed;
Clouds are His chariot, when he flies
On winged storms across the skies.

3 Angels, whom His own breath inspires,
His ministers are flaming fires;
And swift as thought their armies move
To bear His vengeance or His love.

116

Let sinners saved give thanks and sing
Of mercies past, of joys to come;
The Lord their Saviour is and King,
The cross their hope, and heaven their home

117

To God the Father glory be,
And to His sole-begotten Son;
The same, O Holy Ghost, to Thee,
While everlasting ages run.

Just as I am, without one plea, But that Thy blood was shed for me,

And that Thou bid'st me come to Thee, O Lamb of God, I come!

118

2 Just as I am, and waiting not
To rid my soul of one dark blot,
To Thee whose blood can cleanse each spot,
O Lamb of God, I come!

3 Just as I am, though tossed about
With many a conflict, many a doubt,
Fightings within, and fears without,
O Lamb of God, I come!

4 Just as I am, poor, wretched, blind;
Sight, riches, healing of the mind,
Yea, all I need, in Thee to find,
O Lamb of God, I come!

5 Just as I am Thou wilt receive;
Wilt welcome, pardon, cleanse, relieve;
Because Thy promise I believe,
O Lamb of God, I come!

6 Just as I am, Thy love unknown
Has broken every barrier down;
Now, to be Thine, yea, Thine alone,
O Lamb of God, I come!

119

1 Just as thou art—without one trace
Of love, or joy, or inward grace,
Or meetness for the heavenly place,—
O guilty sinner, come!

2 Thy sins I bore on Calvary's tree;
The stripes thy due were laid on Me,
That peace and pardon might be free:
O wretched sinner, come!

3 Burdened with guilt wouldst thou be blest?
Trust not the world; it gives no rest;
I bring relief to hearts oppressed:
O weary sinner, come!

4 Come, leave thy burden at the cross;
Count all thy gains but empty dross;
My grace repays all earthly loss:
O needy sinner, come!

5 Come, hither bring thy boding fears,
Thy aching heart, thy bursting tears;
'Tis mercy's voice salutes thine ears:
O trembling sinner, come!

6 "The Spirit and the bride say, Come;"
Rejoicing saints re-echo, Come!
Who faints,who thirsts,who will,may come:
Thy Saviour bids thee come.

120

1 THERE is a pure and peaceful wave
That rolls around the throne of love,
Whose waters gladden as they lave
The peaceful shores above.

2 While streams which on that tide depend,
Steal from those heavenly shores away,
And on this desert world descend
O'er weary lands to stray.

3 The pilgrim faint and nigh to sink
Beneath his load of earthly woe,
Refreshed beside their verdant brink,
Rejoices in their flow.

4 There, oh my soul, do thou repair
And hover o'er the hallowed spring,
To drink the crystal wave, and there
To lave thy wearied wing.

UXBRIDGE. L. M.

ALLEGRETTO.   DR. LOWELL MASON, 1830.

As-sem-bled at Thy great command, Before Thy face, dread King, we stand:

The voice that marshalled ev-'ry star Has called Thy people from a - far.

121

2 We meet through distant lands to spread
The truth for which the martyrs bled;
·Along the line to either pole,
The anthem of Thy praise to roll.

3 Our prayers assist; accept our praise;
Our hopes revive ; our courage raise;
Our counsels aid; to each impart
The single eye, the faithful heart.

5 Forth with Thy chosen heralds come;
Recall the wandering spirits home;
From Zion's mount send forth the sound,
To spread the spacious earth around.

122

1 WHAT sinners value I resign:
Lord, 'tis enough that Thou art mine:
I shall behold Thy blissful face,
And stand complete in righteousness.

2 This life's a dream, an empty show;
But the bright world to which I go
Hath joys substantial and sincere;
When shall I wake and find me there ?

3 O glorious hour ! O blest abode !
I shall be near and like my God,
And flesh and sin no more control
The sacred pleasures of the soul.

4 My flesh shall slumber in the ground
Till the last trumpet's joyful sound;
Then burst the chains with sweet surprise,
And in my Saviour's image rise.

123

1 ARISE, my soul, on wings sublime,
Above the vanities of time ;
Let faith now pierce the veil, and see
The glories of eternity.

2 Born by a new, celestial birth,
Why should I grovel here on earth ?
Why grasp at vain and fleeting toys,
So near to heaven's eternal joys ?

3 Shall aught beguile me on the road,—
The narrow road that leads to God ?
Or can I love this earth so well,
As not to long with God to dwell ?

4 To dwell with God,—to taste His love
Is the full heaven enjoyed above :
The glorious expectation now
Is heavenly bliss begun below.

124

1 POUR out Thy Spirit from on high;
Lord, Thine assembled servants bless;
Graces and gifts to each supply,   [ness.
And clothe Thy priests with righteous-

2 Wisdom, and zeal, and faith impart,
Firmness with meekness from above,
To bear Thy people on our heart,
And love the souls whom Thou dost love;

3 To watch and pray, and never faint;
By day and night strict guard to keep;
To warn the sinner, cheer the saint,
Nourish Thy lambs, and feed Thy sheep;

4 Then, when our work is finished here,
In humble hope our charge resign;
When the chief Shepherd shall appear.
O God, may they and we be Thine.

125

To Father, Son, and Holy Ghost,
The God whom heaven and earth adore,
Be glory as it was of old,
Is now, and shall be evermore !

DOLCE.   GEO. F. ROOT. 1843.

Great God, to Thee my evening song With humble gra - ti - tude I raise;

Oh, let Thy mercy tune my tongue, And fill my heart with live - ly praise.

126

2 My days unclouded as they pass,
  And every gently-rolling hour,
  Are monuments of wondrous grace,
  And witness to Thy love and power.

3 Thy love and power, celestial guard,
  Preserve me from surrounding harm :
  Can danger reach me while the Lord
  Extends His kind protecting arm !

4 Let this blest hope my eyelids close ;
  With sleep refresh my feeble frame;
  Safe in Thy care may I repose,
  And wake with praises to Thy name.

127

1 SWEET is the light of Sabbath eve,
  And soft the sunbeams lingering there;
  For these blest hours the world I leave,
  Wafted on wings of faith and prayer.

2 The time how lovely and how still;
  Peace shines and smiles on all below;
  The plain, the stream, the wood, the hill,
  All fair with evening's setting glow.

3 Season of rest ! the tranquil soul
  Feels the sweet calm and melts to love;
  And while these sacred moments roll,
  Faith sees the smiling heaven above.

4 Nor will our days of toil be long :
  Our pilgrimage will soon be trod;
  And we shall join the ceaseless song,
  The endless Sabbath of our God.

128

1 LORD, when my thoughts delighted rove
  Amid the wonders of Thy love,
  Sweet hope revives my drooping heart,
  And bids intruding fears depart.

2 For mortal crimes a sacrifice,
  The Lord of life, the Saviour dies;
  What love ! what mercy ! how divine !
  Jesus, and can I call Thee mine?

3 Repentant sorrows fills my heart,
  But mingling joy allays the smart ;
  O, may my future life declare
  This sorrow and the joy sincere.

4 Be all my heart and all my days
  Devoted to my Saviour's praise;
  And let my glad obedience prove
  How much I owe, how much I love.

129

1 THOU Prince of glory, slain for me,
  Breathing forgiveness in thy prayer;
  That loving, melting look I see;
  That bursting sigh, that tender tear.

2 Can I behold that closing eye,
  Still fixed on me, still beaming love;
  And can I see my Saviour die,
  Nor feel one holy passion move?

3 Let me but hear Thy dying voice
  Pronounce forgiveness in my breast;
  My trembling spirit shall rejoice,
  And feel the calm of heavenly rest.

4 Lord, Thine atoning blood apply,
  And life or death is sweet to me;
  In life's last hour, Thy presence nigh,
  From fear shall set my spirit free.

RECITANDO.   GEO. KINGSLEY

When, marshalled on the night-ly plain, The glittering host be-stud the sky,

One Star alone, of all the train, Can fix the sin-ner's wand-'ring eye.

130

2 Hark! hark! to God the chorus breaks
  From every host, from every gem;
  But one alone the Saviour speaks:
    It is the star of Bethlehem.

3 Once on the raging seas I rode;
  The storm was loud, the night was dark;
  The ocean yawned; and rudely blowed
    The wind that tossed my foundering bark.

4 Deep horror then my vitals froze;
  Death-struck, I ceased the tide to stem;
  When suddenly a star arose;
    It was the Star of Bethlehem.

5 It was my guide, my light, my all;
  It bade my dark forebodings cease;
  And through the storm and danger's thrall,
    It led me to the port of peace.

6 Now, safely moored, my perils o'er,
  I'll sing, first in night's diadem,
  Forever and forevermore,
    The Star!—the Star of Bethlehem!

131

1 On, sweetly breathe the lyres above,
  When angels touch the quivering string,
  And wake, to chant Immanuel's love,
    Such strains as angel lips can sing!

2 And sweet, on earth, the choral swell,
  From mortal tongues, of gladsome lays;
  When pardoned souls their raptures tell,
    And, grateful, hymn Immanuel's praise.

3 Jesus, Thy name our souls adore;
  We own the bond that makes us Thine;
  And carnal joys, that charmed before,
    For Thy dear sake we now resign.

4 Our hearts, by dying love subdued,
  Accept Thine offered grace to-day;
  Beneath the cross, with blood bedewed,
    We bow, and give ourselves away.

5 In Thee we trust,—on Thee rely;
  Though we are feeble, Thou art strong;
  Oh, keep us till our spirits fly
    To join the bright, immortal throng!

132

1 SHALL man, O God of light and life!
  Forever moulder in the grave?
  Canst Thou forget Thy glorious work,
    Thy promise, and Thy power to save?

2 In those dark, silent realms of night,
  Shall peace and hope no more arise?
  No future morning light the tomb,
    Nor day-star gild the darksome skies?

3 Cease, cease, ye vain, desponding fears!
  When Christ, our Lord, from darkness
    sprang,
  Death, the last foe, was captive led,
    And heaven with praise and wonder rang.

4 Faith sees the bright eternal doors
  Unfold to make her children way;
  They shall be clothed with endless life,
    And shine in everlasting day.

MODERATO APPETTUOSO. ARR. from BEETHOVEN.

Sweet peace of conscience, heav'nly guest, Come fix thy mansion in my breast;

Dis-pel my doubts, my fears control, And heal the an-guish of my soul.

133

2 Come, smiling hope and joy sincere,
Come, make your constant dwelling here;
Still let your presence cheer my heart,
Nor sin compel you to depart.

3 O God of hope and peace divine,
Make Thou these secret pleasures mine;
Forgive my sins, my fears remove,
And fill my heart with joy and love.

134

1 As, in soft silence, vernal showers
Descend and cheer the fainting flowers,
So in the secrecy of love,
Falls the sweet influence from above.

2 That heavenly influence let me find
In holy silence of the mind,
While every grace maintains its bloom,
Diffusing wide its rich perfume.

3 Nor let these blessings be confined
To me, but poured on all mankind;
Till earth's wild wastes in verdure rise,
And a young Eden bless our eyes.

135

1 My only Saviour! when I feel
O'erwhelmed in spirit, faint, oppressed,
'Tis sweet to tell Thee, while I kneel
Low at Thy feet, Thou art my rest.

2 I'm weary of the strife within;
Strong powers against my soul contest;
Oh, let me turn from self and sin
To Thy dear cross, for there is rest!

3 Oh! sweet will be the welcome day,
When from her toils and woes released,
My parting soul in death shall say,
"Now, Lord! I come to Thee for rest."

136

1 RETURN, O wanderer, return
And seek an injured Father's face;
Those new desires that in thee burn
Were kindled by reclaiming grace.

2 Return, O wanderer, return
And seek a Father's melting heart:
Whose pitying eyes thy grief discern,
Whose hand shall heal thine inward smart.

3 Return, O wanderer, return
Thy Saviour bids thy spirit live;
Go to his bleeding feet and learn
How fondly Jesus can forgive.

4 Return, O wanderer, return,
And wipe away thy falling tear;
'Tis God who says, "no longer mourn;"
'Tis Mercy's voice invites thee near.

137

1 "O, LEARN of Me," the Saviour cried;
"O, learn of Me, ye sons of pride;
For I am lowly, humble, meek;
No haughty looks high thoughts bespeak."

2 Yes, blest Immanuel, Thou wast mild,
Patient and gentle as a child;
And they who would Thy kingdom see,
Must meek and lowly be, like Thee.

WEATHERSFIELD. L. M. (Double.)

ANDANTE.

The ransomed spi - rit to her home, The clime of cloudless beauty flies;

No more on stormy seas to roam, She hails her ha - ven in the skies;

But cheerless are those heavenly fields, That cloudless clime no pleasure yields,

There is no bliss in bowers above, If Thou art absent, ho - ly Love!

138

2 The cherub near the viewless throne,
Hath smote the harp with trembling hand;
And one with incense-fire hath flown,
To touch with flame the angel band:
But tuneless is the quivering string,
No melody can Gabriel bring,
Mute are its arches when above
The harps of heaven wake not to love!

3 Earth, sea and sky one language speak,
In harmony that soothes the soul;
'Tis heard when scarce the zephyrs wake,
And when on thunders thunders roll
That voice is heard, and tumults cease,
It whispers to the bosom peace;
Speak, Thou Inspirer, from above,
And cheer our hearts, celestial Love!

HARRISON.

I send the joys of earth a - way; A-way, ye tempters of the mind.

False as the smooth, de-ceit-ful sea, And empty as the whistling wind.

139

2 Your streams were floating me along,
Down to the gulf of black despair ;
And while I listened to your song, [there.
Your streams had e'en conveyed me

3 Lord, I adore Thy matchless grace,
That warned me of that dark abyss,
That drew me from those treach'rous seas,
And bade me seek superior bliss.

4 Now to the shining realms above,
I stretch my hands and glance my eyes;
O for the pinions of a dove,
To bear me to the upper skies!

5 There, from the bosom of my God,
Oceans of endless pleasures roll:
There would I fix my last abode,
And drown the sorrows of my soul.

140

1 Jesus, and shall it ever be—
A mortal man ashamed of Thee?
Ashamed of Thee, whom angels praise,
Whose glories shine thro' endless days?

2 Ashamed of Jesus! just as soon
Let midnight be ashamed of noon;
'Tis midnight with my soul, till He,
Bright Morning Star, bid darkness flee.

3 Ashamed of Jesus ! that dear Friend
On whom my hopes of heaven depend !
No; when I blush, be this my shame,
That I no more revere His name.

4 Ashamed of Jesus ! yes, I may
When I've no guilt to wash away,
No tear to wipe, no good to crave,
No fears to quell, no soul to save.

5 Till then—nor is my boasting vain—
Till then I boast a Saviour slain!
And O, may this my glory be,
That Christ is not ashamed of me.

141

1 O holy, holy, holy, Lord!
Thou God of Hosts, by all adored:
The earth and heavens are full of Thee,
Thy light, Thy power, Thy majesty.

2 Loud hallelujahs to Thy name,
Angels and Seraphim proclaim:
By all the powers and thrones in heaven
Eternal praise to Thee is given.

3 Apostles join the glorious throng,
And swell the loud, triumphant song:
Prophets and martyrs hear the sound,
And spread the hallelujahs round.

142

1 Thus saith the wisdom of the Lord,—
" Blessed is the man that hears My word;
Keeps daily watch before My gates,
And at My feet for mercy waits.

2 " The soul that seeks Me shall obtain
Immortal wealth, and heavenly gain;
Immortal life is his reward;
Life, and the favor of the Lord."

143

Glory to Thee, O God, most high!
Father, we praise Thy majesty!
The Son, the Spirit, we adore,
One Godhead, blest for evermore !

• 40   ZEPHYR. L. M.

DOLCE.   W. B. BRADBURY.

Come, weary souls, with sin distressed, Come and ac - cept the promised rest;

The Saviour's gracious call o - bey, And cast your gloomy fears a - way.

144

2 Oppressed with guilt—a painful load—
O, come and bow before your God!
Divine compassion, mighty love,
Will all the painful load remove.

3 Here mercy's boundless ocean flows,
To cleanse your guilt and heal your woes;
Pardon and life and endless peace—
How rich the gift; how free the grace!

4 Dear Saviour! let Thy powerful love
Confirm our faith, our fears remove;
O sweetly reign in every breast,
And guide us to eternal rest.

145

1 Behold the Saviour at thy door!
He gently knocks, has knocked before;
Has waited long, is waiting still,—
You treat no other friend so ill.

2 O, lovely attitude! He stands
With melting heart and outstretch'd hands;
O, matchless kindness! and He shows
This matchless kindness to His foes.

3 Admit Him; for the human breast
Ne'er entertained so kind a guest;
Admit Him; or the hour's at hand,
When at His door denied you'll stand.

4 "Open my heart, Lord, enter in;
Slay every foe, and conquer sin:
I now to Thee my all resign;
My body, soul, and all are Thine."

146

1 Stretched on the cross, the Saviour dies!
Hark! His expiring groans arise;
See, from His hands, His feet, His side,
Descends the sacred, crimson tide.

2 And didst Thou bleed?—for sinners bleed?
And could the sun behold the deed?
No; he withdrew his cheering ray,
And darkness veiled the mourning day.

3 Can I survey this scene of woe,
Where mingling grief and mercy flow,
And yet my heart so hard remain,
Unmoved by either love or pain?

4 Come, dearest Lord, Thy grace impart,
To warm this cold, this stupid heart,
Till all its powers and passions move
In melting grief and ardent love.

147

1 Dear Saviour, if these lambs should stray
From Thy secure inclosure's bound,
And lured by worldly joys away,
Among the thoughtless crowd be found:

2 Remember still that they are Thine,
That Thy dear sacred name they bear;
Think that the seal of love divine,
The sign of cov'nant grace they wear.

3 In all their erring, sinful years,
Oh, let them ne'er forgotten be!
Remember all the prayers and tears
Which made them consecrate to Thee.

4 And when these lips no more can pray,
These eyes can weep for them no more,
Turn Thou their feet from folly's way;
The wanderers to Thy fold restore.

My heav'nly home is bright and fair, Nor pain nor death can en-ter there;
Its glitt'ring towers the sun outshine, That heav'nly mansion shall be mine;

CHORUS.

I'm go-ing home, I'm go-ing home, I'm go-ing home to die no more.

To die no more, to die no more, I'm go-ing home, to die no more.

148

2 My Father's house is built on high,
Far, far above the starry sky:
When from this earthly prison free,
That heavenly mansion mine shall be.
  I'm going home, &c.

3 While here, a stranger far from home,
Affliction's waves may round me foam?
And, though like Lazarus, sick and poor,
My heavenly mansion is secure.
  I'm going home, &c.

4 Let others seek a home below,
Which flames devour, or waves o'erflow;
Be mine the happier lot to own
A heavenly mansion near the throne.
  I'm going home, &c.

5 Then fail this earth, let stars decline,
And sun and moon refuse to shine,
All nature sink and cease to be,
That heavenly mansion stands for me.
  I'm going home, &c.

149

1 Hail, sovereign love, that first began
The scheme to rescue fallen man;
Hail, matchless, free, eternal grace,
That gave my soul a Hiding-place.

2 Against the God that rules the sky
I fought with hand uplifted high;
Despised His rich, abounding grace,
Too proud to seek a Hiding-place.

3 But thus the eternal counsel ran:
"Almighty love, arrest that man."
I felt the arrow of distress,
And found I had no Hiding-place.

4 Indignant justice stood in view;
To Sinai's fiery mount I flew:
But Justice cried, with frowning face,
"This mountain is no Hiding-place."

5 Ere long a heavenly voice I heard,
And Mercy's angel form appeared;
She led me on, with gentle pace,
To Jesus, as my Hiding-place.

6 On Him Almighty vengeance fell,
That must have sunk a world to hell.
He bore it for the chosen race,
And thus became their Hiding-place.

7 A few more rolling suns, at most,
Will land me safe on Canaan's coast,
Where I shall sing the song of grace,
And see my glorious Hiding-place.

GERMANY. L. M.

ADAGIO SOSTENUTO.

DR. LOWELL MASON.

From BEETHOVEN.

How sweet the hour of clos - ing day, When all is peace - ful and se - rene,

And when the sun, with cloudless ray, Sheds mellow lus - tre o'er the scene!

150

2 Such is the Christian's parting hour;
  So peacefully he sinks to rest;   [power,
When faith, endued from heaven with
Sustains and cheers his languid breast.

3 Mark but that radiance of his eye,
  That smile upon his wasted cheek;
They tell us of his glory nigh,
  In language that no tongue can speak.

4 Who would not wish to die like those
  Whom God's-own Spirit deigns to bless?
To sink into that soft repose,
  Then wake to perfect happiness?

151 .

1 SAVIOUR, when night involves the skies,
  My soul, adoring turns to Thee;
Thee, self-abased in mortal guise,
  And wrapped in shades of death for me.

2 On Thee my waking raptures dwell,
  When crimson gleams the east adorn;
Thee, Victor of the grave and hell;
  Thee, Source of life's eternal morn.

3 When noon her throne in light arrays,
  To Thee my soul triumphant springs;
Thee, throned in Glory's endless blaze;
  Thee, Lord of lords, and King of kings.

4 O'er earth when shades of evening steal,
  To death and Thee my thoughts I give;
To death, whose power I soon must feel;
  To Thee, with whom I trust to live.

152

1 How sweet to leave the world awhile,
  And seek the presence of our Lord!
Dear Saviour, on Thy people smile,
  And come, according to Thy word.

2 From busy scenes we now retreat,
  That we may here converse with Thee:
Ah, Lord, behold us at Thy feet!
  Let this the " gate of heaven" be.

3 " Chief of ten thousand!" now appear,
  That we by faith may see Thy face;
Oh, speak, that we Thy voice may hear,
  And let Thy presence fill this place!

153

1 SOFT be the gently breathing notes
  That sing the Saviour's dying love;
Soft as the evening zephyr floats;
  Soft as the tuneful lyres above.

2 Soft as the morning dews descend,
  While the sweet lark exulting soars;
So soft to your almighty Friend
  Be every wish your bosom pours.

3 Pure as the sun's enlivening ray
  That scatters life and joy abroad,
Pure as the lucid car of day
  That loud proclaims its Maker God:

4 True as the magnet to the pole,
  So true let your conviction be—
So true let all your sorrows roll
  To Him who bled upon the tree.

MODERATO.

Jesus, the Spring of joys divine, Whence all our hopes and comforts flow;

Je - sus, no oth - er name but Thine Can save us from e - ter - nal woe.

154

2 In vain would boasting reason find
The way to happiness and God;
Her weak directions leave the mind
Bewildered in a dubious road.

3 No other name will heaven approve;
Thou art the true, the living way,
Ordained by everlasting love,
To the bright realms of endless day.

4 Safe lead us through this world of night,
And bring us to the blissful plains,
The regions of unclouded light,
Where perfect joy forever reigns.

155

1 When Jordan hushed his waters still,
And silence slept on Zion's hill;
When Bethlehem's shepherds through the
night
Watched o'er their flocks by starry light;

2 Hark! from the midnight hills around,
A voice of more than mortal sound
In distant hallelujahs stole,
Wild murmuring o'er the raptured soul.

3 On wheels of light, on wings of flame,
The glorious hosts of Zion came;
High heaven with songs of triumph rung,
While thus they struck their harps, and
sung:

4 " O Zion, lift thy raptured eye;
The long expected hour is nigh;
The joys of nature rise again;
The Prince of Salem comes to reign.

5 " He comes to cheer the trembling heart,
Bid Satan and his host depart;
Again the Day star gilds the gloom,
Again the bowers of Eden bloom."

156

1 While o'er the deep Thy servants sail,
Send Thou, O Lord, the prosperous gale;
And on their hearts, where'er they go,
Oh, let Thy heavenly breezes blow!

2 If on the morning's wings they fly,
They will not pass beyond thine eye;
The wanderers' prayer thou bend'st to hear,
And faith exults to know Thee near.

3 When tempests rock the groaning bark,
Oh, hide them safe in Jesus' ark!
When in the tempting port they ride,
Oh, keep them safe at Jesus side!

4 If life's wide ocean smile or roar,
Still guide them to the heavenly shore;
And grant their dust in Christ may sleep,
Abroad, at home, or in the deep.

157

1 'Tis by the faith of joys to come
We walk through deserts dark as night;
Till we arrive at heaven, our home,
Faith is our guide, and faith our light.

2 The want of sight she well supplies;
She makes the pearly gates appear;
Far into distant worlds she pries,
And brings eternal glories near.

3 Cheerful we tread the desert through,
While faith inspires a heavenly ray;
Though lions roar and tempests blow,
And rocks and dangers fill the way.

ALLEGRETTO.   H. K. OLIVER.

Come hith-er, all ye wea-ry souls, Ye hea-vy la-den sin-ners, come.

I'll give you rest from all your toils, And raise you to my heavenly home.

158

2 "They shall find rest who learn of me:
   I'm of a meek and lowly mind;
   But passion rages like the sea,
   And pride is restless as the wind.

3 "Blest is the man whose shoulders take
   My yoke, and bear it with delight:
   My yoke is easy to his neck,
   My grace shall make the burden light."

159

1 TREMBLING, before Thine awful Throne,
   O Lord, in dust my sins I own;
   Justice and mercy for my life
   Contend; O smile, and heal the strife.

2 The Saviour smiles; upon my soul
   New tides of hope tumultuous roll;
   His voice proclaims my pardon found!
   Seraphic transport wings the sound.

3 Earth has a joy unknown in heaven,
   The new-born peace of sins forgiven;
   Tears of such pure and deep delight,
   Ye angels, never dimmed your sight.

4 Loud is the song, the heavenly plain
   Is shaken by the choral strain;
   And dying echoes, floating far,
   Draw music from each chiming star.

5 But I amid your choirs shall shine,
   And all your knowledge will be mine;
   Ye on your harps must lean to hear
   A secret chord that mine will bear.

160

1 So fades the lovely blooming flower,
   Frail, smiling solace of an hour;
   So soon our transient comforts fly,
   And pleasure only blooms to die.

2 Is there no kind, no lenient art
   To heal the anguish of the heart?
   O, let Religion then be nigh;
   Her comforts were not made to die,

3 Then gentle Patience smiles on Pain,
   And dying hope revives again;
   Hope wipes the tear from Sorrow's eye,
   And Faith points upward to the sky.

161

1 MILLIONS within Thy courts have met,
   Millions this day before Thee bow'd;
   Their faces Zionward were set,—
   Vows with their lips to Thee they vow'd.

2 But Thou, soul searching God! hast known
   The hearts of all that bent the knee;
   And hast accepted those alone,
   Who in the spirit worshipped Thee.

3 People of many a tribe and tongue,
   Of various languages and lands,
   Have heard Thy truth, Thy glory sung,
   And offer'd prayer with holy hands.

4 Yet one prayer more;—and be it one,
   In which both heaven and earth accord:
   Fulfil Thy promise to Thy Son:
   Let all that breathes call Jesus Lord!

162

1 DISMISS us with Thy blessing, Lord,
   Help us to feed upon Thy word;
   All that has been amiss forgive,
   And let Thy truth within us live.

2 Though we are guilty, Thou art good;
   Wash all our works in Jesus' blood:
   Give every fettered soul release,
   And bid us all depart in peace.

CON MOTO.   W. B. BRADBURY.

When I survey the wondrous cross On which the Prince of glo-ry died,

My richest gain I count but loss, And pour contempt on all my pride.

163

2 Forbid it, Lord, that I should boast,
  Save in the death of Christ, my God;
All the vain things that charm me most,
  I sacrifice them to His blood.

3 See from His head, His hands, His feet,
  Sorrow and love flow mingled down;
Did e'er such love and sorrow meet?
  Or thorns compose so rich a crown?

4 Were the whole realm of nature mine,
  That were a present far too small;
Love so amazing, so divine,
  Demands my soul, my life, my all.

164

1 When sins and fears prevailing rise,
  And fainting hope almost expires,
Jesus, to Thee I lift my eyes,
  To Thee I breathe my soul's desires.

2 If my immortal Saviour lives.
  Then my immortal life is sure;
His word a firm foundation gives;
  Here let me build and rest secure.

3 Here let my faith unshaken dwell;
  Immovable the promise stands;
Not all the powers of earth or hell
  Can e'er dissolve the sacred bands.

4 Here, O my soul, thy trust repose;
  If Jesus is forever mine,
Not death itself, that last of foes,
  Shall break a union so divine.

165

1 Say, sinner, hath a voice within
  Oft whispered to thy secret soul,
Urged thee to leave the ways of sin,
  And yield thy heart to God's control?

2 Hath something met thee in the path
  Of worldliness and vanity,
And pointed to the coming wrath,
  · And warned thee from that wrath to flee!

3 Sinner, it was a heavenly voice;
  'It was the Spirit's gracious call;
It bade thee make the better choice,
  And haste to seek in Christ thine all.

4 Spurn not the call to life and light;
  Regard in time the warning kind;
That call thou mayst not always slight,
  And yet the gate of mercy find.

166

1 Haste, trav'ler, haste! the night comes on,
  And many a shining hour is gone;
The storm is gathering in the west,
  And thou far off from home and rest.

2 The rising temptest sweeps the sky:
  The rains descend, the winds are high;
The waters swell, and death and fear
  Beset thy path, nor refuge near.

3 O, yes! a shelter you may gain,
  A covert from the wind and rain;
A hiding-place, a rest, a home,
  A refuge from the wrath to come.

4 Then linger not in all the plain;
  Flee for thy life; the mountain gain;
Look not behind; make no delay;
  O speed thee, speed thee on thy way.

GILEAD. L. M. Dr. Lowell Mason.

ANIMATO.

From "Joseph," by Mehul.

Zi - on, awake! thy strength renew, Put on thy robes of beauteous hue;

Church of our God, a - rise and shine Bright with the beams of truth di - vine.

167

2 Church of our God, arise and shine
Bright with the beams of truth divine;
Then shall thy radiance stream afar,
Wide as the heathen nations are.

3 Gentiles and kings thy light shall view;
All shall admire and love thee too,
Shall come like clouds across the sky,
Or doves that to their windows fly.

168

1 O, come, loud anthems let us sing,
Loud thanks to our almighty King; ·
For we our voices high should raise,
When our salvation's Rock we praise.

2 Into his presence let us haste,
To thank Him for His favors past;
To Him address, in joyful songs,
The praise that to His name belongs.

3 For God the Lord, enthroned in state,
Is with unrivalled glory great—
A King superior far to all—
Who by His title God we call,

4 O, let us to His courts repair,
And bow with adoration there;
Down on our knees devoutly, all,
Before the Lord our Maker, fall.

169

1 Sovereign of worlds! display Thy power;
Be this Thy Zion's favored hour;

Bid the bright morning Star arise,
And point the nations to the skies.

2 Set up Thy throne where Satan reigns,—
On Afric's shore, on India's plains,
On wilds and continents unknown,—
And make the nations all Thine own.

3 Speak! and the world shall hear Thy voice;
Speak! and the desert shall rejoice;
Scatter the gloom of heathen night,
And bid all nations hail the light.

170

1 The Lord is King! Lift up thy voice,
O earth, and all ye heavens, rejoice!
From world to world the joy shall ring;
" The Lord omnipotent is King!"

2 The Lord is King! who then shall dare
Resist His will, distrust His care?
Holy and true are all His ways;
Let every creature speak His praise.

3 O, when His wisdom can mistake,
His might decay, His love forsake,
Then may His children cease to sing,
" The Lord omnipotent is King!"

171

To God the Father, God the Son,
And God the Spirit, Three in One,
Be honor, praise, and glory given,
By all on earth, and all in heaven!

MODERATO.   Rev. C. Malan.

My gracious Lord, I own thy right To ev'-ry ser-vice I can pay;

And call it my su-preme de-light To hear Thy dic-tates, and o-bey.

172

2 What is my being but for Thee,—
Its sure support, its noblest end?
'Tis my delight Thy face to see,
And serve the cause of such a Friend.

3 I would not sigh for worldly joy,
Or to increase my worldly good;
Nor future days nor powers employ
To spread a sounding name abroad.

4 'Tis to my Saviour I would live,—
To Him who for my ransom died;
Nor could all worldly honor give
Such bliss as crowns me at His side.

173

1 God of my life, to Thee I call;
Afflicted at Thy feet I fall;
When the great water-floods prevail,
Leave not my trembling heart to fail.

2 Friend of the friendless, and the faint,
Where should I lodge my deep complaint?
Where—but with Him whose open door
Invites the helpless and the poor?

3 Did ever mourner plead with Thee,
And Thou refuse that mourner's plea?
Does not the promise still remain,
That none shall seek Thy face in vain?

4 Poor I may be—despised, forgot,
Yet God, my God, forgets me not;
And he is safe, and must succeed,
For whom the Saviour deigns to plead.

174

1 O spirit of the living God,
In all Thy plenitude of grace,
Where'er the foot of man hath trod,
Descend on our apostate race.

2 Give tongues of fire, and hearts of love,
To preach the reconciling word;
Give power and unction from above,
Where'er the joyful sound is heard.

3 Be darkness, at Thy coming, light;
Confusion—order, in Thy path;
Souls without strength, inspire with might,
Bid mercy triumph over wrath.

4 Baptize the nations; far and nigh
The triumphs of the cross record;
The name of Jesus glorify,
Till every kindred call Him Lord.

175

1 "Go, preach my gospel," saith the Lord;
"Bid the whole earth my grace receive:
"He shall be saved, who trusts my word;
"He shall be damned, who won't believe.

2 "I'll make your great commission known,
"And ye shall prove my gospel true;
"By all the works that I have done:
"By all the wonders ye shall do.

3 "Teach all the nations my commands;
"I'm with you till the world shall end:
"All power is trusted in my hands;
"I can destroy, and I defend."

4 He spake,—and light shone round his head;
On a bright cloud to heaven he rode;
They to the farthest nations spread
The grace of their ascended God.

MIGDOL. L. M.

MODERATO.

DR. LOWELL MASON.

Soon may the last glad song a - rise Through all the millions of the skies,

That song of triumph which records That all the earth is now the Lord's.

176

2 Let thrones, and powers, and kingdoms be
Obedient, mighty God, to Thee;
And over land, and stream, and main,
Wave Thou the scepter of Thy reign.

3 O, let that glorious anthem swell;
Let host to host the triumph tell,
That no one rebel heart remains,
But over all the Saviour reigns.

177

1 Lo, what a glorious Corner Stone
The Jewish builders did refuse;
But God hath built his Church thereon,
In spite of envy and the Jews.

2 Great God, the work is all divine,
The joy and wonder of our eyes;
This is the day that proves it Thine,
The day that saw our Saviour rise.

3 Sinners, rejoice, and saints, be glad;
Hosanna! let His name be blessed;
A thousand honors on His head,
With peace, and light, and glory rest.

4 In God's own name He comes to bring
Salvation to our dying race;
Let the whole Church address their King
With hearts of joy and songs of praise.

178

1 UPON the Gospel's sacred page
The gathered beams of ages shine;
And, as it hastens, every age
But makes its brightness more divine.

2 On mightier wing, in loftier flight,
From year to year does knowledge soar;
And, as it soars, the gospel light
Adds to its influence more and more.

3 More glorious still as centuries roll,
New regions blessed, new powers un-
furled,
Expanding with the expanding soul,
Its waters shall o'erflow the world;

4 Flow to restore, but not destroy;
As when the cloudless lamp of day
Pours out its floods of light and joy,
And sweeps each lingering mist away.

179

1 JESUS! Thy Church, with longing eyes,
For Thine expected coming waits:
When will the promised light arise,
And glory beam on Zion's gates ?

2 E'en now, when tempests round us fall,
And wintry clouds o'ercast the sky,
Thy words with pleasure we recall,
And deem that our redemption 's nigh.

3 O! come, and reign o'er every land;
Let Satan from his throne be hurled;
All nations bow to Thy command,
And grace revive a dying world.

4 Teach us, in watchfulness and prayer,
To wait for Thine appointed hour,
And fit us, by Thy grace, to share
The triumphs of Thy conqu'ring power.

180

2 He saw me ruined in the fall,
Yet loved me, notwithstanding all;
He saved me from my lost estate;
His loving kindness, O, how great!

3 When trouble, like a gloomy cloud,
Has gathered thick and thundered loud,
He near my soul has always stood;
His loving kindness, O, how good!

4 Often I feel my sinful heart
Prone from my Jesus to depart;
But though I have Him oft forgot,
His loving kindness changes not.

5 Soon shall I pass the gloomy vale,
Soon all my mortal powers must fail;
O, may my last, expiring breath
His loving kindness sing in death.

6 Then let me mount and soar away
To the bright world of endless day,
And sing, with rapture and surprise,
His loving kindness in the skies.

181

1 To Thee, O God, in grateful praise,
All nature wakes harmonious lays;
The rolling flood, beast, bird, and bee,
Join in perpetual praise to Thee.

2 The opening flower that scents the morn,
The breeze that bends the golden corn,
The dew-drop trembling in the sun,
Praise Thee, Thou great and Holy One.

3 The mighty orbs that roll on high,
The rainbow arching o'er the sky,
Old ocean heaving deep and free,
Ascribe unceasing praise to Thee.

4 Heaven, earth, and main in one glad song,
Their Maker's glorious praise prolong;
And angels sweep the silver string,
To laud Thy name, eternal King.

5 Our tongues, Great God, adoring Thee,
Shall join the general symphony;
While our Redeemer's lofty praise
Shall be the chorus which we raise.

ALL-SAINTS. L. M.

ANDANTE.   W. KNAPP.

Come, O my soul, in sacred lays At-tempt Thy great Cre-ator's praise:

But, O, what tongue can speak His fame, What verse can reach the lofty theme?

182

2 Enthroned amid the radiant spheres,
 He glory like a garment wears;
 To form a robe of light divine,
 Ten thousand suns around Him shine.

3 In all our Maker's grand designs,
 Almighty power, with wisdom shines;
 His works, through all this wondrous
 Declare the glory of His name.   [frame,

4 Raised on devotion's lofty wing,
 Do thou, my soul, His glories sing;
 And let His praise employ thy tongue,
 Till listening worlds shall join the song.

183

1 If in our daily course our mind
 Be set to hallow all we find,
 New treasures still, of countless price,
 God will provide for sacrifice.

2 Old friends, old scenes will lovelier be
 As more of heaven in each we see:
 Some softening gleam of love and prayer
 Shall dawn on every cross and care.

184

1 JESUS, Thy boundless love to me
 No thought can reach, no tongue declare;
 Unite my thankful heart to Thee,
 And reign without a rival there.

2 O, let Thy love my soul inflame,
 And to Thy service sweetly bind,
 Transfuse it through my inmost frame,
 And mould me wholly to Thy mind.

3 Thy love in sufferings be my peace,
 Thy love in weakness make me strong;
 And when the storms of life shall cease,
 Thy love shall be in heaven my song.

185

1 HAPPY the meek, whose gentle breast,
 Clear as the summer's evening ray,
 Calm as the regions of the blest,
 Enjoys on earth celestial day.

2 His heart no broken friendships sting;
 No jars his peaceful tent invade;
 He rests beneath th' Almighty's wing,
 Hostile to none—of none afraid.

3 Spirit of grace! all meek and mild,
 Inspire our hearts,—our souls possess;
 Repel each passion rude and wild,
 And bless us, as we aim to bless.

186

1 O, DEEM not they are blessed alone
 Whose lives a peaceful tenor keep;
 For God who pities man, has shown
 A blessing for the eyes that weep.

2 The light of smiles shall fill again
 The lids that overflow with tears;
 And weary hours of woe and pain
 Are promises of happier years.

3 And ye who at a friend's low bier
 Now shed the bitter drops like rain,
 Hope that a brighter, happier sphere
 Will give him to your arms again.

4 Nor let the good man's trust depart,
 Though life its common gifts deny,
 Though with a pierced and broken heart,
 And spurned of men, he goes to die.

5 For God has marked each sorrowing day,
 And numbered every secret tear,
 And heaven's long age of bliss shall pay
 For all His children suffer here.

MODERATO

WM. D. BRADBURY.

Sweet hour of prayer! sweet hour of prayer! That calls me from a world of care,
D.C. And oft escaped the tempter's snare By thy return, sweet hour of prayer.

And bids me at my Father's throne Make all my wants and wish-es known.
And oft escaped the tempter's snare By thy re-turn, sweet hour of prayer.

In sea-sons of dis-tress and grief, My soul has of-ten found re-lief.

187

2 Sweet hour of prayer! sweet hour of prayer!
Thy wings shall my petition bear,
To him whose truth and faithfulness,
Engage the waiting soul to bless;
And since he bids me seek his face,
Believe his word, and trust his grace,
I'll cast on him my every care,
And wait for thee, sweet hour of prayer!

3 Sweet hour of prayer! sweet hour of prayer!
May I thy consolations share;
Till from Mount Pisgah's lofty height,
I view my home, and take my flight:
This robe of flesh I'll drop, and rise
To seize the everlasting prize;
And shout, while passing through the air,
Farewell, farewell, sweet hour of prayer.

188

1 O LOVE divine, that stooped to share
Our sharpest pangs, our bitterest tear,
On Thee we cast each earth born care,
We smile at pain while Thou art near!

2 Though long the weary way we tread,
And sorrow crown each lingering year,
No path we shun, no darkness dread,
Our hearts still whispering, Thou art near!

4 When drooping pleasure turns to grief,
And trembling faith is changed to fear,
The murmuring wind, the quivering leaf
Shall softly tell us, Thou art near!

4 On thee we fling our burdening woe,
O love divine, forever dear,
Content to suffer, while we know,
Living and dying, Thou art near!

189

1 THOU art, O God, the Life and Light
Of all this wondrous world we see;
Its glow by day, its smile by night,
Are but reflections caught from Thee;
Where'er we turn, Thy glories shine,
And all things fair and bright are Thine.

Je - sus, my All, to heaven is gone—He whom I fix my hopes upon;

His track I see and I'll pur-sue The narrow way till Him I view.
The King's highway of ho - li - ness, I'll go, for all His paths are peace.

FINE.

End with second strain.

The way the ho - ly prophets went, The way that leads from banishment,

190

3 This is the way I long have sought,
    And mourn'd because I found it not;
    My grief, a burden long has been,
    Because I was not saved from sin.

4 The more I strove against its power,
    I felt its weight and guilt the more;
    Till late I heard my Saviour say,—
    " Come hither, soul, I am the way."

191

1 THERE is a glorious world on high,
    Resplendent with eternal day;
    Faith views the blissful prospect nigh,
    While God's own word reveals the way.

2 There shall the favorites of the Lord
    With never-fading lustre shine;
    Surprising honor—vast reward,
    Conferred on man by love divine.

3 The shining firmament shall fade,
    And sparkling stars resign their light;
    But these shall know no change or shade,
    Forever fair, forever bright.

4 And shall not these cold hearts of ours
    Be kindled at the glorious view?

Come, Lord, awake our active powers,
Our feeble, dying strength renew.

192

1 A POOR wayfaring man of grief
    Hath often crossed me on my way,
    Who sued so humbly for relief,
    That I could never answer, nay.
    I had not power to ask his name,
    Whither he went, or whence he came,
    Yet there was something in his eye
    That won my love, I knew not why.

2 Once when my scanty meal was spread,
    He entered; not a word he spake;
    Just perishing for want of bread,
    I gave him all; he blessed it, brake,
    And ate, but gave me part again;
    Mine was an angel's portion then;
    And while I fed with eager haste,
    The crust was manna to my taste.

3 I spied him where a fountain burst
    Clear from the rock; his strength was gone,
    The heedless water mocked his thirst;
    He heard it, saw it hurrying on:—
    I ran, and raised the sufferer up;
    Thrice from the stream he drained my cup,
    Dipped, and returned it running o'er;
    I drank, and never thirsted more.

Descend from heav'n, immortal Dove; Stoop down and take us on Thy wings;

And mount, and bear us far a - bove The reach of these in - fe - rior things;

CHORUS.

Glo - ry, glo - ry, let us sing, While heaven and earth with glory ring,

Ho - san - na; Ho - san - na! Ho - san - na to the Lamb of God.

193

2 Beyond, beyond this lower sky,
  Up where eternal ages roll,
Where solid pleasures never die,
  And fruits immortal feast the soul.

3 O for a sight, a pleasing sight,
  Of our almighty Father's throne!
There sits our Saviour crowned with light,
  Clothed in a body like our own.

4 Adoring saints around Him stand,
  And thrones and powers before Him
    fall;
The God shines gracious through the
    man,
  And sheds sweet glories on them all.

5 O, what amazing joys they feel,
  While to their golden harps they sing,
And sit on every heavenly hill,
  And spread the triumphs of their King!

54

OLD HUNDRED. L. M.

GUIL. FRANK.

Be Thou, O God, ex - alt - ed high, And as Thy glo - ry fills the sky,

So let it be on earth displayed, Till Thou art here as there obeyed.

194

2 O God, my heart is fixed—'tis bent,
  Its thankful tribute to present;
  And with my heart, my voice I'll raise
  To Thee, my God, in songs of praise.

3 Thy praises, Lord, I will resound
  To all the listening nations round;
  Thy mercy highest heaven transcends,
  Thy truth beyond the clouds extends.

4 Be Thou, O God, exalted high;
  And, as Thy glory fills the sky,
  So let it be on earth displayed,
  Till Thou art here, as there, obeyed.

195

1 FROM all that dwell below the skies,
  Let the Creator's praise arise;
  Let the Redeemer's name be sung,
  Through every land, by every tongue.

2 Eternal are Thy mercies, Lord;
  Eternal truth attends Thy word;
  Thy praise shall sound from shore to shore,
  Till suns shall rise and set no more.

196

1 JESUS shall reign where'er the sun
  Does his successive journeys run;
  His kingdom stretch from shore to shore,
  Till moons shall wax and wane no more.

2 For Him shall endless prayer be made,
  And praises throng to crown His head;
  His name, like sweet perfume, shall rise
  With every morning sacrifice.

3 People and realms, of every tongue,
  Dwell on His love with sweetest song;
  And infant voices shall proclaim
  Their early blessings on His name.

  Let every creature rise and bring
  Peculiar honors to their King,
  Angels descend with songs again,
  And earth repeat the long Amen.

197

1 WHEN as returns this solemn day,
  Man comes to meet his Maker, God,
  What rites, what honors shall he pay?
  How spread His sovereign praise abroad?

2 From marble domes and gilded spires
  Shall curling clouds of incense rise,
  And gems, and gold, and garlands deck
  The costly pomp of sacrifice?

3 Vain, sinful man, creation's Lord,
  Thy golden offerings well may spare;
  But give thy heart, and thou shalt find
  Here dwells a God who heareth prayer.

198

1 LET the seventh angel sound on high
  Let shouts be heard through all the sky;
  Kings of the earth, with glad accord
  Give up your kingdoms to the Lord.

2 Almighty God, Thy power assume,
  Who wast, and art, and art to come;
  Jesus, the Lamb who once was slain,
  Forever live, forever reign.

ORTONVILLE. C. M.

ALLEGRETTO.   DR. T. HASTINGS.

How sweet the name of Je - sus sounds In a be - liev - er's ear! It

soothes his sorrows, heals his wounds, And drives away his fear, And drives away his fear.

199

2 It makes the wounded spirit whole,
  And calms the troubled breast;
  'Tis manna to the hungry soul,
  And to the weary, rest.

3 By Thee my prayers acceptance gain,
  Although with sin defiled;
  Satan accuses me in vain;
  And I am owned a child;

4 Jesus, my Shepherd, Husband, Friend,
  My Prophet, Priest, and King;
  My Lord, my Life, my Way, my End,
  Accept the praise I bring.

5 Weak is the effort of my heart,
  And cold my warmest thought;
  But when I see Thee as Thou art,
  I'll praise Thee as I ought.

6 Till then I would Thy love proclaim
  With every fleeting breath;
  And may the music of Thy name
  Refresh my soul in death.

200

1 MAJESTIC sweetness sits enthroned
  Upon His awful brow;
  His head with radiant glories crowned,
  His lips with grace o'erflow.

2 No mortal can with him compare,
  Among the sons of men:
  Fairer is He than all the fair
  That fill the heavenly train.

3 He saw me plunged in deep distress,
  He flew to my relief;
  For me He bore the shameful cross,
  And carried all my grief.

4 To Him I owe my life and breath,
  And all the joys I have;
  He makes me triumph over death,
  And saves me from the grave.

5 To heaven, the place of His abode,
  He brings my weary feet,
  Shows me the glories of my God,
  And makes my joys complete.

6 Since from His bounty I receive
  Such proofs of love divine,
  Had I a thousand hearts to give,
  Lord, they should all be Thine.

201

1 LORD, I believe a rest remains,
  To all Thy people known;
  A rest where pure enjoyment reigns,
  And Thou art loved alone;—

2 A rest where all our souls' desire
  Is fixed on things above;
  Where fear and sin and grief expire,
  Cast out by perfect love.

3 Oh that I now the rest might know,
  Believe and enter in!
  Now, Saviour! now the power bestow,
  And let me cease from sin.

4 Remove the hardness of my heart,
  The unbelief remove;
  To me the rest of faith impart—
  The Sabbath of Thy love.

TALLIS. C. M. (Chant.) Dr. Lowell Mason.

From Tallis. 1560.

Sing to the Lord, ye heav'n-ly hosts, And thou, O earth, a-dore;

Let death and hell thro' all their coasts, Stand trembling at ·his power.

202

2 His sounding chariot shakes the sky;
He makes the clouds His throne;
There all His stores of lightning lie
Till vengeance darts them down.

3 Think, O my soul, the dreadful day
When this incensed God
Shall rend the sky, and burn the sea,
And send His wrath abroad.

4 What shall the wretch, the sinner do?
He once defied the Lord;
But he shall dread the Thunderer now,
And sink beneath His word.

5 Tempests of angry fire shall roll
To blast the rebel worm,
And beat upon his naked soul
In one eternal storm.

203

1 In heaven the rapturous song began,
And sweet seraphic fire
Through all the shining legions ran,
And strung and tuned the lyre.

2 Swift through the vast expanse it flew,
And loud the echo rolled;
The theme, the song, the joy was new;
'Twas more than heaven could hold.

3 Down through the portals of the sky
The impetuous torrent ran;
And angels flew, with eager joy,
To bear the news to man.

4 Hark! the cherubic armies shout,
And glory leads the song;
Good will and peace are heard throughout
The harmonious heav'nly throng.

5 With joy the chorus we'll repeat,
" Glory to God on high;
Good will and peace are now complete,"
Jesus was born to die.

204

1 SEND forth Thy word, and let it fly,
Armed with Thy Spirit's power,
And thousands shall confess its sway,
And bless the saving hour.

2 Beneath the influence of its grace
The barren wastes shall rise,
With sudden greens and fruits arrayed—
A blooming paradise.

3 Peace, with her olives crowned, shall stretch
Her wings from shore to shore;
No trump shall rouse the rage of war,
No murderous cannon roar.

4 Lord, for these days we wait; these days
Are in Thy word foretold;
Fly swifter, sun and stars, and bring
This promised age of gold.

5 Amen, with joy divine, let earth's
Unnumbered myriads cry;
Amen, with joy divine, let heaven's
Unnumbered choirs reply.

Come, thou De - sire of all Thy saints! Our hum-ble strains at - tend,

While, with our prais - es and complaints, Low at Thy feet we bend.

205

2 How should our songs, like those above,
   With warm devotion rise!
   How should our souls, on wings of love,
   Mount upward to the skies!

3 Come, Lord, Thy love alone can raise
   In us the heavenly flame;
   Then shall our lips resound Thy praise,
   Our hearts adore Thy name.

206

1 BRIGHT Source of everlasting love,
   To Thee our souls we raise;
   And to Thy sovereign bounty rear
   A monument of praise.

2 Thy mercy gilds the path of life
   With every cheering ray,
   Kindly restrains the rising tear,
   Or wipes that tear away.

3 To tents of woe, to beds of pain,
   Our cheerful feet repair,
   And with the gifts Thy hand bestows,
   Relieve the mourners there.

4 The widow's heart shall sing for joy;
   The orphan shall be fed;
   The hungering soul we'll gladly point
   To Christ, the living Bread.

207

1 ASSEMBLED at Thine altar, Lord,
   We lift our hearts in prayer,
   Study the pages of Thy word,
   And learn our duty there.

2 Grant us Thy Spirit's guiding ray;
   Thy presence we implore;
   Dear Saviour, teach us how to pray,
   To love and praise Thee more.

3 So will our worship here below
   Resemble that above,
   Where saints unclouded glory view,
   And sing redeeming love.

208

1 DREAD Sovereign, let my evening song
   Like holy incense rise;
   Assist the offering of my tongue
   To reach the lofty skies.

2 Through all the dangers of the day
   Thy hand was still my guard;
   And still to drive my wants away
   Thy mercy stood prepared.

3 Perpetual blessings from above
   Encompass me around;
   But, oh, how few returns of love
   Hath my Redeemer found!

4 What have I done for him who died
   To save my guilty soul?
   How are my follies multiplied,
   Fast as the minutes roll!

5 Lord! with this sinful heart of mine,
   To Thy dear cross I flee,
   And to Thy grace my soul resign,
   To be renewed by Thee.

6 Sprinkled afresh with pardoning blood
   I lay me down to rest,
   As in the embraces of my God,
   Or on my Saviour's breast.

EMMONS. C. M.

From BURGMULLER.

How sweet, how heavenly is the sight, When those who love the Lord In one an-

other's peace delight, And thus ful - fil His word, And thus fulfil His word!

209

2 When each can feel his brother's sigh,
And with him bear a part!
When sorrows flow from eye to eye,
And joy from heart to heart!

3 When, free from envy, scorn, and pride,
Our wishes all above,
Each can his brother's failings hide,
And show a brother's love!

4 Let love, in one delightful stream,
Through every bosom flow,
And union sweet, and dear esteem,
In every action glow.

5 Love is the golden chain that binds
The happy souls above;
And he's an heir of heaven who finds
His bosom glow with love.

210

1 Messiah! at Thy glad approach
The howling winds are still;
Thy praises fill the lonely waste,
And breathe from every hill.

2 The incense of the spring ascends
Upon the morning gale;
Red o'er the hill the roses bloom,
The lilies in the vale.

3 Renewed, the earth a robe of light,
A robe of beauty, wears;
And in new heavens a brighter Sun
Leads on the promised years.

4 Let Israel to the Prince of Peace
The loud hosanna sing;
With hallelujahs and with hymns,
O Zion, hail thy King.

211

1 The bird let loose in Eastern skies,
Returning fondly home,
Ne'er stoops to earth her wing, nor flies
Where idler warblers roam.

2 But high she shoots through air and light,
Above all low delay,
Where nothing earthly bounds her flight,
Nor shadow dims her way.

3 So grant, me, Lord, from every snare
Of sinful passion free,
Aloft through faith's screner air
To hold my course to Thee.

4 No sin to cloud, no lure to stay
My soul, as home she springs;
Thy sunshine on her joyful way,
Thy freedom in her wings.

212

1 When brighter suns and milder skies
Proclaim the opening year,
What various sounds of joy arise!
What prospects bright appear!

2 Earth and her thousand voices give
Their thousand notes of praise;
And all, that by His mercy live,
To God their offering raise.

3 Thus, like the morning, calm and clear,
That saw the Saviour rise,
The spring of heaven's eternal year
Shall dawn on earth and skies.

4 No winter there, no shades of night,
Obscure those mansions blest,
Where, in the happy fields of light,
The weary are at rest.

ANIMATO.

Je - sus, I love Thy charming name, 'Tis mu-sic to mine ear; Fain would I

sound it out so loud, That heav'n and earth should hear, That heav'n and earth should hear.

213

2 Yes, Thou art precious to my soul,
My transport and my trust;
Jewels to Thee are gaudy toys,
And gold is sordid dust.

3 All my capacious powers can wish,
In Thee do richly meet;
Nor, to mine eyes is light so dear,
Nor friendship half so sweet.

4 Thy grace still dwells upon my heart,
And sheds its fragrance there;
The noblest balm of all its wounds,
The cordial of its care.

5 I'll speak the honors of Thy name
With my last laboring breath;
Then, speechless, clasp Thee in mine arms,
The antidote of death.

214

1 Our journey is a thorny maze;
But we march upward still,
Forget these troubles of the ways,
And reach at Zion's hill.

2 See the kind angels at the gates
Inviting us to come;
There Jesus, the Forerunner, waits
To welcome travellers home.

215

_ The Saviour! O what endless charms
Dwell in the blissful sound!
Its influence every fear disarms,
And spreads sweet comfort round.

2 Here pardon, life, and joys divine,
In rich effusion flow,
For guilty rebels lost in sin,
And doomed to endless woe.

3 The Almighty Former of the skies
Stooped to our vile abode;
While angels viewed with wondering eyes,
And hailed the incarnate God.

4 Oh! the rich depths of love divine!
Of bliss a boundless store!
Dear Saviour, let me call Thee mine;
I cannot wish for more.

5 On Thee alone my hope relies,
Beneath Thy cross I fall;
My Lord, my Life, my Sacrifice,
My Saviour, and my All.

216

1 And did the Holy and the Just,
The Sovereign of the skies,
Stoop down to wretchedness and dust
That guilty man might rise?

2 Yes: the Redeemer left His throne,
His radiant throne on high—
Surprising mercy! love unknown!—
To suffer, bleed, and die.

3 He took the dying traitor's place,
And suffered in his stead;
For man—oh, miracle of grace!—
For man the Saviour bled.

4 Dear Lord, what heavenly wonders dwell
In Thine atoning blood!
By this are sinners saved from hell,
And rebels brought to God.

BOYNTON. C. M. (Double.)

DOLCE.

Dear Saviour, ev - er at my side, How lov - ing Thou must be,

To leave Thy home in heaven, to guard A lit - tle child like me.

Thy beau - ti - ful and shin - ing face I see not though so near;

The sweetness of Thy soft, low voice, I am too deaf to hear.

217

3 I cannot feel Thee touch my hand,
  With pressure light and mild,
  To check me as my mother did,
  When I was but a child.

4 But I have felt Thee in my thoughts,
  Rebuking sin for me;
  And, when my heart loves God, I know
  The sweetness is from Thee.

5 And when, Dear Saviour, I kneel down,
  Morning and night to prayer,
  Something there is within my heart
  Which tells me Thou art there.

6 Yes! when I pray, Thou prayest, too—
  Thy prayer is all for me;
  But when I sleep, Thou sleepest not,
  But watchest patiently.

CHORAL.   JOHN MILTON, (Father of the Poet.)

Our God, our Help in a - ges past, Our Hope in years to come,

Our Shelter in the stormy blast, And our e - ter - nal Home.

218

2 Under the shadow of Thy throne,
Thy saints have dwelt secure;
Sufficient is Thine arm alone,
And our defence is sure.

3 Before the hills in order stood,
Or earth received her frame,
From everlasting Thou art God,
To endless years the same.

4 Thy word commands our flesh to dust,—
" Return, ye sons of men ; "
All nations rose from earth at first,
And turn to earth again.

5 Our God, our help in ages past,
Our hope for years to come,
Be Thou our guard while troubles last,
And our eternal home.

219

1 On, speed thee, Christian! on thy way,
And to thine armor cling;
With girded loins the call obey
Which grace and mercy bring.

2 There is a battle to be fought,
An upward race to run,
A crown of glory to be sought,
A vict'ry to be won.

220

1 LET saints below in concert sing
With those to glory gone;
For all the servants of our King
In earth and heaven are one.

2 One family, we dwell in Him,
One church above, beneath,
Though now divided by the stream,
The narrow stream, of death.

3 One army of the living God,
To His command we bow;
Part of the host have crossed the flood,
And part are crossing now.

4 Some to their everlasting home
This solemn moment fly;
And we are to the margin come,
And soon expect to die.

5 O that we now might see our guide!
O that the word were given!
Come, blessed Lord, the waves divide,
And land us all in heaven.

221

1 OH that the Lord would guide my ways
To keep His statutes still!
Oh that my God would grant me grace
To know and do His will!

2 Oh, send Thy Spirit down, to write
Thy law upon my heart;
Nor let my tongue indulge deceit,
Nor act the liar's part.

3 Order my footsteps by Thy word,
And make my heart sincere;
Let sin have no dominion, Lord,
But keep my conscience clear.

4 Make me to walk in Thy commands—
'Tis a delightful road;
Nor let my head nor heart nor hands
Offend against my God.

62   FOUNTAIN. C. M.

MODERATO.   From MOZART.

There is a Foun-tain filled with blood, Drawn from Im-man-uel's veins;

And sin-ners, plunged be-neath that flood, Lose all their guil-ty stains.

222

2 The dying thief, rejoiced to see
That Fountain in His day;
And there have I, as vile as he,
Washed all my sins away.

3 Dear dying Lamb, Thy precious blood
Shall never loose its power,
Till all the ransomed church of God
Be saved, to sin no more.

4 E'er since, by faith, I saw the stream
Thy flowing wounds supply,
Redeeming love has been my theme,
And shall be, till I die.

5 Then in a nobler, sweeter song,
I'll sing Thy power to save,
When this poor lisping, stammering tongue
Lies silent in the grave.

223

1 WHEN languor and disease invade
This trembling house of clay,
'Tis sweet to look beyond our cage,
And long to fly away:

2 Sweet to look inward, and attend
The whispers of His love;
Sweet to look upward to the place
Where Jesus pleads above:

3 Sweet on His righteousness to stand,
Which saves from second death;
Sweet to experience, day by day,
His Spirit's quickening breath.

4 If such sweetness of the stream,
What must the fountain be,
Where saints and angels draw their bliss
Immed'ately from Thee?

224

1 BLESSED is the man whose softening heart
Feels all another's pain;
To whom the supplicating eye
Was never raised in vain;

2 Whose breast expands with generous
A stranger's woe to feel, [warmth
And bleeds in pity o'er the wound
He wants the power to heal.

3 To gentle offices of love
His feet are never slow;
He views through mercy's melting eye
A brother in a foe.

4 Peace from the bosom of his God,
My peace, to Him I give;
And when he kneels before the throne,
His trembling soul shall live.

225

1 SEE Israel's gentle Shepherd stand,
With all engaging charms;
Hark, how He calls the tender lambs,
And folds them in His arms!

2 "Permit them to approach," He cries,
"Nor scorn their humble name;
For 'twas to bless such souls as these,
The Lord of angels came."

3 We bring them, Lord, in thankful hands,
And yield them up to Thee;
Joyful that we ourselves are Thine,
Thine let our offspring be.

MODERATO.

DR. LOWELL MASON.

My God! the Spring of all my joys, The Life of my de-lights,

The Glo-ry of my brightest days, The Comfort of my nights.

226

2 In darkest shades if He appear,
  My dawning is begun!
He is my soul's sweet morning star,
  And He my rising sun.

3 The opening heavens around me shine
  With beams of sacred bliss,
While Jesus shows His heart is mine,
  And whispers, " I am His! "

4 My soul would leave this heavy clay
  At that transporting word,
Run up with joy the shining way,
  T' embrace my dearest Lord.

5 Fearless of hell and ghostly death,
  I'd break through every foe:
The wings of love and arms of faith,
  Should bear me conqueror through.

227

1 THE Lord our God is clothed with might;
  The winds obey His will;
He speaks, and in his heavenly height
  The rolling sun stands still.

2 Rebel, ye waves, and o'er the land
  With threatening aspect roar;
The Lord uplifts His awful hand,
  And chains you to the shore.

3 Howl, winds of night; your force combine;
  Without His high behest,
Ye shall not, in the mountain pine,
  Disturb the sparrows nest.

4 His voice sublime is heard afar;
  In distant peals it dies;
He yokes the whirlwind to His car,
  And sweeps the howling skies.

5 Ye nations, bend; in reverence bend;
  Ye monarchs, wait His nod,
And bid the choral song ascend
  To celebrate our God.

228

1 A GLORY gilds the sacred page,
  Majestic, like the sun;
It gives a light to every age;
  It gives, but borrows none.

2 The hand that gave it still supplies.
  The gracious light and heat;
His truths upon the nations rise,
  They, rise, but never set.

3 Let everlasting thanks be Thine
  For such a bright display
As makes a world of darkness shine
  With beams of heavenly day.

229

1 As pants the hart for cooling streams,
  When heated in the chase;
So longs my soul, O God, for Thee,
  And Thy refreshing grace.

2 For Thee, my God, the living God,
  My thirsty soul doth pine;
Oh, when shall I behold Thy face,
  Thou Majesty divine?

3 Why restless, why cast down, my soul?
  Trust God; who will employ
His aid for Thee, and change these sighs
  To thankful hymns of joy.

Far from these nar-row scenes of night Un-bounded glo-ries rise,....

And realms of in-fin-ite de-light, Un-known to mor-tal eyes.

230

2 There pain and sickness never come,
And griefs no more complain;
And all who reach that peaceful home
With Jesus ever reign.

3 No cloud these happy regions know,
For ever bright and fair;
For sin, the source of mortal woe,
Can never enter there.

4 Oh, may the heavenly vision fire
Our hearts with ardent love,
Till wings of faith and strong desire
Bear every thought above.

231

1 Hope of our hearts, O Lord, appear,
Thou glorious star of day;
Shine forth and chase the dreary night,
With all our tears, away!

2 Strangers on earth, we wait for Thee;
Oh! leave the Father's throne;
Come with a shout of victory, Lord,
And claim us as Thy own.

3 Oh! bid the bright archangel now,
The trump of God prepare,
To call Thy saints—the quick, the dead,
To meet Thee in the air.

4 No resting place we seek on earth,
No loveliness we see;
Our eye is on the royal crown
Prepared for us and Thee.

5 But, dearest Lord, however bright
That crown of joy above,
What is it to the brighter hope
Of dwelling in Thy love?

232

1 Let worldly minds the world pursue;
What are its charms to me!
Once I admired its trifles too,
But grace has set me free.

2 Its pleasures now no longer please,
No more content afford;
Far from my heart be joys like these,
Now I have seen the Lord.

3 As by the light of opening day
The stars are all concealed,
So earthly pleasures flade away
When Jesus is revealed.

233

1 Hark, the glad sound! the Saviour comes!
The Saviour promised long!
Let every heart prepare a throne,
And every voice a song.

2 On Him the Spirit largely poured
Exerts its sacred fire;
Wisdom and might, and zeal and love,
His holy breast inspire.

3 Our glad hosannas, Prince of Peace,
Thy welcome shall proclaim,
And heaven's eternal arches ring
With Thy beloved name.

234

3 In each event of life, how clear
    Thy ruling hand I see!
Each blessing to my soul most dear,
    Because conferred by Thee.

4 In every joy that crowns my days,
    In every pain I bear,
My heart shall find delight in praise,
    Or seek relief in prayer.

5 When gladness wings my favored hour,
    Thy love my thoughts shall fill;
Resigned when storms of sorrow lower,
    My soul shall meet Thy will.

6 My lifted eye, without a tear,
    The gathering storm shall see;
My steadfast heart shall know no fear;
    That heart will rest on Thee.

235

1 HAVE I that faith which looks to Christ,
    O'ercomes the world and sin,
Receives Him, Prophet, Priest and King,
    And makes the conscience clean?

2 If I this precious grace possess,
    All praise is due to Thee;
If not, I seek it from Thy hands;
    Now grant it, Lord, to me.

CHORAL.   DR. CROFT.

Great God, Thy pen - e - trat - ing eye Per - vades my in - most powers;

With awe profound my wond'ring soul Falls pros - trate and a - dores.

236

2 To be encompassed round with God,
The holy and the just,
Armed with omnipotence to save,
Or crumble me to dust;

3 O, how tremendous is the thought!
Deep may it be impressed;
And may Thy Spirit firmly grave
This truth within my breast.

4 Begirt with Thee, my fearless soul
The gloomy vale shall tread;
And Thou wilt bind the immortal crown
Of glory on my head.

237

1 LORD, I have made Thy word my choice,
My lasting heritage;
There shall my noblest powers rejoice,
My warmest thoughts engage.

2 I'll read the histories of Thy love,
And keep Thy laws in sight,
While through the promises I rove,
With ever fresh delight.

3 'Tis a broad land, of wealth unknown,
Where springs of life arise,
Seeds of immortal bliss are sown,
And hidden glory lies.

4 The best relief that mourners have,
It makes our sorrows blessed;
Our fairest hope beyond the grave,
And our eternal rest.

238

1 How shall the young secure their hearts,
And guard their lives from sin?
Thy word the choicest rules imparts,
To keep the conscience clean.

2 When once it enters to the mind,
It spreads such light abroad,
The meanest souls instruction find,
And raise their thoughts to God.

3 'Tis like the sun, a heavenly light,
That guides us all the day;
And through the dangers of the night,
A lamp to lead our way.

4 Thy word is everlasting truth;
How pure is every page!
That holy book shall guide our youth,
And well support our age.

239

1 I LOVE the Lord: He guides my way
By His revealed will,
And when my erring feet would stray,
His hand is with me still.

2 I love the Lord: He hears my prayer
When stormy troubles rise,
And bids celestial hope look out
On ever-smiling skies.

3 I love the Lord: His grace attends
My pilgrimage below,
And all the streams of grace shall soon
In boundless glory flow.

4 I love the Lord: may each desire
In this united be:
As, Lord, Thy love descends on me,
So raise my heart to Thee.

CHORAL.   FINE.

I'm not ashamed to own my Lord, Nor to de-fend His cause, }
Main-tain the hon-or of His word, The glo-ry of His cross. }
D.C. Nor will He put my soul to shame, Nor let my hope be lost.

D. C.

Je-sus, my God, I know His name, His name is all my trust;

240

3 Firm as His throne His promise stands,
And He can well secure
What I've committed to his hands
Till the decisive hour.

4 Then will He own my worthless name
Before His Father's face,
And in the New Jerusalem
Appoint my soul a place.

241

1 I KNOW that my Redeemer lives,
And ever prays for me;
A token of His love He gives,
A pledge of liberty.

2 I find Him lifting up my head;
He brings salvation near;
His presence makes me free indeed,
And He will soon appear.

3 He wills that I should holy be;
What can withstand His will?
The counsel of His grace in me
He surely shall fulfil.

4 When God is mine, and I am His,
Of paradise possessed,
I taste unutterable bliss,
And everlasting rest.

242

1 HIDE not thy talent in the earth,
However small it be;
Its faithful use, its utmost worth,
God will require of thee.

His own, which He hath lent on trust,
He asks of thee again;
Little or much, the claim is just,
And thine excuses vain.

2 What if the litttle rain should plead,
" So small a drop as I
Can ne'er refresh yon thirsty mead;
I'll tarry in the sky!"
What if a shining beam of noon
Should in its fountain stay,
Because its feeble light alone
Was not enough for day.

3 Doth not each rain drop help to form
The cool, refreshing shower?
And every ray of light to warm
And beautify the flower?
Go, then, and strive to do thy part,
Though humble it may be;
The ready hand, the willing heart,
Are all Heaven asks of thee.

243

1 To our Almighty Maker, God,
New honors be addressed;
His great salvation shines abroad,
And makes the nations blessed.

2 Let the whole earth His love proclaim,
With all her different tongues,
And spread the honors of his name
In melody and songs.

MADAN. C. M.

W. B. BRADBURY.

Our lit - tle bark, on boisterous seas, By cru - el tempests tossed,

Without one cheering beam of hope, Ex - pect - ing to be lost.

244

2 We to the Lord, in humble prayer,
Breathed out our sad distress;
Though feeble, yet with contrite hearts,
We begged return of peace.

3 Then ceased the stormy winds to blow;
The surges ceased to roll;
And soon again a placid sea
Spoke comfort to the soul.

4 O, may our grateful, trembling hearts
Their hallelujahs sing
To Him who hath our lives preserved,
Our Saviour and our King..

245

1 As once the Saviour took His seat—
Attracted by His fame,
And lowly bending at His feet,
An humble suppliant came.

2 Ashamed to lift her streaming eyes
His holy glance to meet,
She poured her costly sacrifice
Upon the Saviour's feet.

3 Oppressed with sin and sorrow's weight,
And sinking in despair,
With tears she washed His sacred feet,
And wiped them with her hair.

4 " Depart in peace," the Saviour said,
" Thy sins are all forgiven! "
The trembling sinner raised her head,
In peaceful hope of heaven.

246

1 IN evil long I took delight,
Unawed by shame or fear,
Till a new object struck my sight,
And stopped my wild career.

2 I saw One hanging on a tree,
In agony and blood,
Who fixed His languid eyes on me,
As near His cross I stood.

3 Sure, never, to my latest breath,
Can I forget that look;
It seemed to charge me with His death,
Though not a word He spoke.

4 Alas! I knew not what I did,
But now my tears are vain;
Where shall my trembling soul be hid?
For I the Lord have slain.

5 A second look He gave, which said,
" I freely all forgive;
This blood is for thy ransom paid;
I'll die that Thou mayst live."

247

1 How oft, alas! this wretched heart
Has wandered from the Lord!
How oft my roving thoughts depart,
Forgetful of His word!

2 Yet sovereign mercy calls, " Return! "
Dear Lord, and may I come?
My vile ingratitude I mourn;
O, take the wanderer home!

3 Almighty Grace, Thy healing power
How glorious, how divine,
That can to life and bliss restore
So vile a heart as mine!

4 Thy pardoning love, so free, so sweet,
Dear Saviour, I adore;
O, keep me at Thy sacred feet,
And let me rove no more.

Early, my God, with - out de - lay, I haste to seek thy face; My thirsty spirit

faints a - way, My thirs - ty spi - rit faints a - way, Without thy cheering grace.

248

2 I've seen Thy glory and Thy power
Through all Thy temple shine;
My God, repeat that heavenly hour,
That vision so divine.

3 Not all the blessings of a feast
Can please my soul so well,
As when Thy richer grace I taste,
And in Thy presence dwell.

4 Not life itself, with all its joys,
Can my best passions move,
Or raise so high my cheerful voice,
As Thy forgiving love.

5 Thus till my last expiring day
I'll bless my God and King;
Thus will I lift my hands to pray,
And tune my lips to sing.

249

1 Thou art my hiding-place, O Lord!
In Thee I put my trust;
Encouraged by Thy holy word,
A feeble child of dust:

2 I have no argument beside,
I urge no other plea;
And 'tis enough, my Saviour died,
My Saviour died for me!

3 When storms of fierce temptation beat,
And furious foes assail,
My refuge is the mercy-seat,
My hope within the vail.

4 From strife of tongues and bitter words,
My spirit flies to Thee;
Joy to my heart the thought affords,
My Saviour died for me.

5 'Mid trials heavy to be borne,
When mortal strength is vain—
A heart with grief and anguish torn—
A body racked with pain—

6 Ah! what could give the sufferer rest,
Bid every murmur flee,
But this, the witness in my breast,
My Saviour died for me!

250

1 Rise, O my soul, pursue the path
By ancient worthies trod;
Aspiring, view those holy men,
Who lived and walked with God.

2 Though dead, they speak in reason's ear,
And in example live;
Their faith, and hope, and mighty deeds,
Still fresh instruction give.

3 'Twas through the Lamb's most precious
blood,
They conquered every foe;
And to His power and matchless grace
Their crowns of life they owe.

4 Lord! may I ever keep in view
The patterns Thou hast given,
And ne'er forsake the blessed road
That led them safe to heaven.

251

Let God the Father and the Son,
And Spirit, be adored,
Where there are works to make him known,
Or saints to love the Lord!

Sal - va - tion! O the joy - ful sound! 'Tis plea - sure to our ears!

A sov'reign balm for ev' - ry wound, A cor - dial for our fears.

252

2 Buried in sorrow and in sin,
   At hell's dark door we lay;
But we arise by grace divine,
   To see a heavenly day.

3 Salvation! let the echo fly
   The spacious earth around,
While all the armies of the sky
   Conspire to raise the sound.

253

1 How glorious is our heavenly King,
   Who reigns above the sky!
How shall a child presume to sing
   His dreadful majesty ?

2 How great His power is, none can tell,
   Nor think how large his grace:
Not men below, nor saints that dwell
   On high before his face.

3 Not angels that stand round the Lord
   Can search His secret will;
But they perform His holy word,
   And sing His praises still.

254

1 Oh! could our thoughts and wishes fly
   Above these gloomy shades,
To those bright worlds beyond the sky
   Which sorrow ne'er invades!

2 There joys unseen by mortal eyes,
   Or reason's feeble ray,
In ever-blooming prospect rise,
   Unconscious of decay.

3 Lord! send a beam of light divine
   To guide our upward aim;
With one reviving touch of Thine
   Our languid hearts inflame.

4 Then shall, on faith's sublimest wing,
   Our ardent wishes rise
To those bright scenes, where pleasures
     spring
   Immortal in the skies.

255

1 There is an eye that never sleeps
   Beneath the wing of night;
There is an ear that never shuts,
   When sink the beams of light.

2 There is an arm that never tires,
   When human strength gives way;
There is a love that never fails,
   When earthly loves decay.

3 That eye is fixed on seraph throngs;
   That arm upholds the sky;
That ear is filled with angel songs;
   That love is throned on high.

4 But there's a power which man can wield
   When mortal aid is vain,
That eye, that arm, that love to reach,
   That listening ear to gain.

5 That power is prayer, which soars on high,
   Through Jesus to the throne;
And moves the hand which moves the world,
   To bring salvation down!

ENGLISH.

Lord, in the morning Thou shalt hear My voice as - cend - ing high;

To Thee will I di - rect my prayer, To Thee lift up mine eye.

256

2 Up to the hills where Christ is gone,
  To plead for all His saints,
Presenting at His Father's throne
  Our songs and our complaints.

3 Thou art a God before whose sight
  The wicked shall not stand;
Sinners shall ne'er be Thy delight,
  Nor dwell at Thy right hand.

4 But to Thy house will I resort,
  To taste Thy mercies there;
I will frequent Thine holy court,
  And worship in Thy fear.

257

.1 COME, Holy Spirit, heavenly Dove,
  With all Thy quickening powers,
Kindle a flame of sacred love,
  In these cold hearts of ours.

2 Look, how we grovel here below,
  Fond of these trifling toys!
Our souls can neither fly nor go
  To reach eternal joys.

3 In vain we tune our formal songs,
  In vain we strive to rise;
Hosannas languish on our tongues,
  And our devotion dies.

4 Dear Lord, and shall we ever live
  At this poor dying rate?
Our love so faint, so cold to Thee,
  And Thine to us so great?

5 Come, Holy Spirit, heavenly Dove,
  With all Thy quickening powers;
Come, shed abroad a Saviour's love,
  And that shall kindle ours.

258

1 YE hearts, with youthful vigor warm,
  To Jesus now draw near,
And turn from every mortal charm,
  A Saviour's voice to hear.

2 He, Lord of all the worlds on high,
  Stoops to converse with you,
And lays His radiant glories by,
  Your welfare to pursue..

3 "The soul who longs to see my face,
  Is sure my love to gain;
And those who early seek my grace,
  Shall never seek in vain."

259

1 PRAYER is the soul's sincere desire,
  Unuttered or expressed;
The motion of a hidden fire
  That trembles in the breast.

2 Prayer is the burden of a sigh,
  The falling of a tear;
The upward glancing of an eye
  When none but God is near.

3 Prayer is the simplest form of speech
  That infant lips can try;
Prayer the sublimest strains that reach
  The Majesty on high.

4 Prayer is the contrite sinner's voice
  Returning from His ways,
While angels in their songs rejoice,
  And say—" Behold, he prays."

5 Prayer is the Christian's vital breath,
  The Christian's native air,
His watchword at the gate of death;
  He enters heaven with prayer.

MINOR.   [Dundee.] From The Scotch Psalter. 1615.

Beneath our feet and o'er our head   Is e-qual warning given;

Beneath us lie the countless dead; A - bove us is the heaven.

260

2 Death rides on every passing breeze,
  He lurks in every flower;
Each season has its own disease,
  Its peril every hour.

3 Our eyes have seen the rosy light
  Of youth's soft cheek decay,
And fate descend in sudden night
  On manhood's middle day.

4 Our eyes have seen the steps of age
  Halt feebly towards the tomb;
And yet shall earth our hearts engage,
  And dreams of days to come?

5 Turn, mortal, turn; thy danger know;
  Where'er thy foot can tread,
The earth rings hollow from below,
  And warns thee of her dead.

6 Turn, Christian, turn; thy soul apply
  To truths divinely given;
The bones that underneath thee lie
  Shall live for hell or heaven.

261

1 Here at Thy table, Lord, we meet
  To feed on food divine;
Thy body is the bread we eat
  Thy precious blood the wine.

2 He that prepares this rich repast
  Himself comes down and dies,
And then invites us thus to feast
  Upon the sacrifice.

3 The bitter torments He endured
  Upon the shameful cross
For us, His welcome guests procured
  These heart-reviving joys.

4 Sure there was never love so free,
  Dear Saviour, so divine;
Well Thou mayst claim that heart of me
  Which owes so much to Thine.

5 Yes, Thou shalt surely have my heart,
  My soul, my strength, my all;
With life itself I'll freely part,
  My Jesus, at Thy call.

262

1 Long have I sat beneath the sound
  Of Thy salvation, Lord;
Yet still how weak my faith is found,
  And knowledge of Thy word!

2 How cold and feeble is my love!
  How negligent my fear!
How low my hope of joys above!
  How few affections there!

3 Great God! thy sovereign power impart
  To give Thy word success;
Write Thy salvation in my heart,
  And make me learn Thy grace.

4 Show my forgetful feet the way
  That leads to joys on high;
Where knowledge grows without decay,
  And love shall never die.

CHANT.

How dread are Thine e - ter - nal years, O ev - er - last - ing Lord;

By prostrate spi - rits, day and night, In - ces - san - tly a - dored.

263

2 Yet I may love Thee too, O Lord,
Almighty as Thou art;
For Thou hast stooped to ask of me
The love of my poor heart.

3 Only to sit and think of God,
O, what a joy it is!
To think the thought, to breathe the name,
Earth has no higher bliss.

4 Father of Jesus! Love's reward!
What rapture will it be,
Prostrate before Thy throne to lie,
And gaze and gaze on Thee.

264

1 Oh, where are kings and empires now
Of old that went and came?
But, Lord, Thy Church is praying yet,
A thousand years the same.

2 We mark her goodly battlements,
And her foundations strong;
We hear within the solemn voice
Of her unending song.

3 For not like kingdoms of the world
Thy holy Church, O God!
Tho' earthquake shocks are threat'ning her,
And temptests are abroad,

4 Unshaken as eternal hills,
Immovable she stands,
A mountain that shall fill the earth,
A house not made with hands.

265

1 STILL on the Lord thy burden roll,
Nor let a care remain;
His mighty arm shall bear thy soul,
And all thy grief sustain.

2 Ne'er will the Lord His aid deny
To those who trust His love;
The men who on His grace rely
Nor earth nor hell shall move.

266

1 WE seek a rest beyond the skies,
In everlasting day;
Thro' floods and flames the passage lies,
But Jesus guards the way.

2 The swelling flood and raging flame
Hear and obey His word;
Then let us triumph in His name;
Our Saviour is the Lord.

267

1 JESUS, the vision of Thy face
Hath overpowering charms;
Scarce shall I feel death's cold embrace,
If Christ be in my arms.

2 Then, while ye hear my heartstrings break,
How sweet my minutes roll!
A mortal paleness on my cheek,
And glory in my soul.

268

To Father, Son, and Holy Ghost,
One God, whom we adore,
Be glory as it was, is now,
And shall be evermore!

{ Sweet land of rest! for thee I sigh; When will the mo-ment come,
{ And dwell with Christ at home,........ And dwell with Christ at home,

When I shall lay my ar-mor by, And dwell with Christ at home. }
When I shall lay my ar-mor by, And dwell with Christ at home. }

269

2 No tranquil joys on earth I know—
No peaceful sheltering dome:
This world's a wilderness of woe—
This world is not my home.

3 To Jesus Christ I sought for rest;
He bade me cease to roam,
But fly for succor to His breast,
And He'd conduct me home.

4 Weary of wandering round and round
This vale of sin and gloom,
I long to leave the unhallowed ground,
And dwell with Christ at home.

270

1 THE Saviour calls! let every ear
Attend the heavenly sound:
Ye doubting souls, dismiss your fear;
Hope smiles reviving round.

2 For every thirsty, longing heart
Here streams of bounty flow;
And life, and health, and bliss impart
To banish mortal woe.

3 Here springs of sacred pleasure rise,
To ease your every pain—
Immortal fountain! full supplies!—
Nor shall you thirst in vain.

271

1 ON Jordan's stormy bank I stand,
And cast a wishful eye
To Canaan's fair and happy land,
Where my possessions lie.

2 O the transporting, rapturous scene
That rises to my sight!
Sweet fields arrayed in living green,
And rivers of delight!

3 All o'er those wide extended plains
Shines one eternal day;
There God, the Sun, forever reigns,
And scatters night away.

4 No chilling winds or poisonous breath
Can reach that healthful shore;
Sickness and sorrow, pain and death,
Are felt and feared no more.

5 When shall I reach that happy place,
And be forever blessed?
When shall I see my Father's face,
And in His bosom rest?

272

1 A PILGRIM through this lonely world,
The blessed Saviour passed;
A mourner all His life was He,
A dying Lamb at last.

2 That tender heart that felt for all,
For all its life-blood gave;
It found on earth no resting place,
Save only in the grave.

3 Such was our Lord; and shall we fear
The cross with all its scorn!
Or love a faithless, evil world,
That wreathed His brow with thorn?

4 No; facing all its frowns or smiles,
Like Him obedient still,
We homeward press thro' storm and calm,
To Zion's blessed hill.

CARMINA SACRA.

Je - sus, im - mor - tal King! arise;   Rise and as - sert Thy sway   Till

earth, sub - dued, its tri - bute bring,   And distant lands o - bey,........And
And distant lands o-

distant lands o - bey,   And   dis - And dis - tant lands o - bey.
bey............................   And dis - tant lands o - bey.

bey,   ·   And   distant lands o - bey,   And dis - tant lands o - bey.

273

2 Ride forth, victorious conqueror! ride,
  Till all Thy foes submit;
And all the powers of hell resign
  Their trophies at Thy feet.

3 Send forth Thy word, and let it fly
  This spacious earth around;
Till every soul beneath the sun
  Shall hear the joyful sound.

4 From sea to sea, from shore to shore,
  May Jesus be adored;
And earth, with all her millions, shout
  Hosannas to the Lord.

274

1 HOSANNA to our conquering King!
  All hail, incarnate love!
Ten thousand songs and glories wait
  To crown Thy head above.

2 Thy victories and Thy deathless fame,
  Through the wide world shall run,

And everlasting ages sing
  The triumphs Thou hast won.

275

1 HOSANNA to the Prince of light,
  Who clothed Himself in clay;
Entered the iron gates of death,
  And tore the bars away.

2 See how the Conqueror mounts aloft,
  And to His Father flies,
With scars of honor in His flesh,
  And triumph in His eyes.

3 Raise your devotion, mortal tongues,
  To reach His blessed abode;
Sweet be the accents of your songs,
  To our incarnate God.

4 Bright angels, strike your loudest strings,
  Your sweetest voices raise;
Let heaven, and all created things,
  Sound our Immanuel's praise.

AFFETTUOSO.   N. D. GOULD.

There is an hour of peaceful rest To mourning wand'rers giv'n; There is a joy for

souls distress'd, A balm for ev'-ry wounded breast; 'Tis found above—in heav'n.

276

2 There is a home for weary souls
  By sin and sorrow driven,
  When tossed on life's tempestuous shoals,
  Where storms arise, and ocean rolls,
  And all is drear; 'tis heaven.

3 There Faith lifts up her cheerful eye
  To brighter prospects given,
  And views the tempest passing by,
  The evening shadows quickly fly,
  And all serene in heaven.

4 There fragrant flowers immortal bloom,
  And joys supreme are given;
  There rays divine disperse the gloom;
  Beyond the confines of the tomb
  Appears the dawn of heaven.

277

1 THIS world is poor from shore to shore,
  And like a baseless vision;
  Its lofty domes and brilliant ore,
  Its gems and crowns, are vain and poor:
  There's nothing rich but heaven.

2 Empires decay and nations die;
  Our hopes to winds are given;
  The vernal blooms in ruin lie;
  Death reigns o'er all beneath the sky:
  There's nothing sure but heaven.

3 Creation's mighty fabric all
  Shall be to atoms riven;
  The skies consume, the planets fall,
  Convulsions rock this earthly ball:
  There's nothing firm but heaven.

4 A stranger, lonely here I roam,
  From place to place am driven;

My friends are gone, and I'm in gloom;
  This world is all a dismal tomb:
  I have no home but heaven.

5 The clouds disperse; the light appears;
  My sins are all forgiven;
  Triumphant grace hath quelled my fears;
  Roll on, thou sun! fly swift my years!
  I'm on my way to heaven.

278

1 AND can mine eyes, without a tear,
  A weeping Saviour see?
  Shall I not weep His groans to hear,
  Who groaned and died for me?

2 Blest Jesus, let those tears of Thine
  Subdue each stubborn foe;
  Come, fill my heart with love divine,
  And bid my sorrows flow.

279

1 THERE is a little, lonely fold,
  Whose flock one Shepherd keeps,
  Through summer's heat and winter's cold,
  With eye that never sleeps.

2 By evil beast, or burning sky,
  Or damp of midnight air,
  Not one in all that flock shall die,
  Beneath that Shepherd's care.

3 For, if unheeding or beguiled
  In danger's path they roam,
  His pity follows through the wild,
  And guards them safely home.

4 O gentle Shepherd, still behold
  Thy helpless charge in me;
  And take a wanderer to Thy fold,
  That trembling turns to Thee.

E. R. BLANCHARD.

There is a place of sa-cred rest, Far, far be-yond the skies,

Where beau-ty smiles e-ter-nal-ly, And plea-sure nev-er dies—

My Father's house, my heavenly home, Where "many mansions" stand,

Prepared by hands di-vine for all Who seek the bet-ter land.

280

2 When tossed upon the waves of life,
  With fear on every side,—
When fiercely howls the gathering storm,
  And foams the angry tide,—
Beyond the storm, beyond the gloom,
  Breaks forth the light of morn,
Bright beaming from my Father's house
  To cheer the soul forlorn.

3 In that pure home of tearless joy
  Earth's parted friends shall meet,
With smiles of love that never fade,
  And blessedness complete.
There, there, adieus are sounds unknown:
  Death frowns not on that scene;

But life and glorious beauty shine
  Untroubled and serene.

281

1 To our Redeemer's glorious name
  Awake the sacred song;
O, may His love—immortal flame—
  Tune every heart and tongue.

2 His love what mortal thought can reach?
  What mortal tongue display?
Imagination's utmost stretch
  In wonder dies away.

3 Dear Lord, while we, adoring, pay
  Our humble thanks to Thee,
May every heart with rapture say,
  "The Saviour died for me."

ARLINGTON. C. M.

Dr. T. Arne.

What shall I ren - der to my God For all His kindness shown?

My feet shall vis - it Thine a - bode, My songs ad - dress Thy throne.

282

2 Among the saints that fill Thy house
  My offerings shall be paid;
There shall my zeal perform the vows
  My soul in anguish made.

3 How much is mercy Thy delight,
  Thou ever-blessed God!
How dear Thy servants in Thy sight!
  How precious is their blood!

4 Here in Thy courts I leave my vow,
  And Thy rich grace record;
Witness, ye saints, who hear me now,
  If I forsake the Lord!

283

1 How vain are all things here below?
  How false and yet how fair!
Each pleasure hath its poison, too,
  And every sweet a snare.

2 The brightest things below the sky
  Give but a flattering light;
We should suspect some danger nigh,
  Where we possess delight.

3 Our dearest joys, and nearest friends—
  The partners of our blood,
How they divide our wavering minds,
  And leave but half for God!

4 Dear Saviour! let Thy beauties be
  My soul's eternal food;
And grace command my heart away
  From all created good.

284

1 Scorn not the slightest word or deed,
  Nor deem it void of power;
There's fruit in each wind-wafted seed,
  That waits its natal hour.

2 A whispered word may touch the heart,
  And call it back to life;
A look of love bid sin depart,
  And still unholy strife.

3 No act falls fruitless, none can tell
  How vast its power may be,
Nor what results infolded dwell
  Within it silently.

4 Work on, despair not, bring thy mite
  Nor care how small it be,
God is with all that serve the right,
  The holy, true, and free.

285

1 Prostrate, dear Jesus, at Thy feet,
  A guilty rebel lies,
And upwards to Thy mercy seat
  Presumes to lift his eyes.

2 If tears of sorrow would suffice
  To pay the debt I owe,
Tears should from both my weeping eyes
  In ceaseless torrents flow.

3 But no such sacrifice I plead,
  To expiate my guilt;
No tears but those which Thou hast shed,
  No blood but Thou hast spilt.

4 Think of Thy sorrows, dearest Lord,
  And all my sins forgive;
Justice will well approve the word
  That bids the sinner live.

To us a Child of hope is born, To us a Son is giv'n;

Him shall the tribes of earth o - bey, Him all the hosts of heav'n.

286

2 His name shall be the Prince of Peace,
For evermore adored;
The Wonderful, the Counsellor,
The great and mighty Lord!

3 His power, increasing, still shall spread;
His reign no end shall know:
Justice shall guard His throne above,
And peace abound below.

4 To us a Child of hope is born,
To us a Son is given;
The Wonderful, the Counsellor,
The mighty Lord of heaven.

287

1 AM I a soldier of the cross,
A follower of the Lamb,
And shall I fear to own His cause
Or blush to speak His name?

2 Must I be carried to the skies
On flowery beds of ease,
While others fought to win the prize,
And sailed through bloody seas?

3 Are there no foes for me to face,
Must I not stem the flood?
Is this vile world a friend to grace,
To help me on to God?

4 Sure I must fight if I would reign;
Increase my courage, Lord;
I'll bear the toil, endure the pain,
Supported by Thy word.

5 Thy saints, in all this glorious war,
Shall conquer, though they die;
They see the triumph from afar,
And seize it with their eye.

6 When that illustrious day shall rise
And all Thy armies shine
In robes of victory through the skies,
The glory shall be Thine.

288

1 On, for a shout of sacred joy
To God, the sovereign King!
Let every land their tongues employ,
And hymns of triumph sing.

2 Jesus, our God, ascends on high;
His heavenly guards around
Attend Him rising through the sky,
With trumpets joyful sound.

3 While angels shout and praise their King,
Let mortals learn their strains;
Let all the earth His honor sing:
O'er all the earth He reigns.

4 Rehearse His praise with awe profound:
Let knowledge lead the song;
Nor mock Him with a solemn sound
Upon a thoughtless tongue.

5 Oh, for a shout of sacred joy
To God, the sovereign King!
Let every land their tongues employ,
And hymns of triumph sing.

WHITFIELD. C. M. 6 l.

Arr. by Geo. Kingsley.

Come, heavenly Love, inspire my song With Thine im - mor - tal flame,

And teach my heart and teach my tongue The Saviour's love - ly name,

And teach my heart and teach my tongue The Saviour's love - ly name.

289

2 The Saviour!—oh, what endless charms
   Dwell in that blissful sound!
   Its influence every fear disarms,
   And spreads delight around.

3 Wrapped in the gloom of dark despair,
   We helpless, hopeless lay:
   But sovereign mercy reached us there,
   And smiled despair away.

4 Th' almighty Former of the skies
   Stoops to our vile abode;
   While angels view with wondering eyes
   And hail th' incarnate God.

5 Incarnate God!—now to thine arms
   I yield my captive soul:
   Oh, let Thine all-subduing charms
   My inmost powers control!

290

1 My Saviour! my almighty Friend!
   When I begin Thy praise,
   Where will the growing numbers end,
   The numbers of Thy grace?

2 Thou art my everlasting trust;
   Thy goodness I adore:
   And since I knew Thy graces first,
   I speak Thy glories more.

3 My feet shall travel all the length
   Of the celestial road;
   And march with courage in Thy strength,
   To see my Father, God.

4 When I am filled with sore distress
   For some surprising sin,
   I'll plead Thy perfect righteousness,
   And mention none but Thine.

5 How will my lips rejoice to tell
   The victories of my King!
   My soul, redeemed from sin and hell,
   Shall Thy salvation sing.

6 Awake, awake, my tuneful powers!
   With this delightful song
   I'll entertain the darkest hours,
   Nor think the season long.

DR. LOWELL MASON.

There is a house not made with hands, E-ter-nal and on high;

And here my wait-ing spi-rit stands Till God shall bid it fly.

291

2 Shortly this prison of my clay
  Must be dissolved and fall:
Then, O my soul, with joy obey
  Thy heavenly Father's call.

3 We walk by faith of joys to come;
  Faith lives upon His word;
But while the body is our home,
  We're absent from the Lord.

4 'Tis pleasant to believe Thy grace,
  But we had rather see;
We would be absent from the flesh,
  And present, Lord, with Thee.

292

1 GOOD is the Lord, the heavenly King,
  Who makes the earth His care,
Visits the pastures every spring,
  And bids the grass appear.

2 The softened ridges of the field
  Permit the corn to spring;
The valleys rich provision yield,
  And the poor laborers sing

3 The various months Thy goodness crowns;
  How bounteous are Thy ways!
The bleating flocks spread o'er the downs,
  And shepherds shout Thy praise.

293

1 SAY, who is she that looks abroad
  Like the sweet, blushing dawn,
When with her living light she paints
  The dew drops of the lawn?

2 Fair as the moon, when in the skies
  Serene her throne she guides,
And o'er the twinkling stars supreme
  In full-orbed glory rides;—

3 Clear as the sun, when from the east
  Without a cloud he springs,
And scatters boundless light and heat
  From his resplendent wings;—

4 Tremendous as a host, that moves
  Majestically slow,
With banners wide displayed, all armed,
  All ardent, for the foe.

5 This is the Church, by Heaven arrayed
  With strength and grace divine:
Thus shall she strike her foes with dread,
  And thus her glories shine.

294

1 PLANTED in Christ, the living Vine,
  This day with one accord,
Ourselves, with humble faith and joy,
  We yield to Thee, O Lord.

2 Joined in one body may we be;
  One inward life partake;
One be our heart; one heavenly hope
  In every bosom wake.

3 In prayer, in effort, tears, and toils,
  One Wisdom be our guide;
Taught by one Spirit from above,
  In Thee may we abide.

4 Then, when among the saints in light
  Our joyful spirits shine,
Shall anthems of immortal praise,
  O Lamb of God, be Thine.

BARBY. C. M.

Wm. Tansur.

Thou boundless source of ev' - ry good, Our best de - sires.. ful - fill.

Help us t' a - dore Thy sov' - reign grace, And mark Thy sov' - reign will.

295

2 In all Thy mercies may our souls
Thy bounteous goodness see;
Nor let the gifts Thy grace imparts
Estrange our hearts from Thee.

3 Teach us in time of deep distress,
To own Thy hand, O God!
And in submissive silence learn
The lessons of Thy rod.

4 In every changing scene of life,
Whate'er that scene may be,
Give us a meek and humble mind,
A mind at peace with Thee.

5 Then may we close our eyes in death,
Free from distracting care;
For death is life—and labor rest,
If Thou art with us there.

296

1 There's nothing round this spacious earth
That suits my large desire;
To boundless joy and solid mirth
My nobler thoughts aspire,—

2 Where pleasure rolls its living flood,
From sin and dross refined,
Still springing from the throne of God,
And fit to cheer the mind.

3 The almighty Ruler of the sphere,
The glorious and the great,
Brings His own all-sufficience there,
To make our bliss complete.

4 Had I the pinions of a dove,
I'd climb the heavenly road;
There sits my Saviour, dressed in love,
And there my smiling God.

297

1 Our Father! through the coming year
We know not what shall be;
But we would leave without a fear
Its ordering all to Thee.

2 It may be we shall toil in vain
For what the world holds fair;
And all the good we thought to gain,
Deceive and prove but care.

3 It may be it shall darkly blend
Our love with anxious fears,
And snatch away the valued friend,
The tried of many years.

4 It may be it shall bring us days
And nights of lingering pain;
And bid us take a farewell gaze
Of these loved haunts of men.

5 But calmly, Lord, on Thee we rest;
No fears our trust shall move;
Thou knowest what for each is best,
And Thou art Perfect Love.

298

1 O Thou whose gently chastening hand
In mercy deals the blow!
Make but Thy servant understand
Wherefore Thou layest me low.

2 I ask Thee not the rod to spare
While thus Thy love I see;
But oh! let every suffering bear
Some message, Lord, from Thee!

ALLEGRETTO.

GEO. KINGSLEY

There is a glo-rious world of light A-bove the star-ry sky,
Where saints de-part-ed, cloth'd in white, A-dore the Lord most high.

299

2 And hark! amid the sacred songs
Those heavenly voices raise,
Ten thousand thousand infant tongues
Unite in perfect praise.

3 Those are the hymns that we shall know,
If Jesus we obey,
That is the place where we shall go,
If found in wisdom's way.

4 Soon will our earthly race be run,
Our mortal frame decay;
Parents and children, one by one,
Must die and pass away.

5 Great God! impress this serious thought,
This day, on every breast;
That both the teachers and the taught
May enter to thy rest.

300

1 In times of peril, pain and strife,
My Lord, I trust in Thee—
And then the ills that checker life
Are made all sweet to me.

2 There's not a cloud that darkling hangs
But hides a beauteous sky;
And when I feel life's bitterest pangs
I know Thy hand is nigh.

3 Submission to Thy holy will
Whenever sorrow springs,
I'll meekly bow—for o'er me still,
Are spread Thy sheltering wings.

4 Forever in Thy name I'll trust
And joyful pass along,
Till heavens bright glories o'er me burst,
And its enraptured song.

301

1 ETERNAL Father, God of love,
To Thee our hearts we raise;
Thy all-sustaining power we prove,
And gladly sing Thy praise.

2 Thine, wholly thine, oh, let us be!
Our sacrifice receive;
Made and preserved, and saved by Thee,
To Thee ourselves we give.

3 Come, Holy Ghost! the Saviour's love
Shed in our hearts abroad;
So shall we ever live and move,
And be with Christ, in God.

302

1 SEE the kind Shepherd, Jesus, stands,
And calls His sheep by name;
Gathers the feeble in His arms,
And feeds each tender lamb.

2 He leads them to the gentle stream,
Where living water flows;
And guides them to the verdant fields,
Where sweetest herbage grows.

3 When, wandering from the peaceful fold,
We leave the narrow way,
Our faithful Shepherd still is near,
To seek us when we stray.

4 The weakest lamb amid the flock
Shall be its Shepherd's care;
While folded in our Saviour's arms,
We're safe from every fear.

CHORAL.

O, 'twas a joy-ful sound to hear Our tribes de-vout-ly say:

"Up, Is-rael, to the tem-ple haste, And keep your fes-tal day."

303

2 At Salem's courts we must appear,
With our assembled powers,
In strong and beauteous order ranged,
Like her united towers.

3 O, pray we then for Salem's peace,
For they shall prosperous be,
Thou holy city of our God,
Who bear true love to Thee.

4 May peace within Thy sacred walls
A constant guest be found;
With plenty and prosperity
Thy palaces be crowned.

304

1 HOLY and reverend is the name
Of our eternal King:
Thrice holy Lord! the angels cry;
Thrice holy! let us sing.

2 The deepest reverence of the mind,
Pay, O my soul to God;
Lift with thy hands a holy heart
To His sublime abode.

3 With sacred awe pronounce His name
Whom words nor thoughts can reach:
A broken heart shall please him more
Than the best forms of speech.

4 Thou holy God, preserve my soul
From all pollution free;
The pure in heart are Thy delight,
And they Thy face shall see.

305

1 BEHOLD, the mountain of the Lord
In latter days shall rise
On mountain tops above the hills,
And draw the wondering eyes.

2 To this the joyful nations round,
All tribes and tongues, shall flow;
"Up to the hill of God," they'll say,
"And to His house, we'll go."

3 The beam that shines from Zion's hill
Shall lighten every land;
The King who reigns in Salem's tower
Shall all the world command.

306

1 NOR eye hath seen, nor ear hath heard,
Nor sense nor reason known,
What joys the Father has prepared
For those that love His Son.

2 But the good Spirit of the Lord
Reveals a heaven to come;
The beams of glory in His word
Allure and guide us home.

3 Pure are the joys above the sky
And all the region peace;
No wanton lips, nor envious eye
Can see or taste the bliss.

4 Those holy gates for ever bar
Pollution, sin, and shame;
None shall obtain admittance there,
But followers of the Lamb.

307

Thee, Father, Son, and Spirit, Thee,
Let heaven and earth adore;
Thou art, Thou wast, and Thou shalt be
God blessed evermore.

That aw-ful day will sure-ly come, Th'appointed hour makes haste,

When I must stand be-fore my Judge, And pass the sol-emn test.

308

2 Thou lovely chief of all my joys,
 Thou sovereign of my heart,
How could I bear to hear Thy voice
 Pronounce the word—Depart!

3 Jesus, I throw my arms around,
 And hang upon Thy breast,
Without a gracious smile from Thee
 My spirit cannot rest.

4 Oh ! tell me that my worthless name
 Is graven on Thy hands;
Show me some promise in Thy book,
 Where my salvation stands.

309

1 THY home is with the humble, Lord!
 The simplest are the best,
Thy lodging is in child-like heart,
 Thou makest there Thy rest.

2 Dear Comforter! Eternal Love!
 If Thou wilt stay with me,
Of lowly thoughts and simple ways
 I'll build a house for Thee.

3 Who made this beating heart of mine,
 But Thou my heavenly guest?
Let no one have it, then, but Thee,
 And let it be Thy rest.

310

1 DEAREST of all the names above,
 My Jesus and my God,
Who can resist Thy heavenly love,
 Or trifle with Thy blood?

2 Till God in human flesh I see,
 My thoughts no comfort find;
The holy, just, and sacred Three
 Are terrors to my mind.

3 But if Immanuel's face appear,
 My hope, my joy begins;
His name forbids my slavish fear,
 His grace removes my sins.

4 While Jews on their own law rely,
 And Greeks of wisdom boast,
I love the incarnate mystery,
 And there I fix my trust.

311

1 O, LORD, another day is flown,
 And we, a lonely band,
Are met once more before Thy throne,
 To bless Thy fostering hand.

2 And wilt Thou lend a listening ear
 To praises low as ours?
Thou wilt; for Thou dost love to hear
 The song which meekness pours.

3 O, let Thy grace perform its part,
 And let contention cease,
And shed abroad in every heart
 Thine everlasting peace.

CHRISTMAS. C. M.

VIGOROSO.

HANDEL.

Awake, my soul, stretch every nerve, And press with vigor on; A

heav'nly race demands thy zeal, And an immortal crown, And an immortal crown.

312

2 A cloud of witnesses around
Hold thee in full survey;
Forget the steps already trod,
And onward urge thy way.

3 'Tis God's all-animating voice
That calls thee from on high;
'Tis His own hand presents the prize
To thine aspiring eye.

4 That prize, with peerless glories bright,
Which shall new lustre boast,
When victors' wreaths and monarchs' gems
Shall blend in common dust.

5 Blest Saviour, introduced by Thee,
Have I my race begun;
And crowned with victory, at Thy feet
I'll lay my honors down.

313

1 Our pilgrim brethren dwelling far,
O God of truth and love,
Light Thou their path with Thine own Star,
Bright beaming from above.

2 Wide as their mighty rivers flow,
Let Thine own truth extend;
Where prairies spread and forests grow,
O Lord, Thy gospel send.

3 Then will a mighty nation own
A union firm and strong;
The sceptre of the eternal throne
Shall rule its councils long.

314

1 Far o'er the land the precious grain
Waves 'neath the sunny sky;
And ripening harvests offer sheaves
For immortality.

2 But who will reap the golden fruit,
And who at last will stand,
A faithful servant, crowned with joy,
O Lord, at Thy right hand?

3 Be ours the work, be ours the joy;
To us the charge be given
To gather souls to Christ, and find
Our garnered sheaves in heaven.

4 Strength to the reapers, mighty God,
Strength to the reapers send,
To bear the burden of the day
And labor till the end.

5 Then songs of triumph shall arise,
Then shall Thy kingdom come,
And echoing anthems greet at last
The heavenly harvest home.

315

1 With songs and honors sounding loud,
Address the Lord on high:
Over the heavens He spreads His cloud,
And waters veil the sky.

2 His hoary frost, His fleecy snow,
Descend and clothe the ground;
The liquid streams forbear to flow,
In icy fetters bound.

3 He sends His word and melts the snow;
The fields no longer mourn;
He calls the warmer gales to blow,
And bids the spring return.

ANDANTE.—LEGATO.   ISAAC SMITH, London. Died about 1800.

Lord, when we bend be - fore Thy throne, And our con - fes - sions pour,

O, may we feel the sins we own, And hate what we de - plore.

316

2 Our broken spirits pitying see;
  True penitence impart;
Then let a healing glance from Thee
  Beam hope on every heart.

3 When we disclose our wants in prayer,
  O, let our wills resign;
And not a thought our bosom share,
  Which is not wholly Thine.

4 Let faith each weak petition fill,
  And lift it to the skies;
And teach our hearts 'tis goodness still
  That grants it, or denies.

317

1 FATHER of mercies, in Thy word
  What endless glory shines!
Forever be Thy name adored,
  For these celestial lines.

2 Here may the wretched sons of want
  Exhaustless riches find;
Riches above what earth can grant,
  And lasting as the mind.

3 Here the Redeemer's welcome voice
  Spreads heavenly peace around,
And life and everlasting joys
  Attend the blissful sound.

4 O, may these heavenly pages be
  My ever dear delight;
And still new beauties may I see,
  And still increasing light.

5 Divine Instructor, gracious Lord,
  Be Thou forever near;
Teach me to love Thy sacred word,
  And view my Saviour there.

318

1 GREAT GOD, how infinite art Thou!
  What worthless worms are we!
Let the whole race of creatures bow,
  And pay their praise to Thee.

2 Thy throne eternal ages stood,
  Ere seas or stars were made:
Thou art the ever-living God,
  Were all the nations dead.

3 Nature and time quite naked lie
  To Thine immense survey,
From the formation of the sky
  To the great burning day.

4 Eternity, with all its years,
  Stands present in Thy view;
To Thee there's nothing old appears;
  Great God, there's nothing new.

319

1 Is there ambition in my heart?
  Search, gracious God, and see;
Or do I act a haughty part?
  Lord, I appeal to Thee.

2 I charge my thoughts, be humble still,
  And all my carriage mild;
Content, my Father, with Thy will,
  And quiet as a child.

3 The patient soul, the lowly mind,
  Shall have a large reward;
Let saints in sorrow lie resigned,
  And trust a faithful Lord.

Must Je - sus bear the cross a - lone, And all the world go free?

No, there's a cross for ev' - ry one, And there's a cross for me.

320

2 How happy are the saints above,
  Who once went sorrowing here;
But now they taste unmingled love,
  And joy without a tear.

3 The consecrated cross I'll bear
  Till death shall set me free,
And then go home my crown to wear,—
  For there's a crown for me.

321

1 Come, humble sinner, in whose breast
  A thousand thoughts revolve,
Come, with your guilt and fear oppressed,
  And make this last resolve:

2 " I'll go to Jesus, though my sin
  Hath like a mountain rose;
I know His courts, I'll enter in,
  Whatever may oppose.

3 Prostrate I'll lie before His throne,
  And there my guilt confess;
I'll tell Him I'm a wretch undone,
  Without His sovereign grace.

4 Perhaps He will admit my plea,
  Perhaps will hear my prayer;
But if I perish, I will pray,
  And perish only there.

5 I can but perish if I go;
  I am resolved to try;
For if I stay away I know
  I must for ever die."

322

1 O, in the morn of life, when youth
  With vital ardor glows,
And shines in all the fairest charms
  That beauty can disclose.

2 Deep in Thy soul, before its powers
  Are yet by vice enslaved,
Be thy Creator's glorious name
  And image deep engraved.

3 True wisdom, early sought and gained,
  In age will give thee rest;
O, then improve the morn of life
  To make its evening blessed.

323

1 We tread the path our Master trod;
  We bear the cross he bore;
And every thorn that wounds our feet
  His temples pierced before.

2 Oft do our eyes with joy o'erflow,
  And oft are bathed in tears;
Yet naught but heaven our hopes can raise,
  And naught but sin our fears.

3 We purge our mortal dross away,
  Refining as we run;
And while we die to earth and sense,
  Our heaven is here begun

324

1 With joy we meditate the grace
  Of our High Priest above;
His heart is made of tenderness,
  His bowels melt with love.

2 Touched with a sympathy within,
  He knows our feeble frame;
He knows what sore temptations mean,
  For he has felt the same.

3 Then let our humble faith address
  His mercy and his power;
We shall obtain delivering grace
  In each distressing hour.

ENGLISH.
by DR. LOWELL MASON.

O for a thou-sand tongues to sing My great Redeemer's praise,

The glo-ries of my God and King, The tri-umphs of His grace.

325

2 My gracious Master, and my God,
Assist me to proclaim,
To spread through all the earth abroad,
The honors of Thy name.

3 Jesus! the name that charms our'fears,
That bids our sorrows cease;
'Tis music in the sinner's ears;
'Tis life, and health, and peace.

4 He breaks the power of reigning sin;
He sets the prisoner free;
His blood can make the foulest clean;
His blood availed for me.

326

1 DAUGHTER of Zion! from the dust
Exalt thy fallen head;
Again in thy Redeemer trust:
He calls thee from the dead.

2 Awake, awake! put on thy strength,
Thy beautiful array;
The day of freedom dawns at length,
The Lord's appointed day.

3 Rebuild thy walls, thy bounds enlarge,
And send thy heralds forth;
Say to the south, "Give up thy charge,"
And keep not back, O north!

4 They come, they come!—thine exiled bands,
Where'er they rest or roam,
Have heard thy voice in distant lands,
And hasten to their home.

327

1 O THOU whose own vast temple stands
Built over earth and sea,

Accept the walls that human hands
Have raised to worship Thee.

2 Lord, from Thine inmost glory send,
Within these courts to 'bide,
The peace that dwelleth, without end,
Serenely by Thy side.

3 May erring minds that worship here
Be taught the better way,
And they who mourn, and they who fear,
Be strengthened as they pray.

4 May faith grow firm, and love grow warm,
And pure devotion rise,
While round these hallowed walls the storm
Of earth-born passion dies.

328

1 Go to the pillow of disease,
Where night gives no repose,
And on the cheek where sickness preys,
Bid health to plant the rose.

2 Go where the friendless stranger lies;
To perish is his doom;
Snatch from the grave his closing eyes,
And bring his blessing home.

3 Thus what our heavenly Father gave
Shall we as freely give;
Thus copy Him who lived to save,
And died that we might live.

329

THE God of mercy be adored,
Who calls our souls from death,
Who saves by His redeeming word
And new-creating breath

DR. RANDALL.

Let ev' - ry mor - tal ear at - tend, And ev' - ry heart re-

joice; The trumpet of the gos - pel sounds With an in - vit - ing

voice, With an in - vit - ing voice, With an in - vit - ing voice.

330

2 Ho! all ye hungry, starving souls,
  That feed upon the wind,
And vainly strive with earthly toys
  To fill an empty mind,—

3 Eternal Wisdom has prepared
  A soul-reviving feast,
And bids your longing appetites
  The rich provision taste.

4 Ho! ye that pant for living streams,
  And pine away and die,—
Here you may quench your raging thirst
  With springs that never dry.

331

1 WELCOME, O Saviour! to my heart;
  Possess thine humble throne;
Bid every rival hence depart,
  And claim me for Thine own.

2 The world and Satan I forsake—
  To Thee I all resign;
My longing heart, O Jesus! take,
  And fill with love divine.

3 O, may I never turn aside,
  Nor from Thy bosom flee;
Let nothing here my heart divide—
  I give it all to Thee.

332

1 FOR mercies countless as the sands,
  Which daily I receive
From Jesus my Redeemer's hands,
  My soul, what canst thou give?

2 Alas! from such a heart as mine,
  What can I bring him forth?
My best is stained and dyed with sin;
  My all is nothing worth.

3 Yet this acknowledgment I'll make
  For all he has bestowed,
Salvation's sacred cup I'll take,
  And call upon my God.

333

1 COME, Lord, in mercy come again,
  With Thy converting power;
The fields of Zion thirst for rain,
  O send a gracious shower.

2 Dear Saviour, come with quick'ning power,
  Thy mourning people cry;
Salvation bring in mercy's hour,
  Nor let the sinner die.

3 Once more let converts throng Thy house,
  And shouts of victory raise;
Then shall our griefs be turned to joy,
  And sighs, to songs of praise.

O Thou, whose ten - der mer - cy hears Con - tri - tion's humble sigh;

Whose hand, in - dul - gent, wipes the tears From sor - row's weep - ing eye.

See, low be - fore Thy throne of grace, A wretch - ed wand' - rer mourn;

Hast Thou not bid me seek Thy face? Hast Thou not said, "Re - turn"?

334

3 And shall my guilty fears prevail
  To drive me from Thy feet?
O, let not this dear refuge fail,
  This only safe retreat.

4 O, shine on this benighted heart,
  With beams of mercy shine;
And let Thy healing voice impart
  A taste of joys divine.

335

1 A MOTHER may forgetful be,
  For human love is frail;
But Thy Creator's love to thee,
  O Zion! can not fail.

2 No! Thy dear name engraven stands,
  In characters of love,
On Thy almighty Father's hands;
  And never shall remove.

3 Before His ever watchful eye
  Thy mournful state appears,
And every groan and every sigh,
  Divine compassion hears.

4 O Zion! learn to doubt no more,
  Be every fear suppressed;
Unchanging truth, and love, and power,
  Dwell in Thy Saviour's breast.

CON SPIRITO.

1. Raise thee, my soul; fly up, and run Through ev' - ry heav'nly street;
2. There, on a high, ma-jes-tic throne, Th'al-mighty Father reigns,

And say, there's naught below the sun, And say, there's naught below the
And sheds His glorious goodness down, And sheds His glorious goodness

sun That's worthy of thy feet, That's wor-thy of thy feet.
down On all the blissful plains, On all the bliss-ful plains.

336

3 Bright, like a sun, the Saviour sits,
  And spreads eternal noon;
No evenings there, nor gloomy nights,
  To want the feeble moon.

4 Amid those ever-shining skies,
  Behold the sacred Dove;
While banished sin and sorrow flies
  From all the realms of love.

5 The glorious tenants of the place
  Stand bending round the throne,
And saints and seraphs sing and praise
  The infinite Three One.

6 Jesus, O, when shall that dear day,
  That joyful hour, appear,
When I shall leave this house of clay
  To dwell among them there?

337

1 To God, our Strength, your voice aloud,
  In strains of glory raise;
High to Jehovah, Jacob's God,
  Exalt the notes of praise.

2 Now let the Gospel trumpet blow
  On each appointed feast,
And teach His waiting church to know
  The Sabbath's sacred rest.

3 This was the statute of the Lord
  To Israel's favored race;
And yet His courts preserve His word,
  And there we wait His grace.

4 With psalms of honor, and of joy,
  Let all His temples ring;
Your various instruments employ,
  And songs of triumph sing.

ANDANTE.   DR. LOWELL MASON

Thy goodness, Lord, our souls confess: Thy goodness we a - dore;

A spring whose blessings nev - er fail, A sea with - out a shore.

338

2 Sun, moon, and stars, Thy love attest
In every golden ray;
Love draws the curtains of the night,
And love returns the day.

3 Thy bounty every season crowns
With all the bliss it yields,
With joyful clusters loads the vines,
With strengthening grain the fields.

4 But chiefly Thy compassions, Lord,
Are in the Gospel seen;
There, like a sun, Thy mercy shines,
Without a cloud between.

339

1 COME, O ye saints, your voices raise
To God, in grateful songs;
And let the memory of His grace
Inspire your hearts and tongues,

2 Her deepest gloom, when sorrow spreads,
And light and hope depart,
His smile celestial morning sheds,
And joy revives the heart.

3 Hear, O my God, in mercy hear;
Attend my plaintive cry;
Be Thou, my gracious Helper, near,
And bid my sorrows fly.

4 Again I hear Thy voice divine;
New joys exulting bound;
My robes of mourning I resign,
And gladness girds me round.

340

1 DEAR Father, to Thy mercy-seat
My soul for shelter flies:
'T is here I find a safe retreat
When storms and tempests rise.

2 My cheerful hope can never die,
If Thou, my God, art near;
Thy grace can raise my comforts high,
And banish every fear.

3 My great Protector, and my Lord,
Thy constant aid impart;
Oh, let Thy kind, Thy gracious word
Sustain my trembling heart!

341

1 WHEN all Thy mercies, O my God,
My rising soul surveys,
Transported with the view, I'm lost
In wonder, love and praise.

2 Unnumbered comforts to my soul
Thy tender care bestowed,
Before my infant heart conceived
From whom those comforts flowed.

3 When, in the slippery paths of youth,
With heedless steps I ran,
Thine arm, unseen, conveyed me safe,
And led me up to man.

4 Through every period of my life,
Thy goodness I'll pursue,
And after death, in distant worlds,
The glorious theme renew.

ANDANTE.   GARDINER.

Hap - py is he who fears the Lord, And fol - lows his commands;

Who lends the poor with - out re - ward, Or gives with lib' - ral hands.

342

2 As pity dwells within his breast
   To all the sons of need,
So God shall answer his request
   With blessings on his seed.

3 No evil tidings shall surprise
   His well-established mind;
His soul to God, his Refuge, flies,
   And leaves his fears behind.

4 In times of general distress,
   Some beams of light shall shine,
To show the world his righteousness,
   And give him peace divine.

343

1 JESUS! our fainting spirits cry,
   When wilt thou show Thy face?
Oh! when our longings satisfy,
   And fill us with Thy grace?

2 We sinners, Lord, with earnest heart,
   With sighs and prayers and tears,
To Thee our inmost cares impart,
   Our burdens and our fears.

3 Thy sovereign grace can give relief,
   Thou Source of peace and light!
Dispel the gloomy cloud of grief,
   And make our darkness bright.

4 Around Thy Father's throne on high,
   All heaven Thy glory sings;
And earth, for which Thou cam'st to die,
   Loud with Thy praises rings.

5 Dear Lord! to Thee our prayers ascend;
   Our eyes Thy face would see;
Oh! let our weary wanderings end,
   Our spirits rest in Thee!

344

1 HAIL, sacred truth, whose piercing rays
   Dispel the shades of night,
Diffusing o'er the mental world
   The healing beams of light.

2 Thy word, O Lord, with friendly aid
   Restores our wandering feet;
Converts the sorrows of the mind
   To joys divinely sweet.

3 O, send Thy light and truth abroad
   In all their radiant blaze,
And bid the admiring world adore
   The glories of Thy grace.

345

1 LORD, I believe; Thy power I own;
   Thy word I would obey;
I wander comfortless and lone,
   When from Thy truth I stray.

2 Lord, I believe; but gloomy fears
   Sometimes bedim my sight;
I look to Thee with prayers and tears
   And cry for strength and light.

3 Lord, I believe; but oft, I know,
   My faith is cold and weak;
Strengthen my weakness, and bestow
   The confidence I seek.

4 Yes, I believe; and only Thou
   Canst give my soul relief;
Lord, to Thy truth my spirit bow;
   Help Thou my unbelief.

God, my sup-port-er and my hope, My help, for-ev-er near,

Thine arm of mer-cy held me up When sinking in de-spair.

346

2 Thy counsels, Lord, shall guide my feet
Through this dark wilderness;
Thy hand conduct me near Thy seat,
To dwell before Thy face.

3 Were I in heaven without my God,
'Twould be no joy to me;
And while this earth is my abode,
I long for none but Thee.

4 Then, to draw near to Thee, my God,
Shall be my sweet employ:
My tongue shall sound Thy works abroad,
And tell the world my joy.

347

1 To Thee, O God, my prayer ascends,
But not for golden stores;
Nor covet I the brightest gems
That shine on eastern shores;

2 Nor that deluding, empty joy,
Men call a mighty name;
Nor greatness, with its pride and state,
My restless thoughts inflame:

3 Nor pleasure's fascinating charms
My fond desires allure;
But nobler things than these from Thee
My wishes would secure.

4 The faith and hope of things unseen
My best affections move—
Thy light, Thy favor, and Thy smiles,
Thine everlasting love.

5 These are the blessings I desire:
Lord, be these blessings mine;
And all the glories of the world
I cheerfully resign.

348

1 GIVE me the wings of faith, to rise
Within the vail, and see
The saints above—how great their joys,
How bright their glories be!

2 Once they were mourning here below,
And wet their couch with tears;
They wrestled hard, as we do now,
With sins, and doubts, and fears.

3 I ask them whence their victory came;
They, with united breath,
Ascribe their conquest to the Lamb,
Their triumph to His death.

4 They marked the footsteps that He trod,
His zeal inspired their breast;
And following their incarnate God,
Possess the promised rest.

5 Our glorious Leader claims our praise
For His own pattern given,
While the long cloud of witnesses
Show the same path to heaven.

349

1 LORD, I address Thy heavenly throne;
Call me a child of Thine,
Send down the Spirit of Thy Son,
To form my heart divine.

2 There shed Thy choicest love abroad,
And make my comforts strong:
Then shall I say, "My Father, God,"
With an unwavering tongue.

WEYBRIDGE. C. M. (Double.)

ALLEGRETTO.   GIORNOVICHI.

O ci - ty of the Lord, be - gin The u - ni - ver - sal song,

And let the scattered vil - la - ges The joy - ful notes pro - long.

Let Kedar's wil - der - ness a - far Lift up the lonely voice;

And let the ten-ants of the rock With accent rude re - joice.

350

3 O, from the streams of distant lands
Unto Jehovah sing;
And joyful from the mountain tops
Shout to the Lord, the King.

4 Let all combined with one accord,
Jehovah's glories raise,
Till in remotest bounds of earth
The nations sound His praise.

351

1 On, who is like the mighty One,
Whose throne is in the sky!

Who compasseth the universe
With His all-searching eye;
At whose creative word appeared
The dry land and the sea:
My spirit thirsts for Thee, O Lord,
My spirit thirsts for Thee!

2 Around Him suns and systems swim
In harmony and light;
Before him harps angelic hymn
His praises day and night,
Yet to the contrite, day and night,
In mercy turneth He:
My spirit thirsts for Thee, O Lord,
My spirit thirsts for Thee.

CHORALMENTE.

MELCHIOR VULPIUS,
Cantor in Weimar. 1610.

Our God is love, and all His saints His im - age bear be - low;

The heart with love to God in - spired, With love to man will glow.

352

2 Our heavenly Father, Lord, art Thou,
Thy favored children we;
O, may we love each other here,
As we are loved by Thee.

3 Heirs of the same immortal bliss,
Our hopes and fears the same;
With bonds of grace our hearts unite,
With mutual love inflame.

4 So may the vain, contentious world
See how true Christians love,
And glorify our Saviour's grace,
And seek that grace to prove.

353

1 Thou art the Way; to Thee alone
From Sin and Death we flee;
And he who would the Father seek,
Must seek Him, Lord, by Thee.

2 Thou art the Truth; Thy word alone
True wisdom can impart;
Thou only canst inform the mind,
And purify the heart.

3 Thou art the Life; the rending tomb
Proclaims Thy conquering arm;
And those who put their trust in Thee
Nor death nor hell shall harm.

4 Thou art the Way, the Truth, the Life;
Grant us that Way to know;
That Truth to keep, that Life to win,
Whose joys eternal flow.

354

1 God moves in a mysterious way
His wonders to perform;
He plants His footsteps in the sea,
And rides upon the storm.

2 Deep in unfathomable mines
Of never-failing skill,
He treasures up His bright designs,
And works His sovereign will.

3 Ye fearful saints, fresh courage take;
The clouds ye so much dread
Are big with mercy, and shall break
In blessings on your head.

4 Judge not the Lord by feeble sense,
But trust Him for His grace;
Behind a frowning providence,
He hides a smiling face.

5 His purposes will ripen fast,
Unfolding every hour;
The bud may have a bitter taste,
But sweet will be the flower.

6 Blind unbelief is sure to err,
And scan His work in vain;
God is His own interpreter,
And He will make it plain.

355.

1 Pity the nations, O our God;
Constrain the earth to come;
Send Thy victorious word abroad,
And bring the strangers home.

2 We long to see Thy churches full,
That all Thy faithful race
May, with one voice, and heart, and soul,
Sing Thy redeeming grace.

WM. BILLINGS.

1. There is a land of pure de - light, Where saints im-mor - tal reign ; }
In - fin - ite day ex - cludes the night,................................ }

And pleasures banish pain. 2. There ev - er - last - ing spring abides, And never-

with'ring flo w'rs; Death, like a narrow sea, divides This heav'nly land from ours.

356

3 Sweet fields, beyond the swelling flood,
  Stand dressed in living green;
  So to the Jews old Canaan stood,
  While Jordan rolled between.

4 But timorous mortals start and shrink
  To cross this narrow sea,
  And linger, shivering, on the brink,
  And fear to launch away.

5 O, could we make our doubts remove,—
  Those gloomy doubts that rise,—
  And see the Canaan that we love
  With unbeclouded eyes,—

6 Could we but climb where Moses stood,
  And view the lanscape o'er,
  Not Jordan's stream, nor death's cold flood
  Should fright us from the shore.

357

1 BRIGHT glories rush upon my sight,
  And charm my wondering eyes—

The regions of immortal light,
  The beauties of the skies!

2 All hail! ye fair, celestial shores,
  Ye lands of endless day!
  A rich delight your prospect pours,
  And drives my griefs away.

3 There's a delightful clearness now;
  My clouds of doubt are gone;
  Fled is my former darkness, too;
  My fears are all withdrawn.

4 Short is the passage, short the space,
  Between my home and me;
  There, there behold the radiant place
  How near the mansions be!

5 Immortal wonders! boundless things
  In those dear worlds appear!
  Prepare me, Lord, to stretch my wings,
  And in those glories share.

GEO. KINGSLEY.

Unheard, the dews a-round me fall, And heav'nly influence shed;

And, si-lent, on this earth-ly ball, Ce-les-tial footsteps tread.

358

2 Night reigns in silence o'er the pole,
And spreads her gems unheard;
Her lessons penetrate the soul,
Yet borrow not a word.

3 Noiseless the sun emits his fire,
And pours his golden streams;
And silently the shades retire
Before his rising beams.

4 O, grant my soul an ear to hear
Thy deep and silent voice;
To bend in lowly, filial fear,
And in Thy love rejoice.

359

1 If human kindness meets return
And owns the grateful tie;
If tender thoughts within us burn,
To feel a friend is nigh; —

2 O, shall not warmer accents tell
The gratitude we owe
To Him who die 1 our fears to quell,
Who bore our guilt and woe?

3 While yet in anguish he surveyed
Those pangs He would not flee,
What love His latest words displayed!
"Meet and remember Me."

4 Remember Thee! Thy death, Thy shame
Our sinful hearts to share!
O memory, leave no other name
But His recorded there.

360

1 Jesus, with all Thy saints above,
My tongue would bear her part;
Would sound aloud thy saving love,
And sing Thy bleeding heart.

2 Blest be the Lamb, my dearest Lord,
Who bought me with his blood;
And quenched his Father's flaming sword,
In his own vital flood.

3 The Lamb, that freed my captive soul
From Satan's heavy chains ;
And sent the lion down to howl,
Where hell and horror reigns.

4 All glory to the dying Lamb,
And never-ceasing praise;
While angels live to know his name,
Or saints to feel his grace.

361

1 When musing sorrow weeps the past,
And mourns the present pain,
'Tis sweet to think of peace at last,
And feel that death is gain.

2 'Tis not that murmuring thoughts arise,
And dread a Father's will;
'Tis not that meek submission flies,
And would not suffer still.

3 It is that heaven-born faith surveys
The path that leads to light,
And longs her eagle plumes to raise,
And lose herself in sight.

4 O, let me wing my hallowed flight
From earth-born woe and care,
And soar above these clouds of night,
My Saviour's bliss to share.

ADAGIO MOLTO.   MODERN HARP.

Calm on the list'-ning ear of night, Come heav'ns melo-dious strains,—

Where wild Ju-de-a stretch-es far Her sil-ver man-tled plains.

362

2 Celestial choirs, from courts above,
'Mid sacred glories there;
And angels with their sparkling lyres,
Make music on the air.

3 The answering hills of Palestine
Send back the glad reply;
And greet, from all their holy heights,
The day-spring from on high.

4 O'er the blue depths of Galilee
There comes a holier calm;
And Sharon waves, in solemn praise,
Her silent groves of palm.

5 "Glory to God!" the sounding skies
Loud with their anthems ring;
"Peace to the earth—good will to men,
From heaven's eternal King."

363

1 JESUS, my sorrow lies too deep
For human ministry;
It knows not how to tell itself
To any but to Thee.

2 Thou dost remember still, amid
The glories of God's throne,
The sorrows of mortality,
For they were once Thine own.

3 Yes! for as if Thou would'st be God,
E'en in Thy misery,
There's been no sorrow but Thine own
Untouched by sympathy.

4 Jesus, my fainting spirit brings
Its fearfulness to Thee;
Thine eye at least can penetrate
The clouded mystery.

5 It is enough, my precious Lord,
Thy tender sympathy!
There is no sorrow e'er so deep
But I may bring to Thee.

364

1 WHAT grace, O Lord, and beauty shone
Around Thy steps below!
What patient love was seen in all
Thy life and death of woe!

2 For ever on Thy burdened heart
A weight of sorrow hung;
Yet no ungentle murmuring word
Escaped Thy silent tongue.

3 Thy foes might hate, despise, revile—
Thy friends unfaithful prove;
Unwearied in forgiveness still,
Thy heart could only love.

4 Oh! give us hearts to love like Thee—
Like Thee, O Lord, to grieve
Far more for other's sins, than all
The wrongs that we receive.

5 One with Thyself, may every eye
In us, Thy brethren, see
That gentleness and grace that spring
From union, Lord, with Thee.

CON SPIRITO.　　　　　　　　　　　　　　O. HOLDEN.

All hail the power of Je-sus' name, Let an-gels prostrate fall;

Bring forth the roy-al di-a-dem, And crown Him Lord of all,

Bring forth the roy-al di-a-dem, And crown Him Lord of all.

365

2 Crown Him, ye morning stars of light,
　Who fixed this floating ball;
　Now hail the strength of Israel's might,
　And crown Him Lord of all.

3 Crown Him, ye martyrs of our God,
　Who from His altar call;
　Extol the stem of Jesse's rod,
　And crown Him Lord of all.

4 Ye chosen seed of Israel's race,
　A remnant weak and small;
　Hail Him who saves you by His grace,
　And crown Him Lord of all.

5 Ye Gentile sinners ne'er forget
　The wormwood and the gall;
　Go, spread your trophies at His feet,
　And crown Him Lord of all.

6 Let every kindred, every tribe,
　On this terrestrial ball,
　To Him all majesty ascribe,
　And crown Him Lord of all.

7 O that with yonder sacred throng,
　We at His feet may fall!

We'll join the everlasting song,
And crown Him Lord of all.

366

1 WHAT heavenly music do I hear,
　Salvation sounding free;
　Ye souls in bondage lend an ear;
　This is the Jubilee.

2 The gospel sounds a sweet release
　To all in misery,
　And bids them welcome home to peace;
　This is the Jubilee.

3 Good news, good news, to Adam's race,
　Let Christians all agree,
　To sing redeeming Love and Grace;
　This is the Jubilee.

4 How sweetly do the tidings roll,
　All round, from sea to sea,
　From land to land, from pole to pole;
　This is the Jubilee.

5 Jesus is on his mercy seat,
　Before Him bend the knee;
　Let heaven and earth his praise repeat,
　This is the Jubilee.

Dr. Lowell Mason.

Father, whate'er of earth-ly bliss Thy sovereign will de - nies,

Accept - ed at Thy throne of grace, Let this pe - ti - tion rise.

367

2 "Give me a calm, a thankful heart,
From every murmur free;
The blessings of Thy grace impart,
And make me live to Thee.

3 "Let the sweet hope that Thou art mine
My life and death attend,
Thy presence through my journey shine;
And crown my journey's end."

368

1 O THAT I knew the secret place
Where I might find my God!
I'd spread my wants before His face,
And pour my woes abroad.

2 I'd tell Him how my sins arise;
What sorrows I sustain;
How grace decays and comfort dies,
And leaves my heart in pain.

3 Arise, my soul, from deep distress,
And banish every fear;
He calls thee to His throne of grace,
To spread thy sorrows there.

369

1 DEAR Refuge of my weary soul,
On Thee, when sorrows rise,
On Thee, when waves of trouble roll,
My fainting hope relies.

2 To Thee I tell each rising grief,
For Thou alone canst heal;

Thy word can bring a sweet relief
For every pain I feel.

3 But O, when gloomy doubts prevail,
I fear to call Thee mine;
The springs of comfort seem to fail,
And all my hopes decline.

4 Yet, gracious God, where shall I flee?
Thou art my only trust;
And still my soul would cleave to Thee,
Though prostrate in the dust.

5 Thy mercy-seat is open still;
Here let my soul retreat,
With humble hope attend Thy will,
And wait beneath Thy feet.

370

1 UNITE, my roving thoughts, unite
In silence soft and sweet;
And thou, my soul, sit gently down
At thy great Sovereign's feet.

2 Jehovah's awful voice is heard;
Yet gladly I attend;
For, lo, the everlasting God
Proclaims Himself my Friend.

3 Harmonious accents to my soul
The sounds of peace convey;
The tempest at His word subsides,
And winds and seas obey.

4 By all its joys, I charge my heart
To grieve His love no more,
But, charmed by melody divine,
To give its follies o'er.

ALLEGRETTO. INGALLS. About 1800.

Lo, what a glo-rious sight appears To our be-liev-ing eyes!

To our.... &c.

The earth and seas are

The earth and seas are passed a-way, The
The earth and seas are passed a-way, The earth and seas are

earth and seas are passed a-way, And the old roll-ing skies.
passed a-way,........ And the............ old roll-ing skies.

earth and seas are passed a-way, And the old roll-ing skies.
passed a - - way, And the old roll-ing skies.

371

2 From the third heaven, where God resides,
That holy, happy place,
The new Jerusalem comes down
Adorned with shining grace.

3 Attending angels shout for joy,
And the bright armies sing,
"Mortals, behold the sacred seat
Of your descending King.

4 "The God of glory down to men
Removes His blest abode;
Men the dear objects of His grace,
And He the loving God.

5 "His own soft hand shall wipe the tears
From every weeping eye;
And pains and groans and griefs and fears,
And death itself, shall die."

6 How long, dear Saviour, O, how long
Shall this bright hour delay?

Fly swifter round, ye wheels of time,
And bring the welcome day.

372

1 SWEET is the memory of Thy grace,
My God, my heavenly King!
Let age to age Thy righteousness
In sounds of glory sing.

2 God reigns on high, but ne'er confines
His goodness to the skies;
Thro' the whole earth His bounty shines,
And every want supplies.

3 How kind are Thy compassions, Lord!
How slow Thine anger moves!
But soon He sends His pardoning word,
To cheer the souls He loves.

4 Creatures, with all their endless race,
Thy power and praise proclaim;
But saints that taste Thy richer grace,
Delight to bless Thy name.

· HALE. C. M.

GEO. KINGSLEY

How sweet to be al-lowed to pray To God, the Ho-ly One;

With fil-ial love and trust to say, "O God, Thy will be done."

373

2 We in these sacred words can find
　A cure for every ill;
They calm and soothe the troubled mind
　And bid all care be still.

3 O let that Will which gave me breath
　And an immortal soul,
In joy or grief, in life or death,
　My every wish control.

4 O, could my heart thus ever pray,
　Thus imitate Thy Son!
　Teach me, O God, with truth to say,
　Thy will, not mine, be done.

374

1 BRIGHT was the guiding star, that led,
　With mild, benignant ray,
The Gentiles to the lowly bed
　Where our Redeemer lay.

2 But, lo! a brighter, clearer light
　Now points to His abode;
It shines thro' sin and sorrow's night,
　To guide us to our Lord.

3 O, haste to follow where it leads;
　The gracious call obey;
Be rugged wilds, or flowery meads,
　The Christian's destined way.

4 O, gladly tread the narrow path,
　While light and grace are given;
Who meekly follow Christ on earth,
　Shall reign with Him in heaven.

375

1 To Thee, before the dawning light,
　My gracious God, I pray;
I meditate Thy name by night,
　And keep Thy law by day.

2 My spirit faints to see Thy grace;
　Thy promise bears me up;
And while salvation long delays,
　Thy word supports my hope.

3 Seven times a day I lift my hands,
　And pay my thanks to Thee;
Thy righteous providence demands
　Repeated praise from me.

4 When midnight darkness veils the skies,
　I call Thy works to mind;
My thoughts in warm devotion rise,
　And sweet acceptance find.

376

1 FAR from the world, O Lord, I flee,
　From strife and tumult far,
From scenes where Satan wages still
　His most successful war.

2 The calm retreat, the silent shade,
　With prayer and praise agree,
And seem by Thy sweet bounty made
　For those who follow Thee.

3 There, if Thy Spirit touch the soul,
　And grace her mean abode,
O, with what peace and joy and love,
　She communes with her God!

4 Author and Guardian of my life,
　Sweet Source of light divine,
And all harmonious names in one,
　My Saviour, Thou art mine.

ANDANTE   SCOTTISH.

Thou dear Redeem - er, dy - ing Lamb, I love to hear of Thee;

No music's like Thy charming name, Nor half so sweet can be.

377

2 O, may I ever hear Thy voice
In mercy to me speak;
And in my Priest will I rejoice,
Thou great Melchisedec.

3 My Jesus shall be still my theme,
While on this earth I stay;
I'll sing my Jesus' lovely name.
When all things else decay.

4 When I appear in yonder cloud,
With all His favored throng,
Then will I sing more sweet, more loud,
And Christ shall be my song.

378

1 BESTOW, O Lord, upon our youth
The gift of saving grace;
And let the seed of sacred truth
Fall in a fruitful place.

2 Grace is a plant, where'er it grows,
Of pure and heavenly root,
But fairest in the youngest shows,
And yields the sweetest fruit.

3 Ye careless ones, O, hear betimes
The voice of sovereign Love; [crimes,
Your youth is stained with numerous
But Mercy reigns above.

4 For you the public prayer is made;
O, join the public prayer;
For you the secret tear is shed;
O, shed yourselves a tear.

379

1 RELIGION is the chief concern
Of mortals here below;
May I its great importance learn,
Its sovereign virtue know.

2 Religion should our thoughts engage,
Amid our youthful bloom;
'Twill fit us for declining age,
And for the awful tomb.

3 O, may my heart, by grace subdued,
Be my Redeemer's throne;
And be my stubborn will subdued
His government to own.

380

1 O, HAPPY is the man who hears
Instruction's warning voice,
And who celestial Wisdom makes
His early, only choice.

2 For she has treasure greater far
Than east or west unfold,
And her reward is more secure
Than is the gain of gold.

3 In her right hand she holds to view
A length of happy years,
And in her left the prize of fame
And honor bright appears.

4 She guides the young with innocence
In pleasure's path to tread;
A crown of glory she bestows
Upon the hoary head.

5 According as her labors rise,
So her rewards increase;
Her ways are ways of pleasantness,
And all her paths are peace.

381

3 There happier bowers than Eden's bloom,
  Nor sin nor sorrow know:
Blest seats! thro' rude and stormy scenes
  I onward press to you.

4 Why should I shrink at pain and woe,
  Or feel at death dismay?
I've Canaan's goodly land in view,
  And realms of endless day.

5 Apostles, martyrs, prophets there,
  Around my Saviour stand;
And soon my friends in Christ below,
  Will join the glorious band.

6 Jerusalem! my happy home!
  My soul still pants for thee;
Then shall my labors have an end,
  When I thy joys shall see.

DR. LOWELL MASON.

There is a land, a hap-py land, Where tears are wiped a-
way From ev'-ry eye, by God's own hand, And
night is turned to day, And night is turned to day.

382

2 There is a Home, a happy home,
   Where the way-worn travellers rest,
   Where toil and languor never come,
   And every mourner's blest.

3 There is a Port, a peaceful port,
   A safe and quiet shore,
   Where weary mariners resort,
   When life's rough voyage is o'er.

4 There is a Crown, a dazzling crown,
   Bedecked with jewels fair;
   And priests and kings of high renown
   That crown of glory wear.

5 That land be mine, that calm retreat,
   That crown of glory bright;
   Then I'll esteem each bitter sweet,
   And every burden light.

383

1 How sad our state by nature is!
   Our sin, how deep it stains!
   And Satan binds our captive minds
   Fast in his slavish chains.

2 But there's a voice of sovereign grace
   Sounds from the sacred word;
   "Ho, ye despairing sinners, come,
   And trust upon the Lord."

3 My soul obeys the almighty call,
   And runs to this relief;
   Would I believe Thy promise, Lord;
   O, help my unbelief.

4 A guilty, weak, and helpless worm,
   On Thy kind arms I fall;
   Be Thou my strength and righteousness,
   My Jesus, and my all.

384

1 O THOU from whom all goodness flows,
   I lift my soul to Thee;
   In all my sorrows, conflicts, woes,
   Good Lord, remember me.

2 When on my aching, burdened heart
   My sins lie heavily,
   Thy pardon grant, new peace impart;
   Good Lord, remember me.

3 When trials sore obstruct my way,
   And ills I cannot flee,
   O let my strength be as my day;
   Good Lord, remember me.

4 When worn with pain, disease, and grief,
   This feeble body see;
   Grant patience, rest and kind relief;
   Good Lord, remember me.

5 When in the solemn hour of death
   I wait Thy just decree;
   Be this the prayer of my last breath—
   Good Lord, remember me.

6 And when before Thy throne I stand,
   And lift my soul to Thee,
   Then with the saints at Thy right hand,
   Good Lord, remember me.

HOWARD. C. M.

Arr. by DR. LOWELL MASON.

O, praise the Lord for He is good, In Him we rest obtain;

His mer - cy has through a - ges stood, And ev - er shall re - main.

385

2 Let all the people of the Lord
His praises spread around;
Let them His grace and love record,
Who have salvation found.

3 Now let the east in Him rejoice,
The west its tribute bring;
The north and south lift up their voice
In honor of their King.

4 O, praise the Lord, for He is good;
In Him we rest obtain;
His mercy has through ages stood,
And ever shall remain.

386

1 Now shall my solemn vows be paid
To that almighty Power
That heard the long requests I made,
In my distressful hour.

2 When on my head huge sorrows fell,
I sought His heavenly aid;
He saved my sinking soul from hell,
And death's eternal shade.

3 If sin lay covered in my heart,
While prayer employed my tongue,
The Lord had shown me no regard,
For I His praises sung.

4 But God—His name be ever blesesd—
Has set my spirit free,
Nor turned from Him my poor request,
Nor turned His heart from me.

387

1 God only is the creature's home,
Though long and rough the road;
Yet nothing less can satisfy
The love that longs for God.

2 How little of that road, my soul!
How little hast thou gone!
Take heart, and let the thought of God
Allure thee further on.

3 Dole not thy duties out to God,
But let thy hand be free:
Look long at Jesus: His own blood,
How was it dealt to thee?

4 The perfect way is hard to flesh;
It is not hard to love;
If thou wert sick for want of God,
How swiftly wouldst thou move!

5 Be docile to thy unseen Guide,
Love Him as He loves thee;
Time and obedience are enough,
And thou like Him shalt be!

388

1 One prayer I have—all prayers in one—
When I am wholly Thine;
Thy will, my God, Thy will be done,
And let that will be mine.

2 All-wise, almighty, and all-good,
In Thee I firmly trust;
Thy ways, unknown or understood,
Are merciful and just.

3 May I remember that to Thee
Whate'er I have I owe;
And back in gratitude from me
May all Thy bounties flow.

DR. LOWELL MASON. 1830.

My God, my Fa-ther, bliss-ful name! O, may I call Thee

mine? May I with sweet as-sur-ance claim A

por-tion so di-vine? A por-tion so di-vine?

389

2 Whate'er Thy providence denies
I calmly would resign;
For Thou art good, and just, and wise:
Oh, bend my will to Thine!

3 Whate'er Thy sacred will ordains,
Oh, give me strength to bear!
And let me know my Father reigns,
And trust His tender care.

4 Thy sovereign ways are all unknown
To my weak, erring sight;
Yet let my soul adoring own
That all Thy ways are right.

390

1 BLEST be the dear, uniting love,
That will not let us part:
Our bodies may far off remove,
We still are one in heart.

2 Joined in one spirit to our Head,
Where He appoints we go;
We still in Jesus' footsteps tread,
And show His praise below.

3 Oh, may we ever walk in Him,
And nothing know beside!
Nothing desire, nothing esteem,
But Jesus crucified!

4 Partakers of the Saviour's grace,
The same in mind and heart,

Not joy, nor grief, nor time, nor place,
Nor life, nor death, can part.

391

1 SINCE all the varying scenes of time
God's watchful eye surveys,
Oh, who so wise to choose our lot,
Or to appoint our ways!

2 Good, when He gives, supremely good;
Nor less when he denies;
Ev'n crosses from His sovereign hand,
Are blessings in disguise.

3 Why should we doubt a Father's love,
So constant and so kind!
To His unerring, gracious will
Be every wish resigned.

392

1 WHEN, rising from the bed of death,
O'erwhelmed with guilt and fear,
I see my Maker face to face—
Oh, how shall I appear!

2 If now, while pardon may be found,
And mercy may be sought,
My heart with inward horror shrinks,
And tremblest at the thought;—

3 When Thou, O Lord! shall stand disclosed
In majesty severe,
And sit in judgment on my soul,
Oh, how shall I appear!

LE BARON. C. M.

MODERATO.

JOSIAH OSGOOD.

How precious is the book divine, By in - spi - ra - tion given!

Bright as a lamp its doctrines shine, To guide our souls to heaven.

393

2 It sweetly cheers our drooping hearts,
In this dark vale of tears;
Life, light, and joy it still imparts,
And quells our rising fears.

3 This lamp, through all the tedious night
Of life, shall guide our way;
Till we behold the clearer light
Of an eternal day.

394

1 WHEN I can read my title clear
To mansions in the skies,
I bid farewell to every fear,
And wipe my weeping eyes.

2 Should earth against my soul engage,
And hellish darts be hurled,
Then I can smile at Satan's rage,
And face a frowning world.

3 Let cares, like a wild deluge, come,
And storms of sorrow fall;
May I but safely reach my home,
My God, my heaven, my all.

4 There shall I bathe my weary soul
In seas of heavenly rest,
And not a wave of trouble roll
Across my peaceful breast.

395

1 THE branch is stooping to thy hand,
And pleasant to behold;
Yet gather not, although its fruit
Be streaked with hues of gold;—

2 For bitter ashes lurk concealed
Beneath that golden skin,
And though the coat be smooth, there lies
But rottenness within.

3 The wings of pleasure fan the bowl,
And bid it overflow;
Yet drugged with poison are its lees,
And death is found below.

396

1 Nor for the summer hour alone,
When skies resplendent shine,
And youth and pleasure fill the throne,
Our hearts and hands we join;

2 But for those stern and wintry days
Of sorrow, pain, and fear,
When Heaven's wise discipline doth make
Our earthly journey drear.

3 Not for this span of life alone,
Which like a blast doth fly,
And, as the transient flowers of grass,
Just blossom, droop and die.

4 But for a being without end
This vow of love we take;
Grant us, O Lord, one home at last,
For Thy great mercy's sake!

397

1 INQUIRE, ye pilgrims for the way
That leads to Zion's hill,
And thither set your steady face,
With a determined will.

2 Come, let us to His temple haste,
And seek His favor there;
Before His footstool humbly bow,
And pour our fervent prayer.

CHORAL.   SCOTTISH.

O, for a clos-er walk with God, A calm and heavenly frame,

A light to shine up-on the road That leads me to the Lamb.

398

2 Where is the blessedness I knew
   When first I saw the Lord;
   Where is the soul-refreshing view
   Of Jesus and His word?

3 Return, O holy Dove; return,
   Sweet Messenger of rest;
   I hate the sins that made Thee mourn,
   And drove Thee from my breast.

4 The dearest idol I have known,
   Whate'er that idol be,
   Help me to tear it from Thy throne,
   And worship only Thee.

5 So shall my walk be close with God,
   Calm and serene my frame;
   So purer light shall mark the road
   That leads me to the Lamb.

399

1 Plunged in a gulf of dark despair,
   We wretched sinners lay,
   Without one cheerful beam of hope,
   Or spark of glimmering day.

2 With pitying eyes, the Prince of grace
   Beheld our helpless grief;
   He saw, and O, amazing love!
   He ran to our relief.

3 Down from the shining seats above,
   With joyful haste He fled,
   Entered the grave in mortal flesh,
   And dwelt among the dead.

4 O, for this love let rocks and hills
   Their lasting silence break,
   And all harmonious human tongues
   The Saviour's praises speak.

5 Angels, assist our mighty joys;
   Strike all your harps of gold;
   But when you raise your highest notes,
   His love can ne'er be told.

400

1 O that the Lord would guide my ways,
   To keep His statutes still!
   O that my God would grant me grace,
   To know and do His will.

2 O send Thy Spirit down—to write
   Thy law upon my heart!
   Nor let my tongue indulge deceit,
   Nor act the liar's part.

3 Make me to walk in Thy commands;
   'Tis a delightful road;
   Nor let my head, or heart, or hands,
   Offend against my God.

401

1 O Thou whose mercy guides my way,
   Though now it seem severe,
   Forbid my unbelief to say,
   There is no mercy here.

2 O, may I, Lord, desire the pain
   That comes in kindness down,
   Far more than sweetest earthly gain
   Succeeded by a frown.

3 Then, though Thou bend my spirit low,
   Love only shall I see;
   The gracious hand that strikes the blow
   Was wounded once for me.

CHINA. C. M.

T. SWAN.

Why do we mourn de - part - ing friends, Or shake at death's a - larms?

'Tis but the voice that Je - sus sends To call them to His arms.

402

2 Are we not tending upward too,
   As fast as time can move?
Nor would we wish the hours more slow,
   To keep us from our Love.

3 The graves of all the saints He blessed,
   And softened every bed;
Where should the dying members rest
   But with the dying Head?

4 Thence He arose, ascending high,
   And showed our feet the way;
Up to the Lord our flesh shall fly
   At the great rising day.

5 Then let the last loud trumpet sound,
   And bid our kindred rise;
Awake, ye nations under ground;
   Ye saints, ascend the skies.

403

1 LIFE is a span, a fleeting hour;
   How soon the vapor flies!
Man is a tender, transient flower,
   That ev'n in blooming dies.

2 The once-loved form, now cold and dead,
   Each mournful thought employs;
And Nature weeps her comforts fled,
   And withered all her joys.

3 Hope looks beyond the bounds of time,
   When what we now deplore
Shall rise in full immortal prime,
   And bloom to fade no more.

4 Then cease, fond Nature, cease thy tears;
   Religion points on high;
There everlasting spring appears,
   And joys that cannot die.

404

1 WHEN blooming youth is snatched away
   By Death's resistless hand,
Our hearts the mournful tribute pay
   Which pity must demand.

2 While pity prompts the rising sigh,
   O, may this truth, impressed
With awful power, " I too, must die,"
   Sink deep in every breast.

3 The voice of this alarming scene
   May every heart obey;
Nor be the heavenly warning vain
   Which calls to watch and pray.

4 O, let us fly, to Jesus fly;
   Whose powerful arm can save;
Then shall our hopes ascend on high,
   And triumph o'er the grave.

405

1 YE mourning saints, whose streaming tears
   Flow o'er your children dead,
Say not, in transports of despair,
   That all your hopes are fled.

2 While, cleaving to that darling dust,
   In fond distress ye lie,
Rise, and with joy and reverence view
   A heavenly parent nigh.

3 "I'll give the mourner," saith the Lord,
   " In My own house a place;
No name of daughters and of sons
   Could yield so high a grace."

O Thou, to whom all crea - tures bow, With - in this earth - ly frame;

Through all the world, how great art Thou! How glo - rious is Thy name!

406

2 When heaven,Thy beauteous work on high,
Employs my wondering sight;
The moon that nightly rules,the sky,
With stars of feebler light:—

3 Lord,what is man, that Thou shouldst deign
To bear him in Thy mind!
Or what his race, that Thou shouldst prove
To them so wondrous kind!

4 O Thou, to whom all creatures bow
Within this earthly frame,
Thro' all the world, how great art Thou!
How glorious is Thy name!

407

1 In vain I trace creation o'er,
In search of solid rest:
The whole creation is too poor,
Too mean to make me blest.

2 Let earth and all her charms depart,
Unworthy of the mind:
In God alone this restless heart
Enduring bliss can find.

3 Thy favor, Lord, is all I want;
Here would my spirit rest:
Oh, seal the rich, the boundless grant,
And make me fully blest!

408

1 See gracious God! before Thy throne
Thy mourning people bend;
'Tis on Thy sovereign grace alone
Our humble hopes depend.

2 Dark, frowning judgments from Thy hand
Thy dreadful power display;
Yet mercy spares this guilty land,
And still we live to pray.

3 How changed, alas! are truths divine,
For error, guilt, and shame!
What impious numbers, bold in sin,
Disgrace the Christian name!

4 Oh, turn us, turn us, mighty Lord,
By Thy resistless grace;
Then shall our hearts obey Thy word,
And humbly seek Thy face.

469

1 Thee we adore, eternal Name!
And humbly own to Thee
How feeble is our mortal frame,
What dying worms are we!

2 The year rolls round, and steals away
The breath that first it gave;
Whate'er we do, where'er we be,
We're travelling to the grave.

3 Great God! on what a slender thread
Hang everlasting things!
Th' eternal state of all the dead
Upon life's feeble strings!

4 Infinite joy, or endless woe
Attends on every breath;
And yet how unconcerned we go
Upon the brink of death!

5 Waken, O Lord, our drowsy sense,
To walk this dangerous road!
And if our souls are hurried hence,
May they be found with God.

GLENN. C. M.

DIVOTO.   T. L. HATELY.

Through sorrow's night and danger's path, A - mid the deep'ning gloom,

We, soldiers of an injured King, Are marching to the tomb.

410

2 There, when the turmoil is no more,
　And all our powers decay,
　Our cold remains in solitude
　　Shall sleep the years away.

3 Our labors done, securely laid
　In this our last retreat,
　Unheeded o'er our silent dust
　　The storms of life shall beat.

4 Yet not thus lifeless, thus inane,
　The vital spark shall lie;
　For o'er life's wreck that spark shall rise
　　To seek its kindred sky.

5 These ashes, too, this little dust
　Our Father's care shall keep,
　Till the last angel rise and break
　　The long and dreary sleep.

6 Then love's soft dew o'er every eye
　Shall shed its mildest rays,
　And the long-silent dust shall burst
　　With shouts of endless praise.

411

1 Thou, O my Jesus, Thou didst me
　Upon the cross embrace;
　For me didst bear the nails and spear,
　　And manifold disgrace;

2 And griefs and torments numberless
　And sweat of agony,
　Yea, death itself; and all for one
　　That was Thine enemy.

3 Then, why, O blessed Jesus Christ,
　Should I not love Thee well?

Not for the hope of winning heaven,
　Nor of escaping hell;

4 Not with the hope of gaining aught,
　Nor seeking a reward;
　But as Thyself hast loved me,
　　O, ever-loving Lord.

5 E'en so I love Thee, and will love,
　And in Thy praise will sing,
　Solely because Thou art my God,
　　And my eternal King.

412

1 Do not I love Thee, O my Lord?
　Behold my heart, and see;
　And turn each cursed idol out
　　That dares to rival Thee.

2 Is not Thy name melodious still
　To mine attentive ear?
　Doth not each pulse with pleasure bound
　　My Saviour's voice to hear?

3 Hast Thou a lamb in all Thy flock
　I would disdain to feed?
　Hast Thou a foe before whose face
　　I fear Thy cause to plead?

4 Would not my heart pour forth its blood
　In honor of Thy name,
　And challenge the cold hand of death
　　To damp the immortal flame?

5 Thou know'st I love Thee, dearest Lord;
　But O, I long to soar
　Far from the sphere of mortal joys,
　　And learn to love Thee more.

MODERATO.

Arr. by DR. LOWELL MASON.

In all my Lord's ap - pointed ways, My journey I'll pur - sue;

Hinder me not, ye much loved saints, For I must go with you.

413

2 Through floods and flames, if Jesus leads,
  I'll follow where He goes;
  Hinder me not!—shall be my cry,
  Though earth and hell oppose.

3 And when my Saviour calls me home,
  Still this my cry shall be—
  Hinder me not—come, welcome death!
  I'll gladly go with Thee.

414

1 How condescending, and how kind
  Was God's eternal Son!
  Our misery reached His heavenly mind,
  And pity brought Him down.

2 This was compassion like a God,
  That when the Saviour knew
  The price of pardon was His blood,
  His pity ne'er withdrew.

3 Here let our hearts begin to melt,
  While we His death record;
  And with our joy for pardoned guilt,
  Mourn that we pierced the Lord.

415

1 Oh help us Lord! each hour of need
  Thy heavenly succor give;
  Help us in thought, and word and deed,
  Each hour on earth we live.

2 Oh help us when our spirits bleed
  With contrite anguish sore;
  And when our hearts are cold and dead,
  Oh help us, Lord, the more.

3 If strangers to Thy fold we call,
  Imploring at Thy feet
  The crumbs that from Thy table fall,
  'Tis all we dare entreat.

4 Oh help us, Jesus! from on high,
  We know no help but Thee;
  Oh! help us so to live and die,
  As Thine in Heaven to be.

416

1 Thou Grace divine, encircling all
  A soundless, shoreless sea!
  Wherein at last, our souls shall fall,
  O Love of God, most free!

2 When over dizzy steeps we go,
  One soft hand blinds our eyes,
  The other leads us safe and slow,
  O Love of God, most wise!

3 The saddened heart, the restless soul,
  The toilsome frame and mind,
  Alike confess Thy sweet control,
  O Love of God, most kind!

4 But not alone Thy care we claim,
  Our wayward steps to win;
  We know Thee by a dearer name,
  O Love of God within.

5 And filled and quickened by Thy breath,
  Our souls are strong and free
  To rise o'er sin, and fear, and death,
  O Love of God, to Thee!

D. DUTTON.

I love to steal a-while a-way From ev'-ry cumb'ring care;

And spend the hours of set-ting day In hum-ble, grate-ful prayer.

417

2 I love in solitude to shed
  The penitential tear,
And all His promises to plead,
  Where none but God can hear.

3 I love to think on mercies past,
  And future good implore,
And all my cares and sorrows cast
  On Him whom I adore.

4 I love by faith to take a view
  Of brighter scenes in heaven;
The prospect doth my strength renew,
  While here by temptests driven.

5 Thus, when life's toilsome day is o'er,
  May its departing ray
Be calm as this impressive hour,
  And lead to endless day.

418

1 COME, ye that know and fear the Lord!
  And raise your souls above;
Let every heart and voice accord,
  To sing that—God is love.

2 This precious truth His word declares,
  And all His mercies prove;
While Christ, the atoning Lamb, appears,
  To show that—God is love.

3 Behold His loving kindness waits
  For those who from Him rove,
And calls of mercy reach their hearts,
  To teach them—God is love.

4 The work begun is carried on
  By power from heaven above;
And every step, from first to last,
  Proclaims that—God is love.

5 O, may we all, while here below,
  The best of blessings prove;
Till warmer hearts, in brighter worlds,
  Shall shout that—God is love.

419

1 LIFT up to God the voice of praise,
  Whose breath our souls inspired;
Loud and more loud the anthems raise,
  With grateful ardor fired.

2 Lift up to God the voice of praise,
  Whose goodness, passing thought,
Loads every moment, as it flies,
  With benefits unsought.

420

1 THERE is a time, we know not when,
  A point, we know not where,
That marks the destiny of men,
  To glory, or despair.

2 And yet the doomed man's path below,
  May bloom as Eden bloomed;
He did not, does not, will not know,
  Or feel that he is doomed.

3 How far may we go on in sin?
  How long will God forbear?
Where does hope end, and where begin
  The confines of despair?

4 An answer from the skies is sent:
  " Ye that from God depart
While it is called TO-DAY, repent,
  And harden not your heart."

ANDANTE SOSTENUTO.
I. B. WOODBURY.

By cool Si - lo - am's sha - dy rill, How sweet the li - ly grows!

How sweet the breath be - neath the hill Of Sha - ron's dew - y rose!

421

2 Lo, such the child whose early feet
  The paths of peace have trod;
Whose secret heart, with influence sweet,
  Is upward drawn to God.

3 By cool Siloam's shady rill
  The lily must decay;
The rose that blooms beneath the hill
  Must shortly fade away.

4 O Thou whose infant feet were found
  Within Thy Father's shrine,
Whose years, with changeless virtue
  Were all alike divine,—   [crowned,

5 Dependent on Thy bounteous breath,
  We seek Thy grace alone,
In childhood, manhood, age, and death,
  To keep us still Thine own.

422

1 ALAS, and did my Saviour bleed,
  And did my Sovereign die?
Would He devote that sacred head
  For such a worm as I?

2 Was it for crimes that I had done,
  He groaned upon the tree!
Amazing pity! grace unknown!
  And love beyond degree!

3 Well might the sun in darkness hide,
  And shut his glories in,
When God, the mighty Maker, died
  For man, the creature's sin.

4 Thus might I hide my blushing face,
  While His dear cross appears;
Dissolve my heart in thankfulness,
  And melt my eyes to tears.

5 But drops of grief can ne'er repay
  The debt of love I owe;
Here, Lord, I give myself away,
  'Tis all that I can do.

423

1 IN the soft season of thy youth,
  In nature's smiling bloom,
Ere age arrives, and trembling waits
  Its summons to the tomb,—

2 Remember thy Creator, God;
  For Him thy powers employ;
Make Him thy fear, thy love, thy hope,
  Thy confidence and joy.

3 He shall defend and guide thy course
  Through life's uncertain sea,
Till thou art landed on the shores
  Of blest eternity.

4 Then seek the Lord betimes, and choose
  The ways of heavenly truth;
The earth affords no lovelier sight
  Than a religious youth.

424

1 Here in Thy presence holy God,
  We meet to seek Thy face;
O let us feel th' eternal word,
  And feast upon Thy grace.

2 O may this be a precious hour
  To every mourning soul;
Impart Thy love, display Thy power,
  And make the wounded whole.

3 Let every soul the Saviour see,
  And taste His love divine;
And every heart forever be
  United, Lord, with Thine.

118

DENFIELD. C. M.

Dr. Lowell Mason.

From Glaser.

Sweet was the time when first I felt The Saviour's pard'ning blood

Applied to cleanse my soul from guilt And bring me home to God.

425

2 Soon as the morn the light revealed,
His praises tuned my tongue;
And when the evening shades prevailed
His love was all my song.

3 In prayer my soul drew near the Lord,
And saw His glory shine;
And, when I read His holy word,
I called each promise mine.

4 Now, when the evening shade prevails,
My soul in darkness mourns;
And when the morn the light reveals,
No light to me returns.

5 Now Satan threatens to prevail,
And make my soul his prey;
Yet, Lord, Thy mercies cannot fail;
O, come without delay.

426

1 Christ leads me through no darker rooms
Than He went through before;
He that into God's kingdom comes
Must enter by this door.

2 Come, Lord, when grace hath made me meet
Thy blessed face to see;
For if Thy work on earth be sweet,
What must Thy glory be?

3 Then I shall end my sad complaints
And weary, sinful days,
And join with those triumphant saints
That sing Jehovah's praise.

4 My knowledge of that life is small;
The eye of faith is dim;
But ' tis enough that Christ knows all,
And I shall be with Him.

427

1 Lord, while for all mankind we pray,
Of every clime and coast,
O hear us for our native land,—
The land we love the most.

2 O, guard our shores from every foe,
With peace our borders bless,
With prosperous times our cities crown,
Our fields with plenteousness.

3 Unite us in the sacred love
Of knowledge, truth and Thee;
And let our hills and valleys shout
The songs of liberty.

4 Lord of the nations, thus to Thee
Our country we commend;
Be Thou her refuge and her trust,
Her everlasting Friend.

428

1 To Christ, in each fresh hour of woe
With confidence repair;
He will all needful grace bestow,
And all thy sorrow share.

2 When dark the troubled surges roll
O'er the bereaved breast,
His power doth still the waves control,
And hush the storm to rest.

3 Christ was a man of sorrows here,
And knew the stings of grief;
He hears affliction's broken prayer;
His love gives sweet relief.

SOUTHERN MELODY.

In Thy great name, O Lord, we come, To worship at Thy feet;

O, pour Thy Ho - ly Spi - rit down On, all that now shall meet.

429

2 We come to hear Jehovah speak,
　To hear the Saviour's voice;
　Thy face and favor, Lord, we seek—
　Now make our hearts rejoice.

3 Teach us to pray and praise, to hear
　And understand Thy word;
　To feel Thy blissful presence near,
　And trust our living Lord.

4 Let sinners now Thy goodness prove,
　And saints rejoice in Thee;
　Let rebels be subdued by love,
　And to the Saviour flee.

430

1 Come let us lift our joyful eyes
　Up to the courts above,
　And smile to see our Father there
　Upon a throne of love.

2 Come, let us bow before His feet,
　And venture near the Lord;
　No fiery cherub guards His seat,
　No double flaming sword.

3 The peaceful gates of heavenly bliss,
　Are opened by the Son;
　High let us raise our notes of praise,
　And reach th' almighty throne.

4 To Thee ten thousand thanks we bring,
　Great Advocate on high,
　And glory to th' eternal King,
　Who lays His anger by.

431

1 JESUS, the only thought of Thee;
　With sweetness fills my breast;
　But sweeter far it were to see,
　And on Thy beauty feast.

2 No sound, no harmony so gay,
　Can art or music frame;
　No thoughts can reach, no words can say
　The sweets of Thy blest name.

3 Jesus, our hope when we repent,
　Sweet source of all our grace,
　Sole comfort in our banishment,
　Oh! what when face to face!

4 Come then, dear Lord, possess my heart,
　Chose thence the shades of night;
　Come pierce it with Thy flaming dart,
　And ever-shining light!

432

1 Within these doors assembled now,
　We wait Thy blessing, Lord;
　Appear within our midst we pray,
　According to Thy word.

2 O breathe upon the lifeless soul,
　And raise the drooping heart;
　And let us see Thy smiling face
　Ere we from hence depart.

WM. MATHER.

For-ev-er here my rest shall be, Close to Thy bleed-ing side;

This all my hope, and all my plea— For me the Sa-viour died.

433

2 My dying Saviour, and my God,
 Fountain for guilt and sin,
Sprinkle me ever with Thy blood,
 And cleanse and keep me clean.

3 Wash me, and make me thus Thine own:
 Wash we, and mine Thou art;
Wash me, but not my feet alone,—
 My hands, my head, my heart.

4 Th' atonement of Thy blood apply,
 Till faith to sight improve;
Till hope in full fruition die, •
 And all my soul be love.

434

1 TRY us, O God, and search the ground
 Of every sinful heart;
Whate'er of sin in us is found,
 Oh bid it all depart.

2 Help us to help each other, Lord,
 Each other's cross to bear;
Let each his friendly aid afford,
 And feel his brother's care.

3 Help us to build each other up,
 Our heart and life improve;
Increase our faith, confirm our hope,
 And perfect us in love.

4 Up into Thee, our living Head,
 Let us in all things grow;
Till Thou hast made us free indeed,
 And spotless here below.

435

1 As by the light of opening day
 The stars are all concealed,
So earthly pleasures fade away
 When Jesus is revealed.

2 These pleasures now no longer please,
 No more content afford;
Far from my heart be joys like these,
 For I have seen the Lord.

3 Now, Lord, I would be Thine alone,
 And wholly live to Thee;
But may I hope that Thou wilt own
 A worthless one like me.

4 Yes; though of sinners I'm the worst,
 I cannot doubt Thy will;
For if Thou hadst not loved me first,
 I had refused Thee still.

436

1 I WAS a grovelling creature once,
 And basely cleaved to earth;
I wanted spirit to renounce
 The clod that gave me birth.

2 But God has breathed upon a worm,
 And sent me from above
Wings such as clothe an angel's form—
 The wings of joy and love.

3 With these to Pisgah's top I fly,
 And there delighted stand,
To view beneath a shining sky,
 The spacious promised land.

4 The Lord of all the vast domain
 Has promised it to me;
The length and breadth of all the plain,
 As far as faith can see.

5 How glorious is my privilege!
 To Thee for help I call;
I stand upon a mountain's edge;
 O, save me, lest I fall.

ALLEGRETTO.   WM. B. BRADBURY. 1845.

When morning's first and hal-lowed ray Breaks, with its trembling light,

To chase the pear-ly drops a-way, Bright tear-drops of the night;—

437

2 My heart, O Lord! forgets to rove,
  But rises gladly free,
  On wings of everlasting love,
  And finds its home in Thee.

3 When evening's silent shades descend,
  And nature sinks to rest,
  Still, to my Father and my Friend,
  My wishes are addressed.

4 Though tears may dim my hours of joy,
  And bid my pleasures flee,
  Thou reign'st where grief cannot annoy;
  I will be glad in Thee.

438

1 ACCORDING to Thy gracious word,
  In meek humility,
  This will I do, my dying Lord,
  I will remember Thee.

2 Thy body, broken for my sake,
  My bread from heaven shall be;
  Thy testamental cup I take,
  And thus remember Thee.

3 When to the cross I turn mine eyes,
  And rest on Calvary,
  O Lamb of God, my Sacrifice,
  I must remember Thee.

4 And when these failing lips grow dumb,
  And mind and memory flee,
  When Thou shalt in Thy kingdom come,
  ɔ Jesus, remember me.

439

1 REMEMBER thy Creator now,
  In these thy youthful days;
  He will accept thy earliest vow,
  And listen to thy praise.

2 Remember thy Creator now,
  And seek Him while He's near;
  For evil days will come, when thou
  Shalt find no comfort near.

3 Remember thy Creator now;
  His willing servant be:
  Then, when thy head in death shall bow,
  He will remember thee.

4 Almighty God! our hearts incline
  Thy heavenly voice to hear;
  Let all our future days be Thine,
  Devoted to Thy fear.

440

1 IN trouble and in grief, O God,
  Thy smile hath cheered my way,
  And joy hath budded from each thorn
  That round my footsteps lay.

2 The hours of pain have yielded good
  Which prosperous days refused;
  As herbs, though scentless when entire,
  Spread fragrance when they're bruised.

3 The oak strikes deeper as its boughs
  By furious blasts are driven;
  So life's tempestuous storms the more
  Have fixed my heart in heaven.

4 All-gracious Lord, whate'er my lot
  In other times may be,
  I'll welcome still the heaviest grief
  That brings me near to Thee.

DOWNS. C. M.

DR. LOWELL MASON.

In Thee, great God, with songs of praise, Our favored realms re-joice,

And, blessed with Thy sal-va-tion, raise ,To heaven their cheerful voice.

441

2 In deep distress, our injured land
Implored Thy power to save;
For life we prayed: Thy bounteous hand
The timely blessing gave.

3 On Thee, in want, in woe, or pain,
Our hearts alone rely;
Our rights Thy mercy will maintain,
And all our wants supply.

4 Thus, Lord, Thy wondrous power declare,
And still exalt Thy fame;
While we glad songs of praise prepare
For Thine almighty name.

442

1 O, WHAT amazing words of grace
Are in the gospel found!
Suited to every sinner's case,
Who knows the joyful sound.

2 Poor, sinful, thirsty, fainting souls
Are freely welcome here;
Salvation like a river rolls,
Abundant, free, and clear.

3 Come, then, with all your wants and wounds,
Your every burden bring;
Here love, unchanging love, abounds,—
A deep, celestial spring.

4 Whoever will—O, gracious word!—
Shall of the stream partake;
Come, thirsty souls, and bless the Lord
And drink for Jesus' sake.

5 Millions of sinners, vile as you,
Have here found life and peace,
Come, then, and prove its virtues too,
And drink, adore, and bless.

443

1 THERE is a way that seemeth right;
The steps go on with ease;
And conscience slumbers while the soul
Forsakes the path of peace.

3 There is a way that leads to death,—
God hath the warning given;
And multitudes pursue that way,
Still dreaming on of heaven.

3 Then let me tremble at the word
That shows this danger nigh;
And wake, and pray, and keep the path,
That leads to joys on high.

4 For God will teach the contrite mind
The way of death to shun;
He ne'er will leave a praying soul
By sin to be undone.

444

1 RETURN, O wand'rer, to thy home,
Thy Father calls for thee;
No longer now an exile roam,
In guilt and misery.

2 Return, O wand'rer, to thy home,
'Tis Jesus calls for thee;
The Spirit and the Bride say—come;
Oh! now for refuge flee.

3 Return, O wand'rer, to thy home,
'Tis madness to delay;
There are no pardons in the tomb,
And brief is mercy's day.

O for a shout of sa-cred joy To God, the sov'reign King; Let

Let ev-'ry land their

ev-'ry land their tongues employ, Let ev'ry land their tongues employ, And hymns of triumph

Let ev-'ry land their tongues employ, And hymns.... of tri - - - - umph
tongues.... em-ploy,........ And hymns of triumph sing,...... And hymns of tri-umph

sing, Let ev-'ry land their tongues employ, And hymns of tri-umph sing.

445

2 Faith grasps the blessings she desires;
Hope points the upward gaze;.
And Love, celestial Love, inspires
The eloquence of praise.

3 But sweeter far the still small voice,
Unheard by human ear,
When God has made the heart rejoice,
And dried the bitter tear.

4 No accents flow, no words ascend;
All utterance faileth there;
But sainted spirits comprehend,
And God accepts the prayer!

446

1 THERE's not a star whose twinkling light
Shines on the distant earth,
And cheers the silent gloom of night,
But goodness gave it birth;

2 There's not a cloud whose dews distil
Upon the parching clod,

And clothe with verdure vale and hill,
That is not sent by God.

3 There's not a place in earth's vast round,
In ocean's deep, or air,
Where skill and wisdom are not found,
For God is everywhere.

4 Around, beneath, below, above,
Wherever space extends,
There God displays His boundless love,
And power with mercy blends.

447

1 BEFORE the rosy dawn of day
To Thee, my God, I'll cling;
Awake my soft and tuneful lyre,
Awake each charming string.

2 Awake and let thy flowing strain
Glide through the midnight air,
While high amidst the silent orbs,
The silver moon rolls clear.

SCOTTISH.

As o'er the past my mem'ry strays, Why heaves the se-cret sigh?

'Tis that I mourn de-part-ed days, Still un-pre-pared to die.

448

2 The world and worldly things beloved,
   My anxious thoughts employed;
   And time unhallowed, unimproved,
   Presents a fearful void.

3 Yet, holy Father, wild despair
   Chase from my laboring breast,
   Thy grace it is which prompts the prayer,
   That grace can do the rest.

4 My life's brief remnant all be Thine!
   And when Thy sure decree
   Bids me this fleeting breath resign,
   O speed my soul to Thee.

449

1 ONE more petition, O our God,
   We lay before Thy throne;
   That Thou wouldst bless us as we part,
   And our weak efforts own.

2 O ever may the love of God
   Within our bosoms glow;
   And love to man in all our acts,
   The humble Christian show.

3 That when Thou makest up Thy gems
   In yonder world of bliss,
   It may be known that not in vain
   Our mission was in this.

450

1 AND now, my soul, another year
   Of thy short life is past;
   I cannot long continue here,
   And this may be my last.

2 Much of my hasty life is gone,
   Nor will return again;
   And swift my passing moments run—
   The few that yet remain.

3 Awake, my soul; with utmost care
   Thy true condition learn:
   What are my hopes? how sure? how fair?
   What is thy great concern?

4 Behold, another year begins;
   Set out afresh for heaven;
   Seek pardon for thy former sins,
   In Christ so freely given.

451

1 I SAW One hanging on a tree,
   In agony and blood,
   Who fixed his languid eyes on me,
   As near the cross I stood.

2 Sure, never till my latest breath,
   Can I forget that look:
   It seemed to charge me with his death,
   Though not a word He spoke.

3 Alas! I knew not what I did,
   But now my tears are vain;
   Where shall my trembling soul be hid,
   For I the Lord have slain.

4 A second look He gave, that said,
   " I freely all forgive:
   This blood is for thy ransom paid
   I die that thou may'st live."

ALLEGRETTO. PAER.

Come, let us join our cheerful songs With angels round the throne;

Ten thousand thousand are their tongues, But all their joys are one!

452

2 "Worthy the Lamb that died," they cry,
"To be exalted thus;"
"Worthy the Lamb," our lips reply,
"For he was slain for us."

3 Jesus is worthy to receive
Honor and power divine;
And blessings, more than we can give,
Be, Lord, forever Thine.

4 Let all that dwell above the sky,
And earth, and air, and seas,
Conspire to lift Thy glories high,
And speak Thine endless praise.

5 The whole creation join in one,
To bless the sacred name
Of Him that sits upon the throne,
And to adore the Lamb.

453

1 SPIRIT divine, attend our prayer,
Now make this place Thy home;
Descend, with all Thy gracious power;
O come great Spirit, come!

2 Come as the light; to us reveal
Our sinfulness and woe;
And lead us in the paths of life,
Where all the righteous go.

3 Come as the fire, and purge our hearts
Like sacrificial flame;
Let every soul an offering be
To our Redeemer's name.

4 Come as a dove, and spread Thy wings,—
The wings of peaceful love,—
And let the church on earth become
Blest as the church above.

454

1 COME, happy souls, approach your God
With new melodious songs;
Come, render to Almighty grace
The tribute of your tongues.

2 The hands of Jesus were not armed
With an avenging rod,
Some dread commission to perform
From an offended God.

3 So strange, so boundless was His love
To guilty, dying men,
The Father sent His equal Son,
To give them life again.

4 Ye sinners, come and heal your wounds,
And let your tears be dry;
Trust in the mighty Saviour's name,
And you shall never die.

455

1 BLEST Jesus, while in mortal flesh
I hold my frail abode,
Still would my spirit rest on Thee,
My Saviour and my God.

2 On Thy dear cross I fix my eyes,
Then raise them to Thy seat;
Till love dissolves my inmost soul,
At my Redeemer's feet.

3 Be dead, my heart, to worldly charms;
Be dead to every sin;
And tell the boldest foe without.
That Jesus reigns within.

DR. LOWELL MASON.

Sweet day! so cool, so calm, so bright, Bri - dal of earth and sky; The dew shall weep thy fall to - night, For thou, a - las! must die, For thou, a - las! must die.

456

2 Sweet Rose! in air whose odors wave,
  And color charms the eye;
Thy root is even in the ground,
  And thou, alas! must die.

3 Sweet Spring! of days and roses made,
  Whose charms for beauty vie,
Thy days depart, thy roses fade,
  Thou too, alas! must die.

4 Only a sweet and holy soul
  Hath tints that never fly:
While flowers decay, and seasons roll,
  It lives, and cannot die.

457

1 How sweet and awful is the place,
  With Christ within the doors,
While everlasting love displays
  The choicest of her stores!

2 While all our hearts, and all our songs,
  Join to admire the feast;
Each of us cry, with thankful tongues,
  " Lord, why was I a guest?

3 " Why was I made to hear Thy voice,
  And enter while there 's room—

  When thousands make a wretched choice,
    And rather starve than come?"

4 ' Twas the same love that spread the feast
  That sweetly forced us in;
Else we had still refused to taste, · ·
  And perished in our sin.

458

1 THINK gently of the erring one!
  And let us not forget,
However darkly stained by sin,
  He is our brother yet.

2 Heir of the same inheritance,
  Child of the self-same God;
He hath but stumbled in the path,
  We have in weakness trod.

3 Speak gently to the erring one:
  Thou yet mayst lead him back,
With holy words, and tones of love,
  From misery's thorny track.

4 Forget not, brother, thou hast sinned,
  And sinful yet mayst be;
Deal gently with the erring heart,
  As God has dealt with thee.

SHARON. C. M. (Double.)   127

Happy's the child whose tender years Receive instruc - tions well,

Who hates the sinner's path and fears The road that leads to hell.
A flower that's offered in the bud Is no vain sa - cri - fice.

When we de - vote our youth to God, 'Tis pleasing in His eyes;

459

3 'Tis easier work, if we begin
  To fear the Lord betimes;
While sinners who grow old in sin,
  Are hardened in their crimes.

4 To Thee, almighty God, to Thee
  Our childhood we resign;
'Twill please us to look back and see
  That our whole lives were Thine.

460

1 Who is thy neighbor? he whom thou
  Hast power to aid or bless;
Whose aching heart or burning brow
  Thy soothing hand may press.

2 Thy neighbor? 'tis the fainting poor,
  Whose eye with want is dim;
O enter thou his humble door
  With aid and peace for him.

3 Thy neighbor? he who drinks the cup
  When sorrow drowns the brim;

With words of high sustaining hope,
  Go thou and comfort him.

4 Thy neighbor? 'tis the weary slave,
  Fettered in mind and limb;
He hath no hope this side the grave,
  Go thou and ransom him.

5 Thy neighbor? pass no mourner by;
  Perhaps thou canst redeem
A breaking heart from misery;
  Go, share thy lot with him.

461

1 QUENCH not the Spirit of the Lord,
  The holy One from heaven;
The Comforter, beloved, adored,
  To man in mercy given.

2 Quench not the Spirit of the Lord;
  He will not always strive:
O tremble at that awful word
  Sinner! awake and live.

ST. ANN'S. C. M.

DR. WM. CROFT.

O, how I love Thy ho-ly law! 'Tis dai-ly my de-light;

And thence my me-di-ta-tions draw Di-vine ad-vice by night.

462

2 My waking eyes prevent the day
To meditate Thy word;
My soul with longing melts away
To hear Thy gospel, Lord.

3 How doth Thy word my heart engage!
How well employ my tongue!
And in my tiresome pilgrimage
Yields me a heavenly song.

4 When nature sinks, and spirits droop,
Thy promises of grace
Are pillars to support my hope,
And there I write Thy praise.

463

1 Not in the church-yard shall he sleep,
Amid the silent gloom;
His home was on the mighty deep,
And there shall be his tomb.

2 He loved his own bright, deep blue sea;
O'er it he loved to roam;
And now his winding sheet shall be
That same bright ocean's foam.

3 No village bell shall toll for him
Its mournful, solemn dirge;
The winds shall chant a requiem
To him beneath the surge.

4 For him break not the grassy turf,
Nor turn the dewy sod;
His dust shall rest beneath the surf,
His spirit with its God.

464

1 ARISE, O King of grace, arise,
And enter to Thy rest;
Lo, Thy church waits with longing eyes,
Thus to be owned and blessed.

2 Enter, with all Thy glorious train,
Thy Spirit and Thy word;
All that the ark did once contain
Could no such grace afford.

3 Here, mighty God, accept our vows,
Here let Thy praise be spread;
Bless the provisions of Thy house,
And fill Thy poor with bread.

4 Here let the Son of David reign,
Let God's Anointed shine;
Justice and truth His court maintain,
With love and power divine.

5 Here let Him hold a lasting throne,
And, as His kingdom grows,
Fresh honors shall adorn His crown,
And shame confound His foes.

465

1 O GOD, my heart is fully bent
To magnify Thy name;
My tongue with cheerful songs of praise
Shall celebrate Thy fame.

2 Because Thy mercy's boundless height
The highest heaven transcends,
And far beyond the aspiring clouds
Thy faithful truth extends.

3 Be Thou, O God, exalted high,
Above the starry frame,
And let the world with one consent,
Confess Thy glorious name.

REV. D. F. FORD.

Great is the Lord; His works of might De-mand our no - - blest
songs; Let His as - sem - bled saints u - nite Their
har - mo - ny of tongues, Their har - mo - ny of tongues.

466

2 Great is the mercy of the Lord;
He gives His children food,
And, ever mindful of His word,
He makes His promise good.

3 His Son, the great Redeemer, came,
To seal His covenant sure;
Holy and reverend is His name;
His ways are just and pure.

4 They who would grow divinely wise,
Must with His fear begin;
Our fairest proof of knowledge lies
In hating every sin.

467

1 O GOD, we praise Thee, and confess
That Thou, the only Lord
And everlasting Father art,
By all the earth adored.

2 To Thee all angels cry aloud;
To Thee the powers on high,
Both cherubim and seraphim,
Continually do cry:

3 O holy, holy, holy Lord,
Whom heavenly hosts obey,

The world is with the glory filled
Of Thy majestic sway.

4 The apostles' glorious company,
And prophets crowned with light,
With all the martyrs' noble host,
Thy constant praise recite.

468

1 No change of time shall ever shock
My trust, O Lord, in Thee;
For Thou hast always been my Rock,—
A sure Defence for me.

2 Thou our Deliverer art, O God;
Our trust is in Thy power;
Thou art our Shield from foes abroad,
Our Safeguard, and our Tower.

3 To Thee will we address our prayer,
To whom all praise we owe;
So shall we, by Thy watchful care,
Be saved from every foe.

4 Then let Jehovah be adored,
On whom our hopes depend;
For who, except the mighty Lord,
His people can defend?

IDDO. C. M.

DR. LOWELL MASON.

ANDANTINO AMOROSO.

From NAGELI.

1. From Thee, my God, my joys shall rise, And run e - ternal rounds, } 2. There,
Be - yond the li - mits of the skies And all cre - ated bounds. }
3. The ho - ly triumphs of my soul Shall death itself outbrave, } 4. Mill-
Leave dull mor - ta - li - ty behind, And fly be - yond the grave. }

where my blessed Jesus reigns, In heaven's unmeasur'd space, I'll spend a long e-
ions of years my wond'ring eyes Shall o'er Thy beauties rove, And endless a - ges

ter - n. - ty In pleasure and in praise. In pleasure and in praise.
I'll a - dore The glo - ries of Thy love. The glo - ries of Thy love.

469

5 Haste, my Beloved; fetch my soul
  Up to Thy blest abode;
 Fly, for my spirit longs to see
  My Saviour and my God.

470

1 BEGIN the high, celestial strain,
  My raptured soul, and sing
 A sacred hymn of grateful praise
  To heaven's almighty King.

2 Ye curling fountains, as ye roll ·
  Your silver waves along,
 Repeat to all your verdant shores
  The subject of the song.

3 Bear it ye breezes, on your wings,
  To distant climes away,
 And round the wide-extended world
  The lofty theme convey.

4 Take up the burden of His name,
  Ye clouds, as ye arise,
 To deck with gold the opening morn,
  Or shade the evening skies.

5 Long let it warble round the spheres,
  And echo through the sky;
 Let angels, with immortal skill,
  Improve the harmony;

6 While we, with sacred rapture fired,
  The blest Creator sing,
 And chant our consecrated lays
  To heaven's eternal King.

1. There's not a star whose twinkling light Shines on the dis-tant earth,
2. There's not a place in earth's vast round In ocean's deep, or air,

And cheers the si-lent gloom of night, But goodness gave it birth;
Where skill and wisdom are not found, For God is ev-'ry-where;

There's not a cloud whose dews di-stil Up-on the parching clod,
Around, beneath, be-low, a-bove, Wherev-er space ex-tends,

And clothe with verdure vale and hill, That is not sent by God.
There God displays His boundless love, And pow'r with mer-cy blends.

472

1 ETERNAL Spirit! God of truth,
  Our contrite hearts inspire;
Revive the flame of heavenly love,
  And feed the pure desire.

2 'T is Thine to sooth the sorrowing mind,
  With guilt and fear oppressed;
'T is Thine to bid the dying live,
  And give the weary rest.

3 Subdue the power of every sin,
  Whate'er that sin may be,
That we, with humble, holy heart,
  May worship onlyThee.

4 Then with our spirits witness bear
  That we are sons of God,
Redeemed from sin, from death, and hell,
  Through Christ's atoning blood.

ALLEGRO.

Behold the glo-ries of the Lamb, A-mid His Father's throne;

A-mid His Father's throne; Pre-pare new hon-ors for His name,

Pre-pare new hon-ors to His name, And songs be-fore un-known.

473

2 Let elders worship at His feet,
  The church adore around;
With vials full of odors sweet,
  And harps of sweeter sound.

3 Those are the prayers of all the saints,
  And these the hymns they raise;
Jesus is kind to our complaints;
  He loves to hear our praise.

4 Now to the Lamb that once was slain,
  Be endless blessings paid;
Salvation, glory, joy remain
  Forever on Thy head.

5 The worlds of nature and of grace
  Are put beneath Thy power;
Then shorten these delaying days,
  And bring the promised hour.

474

1 THE glorious universe around,
  The heavens with all their train,
Sun, moon, and stars, are firmly bound
  In one mysterious chain.

2 The earth, the ocean, and the sky,
  To form one world agree,
Where all that walk, or swim, or fly,
  Compose one family.

3 In one fraternal bond of love,
  One fellowship of mind,
The saints below and saints above
  Their bliss and glory find.

4 Here in their house of pilgrimage,
  Thy statutes are their song;
There, through one bright, eternal age,
  Thy praises they prolong.

475

1 O THOU, the heaven's eternal King!
  Lord of the starry spheres!
Who with the Father equal art
  From everlasting years.

2 Eternal Shepherd! who Thy flock
  In Thy pure Font dost lave,
Where souls are cleansed, and all their guilt
  Buried as in a grave.

3 Anoint me with Thy heavenly grace,
  Adopt me for Thine own—
That I may see Thy glorious face,
  And worship at Thy throne!

MODERATO.

How sweet the ev'ning shadows fall, Advanc-ing from the west!

As ends the wea-ry week of toil, And comes the day of rest.

476

2 Bright o'er the earth the star of eve
Her radiant beauty sheds;
And myriad sisters calmly weave
Their light around our heads.

3 Rest, man, from labor; rest from sin;
The world's hard contest close;
The holy hours with God begin;
Yield thee to sweet repose.

4 Bright o'er the earth the morning ray
Its sacred light will cast—
Fair emblem of the glorious day
That evermore shall last.

477

1 Now that the sun is gleaming bright,
Implore we, bending low,
That He, the uncreated light,
May guide us as we go.

2 No sinful word, nor deed of wrong,
Nor thoughts that idly rove;
But simple truth be on our tongue,
And in our hearts be love.

3 And while the hours in order flow,
O Christ, securely fence
Our gates beleaguared by the foe,
The gate of every sense.

4 And grant that to Thine honor, Lord,
Our daily toil may tend;
That we begin it at Thy word,
And in Thy favor end.

478

1 When brighter suns and milder skies
Proclaim the opening year,
What various sounds of joy arise!
What prospects bright appear!

2 Earth and her thousand voices give
Their thousand notes of praise;
And all, that by His mercy live,
To God their offering raise.

3 The streams, all beautiful and bright,
Reflect the morning sky;
And there, with music in his flight,
The wild bird soars or high.

4 Thus, like the morning, calm and clear,
That saw the Saviour rise,
The spring of heaven's eternal year
Shall dawn on earth and skies.

479

1 O most delightful hour by man
Experienced here below,
The hour that terminates his span,
His folly, and his woe.

2 Worlds should not bribe me back to tread
Again life's dreary waste,
To see again my day o'erspread
With all the gloomy past.

3 My home henceforth is in the skies;
Earth, seas, and sun, adieu!
All heaven unfolded to my eyes,
I have no sight for you.

4 So speaks the Christian, firm possessed
Of faith's supporting rod,
Then breathes his soul into its rest,
The bosom of his God.

MODERATO.   SACRED CHOIR.

Be Thou, my God, by night, by day, My Guide, my Guard from sin ;

My Life, my Trust, my Light di - vine, To keep me pure with - in.

480

2 Pure as the air, when day's first light
  A cloudless sky illumes;
And active as the lark that soars
  Till heaven shines round its plumes—

3 So may my soul, upon the wings
  Of faith, unwearied rise,
Till at the gate of heaven it sings,
  'Midst light from Paradise.

481

1 HELP, Lord, for men of virtue fail;
  Religion loses ground;
The sons of violence prevail,
  And treacheries abound.

2 Their oaths and promises they break,
  Yet act the flatterer's part;
With fair, deceitful lips they speak,
  And with a double heart.

3 Lord, when iniquities abound,
  And blasphemy grows bold,
When faith is hardly to be found,
  And love is waxing cold,—

4 Is not Thy chariot hastening on ?
  Hast Thou not given the sign ?
May we not trust and live upon
  A promise so divine?

482

1 O PURE reformers! not in vain
  Your trust in human kind;
The good which bloodshed could not gain,
  Your peaceful zeal shall find.

2 The truths ye urge are borne abroad
  By every wind and tide;
The voice of nature and of God
  Speaks out upon your side.

3 The weapons which your hands have found
  Are those which heaven hath wrought,
Light,'Truth and Love—your battle-ground
  The free, broad field of Thought.

4 Press on! and if we may not share
  The glory of your fight,
We'll ask at least, in earnest prayer,
  God's blessing on the Right.

483

1 THROUGH all the changing scenes of life,
  In trouble and in joy,
The praises of my God shall still
  My heart and tongue employ.

2 O, magnify the Lord with me,
  With me exalt His name;
When, in distress, to Him I called,
  He to my rescue came.

3 The hosts of God encamp around
  The dwellings of the just;
Deliverance He affords to all
  Who on His succor trust.

4 O, make but trial of His love,
  Experience will decide
How blest are they, and only they,
  Who in His truth confide.

5 Fear Him, ye saints, and you will then
  Have nothing else to fear;
Make you His service your delight,
  He'll make your wants His care.

O, for that ten-der-ness of heart That bows be-fore the Lord!

Own-ing how just and good Thou art, And trem-bling at Thy word.

484

2 Oh, for those humble, contrite tears
Which from repentance flow!
Oh, for that sense of guilt which fears
The long-suspended blow!

3 Saviour, to me in pity give,
For me, the deep distress—
The pledge Thou wilt at last receive;
And bid me die in peace.

4 Oh, fill my soul with faith and love,
And strength to do Thy will!
Raise my desires and hopes above;
Thyself to me reveal.

485

1 From busy toil and heavy care
We turn the weary mind,
And in the place of noontide prayer
Our sanctuary find.

2 The voice that stilled the stormy waves
On distant Galilee,
Speaks once again, and at the sound,
Retires another sea.

3 The restless waves of care and strife,
Obey the mighty voice;
Peace broods the mighty waters o'er,
And all our souls rejoice.

4 These heaven-bright hours too soon are past;
Grant, Lord, this greater boon, [past;
A place where worship never ends,
Nor night succeeds to noon.

486

1 The dead are like the stars by day,
Withdrawn from mortal eye,
Yet holding unperceived their way
Through the unclouded sky.

2 By them, through holy hope and love,
We feel, in hours serene,
Connected with a world above,
Immortal and unseen.

3 For death his sacred seal hath set
On bright and by-gone hours;
And they we mourn are with us yet,
Are more than ever ours;—

4 Ours, by the pledge of love and faith,
By hopes of heaven on high;
By trust, triumphant over death,
In immortality.

487

1 There is an hour of hallowed peace
For those with cares oppressed,
When sighs and sorrowing tears shall cease,
And all be hushed to rest.

2 'Tis then the soul is freed from fears
And doubts which here annoy;
Then they who oft have sown in tears,
Shall reap again in joy.

3 There is a home of sweet repose,
Where storms assail no more;
The stream of endless pleasure flows
On that celestial shore.

4 There smiling peace with love appears
And bliss without alloy;
There they who oft have sown in tears,
Now reap eternal joy.

ELIZABETHTOWN. C. M.

ANDANTINO.

SACRED CHOIR.

She loved her Saviour, and to Him Her costliest present brought;

To crown His head or grace His name, No gift too rare she thought.

488

2 So let the Saviour be adored,
    And not the poor despised,
Give to the hungry from your board,
    But all, give all to Christ.

3 Go, clothe the naked, lead the blind,
    Give to the weary rest;
For sorrow's children comfort find,
    And help for all distressed;—

4 But give to Christ alone thy heart,
    Thy faith, thy love supreme;
Then for His sake thine alms impart,
    And so give all to Him.

489

1 DELIGHTFUL work, young souls to win,
    And turn the rising race
From the deceitful paths of sin,
    To seek redeeming grace.

2 Children our kind protection claim,
    And God will well approve
When infants learn to lisp His name,
    And their Creator love.

3 Be ours the bliss in wisdom's way
    To guide untutored youth,
And lead the mind that went astray
    To virtue and to truth.

4 Almighty God, Thy influence shed
    To aid this good design;
The honors of Thy name be spread,
    And all the glory Thine.

490

1 WHY should the children of a King
    Go mourning all their days?
Great Comforter descend and bring
    Some tokens of Thy grace.

2 Dost Thou not dwell in all the saints,
    And seal the heirs of heaven?
When wilt Thou banish my complaints,
    And show my sins forgiven?

3 Assure my conscience of her part
    In the Redeemer's blood;
And bear Thy witness with my heart,
    That I am born of God.

4 Thou art the earnest of His love,
    The pledge of joys to come;
And Thy soft wings, celestial Dove,
    Will safe convey me home.

491

1 LIFT up to God, the voice of praise,
    Whose breath our souls inspired;
Loud and more loud the anthems raise,
    With grateful ardor fired!

2 Lift up to God the voice of praise,
    Whose goodness, passing thought,
Loads every moment as it flies,
    With benefits unsought!

3 Lift up to God the voice of praise,
    From whom salvation flows;
Who sent His Son our souls to save
    From everlasting woes.

4 Lift up to God the voice of praise,
    For hope's transporting ray,
Which lights thro' darkest shades of death
    To realms of endless day.

MODERATO.

A - maz - ing grace ! how sweet the sound, That saved a wretch like me!

I once was lost, but now am found, Was blind, but now I see,

FINE.

Close with second strain.

Was blind, but now I see, Was blind, but now I see :

492

2 'Twas grace that taught my heart to fear,
And grace my fears relieved:
How precious did that grace appear,
The hour I first believed!

3 Through many dangers, toils and snares,
I have already come;
'Tis grace has brought me safe thus far,
And grace will lead me home.

4 The Lord has promised good to me,
His word my hope secures;
He will my shield and portion be,
And long as life endures.

5 The earth shall soon dissolve like snow,
The sun forbear to shine;
But God, who called me here below,
Will be forever mine.

493

1 EARTH has engrossed my love too long!
'Tis time I lift mine eyes
Upward, dear Father, to Thy throne,
And to my native skies.

2 There the blessed Man, my Saviour sits;
The God! how bright he shines!
And scatters infinite delights
On all the happy minds.

3 Jesus, the Lord, their harps employs;
Jesus, my love, they sing!
Jesus, the life of all our joys,
Sounds sweet from every string.

4 Now let me mount and join their song,
And be an angel, too!
My heart, my hand, my ear, my tongue
Here's joyful work for you.

5 I would begin the music here,
And so my soul should rise;
O for some heavenly notes to bear
My passions to the skies!

6 There ye that love my Saviour sit,
There I would fain have place,
Among your thrones; or at your feet,
So I might see His face.

138 ODLIN. C. M.

From a Scotch Tune,
by DR LOWELL MASON.

What is the thing of greatest price, The whole cre - a - tion round?

That which was lost in Pa - ra - dise, That which in Christ is found.

494

2 The soul of man, Jehovah's breath,
That keeps two worlds at strife;
Hell moves beneath to work its death,
Heaven stoops to give it life.

3 God, to reclaim it, did not spare
His well-beloved Son;
Jesus, to save it, deigned to bear
The sins of all in One.

4 And is this treasure borne below
In earthly vessels frail?
Can none its utmost value know
Till flesh and spirit fail?

5 Then let us gather round the cross,
This knowledge to obtain;
Not by the soul's eternal loss,
But everlasting gain.

495

1 O DEAREST Lamb, take Thou my heart!
Where can such sweetness be,
As I have tasted in Thy love,
As I have found in Thee?

2 If love, that mildest flame can rest
In hearts so hard as mine,
Come, gentle Saviour, to my breast,
Its love shall all be Thine.

3 Now the gay world with treacherous art
Shall tempt my heart in vain;
I have conveyed away that heart,
Ne'er to return again.

4 'Tis heaven on earth to taste His love,
To feel His quickening grace,
And all the heaven I hope above,
Is but to see His face.

496

1 WITH tears of anguish I lament,
Here, at Thy feet, my God,
My passion, pride and discontent,
And vile ingratitude.

2 Sure, there was ne'er a heart so base,
So false as mine has been;
So faithless to its promises,
So prone to every sin!

3 How long, dear Saviour, shall I feel
These struggles in my breast?
When wilt Thou bow my subborn will,
And give my conscience rest?

4 Break, sovereign Grace, oh, break the
And set the captive free! [charm,
Reveal, almighty God, thine arm,
And haste to rescue me.

497

1 O HAPPY land! O happy land!
Where saints and angels dwell;
We long to join that glorious band,
And all their anthems swell.

2 But every voice in yonder throng
On earth has breathed a prayer:
No lips untaught may join that song,
Or learn the music there.

3 Thou heavenly Friend! thou heavenly
Oh, hear us when we pray! [Friend.
Now let Thy pardoning grace descend,
And take our sins away.

4 Be all our fresh, our youthful days
To Thy blest service given;
Then we shall meet to sing Thy praise,
A ransomed band in heaven.

MODERATO.   ANCIENT LYRE.

Spi - rit of power and might, be - hold A world by sin destroyed;

Cre - a - tor, Spi - rit, as of old, Move on the form - less void.

498

2 Give Thou the word; that healing sound
  Shall quell the deadly strife,
  And earth again, like Eden crowned,
  Produce the tree of life.

3 If sang the morning stars for joy
  When nature rose to view,
  What strains will angel harps employ
  When Thou shalt all renew!

4 And if the sons of God rejoice
  To hear a Saviour's name,
  How will the ransomed raise their voice,
  To whom that Saviour came!

5 Lo! every kindred, tongue, and tribe,
  Assembling round the throne,
  The new creation shall ascribe
  To sovereign love alone.

499

1 JESUS, assembled in Thy name,
  We bow the suppliant knee;
  And, as the ancient mothers came,
  We bring our charge to Thee.

2 O Thou good Shepherd of the sheep,
  Who didst Thy life lay down,
  These objects of Thy goodness keep,
  And guard them as Thine own.

3 Fold them within Thy kind embrace,
  And feed them with Thy love,
  Till they are called to see Thy face
  In brighter worlds above.

500

1 WITH joy we hail the sacred day
  Which God has called his own;
  With joy the summons we obey
  To worship at His throne.

2 Thy chosen temple, Lord, how fair!
  Where willing votaries throng
  To breathe the humble, fervent prayer,
  And pour the choral song.

3 Spirit of grace, O, deign to dwell
  Within Thy church below;
  Make her in holiness excel,
  With pure devotion glow.

501

1 I HEARD the voice of Jesus say,
  "Come unto me and rest;
  Lay down, thou weary one, lay down
  Thy head upon my breast."

2 I came to Jesus as I was,
  Weary, and worn, and sad;
  I found in Him a resting place,
  And He has made me glad.

3 I heard the voice of Jesus say,
  "Behold, I freely give
  The living water! thirsty one
  Stoop down, and drink, and live."

4 I came to Jesus, and I drank
  Of that life-giving stream:
  My thirst was quenched, my soul revived,
  And now I live in Him.

5 I heard the voice of Jesus say,
  "I am this dark world's light:
  Look unto me; thy morn shall rise,
  And all thy day be bright."

6 I looked to Jesus and I found
  In Him my Star, my Sun;
  And in that light of light I'll walk
  Till all my journey's done.

140 BELIEF. C. M. (Double.)

W. B. BRADBURY. FINE.

O, who, in such a world as this, Could bear his lot of pain?
Did not one radiant hope of bliss Un-clouded yet re-main?
D. C.—Hope that u-nites the soul to heaven By faith's en-dearing ties.

That hope the sovereign Lord has given, Who reigns a-bove the skies:

502

3 Each care, each ill of mortal birth,
Is sent in pitying love
To lift the lingering heart from earth,
And speed its flight above.

4 And every pang that wrings the breast,
And every joy that dies,
Tell us to seek a purer rest,
And trust to holier ties.

503

1 WHILE thro' this changing world we roam,
From infancy to age,
Heaven is the Christian pilgrim's home,
His rest at every stage.

2 Thither his raptured thoughts ascends,
Eternal joys to share;
There his adoring spirit bends,
While here he kneels in prayer.

3 From earth his freed affections rise
To fix on things above,
Where all his hope of glory lies,
And love is perfect love.

4 O, there may we our treasure place,
There let our hearts be found;
That still, where sin abounded, grace
May more and more abound.

5 Henceforth our conversation be
With Christ before the throne;
Ere long, we eye to eye shall see,
And know as we are known.

504

1 OH, wondrous is Thy mercy, Lord!
We hear Thy word of grace,
" Forbid them not"—oh, rich the word
That calls our infant race!

2 Our infant race we bring to Thee;
Receive them as Thine own!
Now and forever may they be
Thine wholly, Thine alone.

505

1 THE promise of my Father's love
Shall stand forever good;
He said—and gave His soul to death,
And sealed the grace with blood.

2 I call that legacy my own,
Which Jesus did bequeath;
'Twas purchased with a dying groan,
And ratified in death.

3 The light and strength, the pard'ning grace
And glory shall be mine:
My life and soul—my heart and flesh,
And all my powers are Thine.

506

1 Yes, there are joys that cannot die,
With God laid up in store—
Treasures, beyond the changing sky,
More bright than golden ore.

2 To that bright world my soul aspires,
With rapturous delight;
O for the Spirit's quickening powers,
To speed me in my flight.

MODERATO.   DR. LOWELL MASON.

Dark was the night, and cold the ground, On which the Lord was laid.

His sweat like drops of blood ran down; In a - go - ny He prayed.

507

2 " Father, remove this bitter cup,
    If such Thy sacred will;
    If not, content to drink it up,
    Thy pleasure to fulfil."

3 Go to the garden, sinner; see
    Those precious drops that flow;
    The heavy load He bore for thee;
    For thee He lies so low.

4 Then learn of Him the cross to bear;
    Thy Father's will obey;
    And, when temptations press thee near,
    Awake to watch and pray.

508

1 SPIRIT of peace, celestial Dove,
    How excellent Thy praise!
    No richer gift than Christian love
    Thy gracious power displays.

2 Sweet as the dew on herb and flower,
    That silently distils,
    At evening's soft and balmy hour,
    On Zion's fruitful hills,—

3 So with mild influence from above,
    Shall promised grace descend,
    Till universal peace and love
    O'er all the earth extend.

4 Spirit of peace, celestial Dove,
    How excellent Thy praise!
    No richer gift than Christian love
    Thy gracious power displays.

509

1 BEHOLD the Saviour of mankind
    Nailed to the shameful tree;
    How vast the love that Him inclined
    To bleed and die for thee!

2 Hark, how he groans! while nature shakes,
    And earth's strong pillars bend;
    The temple's veil in sunder breaks,
    The solid marbles rend.

3 'Tis done; the precious ransom 's paid;
    " Receive My soul," He cries:
    See where He bows His sacred head;
    He bows His head and dies.

4 Though far unequal our low praise
    To Thy vast sufferings prove,
    O Lamb of God, thus all our days,
    Thus will we grieve and love.

510

1 WE ask not, Lord, Thy cloven flame,
    Or tongues of various tone;
    But long Thy praises to proclaim
    With fervor, in our own.

2 We neither have nor seek the power
    Ill demons to control;
    But Thou in dark temptation's hour
    Shalt chase them from the soul.

3 No heavenly harpings soothe our ear,
    No mystic dreams we share;
    Yet hope to feel Thy comfort near,
    And bless Thee in our prayer.

4 When tongues shall cease, and powers de-
    And knowledge empty prove,   [cay,
    Do Thou thy trembling servants stay
    With faith, and hope, and love.

142   SWANWICK. C. M.

MODERATO.   LUCAS.

A - rise, ye people, and adore, Exulting strike the chord; Let all the

earth, from shore to shore, Confess th'almighty Lord, Confess th'almighty Lord.

511

2 Glad shouts aloud, wide echoing round,
  The ascending God proclaim;
  The angelic choir respond the sound,
  And shake creation's frame.

3 They sing of death and hell o'erthrown
  In that triumphant hour;
  And God exalts His conquering Son
  To His right hand of power.

4 O, shout, ye people, and adore;
  Exulting strike the chord;
  Let all the earth, from shore to shore,
  Confess the Almighty Lord.

512

1 To celebrate Thy praise, O Lord,
  I will my heart prepare;
  To all the listening world, Thy works,
  Thy wondrous works, declare.

2 The thought of them shall to my soul
  Exalted pleasures bring;
  While to Thy name, O Thou Most High,
  Triumphant praise I sing.

3 God is a constant, sure defence
  Against oppressing rage;
  As troubles rise, His needful aids
  In our behalf engage.

4 To celebrate Thy praise, O Lord,
  I will my heart prepare;
  To all the listening world, Thy works,
  Thy wondrous works, declare.

513

1 THY works of glory, mighty Lord,
  Thy wonders in the deeps,
  The sons of courage shall record,
  Who trade in floating ships.

2 At Thy command the winds arise,
  And swell the towering waves;
  The men astonished mount the skies,
  And sink in gaping graves.

3 Sailors rejoice to lose their fears,
  And see the storm allayed;
  Now to their eyes the port appears;
  There let their vows be paid.

4 O that the sons of men would praise
  The goodness of the Lord,
  And those who see Thy wondrous ways
  Thy wondrous love record.

514

1 NOT to the terrors of the Lord,
  The tempest, fire and smoke;
  Not to the thunder of that word
  Which God on Sinai spoke;

2 But we are come to Zion's hill,
  The city of our God,
  Where milder words declare His will,
  And spread His love abroad.

3 Behold the innumerable host
  Of angels clothed in light!
  Behold the spirits of the just,
  Whose faith is turned to sight!

4 The saints on earth, and all the dead,
  But one communion make;
  All join in Christ, their living Head,
  And of His grace partake.

TAPPAN. C. M.

Geo. Kingsley.

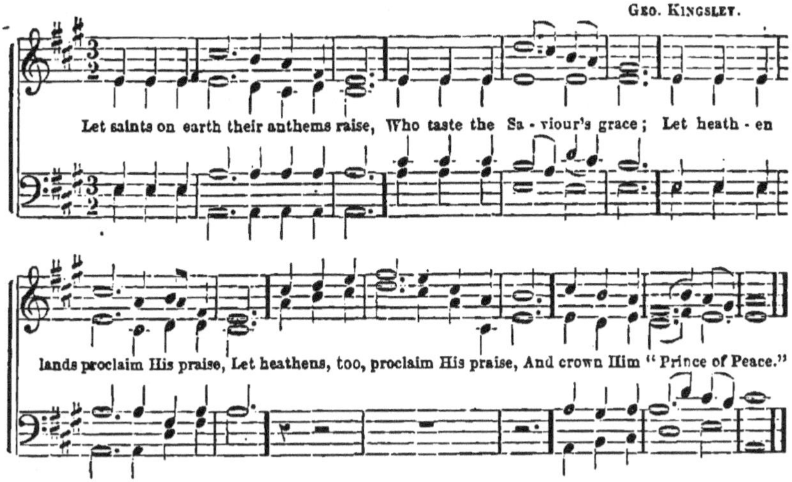

515

2 Praise Him who laid His glory by
For man's apostate race;
Praise Him who stooped to bleed and die,
And crown Him "Prince of Peace."

3 Ye nations lay your weapons down,
Let war for ever cease;
Immanuel for your Sovereign own,
And crown Him "Prince of Peace."

516

1 Yes, I will bless Thee, O my God,
Through all my fleeting days;
And to eternity prolong
Thy vast, Thy boundless praise.

2 Nor shall my tongue alone proclaim
The honors of my God;
My life, with all its active powers,
Shall spread Thy praise abroad.

3 Nor will I cease Thy praise to sing,
When death shall close mine eyes;
My thoughts shall then to nobler heights,
And sweeter raptures rise.

4 Then shall my lips in endless praise,
Their grateful tribute pay;
The theme demands an angel's tongue,
And an eternal day.

517

1 Let children hear the mighty deeds,
Which God performed of old,—
Which in our younger years we saw,
And which our fathers told.

2 He bids us make his glories known,
His works of power and grace;
And we'll convey his wonders down
Through every rising race.

3 Our lips shall tell them to our sons,
And they again to theirs,
That generations yet unborn
May teach them to their heirs.

4 Thus they shall learn, in God alone
Their hope securely stands,
That they may ne'er forget His works,
But practice His commands.

518

1 Sing we the song of those who stand
Around the eternal throne.
Of every kindred, clime, and land,
A multitude unknown.

2 Life's poor distinctions vanish here;
To-day, the young, the old,
Our Saviour and His flock appear,
One Shepherd and one fold.

3 Toil, trial, suffering still await
On earth the pilgrim throng;
Yet learn we in our low estate,
The Church triumphant's song.

4 Worthy the Lamb for sinners slain,
Cry the redeemed above,
Blessing and honor to obtain,
And everlasting love.

5 Worthy the Lamb, on earth we sing,
Who died our souls to save.
Henceforth, O Death! where is thy sting?
Thy victory, O Grave?

All that I was, my sin, my guilt, My death was all my own;

All that I am I owe to Thee, My gra-cious God, a-lone.

519

2 The evil of my former state
Was mine, and only mine,
The good in which I now rejoice
Is Thine, and only Thine.

3 The darkness of my former state,
The bondage—all was mine:
The light of life in which I walk,
The liberty—is Thine.

4 Thy grace first made me feel my sin,
And taught me to believe:
Then, in believing, peace I found,
And now, I live, I live!

5 All that I am e'en here on earth,
All that I hope to be
When Jesus comes and glory dawns,—
I owe it, Lord, to Thee.

520

1 COME in, Thou blessed of the Lord,
Stranger nor foe art Thou:
We welcome Thee with warm accord,
Our Friend, our Brother now.

2 The hand of fellowship, the heart
Of love, we offer Thee;
Leaving the world, Thou dost but part
From lies and vanity.

3 Come with us—we will do Thee good,
As God to us hath done:
Stand but in Him, as those have stood
Whose faith the victory won.

4 And when, by turns, we pass away,
And star by star grows dim,
May each, translated into day,
Be lost and found in Him.

521

1 How few the word of God regard,
Or seek their Maker's face!
In vain the gospel is proclaimed,
If not enforced by grace.

2 Almighty God, exert Thy power,
And melt the stony breast;
Then shall Thy justice be adored,
Thy mercy stand confessed.

3 The scorner then shall mourn in dust,
And put his sins away;
No more resist his Maker's hands,
But lift his own to pray

522

1 I WOULD be Thine; O take my heart,
And fill it with Thy love;
Thy sacred image, Lord, impart,
And seal it from above.

2 I would be Thine; but while I strive
To give myself away,
I feel rebellion still alive,
And wander while I pray.

3 I would be Thine; but, Lord, I feel
Evil still lurks within:—
Do Thou Thy majesty reveal,
And overcome my sin.

4 I would be Thine; I would embrace
The Saviour, and adore;
Inspire with faith, infuse Thy grace,
And now my soul restore.

ALLEGRETTO.

Great God, the na - tions of the earth Are by cre - a - tion Thine;

And in Thy works, by all be - held, Thy radiant glo - ries shine.

523

2 But, Lord, Thy richer love has sent
Thy gospel to mankind;
Unveiling what rich stores of grace
Are treasured in Thy mind.

3 Lord, when shall these glad tidings spread
The spacious earth around
Till every tribe and every soul
Shall hear the joyful sound.

4 Smile, Lord, on each divine attempt
To spread the gospel rays;
And build, on sin's demolished throne,
The temples of Thy praise.

524

1 What worthy anthem can I sing
To my dear Saviour's praise?
What worthy offering can I bring
Or cloud of incense raise?

2 What willing service can I pay
To recompence His love?
What life of mine can mount the way
To this blest home above?

3 Dear Saviour, nothing I can bring
Is worth one smile of Thine;
But Thy redeeming grace I'll sing,
And praise Thy love divine.

4 Then shew me still Thy smiling face;
Help me to live to Thee;
To run with joy the heavenly race
And Thy full glory see.

525

1 Lord, I approach the mercy-seat,
Where Thou dost answer prayer;
There humbly fall before Thy feet,—
For none can perish there.

2 Thy promise is my only plea;
With this I venture nigh;
Thou callest burdened souls to Thee,
And such, O Lord, am I.

3 Bowed down beneath a load of sin,
By Satan sorely pressed;
By wars without and fears within,
I come to Thee for rest.

4 Be Thou my shield and hiding-place;
That, sheltered near Thy side,
I may rejoice in Jesus' grace,—
In Jesus crucified.

5 O, wondrous love! to bleed and die,
To bear the cross and shame,
That guilty sinners, such as I,
Might plead Thy gracious name.

526

1 Eternal Source of joys divine,
To Thee my soul aspires;
O! could I say—the Lord is mine!
'Tis all my soul desires.

2 My hope, my trust, my life, my Lord,
Assure me of Thy love;
O! speak the kind, transporting word,
And bid my fears remove.

3 Then shall my thankful powers rejoice,
And triumph in my God,
Till heavenly rapture tune my voice
To spread Thy praise abroad.

ALLEGRETTO.

ROBERT HARRISON. 1760—1812.

Our Heav'n-ly Fa - ther calls, And Christ in - vites us near,

With both our friendship sweet shall be, And our com - mu - nion dear.

527

2 God pities all our griefs;
He pardons every day,—
Almighty to protect our souls,
And wise to guide our way.

3 How large His bounties are!
What various stores of good,
Diffused from our Redeemer's hand,
And purchased with His blood!

4 Jesus, our living Head!
We bless Thy faithful care—
Our Advocate before the Throne,
And our Forerunner there.

5 Here fix my roving heart;
Here wait my warmest love;
Till the communion be complete,
In nobler scenes above.

528

1 Lord, lead my heart to learn,
Prepare my ears to hear,
And let me useful knowledge seek
In Thy most holy fear.

2 If unforgiven sin
Within my bosom lies,
Or evil motives linger there
To offend Thy perfect eyes,—

3 Remove them far away,
Inspire me with Thy love,
That I may please Thee here below,
And dwell with Thee above.

529

1 Love is the strongest tie
That can our hearts unite;
Love makes our service liberty,
Our every burden light.

2 We run in God's commands,
When love directs the way;
With willing hearts, and active hands,
Our Maker's will obey.

530

1 Thou Holy Spirit, art
Of truth the promised seal;
Convincing power Thou dost impart,
And Jesus' grace reveal.

2 O breathe Thy quickening breath,
And light and life afford;
Instruct us how to live by faith,
And glorify the Lord.

531

1 Along my earthly way,
How many clouds are spread!
Darkness with scarce one cheerful ray,
Seems gathering o'er my head.

2 Yet, Father, Thou art Love;
Oh, hide not from my view!
But when I look, in prayer, above,
Appear in mercy through!

532

The Father and the Son,
And Spirit we adore;
We praise, we bless, we worship Thee,
Both now and evermore!

RECITANDO.

Come, Ho - ly Spi - rit, come! Let Thy bright beams a - rise;

Dis - pel the sor - row from our minds, The darkness from our eyes.

533

2 Convince us of our sin;
  Then lead us to Jesus' blood,
And to our wondering view reveal
  The secret love of God.

3 Revive our drooping faith,
  Our doubts and fears remove,
And kindle in our breasts the flame
  Of never-dying love.

534

1 "FOREVER with the Lord!"
  Amen! so let it be;
Life from the dead is in that word;
  'Tis immortality.

2 Here in this body pent,
  Absent from Him I roam,
Yet nightly pitch my moving tent
  A day's march nearer home.

3 My Father's house on high,
  Home of my soul, how near,
At times to faith's discerning eye
  Thy golden gates appear!

4 "Forever with the Lord!"
  Father, if 'tis Thy will,
The promise of that faithful word
  E'en here to me fulfil.

5 Be Thou at my right hand;
  Then can I never fail;
Uphold Thou me, and I shall stand;
  Fight, and I must prevail.

535

1 THE Spirit, in our hearts,
  Is whispering, "Sinners, come,
The bride, the church of Christ, proclaims
  To all His children, come.

2 Let him that heareth say
  To all about him, Come!
Let him that thirsts for righteousness
  To Christ, the Fountain, come.

3 Yes, whosoever will
  O, let him freely come,
And freely drink the stream of life;
  'Tis Jesus bids him come.

4 Lo, Jesus, who invites,
  Declares, "I quickly come;"
Lord, even so: I wait Thy hour;
  Jesus, my Saviour, come!

536

1 LORD, at this closing hour,
  Establish every heart
Upon Thy word of truth and power,
  To keep us when we part.

2 Peace to our brethren give;
  Fill all our hearts with love;
In faith and patience may we live,
  And seek our rest above.

3 Through changes, bright or drear,
  We would Thy will pursue;
And toil to spread Thy kingdom here,
  Till we its glory view.

4 To God, the Only Wise,
  In every age adored,
Let glory from the church arise
  Through Jesus Christ our Lord.

537

Praise to the Father be;
Praise to the Son, who rose;
Praise to the blessed Comforter,
While time unending flows.

148   ST. THOMAS. S. M.

A. WILLIAMS.

O Lord, our God, a - rise; The cause of truth maintain,

And wide o'er all the peopled world Ex-tend her blessed reign.

538

2 Thou Prince of life, arise,
Nor let Thy glory cease;
Far spread the conquests of Thy grace,
And bless the earth with peace.

3 O Holy Spirit, rise,
Expand Thy heavenly wing,
And o'er a dark and ruined world,
Let light and order spring.

4 O, all ye nations, rise;
To God the Saviour sing;
From shore to shore, from earth to heaven,
Let echoing anthems ring.

539

1 Now living waters flow
To cheer the humble soul;
From sea to sea the rivers go,
And spread from pole to pole.

2 Now righteousness shall spring,
And grow on earth again;
Jesus, Jehovah, be our King,
And o'er the nations reign.

3 Jesus shall rule alone,
The world shall hear His word;
By one blessed name shall He be known,
The universal Lord.

540

1 In expectation sweet
We wait, and sing, and pray,
Till Christ's triumphal car we meet,
And see an endless day.

2 He comes! the Conqueror comes!
Death falls beneath His sword;

The joyful prisoners burst their tombs,
And rise to meet their Lord.

3 The trumpet sounds! awake!
Ye dead to judgment come!
The pillars of creation shake,
While hell receives her doom.

4 Thrice happy morn for those
Who love the ways of peace;
No night of sorrow e'er shall close
Or shade their perfect bliss.

541

1 Behold, what wondrous grace
The Father hath bestowed
On sinners of a mortal race,
To call them sons of God?

2 Nor doth it yet appear
How great we must be made;
But when we see our Saviour here,
We shall be like our Head.

3 If in my Father's love
I share a filial part,
Send down Thy Spirit like a dove,
To rest upon my heart.

4 We would no longer lie,
Like slaves, beneath the throne;
My faith shall Abba Father cry,
And Thou the kindred own.

542

To God the Father, Son,
And God the Holy Ghost,
By saints on earth be honor done,
And by the heavenly host.

DOLCE.   From Nageli.

Sweet is the task, O Lord, Thy glo - rious acts to sing;

To praise Thy name, and hear Thy word, And grate - ful off - 'rings bring.

.543

2 Sweet at the dawning hour,
Thy boundless love to tell;
And when the night wind shuts the flower,
Still on the theme to dwell.

3 Sweet on this day of rest,
To join in heart and voice,
With those who love and serve Thee best,
And in Thy name rejoice.

4 To songs of praise and joy,
Be every Sabbath given,
That such may be our blest employ
Eternally in heaven.

544

1 Within these walls be peace;
Love through our borders found;
In all our little palaces
Prosperity abound.

2 God scorns not humble things;
Here, though the proud despise,
The children of the King of kings
Are training for the skies.

3 May none who thus are taught,
From glory be cast down,
But all, thro' faith and patience brought
To an immortal crown.

545

1 While my Redeemer's near,
My Shepherd and my Guide,
I bid farewell to anxious fear;
My wants are all supplied.

2 To ever-fragrant meads,
Where rich abundance grows,
His gracious hand, indulgent leads,
And guards my sweet repose.

3 Dear Shepherd, if I stray,
My wandering feet restore;
To Thy fair pastures guide my way,
And let me rove no more.

546

1 Who can forbear to sing,
Who can refuse to praise,
When Zion's high, celestial King
His saving power displays?

2 When sinners at his feet,
By mercy conquered, fall;
When grace, and truth, and justice meet,
And peace unites them all?

3 Who can forbear to praise,
When angel-notes prolong
O'er sinners turning from their ways,
The high, seraphic song?

547

1 Blessed are the sons of peace,
Whose hearts and hopes are one;
Whose kind designs to serve and please
Through all their actions run.

2 Blessed is the pious house
Where zeal and friendship meet;
Their songs of praise, their mingled vows,
Make their communion sweet.

3 Thus on the heavenly hills
The saints are blessed above,
Where joy like morning dew distils,
And all the air is love.

STATE STREET. S. M.

MODERATO.

J. C. WOODMAN.

How sweet the melt-ing lay Which breaks up-on the ear,

When at the hour of ris-ing day, Christians u-nite in prayer.

548

2 The breezes waft their cries
Up to Jehovah's throne;
He listens to their humble sighs,
And sends his blessings down.

3 So Jesus rose to pray
Before the morning light,
Once on the chilling mount did stay,
And wrestle all the night.

4 So Jesus still doth pray
Before the morning bright,
On heavenly mountains far away,
While we toil here in night.

5 Leave, Lord, Thy vigil there;
Descend upon life's wave;
Come to the bark through midnight air;
The storm shall cease to rave.

549

1 OUR times are in Thy hand,
O God, we wish them there;
Our life, our friends, our souls we leave
Entirely to Thy care.

2 Our times are in Thy hand,
Whatever they may be,
Pleasing or painful, dark or bright,
As best may seem to Thee.

3 Our times are in Thy hand,
Jesus the crucified;
The hand our many sins have pierced,
Is now our guard and guide.

4 Our times are in Thy hand,
We'll always trust in Thee,
Till we have left this weary land,
And all Thy glory see.

550

1 COME to the land of peace;
From shadows come away;
Where all the sounds of weeping cease,
And storms no more have sway.

2 Fear hath no dwelling here;
But pure repose and love
Breathe through the bright celestial air
The spirit of the dove.

3 Come to the bright and blest,
Gathered from every land,
For here thy soul shall find its rest,
Amid the shining band.

551

1 STILL with Thee, O my God,
I would desire to be;
By day, by night, at home, abroad,
I would be still with Thee:

2 With Thee, when dawn comes in
And calls me back to care;
Each day returning to begin
With Thee, my God, in prayer:

3 With Thee, amid the crowd
That throngs the busy mart,
To hear Thy voice, 'mid clamor loud,
Speak softly to my heart:

4 With Thee, when day is done,
And evening calms the mind:
The setting as the rising sun
With Thee my heart would find:

5 With Thee, when darkness brings
The signal of repose;
Calm in the shadow of Thy wings,
Mine eyelids I would close.

1. Come, we who love the Lord, And let our joys be known; Join in a song with sweet ac-cord, And thus surround the throne. 2. Let those refuse to sing Who nev-er knew our God; But children of the heavenly King May speak their joys abroad, May speak their joys abroad.

552

3 The hill of Zion yields
A thousand sacred sweets,
Before we reach the heavenly fields,
Or walk the golden streets.

4 Then let our songs abound,
And every tear be dry;
We're marching thro' Immanuel's ground
To fairer worlds on high

553

1 I STAND on Zion's mount,
And view my starry crown;
No power on earth my hope can shake,
Nor hell can thrust me down.

2 The lofty hills and towers
That lift their heads on high,
Shall all be levelled low in dust;
Their very names shall die.

DR. GREEN.

DOLCE.

Mine eyes and my de-sire Are ev-er to the Lord;

I love to plead His pro-mis-es, And rest up-on His word.

554

2 Turn, turn Thee to my soul;
Bring Thy salvation near;
When will Thy hand release my feet
Out of the deadly snare?

3 When shall the sovereign grace
Of my forgiving God
Restore me from those dangerous ways
My wandering feet have trod?

4 O, keep my soul from death,
Nor put my hope to shame;
For I have placed my only trust
In my Redeemer's name.

555

1 I saw, beyond the tomb,
The awful Judge appear,
Prepared to scan with strict account
My blessings wasted here.

2 His wrath, like flaming fire,
Burned to the lowest hell;
And in that hopeless world of woe
He bade my spirit dwell.

3 My friends—now friends no more—
At infinite remove,
Left me to gain their rich reward,
And taste forgiving love.

4 Then to the Lord I prayed,
And raised a bitter cry:
"Hear me, O God, and save my soul,
Lest I forever die."

5 He heard my humble cry,
He saved my soul from death;
To Him I'll give my heart and hands,
And consecrate my breath.

556

1 Lord, what a feeble piece
Is this our mortal frame!
Our life, how poor a trifle 'tis,
That scarce deserves the name!

2 Alas! the brittle clay
That built our body first!
And every month and every day,
'Tis mouldering back to dust.

3 Our moments fly apace,
Nor will our minutes stay;
Just like a flood our hasty days
Are sweeping us away.

4 Well, if our days must fly,
We'll keep their end in sight;
We'll spend them all in wisdom's way,
And let them speed their flight.

5 They'll waft us sooner o'er
This life's tempestuous sea;
Soon we shall reach the peaceful shore
Of blest eternity.

557

1 Another day is past,
The hours forever fled,
And time is bearing us away
To mingle with the dead.

2 Our minds in perfect peace
Our Father's care shall keep;
We yield to gentle slumber now,
For Thou canst never sleep.

LEACH.

The har-vest dawn is near, The year de-lays not long;

And he who sows with many a tear Shall reap with many a song.

558

2 Sad to his toil he goes,
His seed with weeping leaves;
But He shall come, at twilight's close,
And bring His golden sheaves.

559

1 Nor all the blood of beasts,
On Jewish altars slain,
Could give the guilty conscience peace,
Or wash away the stain.

2 But Christ, the heavenly Lamb,
Takes all our guilt away;
A sacrifice of nobler name,
And richer blood than they.

3 My faith would lay her hand
On that dear head of Thine,
While as a penitent I stand,
And there confess my sin.

4 Believing, we rejoice
To see the curse remove;
We bless the Lamb with cheerful voice,
And sing His bleeding love.

560

1 "The Lord is risen indeed;"
Then hell has lost his prey;
With Him is risen the ransomed seed
To reign in endless day.

2 "The Lord is risen indeed;"
He lives, to die no more;

He lives the sinner's cause to plead,
Whose curse and shame He bore.

3 "The Lord is risen indeed;"
Attending angels, hear;
Up to the courts of heaven, with speed,
The joyful tidings bear.

4 Then take your golden lyres,
And strike each cheerful chord;
Join all the bright, celestial choirs,
To sing our risen Lord.'

561

1 The praises of my tongue
I offer to the Lord,
That I was taught and learned so young
To read His holy word.

2 Dear Lord, this book of Thine
Informs me where to go
For grace to pardon all my sin,
And make me holy too.

3 O, may Thy spirit teach
And make my heart receive
Those truths which all Thy servants preach,
And all Thy saints believe.

4 Then shall I praise the Lord
In a more cheerful strain,
That I was taught to read His word,
And have not learned in vain.

562

Give to the Father praise,
Give glory to the Son;
And to the Spirit of His grace,
Be equal honor done.

LISBON. S. M.

Dr. Lowell Mason.
From Read.

Wel - come, sweet day of rest, That saw the Lord a - rise;

Wel - come to this re - viv - ing breast, And these re - joic - ing eyes;

Wel - come to this re - viv - ing breast, And these re - joic - ing eyes.

563

2 The King himself comes near,
    And feasts His saints to-day;
Here we may sit, and see Him here,
    And love, and praise, and pray.

3 One day amid the place
    Where my dear God hath been,
Is sweeter than ten thousand days
    Of pleasurable sin.

4 My willing soul would stay
    In such a frame as this,
And sit and sing herself away
    To everlasting bliss.

564

1 Great is the Lord our God,
    And let His praise be great;
He makes His churches His abode,
    His most delightful seat.

2 These temples of His grace,
    How beautiful they stand!
The honors of our native place,
    And bulwarks of our land.

3 In Zion God is known,
    A refuge in distress;

How bright has His salvation shone
    Through all her palaces.

4 Oft have our fathers told,
    Our eyes have often seen,
How well our God secures the fold,
    Where His own sheep have been.

5 In every new distress
    We'll to His house repair;
We'll think upon His wondrous grace,
    And seek deliverance there.

565

1 Let every creature join
    To praise the eternal God;
Ye heavenly hosts, the song begin,
    And sound His name abroad.

2 Thou sun, with golden beams,
    And moon, with paler rays,
Ye starry lights, ye twinkling flames,
    Shine to your Maker's praise.

3 By all His works above
    His honors be expressed;
But saints, that taste His saving love,
    Should sing His praises best.

DOLCE. BEETHOVEN.

The Lord my shepherd is; I shall be well supplied;

Since He is mine and I am His, What can I want be-side?

566

2 He leads me to the place
 Where heavenly pasture grows,
Where living waters gently pass,
 And full salvation flows.

3 If e'er I go astray,
 He doth my soul reclaim,
And guides me in His own right way,
 For His most holy name.

4 While He affords His aid,
 I cannot yield to fear;
Tho' I should walk thro' death's dark shade,
 My Shepherd's with me there.

5 The bounties of Thy love
 Shall crown my following days;
Nor from Thy house will I remove,
 Nor cease to speak Thy praise.

567

1 OUR heavenly Father, hear
 The prayer we offer now;
Thy name be hallowed far and near;
 To Thee all nations bow!

2 Thy kingdom come; Thy will
 On earth be done in love,
As saints and seraphim fulfil
 Thy perfect law above!

3 Our daily bread supply,
 While by Thy word we live;
The guilt of our iniquity
 Forgive as we forgive.

4 From dark temptation's power,
 From Satan's wilds, defend;
Deliver in the evil hour,
 And guide us to the end.

568

1 O, WHERE shall rest be found,—
 Rest for the weary soul?
'Twere vain the ocean depths to sound,
 Or pierce to either pole.

2 The world can never give
 The bliss for which we sigh;
'Tis not the whole of life to live,
 Nor all of death to die.

3 Beyond this vale of tears
 There is a life above,
Unmeasured by the flight of years;
 And all that life is love.

4 There is a death whose pang
 Outlasts the fleeting breath;
O, what eternal horrors hang
 Around the second death!

5 Lord God of truth and grace,
 Teach us that death to shun,
Lest we be banished from Thy face,
 And evermore undone.

569

1 BLESSED are the pure in heart,
 For they shall see our God;
The secret of the Lord is theirs;
 Their soul is Christ's abode.

2 Still to the lowly soul
 He doth Himself impart,
And for His cradle and His throne
 Chooseth the pure in heart.

156   HOLBROOK. S. M.

One sweet-ly sol-emn tho't Comes to me o'er and o'er:

Near-er my parting hour am I Than e'er I was be-fore.

570

2 Nearer my Father's house,
Where many mansions be;
Nearer the throne where Jesus reigns,—
Nearer the crystal sea;

3 Nearer my going home,
Laying my burden down,
Leaving my cross of heavy grief,
Wearing my starry crown;

4 Nearer that hidden stream,
Winding through shades of night,
Rolling its cold, dark waves between
Me and the world of light.

5 Jesus! to Thee I cling:
Strengthen my arm of faith;
Stay near me while my way-worn feet
Press through the stream of death.

571

1 SERENE I laid me down,
Beneath His guardian care:
I slept—and I awoke, and found
My kind Preserver near.

2 Thus dost Thine arm support
This weak, defenceless frame;
But whence these favors, Lord, to me,
All worthless as I am?

3 O, how shall I repay
The bounties of my God?
This feeble spirit pants beneath
The pleasing, painful load.

4 My life I would anew
Devote, O Lord to Thee;
And in Thy service I would spend
A long eternity.

572

1 COME, children, come to God;
Cast all your sins away;
Seek ye the Saviour's cleansing blood;
Repent, believe, obey.

2 Say not ye cannot come;
For Jesus bled and died,
That none who ask in humble faith
Should ever be denied.

3 Say not ye will not come;
When God vouchsafes to call;
For fearful will their end be found
On whom His wrath shall fall.

4 Come, then, whoever will;
Come, while 'tis called to-day;
Seek ye the Saviour's cleansing blood:
Repent, believe, obey.

573

1 To Thee, O God in heaven,
This little one we bring,
Giving to Thee what Thou hast given—
Our dearest offering.

2 Into a world of toil
Its little feet will roam,
Where sin its purity may soil,
Where care and grief may come.

3 O, then, let Thy pure love,
With influence serene,
Come down, like water, from above,
To comfort and make clean.

DR. LOWELL MASON. 1830.

Thy boun - ties, gra - cious God, With gra - ti - tude we own;

We praise Thy pro - vi - den - tial care, That showers its bless - ings down.

574

2 With joy Thy people bring
Their offerings round Thy throne;
With thankful souls, behold, we pay
A tribute of Thine own.

3 O may this sacrifice
To Thee, the Lord, ascend,
An odor of a sweet perfume,
Presented by His hand.

575

1 Sow in the morn thy seed;
At eve hold not thine hand;
To doubt and fear give thou no heed;
Broadcast it o'er the land;

2 Beside all waters sow,
The highway furrows stock,
Drop it where thorns and thistles grow,
Scatter it on the rock.

3 The good, the fruitful ground
Expect not here nor there;
O'er hill and dale by plots 'tis found;
Go forth, then, everywhere;

4 And duly shall appear,
In verdure, beauty, strength,
The tender blade, the stalk, the ear,
And the full corn at length.

5 Thou canst not toil in vain;
Cold, heat, and moist, and dry,
Shall foster and mature the grain,
For garners in the sky.

6 Thence, when the glorious end,
The day of God is come,
The angel reapers shall descend,
And Heaven cry, "Harvest home!"

576

1 ARISE, ye saints, arise!
The Lord our leader is;
The foe before His banner flies,
For victory is His.

2 We hope to see the day
When all our toils shall cease;
When we shall cast our arms away,
And dwell in endless peace.

3 This hope supports us here,
It makes our burdens light;
'Twill serve our drooping hearts to cheer,
Till faith shall end in sight;

4 Till of the prize possessed,
We hear of war no more;
And oh, sweet thought! forever rest
On yonder peaceful shore!

577

1 Now is the accepted time;
Now is the day of grace;
Now, sinners, come, without delay,
And seek the Saviour's face.

2 Now is the accepted time;
The Saviour calls to-day;
To-morrow it may be too late;
Then why should you delay?

3 Now is the accepted time;
The gospel bids you come;
And every promise in His word
Declares there yet is room.

The day is draw-ing nigh, Still bright-er far than this,

When con-verts like a cloud shall fly To seek the realms of bliss.

578

2 What blessed scenes of joy
Shall burst upon our sight,
When sinners up to Zion's hill
Like doves shall speed their flight.

3 Beneath Thy balmy wing,
O, Son of righteousness,
These happy souls shall sit and sing
The wonders of Thy grace,

579

1 LORD God, the Holy Ghost!
In this accepted hour,
As on the day of Pentecost,
Descend in all Thy power.

2 We meet with one accord,
In this Thy holy place,
And wait the promise of our Lord,
The Spirit of all grace.

3 Like mighty rushing wind
Upon the waves beneath,
Move with one impulse every mind,
One soul, one feeling breathe.

4 Wake with Thy sovereign breath,
The souls now dark and dead,
And o'er this silent field of death,
Thy living influence shed.

580

1 A FEW more years shall roll,
A few more seasons come;
And we shall be with those that rest,
Asleep within the tomb:

2 Then, O my Lord, prepare
My soul for that great day;
Oh, wash me in Thy precious blood,
And take my sins away!

3 A few more storms shall beat
On this wild rocky shore;
And we shall be where tempests cease,
And surges swell no more:

4 Then, O my Lord, prepare
My soul for that calm day;
Oh, wash me in Thy precious blood,
And take my sins away!

581

1 MOURN for the thousands slain,
The youthful and the strong;
Mourn for the wine-cup's fatal reign,
And the deluded throng.

2 Mourn for the tarnished gem—
For reason's light divine,
Quenched from the soul's bright diadem,
Where God hath bid it shine.

3 Mourn for the ruined soul—
Eternal life and light
Lost by the fiery, maddening bowl,
And turned to hopeless night.

4 Mourn for the lost—but call,
Call to the strong, the free;
Rouse them to shun that dreadful fall,
And to the refuge flee.

5 Mourn for the lost—but pray,
Pray to our God above,
To break the fell destroyer's sway,
And show His saving love.

DR. LOWELL MASON. 1840.

With hum-ble heart and tongue, My God, to Thee I pray;

Oh! bring me now, while I am young, To Thee, the liv - - ing way.

582

2 Make an unguarded youth
The object of Thy care;
Help me to choose the way of truth,
And fly from every snare.

3 My heart, to folly prone,
Renew by power divine;
Unite it to Thyself alone,
And make me wholly Thine.

4 O, let Thy word of grace
My warmest thoughts employ;
Be this through all my following days,
My treasure and my joy.

5 May Thy young servant learn
By this to cleanse his way;
And may I here the path discern
That leads to endless day.

583

1 LET party names no more
The Christian world o'erspread;
Gentile and Jew, and bond and free,
Are one in Christ, their Head.

2 Among the saints on earth
Let mutual love be found;
Heirs of the same inheritance,
With mutual blessings crowned.

3 Thus will the church below
Resemble that above;
Where streams of pleasure ever flow,
And every heart is love.

584

1 GREEN pastures and clear streams,
Freedom and quiet rest,
Christ's flock enjoy beneath His beams,
Or in His shadow blessed.

2 The mountain and the vale,
Forest and field, they range;
The morning dew, the evening gale,
Bring health in every change.

3 The wounded and the weak,
He comforts, heals, and binds;
The lost He came from heaven to seek,
And saves them when He finds.

4 Conflicts and trials done,
His glory they behold,
Where Jesus and His flock are one,
One Shepherd and one fold.

585

1 O LORD, Thy perfect word
Directs our steps aright,
Nor can all other books afford
Such profit and delight.

2 Celestial beams it sheds
To cheer this vale below;
To distant lands its glory spreads,
And streams of mercy flow.

3 True wisdom it imparts,
Commands our hope and fear;
Oh, may we hide it in our hearts,
And feel its influence there.

ST. BRIDES. S. M.

DR. HOWARD.

From low-est depths of woe, To God I send my cry;

Lord, hear my sup-pli-cat-ing voice, And gracious-ly re-ply.

586

2 My soul with patience waits
For Thee, the living Lord;
My hopes are on Thy promise built,
Thy never-failing word.

3 My longing eyes look out
For Thy enlivening ray,
More duly than the morning watch
To spy the dawning day.

4 Let Israel trust in God;
No bounds His mercy knows;
The plenteous Source and Spring from
Eternal succor flows.   [whence

587

1 Thou Judge of quick and dead,
Before whose bar severe,
With holy joy, or guilty dread,
We all shall soon appear :

2 Our cautioned souls prepare
For that tremendous day;
And fill us now with watchful care,
And stir us up to pray.

3 O, may we thus be found
Obedient to Thy word;
Attentive to the trumpet's sound,
And looking for our Lord.

*4 O, may we all insure
A lot among the blessed:
And watch a moment to secure
An everlasting'rest.

588

1 How heavy is the night
That hangs upon our eyes;
Till Christ, with His reviving light,
Over our souls arise !

2 Our guilty spirits dread
To meet the wrath of heaven;
But in His righteousness arrayed,
We see our sins forgiven.

3 Unholy and impure
Are all our thoughts and ways;
His hands infected nature cure
With sanctifying grace.

4 Lord, we adore Thy ways
To bring us near to God—
Thy sovereign power, Thy healing grace,
And Thine atoning blood.

589

1 Thy piercing eye, O Lord,
My every thought surveys,
Darkness and light alike reveal,
My sinful thoughts and ways.

2 This knowledge of my guilt,
Doth magnify Thy grace,
While bathed in tears, I upward look,
To my Redeemer's face.

3 Mercy and truth are met,
In His benignant eye,
His righteousness to faith revealed,
Brings full salvation nigh.

4 The God who hates my sin,
Christ's righteousness will own
And clothed in that, I shall appear,
Complete before His throne.

REV. E. W. DUNBAR.

O, sing to me of heav'n, When I am called to die,
CHO. There'll be no more sor-row there— There'll be no more sor-row there—

Sing songs of ho-ly ec-sta-cy, To waft my soul on high!
In heaven a-bove, where all is love, There'll be no more sor-row there.

590

2 When cold and sluggish drops
Roll off my marble brow,
Break forth in songs of joyfulness,
Let heaven begin below.

3 When the last moment comes,
O, watch my dying face,
To catch the bright seraphic glow,
Which o'er each feature plays.

4 Then to my raptured ear,
Let one sweet song be given;
Let music charm me last on earth
And greet me first in heaven.

5 Then close my sightless eyes,
And lay me down to rest,
And clasp my cold and icy hands,
Upon my lifeless breast.

6 Then round my senseless clay,
Assemble those I love—
And sing of heaven, delightful heaven,
My glorious home above.

591

1 My Father's house on high!
Home of my soul! how near,
At times, to faith's foreseeing eye
Thy golden gates appear!

2 Ah! then my spirit faints
To reach the land I love,
The bright inheritance of saints.
Jerusalem above.

3 Yet clouds will intervene,
And all my prospects fly;
Like Noah's dove I flit between
Rough seas and stormy sky.

4 Anon the clouds depart,
The winds and waters cease;
While sweetly o'er my gladdened heart
Expands the bow of peace.

5 I hear at morn and even,
At noon and midnight hour,
The choral harmonies of heaven
Earth's Babel-tongues o'erpower.

6 Then, then I feel that He—
Remembered or forgot—
The Lord is never far from me,
Though I perceive Him not.

592

1 HARK! through the courts of heaven
Angelic voices sound;
He that was dead now lives again;
He that was lost is found.

2 God of unfailing grace,
Send down Thy Spirit now;
Oh, raise the lowly soul to hope,
And make the lofty bow.

3 In countries far from home,
On earthly husks who feed,
Back to their Father's house, O Lord,
Their wandering footsteps lead.

4 Then at each soul's return,
The heavenly harp shall sound:
He that was dead now lives again;
He that was lost is found.

SILVER STREET. S. M.

I. SMITH.

Come, sound His praise a - broad, And hymns of glo - ry sing;

Je - ho - vah is the sov - 'reign God, The u - ni - ver - sal King.

593

2 He formed the deeps unknown;
   He gave the seas their bound;
The watery worlds are all His own,
   And all the solid ground.

3 Come, worship at His throne.
   Come, bow before the Lord;
We are His work, and not our own;
   He formed us by His word.

4 To-day attend His voice,
   Nor dare provoke His rod;
Come, like the people of His choice,
   And own your gracious God.

594

1 GRACE! 'tis a charming sound,
   Harmonious to my ear;
Heaven with the echo shall resound,
   And all the earth shall hear.

2 Grace first contrived a way
   To save rebellious man;
And all the steps that grace display
   Which drew the wondrous plan.

3 Grace taught my wandering feet
   To tread the heavenly road;
And new supplies each hour I meet,
   While pressing on to God.

4 Grace all the work shall crown,
   Through everlasting days;
It lays in heaven the topmost stone,
   And well deserves the praise.

595

1 How beauteous are their feet
   Who stand on Zion's hill!
Who bring salvation on their tongues,
   And words of peace reveal.

2 How charming is their voice!
   How sweet the tidings are!—
"Zion, behold thy Saviour King!
   He reigns and triumphs here."

3 How happy are our ears,
   That hear this joyful sound,
Which kings and prophets waited for,
   And sought, but never found.

4 How blessed are our eyes,
   That see this heavenly light!
Prophets and kings desired it long,
   But died without the sight.

596

1 GREAT GOD, at Thy command
   Seasons in order rise:
Thy power and love in concert reign
   Through earth, and seas, and skies.

2 How balmy is the air!
   How warm the sun's bright beams!
While, to refresh the ground, the rains
   Descend in gentle streams.

3 With grateful praise we own
   Thy kind, providing hand,
While grass, and herbs, and waving corn
   Adorn and bless the land.

4 But greater still the gift
   Of Thine incarnate Son;
By Him forgiveness, peace and joy
   Through endless ages run.

PIA.   M. S. PIKE.

Home at last! home at last! From an earth - ly shore;

FINE.

For O, I've join'd the ransom'd ones, Who passed on long be - fore.

Here each tear is wiped a - way By God, the Ho - ly One;

D. C.

There's naught but songs of joy and praise Round the E - ter - nal's throne.

597

2 Th' pure in heart ! th' pure in heart !
  Robed in spotless white,
Are here with starry crowns of joy,
  All gloriously bright.
Some I loved so long ago,
  Who left me sad and lone,
I meet among the heavenly host,
  Within our Father's home.
Home at last ! home at last !
  From an earthly shore,
For O, I've joined the ransomed ones
  Who passed on long before.

3 Safe at home ! safe at home !
  O, let the echo go,
To soothe the hearts that mourn me yet,
  In that first home below.

His dear arms are round me now,
  Who was for sinners slain;
Through Him I've won eternal life;
  For me to die was gain.
Safe at home ! safe at home !
  From an earthly shore;
I'll bless and praise Thee, O my God,
  Forever, evermore.

598

Ye angels round the throne,
  And saints that dwell below,
Adore the Father, love the Son,
  And bless the Spirit too.

SHIRLAND. S. M.

STANLEY.

Be - hold, the morn - ing sun Be - gins his glo - rious way;

His beams thro' all the na - tions run, And life and light con - vey.

599

2 But where the gospel comes,
   It spreads diviner light;
It calls dead sinners from their tombs,
   And gives the blind their sight.

3 How perfect is Thy word,
   And all Thy judgments just!
Forever sure Thy promise, Lord,
   And men securely trust.

4 My gracious God, how plain
   Are Thy directions given!
O, may I never read in vain,
   But find the path to heaven.

600

1 Now let our voices join
   To form one pleasant song;
Ye pilgrims in Jehovah's ways,
   With music pass along.

2 How straight the path appears!
   How open and how fair!
No lurking gins to entrap our feet,
   No fierce destroyer there.

3 But flowers of paradise
   In rich profusion spring; •
The sun of glory gilds the path,
   And dear companions sing.

4 Reduce the nations, Lord;
   Teach all their kings Thy ways,
That earth's full choir the notes may swell,
   And heaven resound the praise.

601

1 " Is this a fast for Me? "—
   Thus saith the Lord, our God;—
" A day for man to vex his soul,
   And feel affliction's rod?

2 " Shall day like this have power
   To stay the avenging hand,
Efface transgression or avert
   My judgments from the land?

3 " No ; is not this alone
   The sacred fast I choose—
Oppression's yoke to burst in twain,
   The bands of guilt unloose?

4 " To nakedness and want
   Your food and raiment deal,
To dwell your kindred race among,
   And all their sufferings heal?

5 " Then, like the morning ray,
   Shall spring your health and light;
Before you, righteousness shall shine;
   Behind, My glory bright."   •

602

1 COME at the morning hour,
   Come, let us kneel and pray;
Prayer is the Christian pilgrim's staff
   To walk with God all day.

2 At noon, beneath the Rock
   Of Ages, rest and pray;
Sweet is that shelter from the sun
   In the weary heat of day.

3 At evening in Thy home,
   Around its altar, pray;
And finding there the house of God,
   With heaven then close the day.

Dr. Boyce.

My soul, be on thy guard! Ten thousand foes . a - rise;

The hosts of sin are pressing hard To draw thee from the skies.

603

2 O, watch, and fight, and pray;
   The battle ne'er give o'er;
Renew it boldly every day,
   And help divine implore.

3 Ne'er think the victory won,
   Nor lay thine armor down;
Thy arduous work will not be done
   Till thou obtain thy crown.

4 Fight on, my soul, till death
   Shall bring thee to thy God;
He'll take thee at thy parting breath
   Up to His blest abode.

604

1 Awake, and sing the song
   Of Moses and the Lamb;
Wake every heart and every tongue,
   To praise the Saviour's name.

2 Sing of His dying love ;
   Sing of His rising power;
Sing how He intercedes above,
   For us, whose sins He bore.

3 Sing, till we feel our heart
   Ascending with our tongue;
Sing, till the love of sin depart,
   And grace inspire our song.

4 Soon shall we hear Him say ; —
   " Ye blessed children come! "
Soon will He call us hence away
   To our eternal home.

605

1 Soldiers of Christ, arise,
   And put your armor on;
Strong in the strength which God supplies
   Through His eternal Son.

2 Strong in the Lord of Hosts,
   And in His mighty power;
Who in the strength of Jesus trusts
   Is more than conqueror.

3 Stand, then, in His great might,
   With all His strength endued;
But take, to arm you for the fight,
   The panoply of God.

4 That, having all things done,
   And all your conflicts past,
Ye may o'ercome, through Christ alone,
   And stand entire at last.

606

1 Ye servants of the Lord,
   Each in his office wait;
Observant of His heavenly word,
   And watchful at His gate.

2 Let all your lamps be bright,
   And trim the golden flame;
Gird up your loins, as in His sight,
   For awful is His name.

3 " Watch! " 'Tis your Lord's command;
   And while we speak, He's near;
Mark the first signal of His hand,
   And ready all appear.

4 O, happy servant he,
   In such a posture found;
He shall his Lord with rapture see,
   And be with honor crowned.

OLMUTZ. S. M.   Dr. Lowell Mason.
From a Gregorian.

Blest be the tie that binds Our hearts in Chris-tian love;

The fel-low-ship of kin-dred minds Is like to that a-bove.

607

2 Before our Father's throne
  We pour our ardent prayers;
Our fears, our hopes, our aims are one,
  Our comforts and our cares.

3 We share our mutual woes, ·
  Our mutual burdens bear;
And often for each other flows
  The sympathizing tear.

4 When we asunder part,
  It gives us inward pain;
But we shall still be joined in heart,
  And hope to meet again.

5 This glorious hope revives
  Our courage by the way,
While each in expectation lives,
  And longs to see the day.

6 From sorrow, toil, and pain,
  And sin we shall be free,
And perfect love and friendship reign
  Through all eternity.

608

1 I love Thy kingdom, Lord,
  The house of Thine abode,
The church our blest Redeemer saved
  With His own precious blood.

2 I love Thy church, O God;
  Her walls before Thee stand,
Dear as the apple of Thine eye,
  And graven on Thy hand.

3 If e'er my heart forget
  Her welfare or her woe,
Let every joy this heart forsake,
  And every grief o'erflow.

4 Beyond my highest joy,
  I prize her heavenly ways,
Her sweet communion, solemn vows,
  Her hymns of love and praise.

5 Sure as Thy truth shall last,
  To Zion shall be given
The brightest glories earth can yield,
  And brighter bliss of heaven.

609

1 Your harps, ye trembling saints,
  Down from the willows take;
Loud to the praise of love divine
  Bid every string awake.

2 Though in a foreign land,
  We are not far from home;
And nearer to our house above
  We every moment come.

3 His grace will to the end
  Stronger and brighter shine;
Nor present things, nor things to come,
  Shall quench the spark divine.

4 Soon shall our doubts and fears
  Subside at His control;
His loving kindness shall break through
  The midnight of the soul.

5 Blest is the man, O God,
  That stays himself on Thee;
Who waits for Thy salvation, Lord,
  Shall Thy salvation see.

IOWA. S. M. (Kentucky.) 167

Shall we go on to sin, Be - cause Thy grace a - bounds?

Or cru - ci - fy the Lord a - gain, And o - pen all His wounds?

610

2 Forbid it, mighty God;
Nor let it e'er be said
That we whose sins are crucified,
Should raise them from the dead.

3 We will be slaves no more,
Since Christ has made us free,—
Has nailed our tyrants to His cross,
And bought our liberty.

611

1 Ah! whither should I go,
Burdened, and sick, and faint?
To whom should I my troubles show,
And pour out my complaint?

2 My Saviour bids me come,
Ah! why do I delay?
He calls the weary sinner home,
And yet from Him I stay!

3 Oh! break the fatal chain,
And all my bonds remove;
Nor let one bosom-sin remain,
To keep me from Thy love.

612

1 Can sinners hope for heaven,
Who love this world so well?
Or dream of future happiness,
While on the road to hell?

2 Shall they hosannahs sing,
With an unhallowed tongue?
Shall palms adorn the guilty hand
Which does its neighbor wrong?

3 Can sin's deceitful way
Conduct to Zion's hill?
Or those expect with God to reign
Who disregard his will?

4 Thy grace, O God, alone,
Good hope can e'er afford!
The pardoned and the pure shall see
The glory of the Lord.

613

1 My son, know thou the Lord;
Thy father's God obey;
Seek His protecting care by night,
His guiding hand by day.

2 Call when he may be found,
And seek Him while He's near;
Serve Him with all thy heart and mind,
And worship Him in fear,

3 Judgments that fill the soul with awe
Are written by the Lord
For him that breaks his father's law
Or mocks his mother's word.

614

1 Give me a sober mind,
A quick discerning eye,
The first approach of sin to find,
And all occasions fly.

2 Still may I cleave to Thee,
And never more depart,
But watch with godly jealousy
Over my evil heart.

3 Thus may I pass my days
Of sojourning beneath,
And languish to conclude my race,
And render up my breath.

GERAR. S. M.

MODERATO.

DR. LOWELL MASON.

How charming is the place Where my Redeemer, God, Unveils the beauties

of His face, Unveils the beauties of His face, And sheds His love abroad.

615

2 Not the fair palaces
To which the great resort,
Are once to be compared with this,
Where Jesus holds His court.

3 Here on the mercy seat,
With radiant glory crowned,
Our joyful eyes behold Him sit,
And smile on all around.

4 Give me, O Lord, a place
Within Thy blest abode,
Among the children of Thy grace,
The servants of my God.

616

1 THOU Lord of all above,
And all below the sky,
Prostrate before Thy feet I fall,
And for Thy mercy cry.

2 Forgive my follies past,
The crimes which I have done;
Oh, bid a contrite sinner live,
Through Thine incarnate Son.

3 Guilt, like a heavy load,
Upon my conscience lies;
To Thee I make my sorrows known,
And lift my weeping eyes.

4 The burden which I feel,
Thou only canst remove;
Do Thou display Thy pardoning grace
And Thine unbounded love.

5 One gracious look of Thine
Will ease my troubled breast:
Oh! let me know my sins forgiven,
And I shall then be blest.

617

1 O FOR the death of those
Who slumber in the Lord!
O, be like theirs my last repose,
Like theirs my last reward.

2 Their bodies in the ground,
In silent hope may lie,
Till the last trumpet's joyful sound
Shall call them to the sky.

3 Their ransomed spirits soar,
On wings of faith and love,
To meet the Saviour they adore,
And reign with Him above.

4 O for the death of those
Who slumber in the Lord!
O, be like theirs my last repose,
Like theirs my last reward.

618

1 WHERE shall the man be found
Who fears to offend his God,
Who loves the gospel's joyful sound,
And trembles at the rod?

2 The Lord shall make him know
The secrets of his heart;
The wonders of His covenant show,
And all His love impart.

3 The dealings of His hand
Are truth and mercy, still,
With such as to His covenant stand,
And love to do His will.

MODERATO.
From CORELLI. 1690.

When, o-verwhelmed with grief, My heart with-in me dies,

Helpless and far from all re-lief, To heaven I lift mine eyes.

619

2 O, lead me to the Rock
That's high above my head,
And make the covert of Thy wings
My shelter and my shade.

3 Within Thy presence, Lord,
Forever I'll abide;
Thou art the Tower of my defence,
The refuge where I hide.

4 Thou givest me the lot
Of those that fear Thy name;
If endless life be their reward,
I shall possess the same.

620

1 My few revolving years,
How swift they glide away!
How short the term of life appears!
When past, 'tis but a day;—

2 A dark and cloudy day
Made up of grief and sin;
A host of dangerous foes without,
And guilt and fear within.

3 Lord, through another year,
If Thou permit my stay,
With watchful care may I pursue
The true and living way.

621

1 My former hopes are fled,
My terror now begins;
I feel, alas! that I am dead
In trespasses and sins.

2 Ah! whither shall I fly?
I hear the thunder roar;
The law proclaims destruction nigh
And vengeance at the door.

3 When I review my ways,
I dread impending doom;
But sure a friendly whisper says,
" Flee from the wrath to come."

4 I see, or think I see,
A glimmering from afar;
A beam of day that shines for me,
To save me from despair.

5 Forerunner of the sun,
It marks the pilgrim's way;
I'll gaze upon it while I run,
And watch the rising day.

622

1 And will the judge descend,
And must the dead arise,
And not a single soul escape
His all-discerning eyes?

2 How will my heart endure
The terrors of that day,
When earth and heaven before his face
Astonished shrink away?

3 But, ere the trumpet shakes
The mansions of the dead,
Hark, from the Gospel's cheering sound
What joyful tidings spread!

4 Ye sinners! seek his grace
Whose wrath ye cannot bear;
Fly to the shelter of his cross,
And find salvation there.

GOLDEN HILL. S. M.

MODERATO.   WESTERN TUNE.

Did Christ o'er sin-ners weep, And shall our cheeks be dry?

Let floods of pen-e-ten-tial grief Burst forth from ev-'ry eye.

623

2 The Son of God in tears
  Angels with wonder see;
Be thou astonished, O my soul;
He shed those tears for thee.

3 He wept that we might weep;
  Each sin demands a tear;
In heaven alone no sin is found,
And there's no weeping there.

624

1 And must this body die,
  This mortal frame decay?
And must these active limbs of mine
Lie mouldering in the clay?

2 Corruption, earth and worms
  Shall but refine this flesh,
Till my triumphant spirit comes,
To put it on afresh.

3 God, my Redeemer, lives,
  And often, from the skies,
Looks down and watches all my dust,
Till he shall bid it rise.

4 Arrayed in glorious grace
  Shall these vile bodies shine,
And every shape, and every face,
Look heavenly and divine.

5 These lively hopes we owe
  To Jesus' dying love;
We would adore His grace below,
And sing His power above.

6 Dear Lord, accept the praise
  Of these our humble songs,
Till tunes of nobler sound we raise
With our immortal tongues.

625

1 And canst thou, sinner, slight
  The call of love divine?
Shall God, with tenderness invite,
And gain no thought of thine?

2 Wilt thou not cease to grieve
  The Spirit from thy breast,
Till He thy wretched soul shall leave
With all thy sins oppressed?

3 To-day, a pardoning God
  Will hear the suppliant pray;
To-day, a Saviour's cleansing blood
Will wash thy guilt away.

4 But grace so dearly bought,
  If yet thou wilt despise,
Thy fearful doom with vengeance fraught,
Will fill thee with surprise.

626

1 Blest Comforter, divine,
  Let rays of heavenly love
Amid our gloom and darkness shine,
To guide our souls above.

2 Draw, with Thy still small voice,
  From every sinful way,
And bid the mourning saint rejoice,
Though earthly joys decay.

3 By Thine inspiring breath,
  Make every cloud of care,
And e'en the gloomy vale of death,
A smile of glory wear.

ANDANTE.   Arr. by Dr. LOWELL MASON.

If through un - ruf - fled seas, Tow'rd heav'n we calm - ly sail,

With grateful hearts, O God, to Thee, We'll own the fost'ring gale,

With grateful hearts, O God, to Thee, We'll own the fost'ring gale.

627

2 But should the surges rise,
  And rest delay to come,
Blessed be the sorrow, kind the storm,
  Which drives us nearer home.

3 Soon shall our doubts and fears
  All yield at Thy control;
Thy tender mercies shall illume
  The midnight of the soul.

4 Teach us, in every state,
  To make Thy will our own,
And when the joys of sense depart,
  To live by faith alone.

628

1 My spirit on Thy care,
  Blest Saviour, I recline;
Thou wilt not leave me to despair,
  For Thou art love divine.

2 In Thee I place my trust;
  On Thee I calmly rest:
I know Thee good, I know Thee just,
  And count Thy choice the best.

3 Whate'er events betide,
  Thy will they all perform;

Safe in Thy breast my head I hide,
  Nor fear the coming storm.

4 Let good or ill befall,
  It must be good for me—
Secure of having Thee in all,
  Of having all in Thee.

629

1 My God, my Life, my Love.
  To Thee, to Thee I call;
I cannot live if Thou remove,
  For Thou art all in all.

2 To Thee, and Thee alone,
  The angels owe their bliss:
They sit around their gracious throne
  And dwell where Jesus is.

3 Nor earth, nor all the sky,
  Can one delight afford—
No, not a drop of real joy—
  Without Thy presence, Lord.

4 Thou art the sea of love,
  Where all my pleasures roll;
The circle where my passions move,
  And centre of my soul.

HASTINGS.

Raise your tri - umphant songs To an im - mor - tal tune; Let

the wide earth resound the deeds Ce - les - tial grace has done.

Let the wide earth resound the deeds Ce - les - tial grace has done.
Let the wide earth resound the deeds Celestial grace has done.

630

2 Sing how eternal love
   Its chief Beloved chose,
And bade Him raise our wretched race
   From their abyss of woes..

3 His hand no thunder bears;
   No terror clothes His brow;
No bolts to drive our guilty souls
   To fiercer flames below.

4 'T was mercy filled the throne,
   And wrath stood silent by,
When Christ was sent with pardons down
   To rebels doomed to die.

5 Now, sinners, dry your tears;
   Let hopeless sorrow cease:
Bow to the sceptre of His love,
   And take the offered peace.

6 Lord, we obey Thy call;
   We lay an humble cla'm
To the salvation Thou hast brought,
   And love and praise Thy name.

631

1 THE Church has waited long,
   Her absent Lord to see;
And still in loneliness she waits,
   A friendless stranger she.

2 How long, O Lord our God,
   Holy and true and good,
Wilt thou not judge Thy suffering church,
   Her sighs and tears and blood?

3 Saint after saint on earth
   Has lived, and loved and died;
And as they left us one by one,
   We laid them side by side.

4 We laid them down to sleep,
   But not in hope forlorn;
We laid them but to ripen there,
   Till the last glorious morn.

5 We long to hear Thy voice,
   To see Thee face to face,
To share Thy crown and glory then,
   As now we share Thy grace.

6 Come, Lord! and wipe away
   The curse, the sin, the stain,
And make this blighted world of ours
   Thine own fair world again.

632

1 FAR as Thy name is known,
   The world declares Thy praise;
Thy saints, O Lord, before Thy throne,
   Their songs of honor raise.

2 With joy let Judah stand
   On Zion's chosen hill,
Proclaim the wonders of Thy hand,
   And counsels of Thy will.

3 Let strangers walk around
   The city where we dwell,
Compass and view the holy ground,
   And mark the building well—

4 How decent and how wise!
   How glorious to behold:
Beyond the pomp that charms the eyes,
   And rites adorned with gold.

CON SPIRITO.   OLD ENGLISH.

Give   to   the winds thy fears, Hope, and   be   un - dismayed;

God hears thy sighs and counts thy tears,—God shall lift up   thy head.

633

2 Through waves, and clouds, and storms,
  He gently clears thy way;
Wait thou His time; so shall this night
Soon end in joyous day.

3 Far, far above thy thought
  His counsel shall appear,
When fully He the work hath wrought,
  That caused thy needless fear.

4 What though thou rulest not!
  Yet heaven, and earth, and hell
Proclaim, God sitteth on the throne,
  And ruleth all things well.

634

1 A CHARGE to keep I have,
  A God to glorify,
A never-dying soul to save,
  And fit it for the sky.

2 To serve the present age,
  My calling to fulfil;
O, may it all my powers engage
  To do my Master's will.

3 Arm me with jealous care
  As in Thy sight to live;
And O, Thy servant, Lord, prepare
A strict account to give.

4 Help me to watch and pray,
  And on Thyself rely,
Assured, if I my trust betray,
  I shall forever die.

635

1 WE come with joyful song,
  To hail this happy morn;
Glad tidings from an angel's tongue,
  "This day is Jesus born!"

2 What transports doth his name
  To sinful men afford!
His glorious titles we proclaim—
  A Saviour—Christ—the Lord!

3 Glory to God on high,
  All hail the happy morn:
We join the anthems of the sky—
  And sing—"the Saviour's born!"

636

1 STAND up and bless the Lord,
  Ye people of His choice;
Stand up and bless the Lord your God,
  With heart and soul and voice.

2 Though high above all praise,
  Above all blessing high,
Who would not fear His holy name,
  And laud and magnify?

3 O! for the living flame,
  From His own altar brought,
To touch our lips, our minds inspire,
  And wing to heaven our thought!

4 God is our strength and song,
  And His salvation ours;
Then be His love in Christ proclaimed,
  With all our ransomed powers.

5 Stand up and bless the Lord,
  The Lord your God adore;
Stand up and bless His glorious name,
  Henceforth for ever more.

How gen-tle God's commands! How kind His pre-cepts are;

Come, cast your bur-dens on the Lord, And trust His con-stant care.

637

2 Beneath His watchful eye
  His saints securely dwell;
That hand which bears all nature up,
  Shall guard His children well.

3 Why should this anxious load
  Press down your weary mind?
Haste to your heavenly Father's throne,
  And sweet refreshment find.

4 His goodness stands approved,
  Through each succeeding day;
I'll drop my burden at His feet,
  And bear a song away.

638

1 Is this the kind return,
  And these the thanks we owe,
Thus to abuse the eternal love,
  Whence all our blessings flow?

2 To what a stubborn frame
  Has sin reduced our mind!
What strange, rebellious wretches we,
  And God as strangely kind.

3 Turn, turn us, mighty God,
  And mould our souls afresh;   [stone,
Break, Sovereign Grace, these hearts of
  And give us hearts of flesh.

4 Let old ingratitude
  Provoke our weeping eyes;
And hourly, as new mercies fall,
  Let hourly thanks arise.

639

1 LIKE Noah's weary dove,
  That soared the earth around,
But not a resting place above
  The cheerless waters found;

2 O cease, my wandering soul,
  On restless wing to roam;
All the wide world, to either pole,
  Has not for thee a home.

3 Behold the ark of God;
  Behold the open door;
Hasten to gain that dear abode,
  And rove, my soul, no more.

4 There, safe thou shalt abide;
  There, sweet shall be thy rest;
And every longing satisfied,
  With full salvation blessed.

5 And when the waves of ire
  Again the earth shall fill,
The ark shall ride the sea of fire,
  Then rest on Zion's hill.

640

1 THE day is past and gone;
  The evening shades appear; .
O, may I ever keep in mind
  The night of death draws near.

2 I lay my garments by,
  Upon my bed to rest;
So death will soon remove me hence,
  And leave my soul undressed.

3 Lord, keep me safe this night,
  Secure from all my fears;
May angels guard me while I sleep,
  Till morning light appears.

THATCHER. S. M.

HANDEL.

'Tis God the Spi-rit leads In paths be-fore un-known; The
work to be per-form'd is ours, The strength is all His own.

641

2 Supported by His grace,
We still pursue our way;
And hope at last to reach the prize,
Secure in endless day.

3 'Tis He that works to will;
'Tis He that works to do;
His is the power by which we act
His be the glory too

642

1 REVIVE Thy work, O Lord.
And send salvation down :
Let the sharp arrows of Thy word,
Now pierce the hearts of stone.

2 Ride in Thy prosperous car;
Regain Thy people lost;
Let Thy right hand conduct the war,
Let victory crown Thy host.

643

1 AWAKE, O sleeper ! and behold
There stands a loving One,
With shining feet begirt with gold,
And raiment like the sun.

2 There's music in His heavenly voice,
And when He speaks to thee
It bids thy saddened heart rejoice
And sets thy spirit free.

644

1 LORD, keep us safe this night,
Secure from all our fears;
May angels guard us while we sleep,
Till morning light appears.

2 And if we early rise,
And view the unwearied sun,
May we set out to win the prize,
And after glory run.

3 And when our days are past,
And we from time remove,
O may we in Thy bosom rest,—
The bosom of Thy love.

645

1 REST for the toiling hand,
Rest for the anxious brow,
Rest for the weary way-worn feet,
Rest from all labor now;—

2 Rest for the fevered brain,
Rest for the throbbing eye;
Thro' these parched lips of thine no more
Shall pass the moan or sigh.

3 Soon shall the trump of God
Give out the welcome sound,
That shakes thy silent chamber-walls,
And breaks the turf-sealed ground.

4 Ye dwellers in the dust
Awake ! come forth and sing;
Sharp has your frost of winter been,
But bright shall be your spring.

5 'Twas sown in weakness here;
'Twill then be raised in power :
That which was sown an earthly seed,
Shall rise a heavenly flower !

646

To the eternal Three,
In will and essence One,
Be universal honors paid,
Coequal honors done.

J. ZUNDEL.

I was a wandering sheep, I did not love the fold;

I did not love my Shepherd's voice, I would not be con-trolled;

I was a wayward child, I did not love my home;

I did not love my Father's voice; I loved a-far to roam.

647

2 The Shepherd sought His sheep,
  The Father sought His child;
They followed me o'er vale and hill,
  O'er deserts waste and wild:
They found me nigh to death,
  Famished and faint and lone;
They bound me with the bands of love,
  They saved the wandering one.

3 They spoke in tender love,
  They raised my drooping head;
They gently closed my bleeding wounds,
  My fainting soul they fed:

They washed my filth away,
  They made me clean and fair;
They brought me to my home in peace,
  The long-sought wanderer.

4 Jesus, my Shepherd is,
  'Twas He that loved my soul,
'Twas He that washed me in His blood,
  'Twas He that made me whole:
'Twas He that sought the lost,
  That found the wandering sheep,
'Twas He that brought me to the fold—
  'Tis He that still doth keep.

Dr. Lowell Mason. 1832.

O Lord, Thy work re - vive, In Zi - on's gloomy hour, And

make her dy - ing gra - ces live By Thy re - stor - ing power.

648

2 Awake Thy chosen few
To fervent, earnest prayer;
Again their sacred vows renew,
Thy blessed presence share.

3 Thy Spirit then will speak
Through lips of feeble clay,
And hearts of adamant will break,
And rebels will obey.

4 Lord, lend Thy gracious ear;
O, listen to our cry:
O, come and bring salvation here :
Our hopes on Thee rely.

649

1 Jesus invites His saints
To meet around His board;
Here pardoned rebels sit, and hold
Communion with their Lord.

2 For food He gives His flesh;
He bids us drink His blood;
Amazing favor, matchless grace,
Of our descending God !

3 This holy bread and wine
Maintains our fainting breath,
By union with our living Lord,
And interest in His death.

• 4 We are but several parts
Of the same broken bread;
One body hath its several limbs,
But Jesus is the Head.

5 Let all our powers be joined
His glorious name to raise,
Pleasure and love fill every mind,
And every voice be praise.

650

1 The pity of the Lord,
To those that fear His name,
Is such as tender parents feel :
He knows our feeble frame. '

2 He knows we are but dust,
Scattered by every breath;
His anger, like a rising wind,
Can send us swift to death.

3 Our days are as the grass,
Or like the morning flower;
If one sharp blast sweeps o'er the field,
It withers in an hour.

4 But Thy compassions, Lord,
To endless years endure;
And children's children ever find
Thy words of promise sure.

651

1 Come, Holy Spirit, come,
With energy divine,
And on this poor benighted soul
With beams of mercy shine.

2 Melt, melt this frozen heart;
This stubborn will subdue;
Each evil passion overcome,
And form me all anew.

3 Mine will the profit be,
But Thine shall be the praise;
And unto Thee I will devote
The remnant of my days.

ROWSON. S. M.

AFFETUOSO.　　　　　　　　　　PLEYEL. (Chants Chrétiens.)

My Maker and my King, To Thee my all I owe; Thy sovereign bounty

is the spring Whence all my blessings flow, Whence all my blessings flow.

652

2 The creature of Thy hand,
On Thee alone I live;
My God, Thy benefits demand
More praise than I can give.

3 O let Thy grace inspire
My soul with strength divine;
Let all my powers to Thee aspire,
And all my days be Thine.

653

1 To bless Thy chosen race,
In mercy, Lord, incline;
And cause the brightness of Thy face
On all Thy saints to shine;—

2 That so Thy wondrous way
May through the world be known;
While distant lands their homage pay,
And Thy salvation own.

3 Let all the nations join
To celebrate Thy fame;
And all the world, O Lord, combine
To praise Thy glorious name.

654

1 GREAT GOD, accept a heart
That pants to sing Thy praise;
Thou, who without beginning art
And without end of days:

2 Thy goodness is displayed,
On all Thy works impressed;
Thou lovest all Thy hands have made,
But man Thou lovest best.

3 Gracious art Thou to all
Who truly turn to Thee;
O hear me, then, for pardon call,
And show Thy grace to me:

4 Through mercy reconciled,
For Jesus' sake forgiven;
Receive, O Lord, Thy favored child,
To sing Thy praise in heaven.

655

1 DEAR Saviour, we are Thine
By everlasting bonds;
Our names, our hearts, we would resign;
Our souls are in Thy hands.

2 To Thee we still would cleave,
With ever-growing zeal:
If millions tempt us Christ to leave,
O let them ne'er prevail.

3 Thy Spirit shall unite
Our souls to Thee our Head;
Shall form us to Thy image bright,
That we Thy paths may tread.

4 Since Christ and we are one,
'Why should we doubt or fear ;
If He in heaven hath fixed His throne,
He'll fix His members there.

656

1 LORD in the strength of grace
With a glad heart and free,
Myself, my residue of days,
I consecrate to Thee.

2 Thy ransomed servant, I,
Restore to Thee Thine own;
And from this moment live or die,
To serve my God alone.

ANDANTE.

DR. LOWELL MASON.

Our Heavenly Fa - ther calls, And Christ in - vites us near;

The Spi - rit makes our friend-ship sweet, And our com - mu - nion dear.

657

2 God pities all our griefs;
He pardons every day;
Almighty to protect our souls,
And wise to guide our way.

3 How large His bounties are!
What various stores of good,
Diffused from our Redeemer's hand,
And purchased with His blood!

4 Jesus, our living Head,
We bless Thy faithful care;
Our Advocate before the throne,
And our Forerunner there.

658

1 Jesus, my truth, my way,
My sure unerring light,
On Thee my feeble steps I stay,
Which Thou wilt guide aright.

2 My wisdom and my guide,
My counsellor Thou art;
O never let me leave Thy side,
Or from Thy paths depart.

3 O make me all like Thee,
Before I hence remove;
Settle, confirm, and 'stablish me,
And build me up in love.

4 Let me Thy witness live,
When sin is all destroyed;
And then my spotless soul receive,
And take me home to God.

659

1 Ah, how shall fallen man
Be just before his God?
If he contend in righteousness,
We sink beneath His rod.

2 If He our ways should mark
With strict inquiring eyes,
Could we for one of thousand faults
A just excuse devise?

3 The mountains, in Thy wrath,
Their ancient seats forsake;
The trembling earth deserts her place,—
Her rooted pillars shake.

4 Ah, how shall guilty man
Contend with such a God?
None—none can meet Him, and escape,
But through the Saviour's blood.

660

1 As strangers here below,
With various woes oppressed,
We must through tribulation go
To our eternal rest.

2 Thus Christ our glorious Head,
Ascended to His throne:—
Why should His servants fear to tread
The way their Lord hath gone?

3 The path to glory lies
Through conflict and distress:—
But joyful we at length shall rise,
The kingdom to possess.

How ten - der is Thy hand, O Thou most gracious Lord!

Af - flictions came at Thy command, And left us at Thy word.

661

2 How gentle was the rod
That chastened us for sin!
How soon we found a smiling God
Where deep distress had been!

3 A Father's hand we felt,
A Father's love we knew:
'Mid tears of penitence we knelt,
And found his promise true.

4 Now will we bless the Lord,
And in his strength confide:
Jehovah ever be adored,
There is no God beside.

662

1 OUR children Thou dost claim,
O Lord our God, as Thine;
Ten thousand blessings to Thy name,
For goodness so divine.

2 Thee let the fathers own,
Thee let the sons adore;
Joined to the Lord in solemn vows,
To be forgot no more.

3 How great Thy mercies, Lord!
How plenteous is Thy grace,
Which, in the promise of Thy love,
Includes our rising race.

4 Our offspring, still Thy care,
Shall own their father's God ;
To latest times Thy blessings share,
And sound Thy praise abroad.

663

1 WHEN on the brink of death
My trembling soul shall stand,
Waiting to pass that awful flood,
Great God! at Thy command ;—

2 When every scene of life
Stands ready to depart ;
And the last sigh that shakes the frame
Shall rend this bursting heart;—

3 Thou Source of joy supreme,
Whose arm alone can save,—
Dispel the darkness that surrounds
The entrance to the grave.

4 Lay Thy supporting hand
Beneath my sinking head;
And with a ray of love divine
Illume my dying bed.

5 Leaning on Jesus' breast,
May I resign my breath ;
And in his kind embraces lose
The bitterness of death.

664

1 ALL yesterday is gone;
To-morrow's not our own;
O sinner, come, without delay,
And bow before the throne.

2 O hear God's voice to-day,
And harden not your heart;
To-morrow, with a frown, he may
Pronounce the word,—Depart.

With joy we lift our eyes To those bright realms a - bove;

That glorious temple in the skies Where dwells e - ter - nal Love.

665

2 Before Thy throne we bow,
O Thou almighty King;
Here we present the solemn vow,
And hymns of praise we sing.

3 While in Thy house we kneel,
With trust and holy fear,
Thy mercy and Thy truth reveal,
And lend a gracious ear.

4 Lord, teach our hearts to pray,
And tune our lips to sing;
Nor from thy presence cast away
The sacrifice we bring.

666

1 ENTHRONED is Jesus now,
Upon his heavenly seat;
The kingly crown is on his brow,
The saints are at His feet.

2 In shining white they stand,—
A great and countless throng;
A palmy sceptre in each hand,
On every lip a song.

3 They sing the Lamb of God,
Once slain on earth for them;
The Lamb, through whose atoning blood,
Each wears his diadem.

4 Thy grace, O Holy Ghost,
Thy blessed help supply,
That we may join that radiant host,
Triumphant in the sky.

667

1 A CONQUEROR am I,
Through Him who died for me;
My crown I see with joyful eye
Across the stormy sea.

2 Weak is mine arm to meet
The shock of haughty foes;
But kneeling at my Saviour's feet,
No fear my spirit knows.

3 There, sheltered by the wing
Of His unbounded love,
While His eternal might I sing
He cheers me from above.

4 So with a conqueror's song
I march along the way: [throng,
And soon shall meet the blood-bought
And reign through endless day.

668

1 My soul, with joy attend,
While Jesus silence breaks;
No angel's harp such music yields,
As what my Shepherd speaks:

2 "I know my sheep," he cries,
"My soul approves them well:
Vain is the treacherous world's disguise,
And vain the rage of hell.

3 "I freely feed them now
With tokens of my love;
But richer pastures I prepare,
And sweeter streams above."

4 Enough, my gracious Lord,
Let faith triumphant cry;
My heart can on this promise live,
Can on this promise die.

I'll praise my Maker while I've breath, And when my voice is lost in death,

Praise shall employ my nobler powers; My days of praise shall ne'er be past,

While life, and thought, and be-ing last, Or im-mor-tal-i-ty en-dures.

669

2 Happy the man whose hopes rely
  On Israel's God; He made the sky,
    And earth, and seas, with all their train;
His truth forever stands secure;
He saves the oppressed, He feeds the poor:
    And none shall find His promise vain.

3 I'll praise Him while He lends me breath.
  And when my voice is lost in death,
    Praise shall employ my nobler powers;
My days of praise shall ne'er be past,
While life, and thought, and being last,
  Or immortality endures.

670

1 Of all the thoughts of God, that are
Borne inward unto souls afar,
  Along the Psalmist's music deep,
Now tell me if that any is,
For gift or grace, surpassing this—
  "He giveth His beloved sleep."

2 His dews drop mutely on the hill,
His cloud above it saileth still,
  Though on its slope men toil and reap;
More softly than the dew is shed,
Or cloud is floated overhead,
  "He giveth His beloved sleep."

3 And friends, dear friends, when it shall be,
That this low breath is gone from me,
  When round my bier ye come to weep,
Let one, most loving of you all,
Say "Not a tear must o'er her fall;
  "He giveth His beloved sleep."

671

1 GREAT GOD, this sacred day of Thine
Demands our soul's collected powers;
May we employ in work divine
These solemn, these devoted hours;
O, may our souls adoring own
The grace which calls us to Thy throne.

2 Hence, ye vain cares and trifles fly;
  Where God resides appear no more;
Omniscient God, Thy piercing eye
  Can every secret thought explore;
O, may Thy grace our hearts refine,
And fix our thoughts on things divine.

3 Thy Spirit's powerful aid impart;
  O, may Thy word, with life divine,
Engage the ear, and warm the heart;
  Then shall the day indeed be Thine;
Then shall our souls, adoring, own
The grace which calls us to Thy throne.

MODERATO.
H. BOND.

Let all the earth their voices raise To sing the choicest psalm of praise,

To sing and bless Jehovah's name; His glo-ry let the heathen know,

His wonders to the nations show, And all His saving works proclaim.

672

2 He framed the globe, He built the sky,
He made the shining worlds on high,
  And reigns complete in glory there:
His beams are majesty and light;
His beauties, how divinely bright!
His temple, how divinely fair!

3 Come the great day, the glorious hour,
When earth shall feel His saving power,
  And barbarous nations fear His name:
Then shall the race of man confess
The beauty of His holiness, .
And in His courts His grace proclaim.

673

1 THERE is a glorious land afar,
Beyond the brightest burning star,
  Where peace interminably reigns,—
Where soft and balmy breezes blow,
And golden rivers gently flow,
  And gladness smiles o'er all the plains.

2 No groveling thought, no treach'rous smile,
No word unkind, no act of guile,
  Will e'er disturb the sacred rest;
On every peaceful brow will shine
A living beauty, all divine,
  And love pervade the sinless breast.

674

1 THINK, mighty God, on feeble man;
How few his hours, how short his span !
  Short from the cradle to the grave;
Who can secure his vital breath
Against the bold demands of death,
  With skill to fly, or power to save?

2 Lord, shall it be forever said,
" The race of man was only made
  For sickness, sorrow, and the dust?"
Are not Thy servants, day by day,
Sent to their graves, and turned to clay ?
  Lord, where's Thy kindness to the just !

3 Hast Thou not promised to Thy Son
And all His seed a heavenly crown ?
  But flesh and sense indulge despair;
Forever blessed be the Lord,
That faith can read His holy word,
  And find a resurrection there.

4 Forever blessed be the Lord,
Who gives His saints a long reward
  For all their toil, reproach, and pain;
Let all below, and all above,
Join to proclaim Thy wondrous love,
  And each repeat their loud amen.

NASHVILLE. L. P. M. From an old Melody,
by Dr. LOWELL MASON.

I love the vol - ume of Thy word ; ·What light and joy those leaves afford

CLOSE.

D. S.

To souls be-night - ed and distressed ! ⎰ Thy precepts guide my doubtful way, ⎱
Thy promise leads my heart to rest. ⎰ Thy fear for - bids my feet to stray, ⎱

D. S.

675

2 Thy threatenings wake my slumbering
eyes,
And warn me where my danger lies;
But 'tis Thy blessed Gospel, Lord,
That makes my guilty conscience clean,
Converts my soul, subdues my sin,
And gives a free, but large reward.

3 Who knows the errors of his thoughts ?
My God forgive my secret faults,
And from presumptuous sins restrain:
Accept my poor attempts of praise,
That I have read Thy book of grace,
And book of nature not in vain.

676

1 WITH grateful hearts, with joyful tongues,
To God we raise united songs;
His power and mercy we proclaim;
This land through every age shall own
Jehovah here has fixed His throne,
And triumph in His mighty name.

2 Long as the moon her course shall run,
Or man behold the circling sun,
O, still may God amid us reign;
Crown our just counsels with success,
With peace and joy our borders bless,
And all our sacred rights maintain.

677

1 JUDGES, who rule the world by laws,
Will ye despise the righteous cause,
When the oppressed before you stands

Dare ye condemn the righteous poor,
And let rich sinners go secure,
While gold and greatness bribe your
hands ?

2 Have ye forgot, or never knew,
That God will judge the judges, too ?
High in the heavens His justice reigns;
Yet you invade the rights of God,
And send your bold decrees abroad,
To bind the conscience in your chains!

3 Th' Almighty thunders from the sky—
Their grandeur melts, their titles die—
They perish like dissolving frost:
As empty chaff, when whirlwinds rise,
Before the sweeping tempest flies,
So shall their hopes and names be lost.

4 Thus shall the vengeance of the Lord
Safety and joy to saints afford;
And all that hear shall join and say—
"Sure there's a God that rules on high,'
A God that hears his children cry,
And will their sufferings well repay."

678

Now to the great and sacred Three,
The Father, Son, and Spirit, be
Eternal praise and glory given,
Through all the worlds where God is known,
By all the angels near the throne,
And all the saints in earth and heaven.

DR. LOWELL MASON.

That warning voice, O sinner, hear; And while salvation lingers near, The

heav'nly call obey; { Flee from destruction's downward path, }
{ Flee from the threat'ning storm of wrath } That rises o'er thy way.

679

2 Soon night comes on, with thickening
   shade;
The tempest hovers o'er thy head,
  The winds their fury pour;
The lightnings rend the earth and skies,
The thunders roar, the flames arise;
  What terrors fill that hour!

3 That warning voice, O sinner, hear,
Whose accents linger on thine ear;
  Thy footsteps now retrace;
Renounce thy sins, and be forgiven;
Believe, become an heir of heaven,
  And sing redeeming grace.

680

1 WHEN, Lord, to this our western land,
Led by Thy providential hand,
  Our wandering fathers came,
Their ancient homes, their friends in youth,
Sent forth the heralds of Thy truth,
  To keep them in Thy name.

2 Then, through our solitary coast,
The desert features soon were lost,
  Thy temples there arose;
Our shores, as culture made them fair,
Were hallowed by Thy rites, by prayer,
  And blossomed as the rose.

3 And O, may we repay this debt
To regions solitary yet
  Within our spreading land;
There, brethren, from our common home,
Still westward, like our fathers, roam,
  Still guided by Thy hand.

4 Saviour, we own this debt of love;
O, shed Thy Spirit from above,
  To move each Christian breast,
Till heralds shall Thy truth proclaim,
And temples rise, to fix Thy name
  Through all our desert west.

681

1 SOFT are the fruitful showers that bring
The welcome promise of the spring;
  And soft the vernal gale;
Sweet the wild warblings of the grove,
The voice of nature and of love,
  That gladden every vale.

2 But softer in the mourner's ear
Sounds the mild voice of mercy near,
  That whispers sins forgiven;
And sweeter far the music swells
When to the raptured soul she tells
  Of peace and promised heaven.

3 Fair are the flowers that deck the ground;
And groves and gardens blooming round,
  Unnumbered charms unfold;
Bright is the sun's meridian ray,
And bright the beams of setting day,
  That robe the clouds in gold.

4 But far more fair the pious breast,
In richer robes of goodness dressed,
  Where heaven's own graces shine;
And brighter far the prospects rise,
That burst on faith's delighted eyes,
  From glories all divine.

O Thou that hear'st the prayer of faith, Wilt Thou not save a soul from death,

That casts it - self on Thee? I have no re - fuge of my own,

But fly to what my Lord hath done And suf - fered once for me.

682

2 Slain in the guilty sinner's stead,
His spotless righteousness I plead,
 And His availing blood:
Thy merit, Lord, my robe shall be;
Thy merit shall atone for me,
 And bring me near to God.

3 Then snatch me from eternal death;
The Spirit of adoption breathe;
 His consolations send;
By Him some word of life impart,
And sweetly whisper to my heart,
 "Thy Maker is thy Friend."

683

1 Thy mercy heard my infant prayer,
Thy love, with all a mother's care,
 . Sustained my childish days:
Thy goodness watched my ripening youth,
And formed my heart to love Thy truth,
 And filled my lips with praise.

2 Then even in age and grief, Thy name
Shall still my languid heart inflame,
 And bow my faltering knee:
Oh! yet this bosom feels the fire,
This trembling hand and drooping lyre
 Have yet a strain for Thee!

3 Yes! broken, tuneless, still, O Lord,
This voice transported shall record
 Thy goodness tried so long;
Till, sinking slow, with calm decay,
Its feeble murmurs melt away
 Into a seraph's song.

684

1 How happy is the pilgrim's lot!
How free from every anxious thought,
 From every worldly hope and fear!
Confined to neither court nor cell,
His soul disdains on earth to dwell—
 He only sojourns here.

2 This happiness in part is mine,
Already saved from low design,
 From every creature-love;
Blest with the scorn of finite good,
My soul is lightened of its load,
 And seeks the things above.

3 There is my house and portion fair:
My treasure and my heart are there,
 And my abiding home;
For me my elder brethren stay,
And angels beckon me away,
 And Jesus bids me come.

MODERATO.

Awaked by Si - nai's aw - ful sound, My soul in bonds of guilt I found, And knew not where to go; E - ter - nal truth did loud proclaim: "The sinner must be born again,' Or sink to endless woe.

685

2 When to the law I trembling fled,
It poured its curses on my head;
I no relief could find.
This fearful truth increased my pain,
"The sinner must be born again,"
And whelmed my tortured mind.

3 Again did Sinai's thunder roll,
And guilt lay heavy on my soul,
A vast, oppressive load;
Alas! I read and saw it plain,
"The sinner must be born again,"
Or drink the wrath of God.

4 But while I thus in anguish lay,
The bleeding Saviour passed that way,
My bondage to remove;
The sinner, once by justice slain,
Now by His grace is born again,
And sings redeeming love.

686

1 When Thou, my righteous Judge shalt come
To fetch Thy ransomed people home,
Shall I among them stand?
Shall such a worthless worm as I,
Who sometimes am afraid to die,
Be found at Thy right hand?

2 I love to meet among them now,
Before Thy gracious feet to bow,
Though vilest of them all:
But can I bear the piercing thought,
What if my name should be left out,
When Thou for them shalt call.

3 O Lord, prevent it by Thy grace;
Be Thou my only hiding-place,
In this the accepted day:
Thy pardoning voice, O let me hear,
To still my unbelieving fear;
Nor let me fall, I pray.

4 Let me among Thy saints be found,
Whene'er the archangel's trump shall
    To see Thy smiling face;   [sound,
Then loudest of the crowd I'll sing,
While heaven's resounding mansions ring
With shouts of sovereign grace.

687

To Father, Son, and Holy Ghost,
The God, whom heaven's triumphant host
    And saints on earth adore,
Be glory as in ages past,
As now it is, and so shall last,
    When time shall be no more.

My days, my weeks, my months and years Fly ra - pid as the whirling spheres Around the stead - y pole; Time, like the tide, its motion keeps, Flowing for - ev - er to the deeps, Where ceaseless ages roll.

688

2 The grave is near the cradle seen,
How swift the moments pass between
  And whisper as they fly—
Unthinking man remember this,
That, 'mid thy sublunary bliss,
  Thou soon must fade and die!

3 My soul attend the solemn call,
Thine earthly tent must quickly fall,
  And thou must take thy flight,
Beyond the vast ethereal blue,
To love and sing as angels do,
  Or sink in endless night.

4 But shall my soul be then extinct,
And cease to be, or cease to think?
  It cannot, cannot be:
Thou! my immortal, cannot die,
What wilt thou do, or whither fly,
  When death shall set thee free?

5 Will mercy then its arms extend?
Will Jesus be thy guardian friend?
  And heaven thy dwelling place?
Or shall insulting fiends appear,
To drag thee down to black despair,
  Beyond the reach of grace?

689

1 O Love divine, how sweet Thou art!
When shall I find my willing heart
  All taken up in Thee?
I thirst, I faint, I die to prove
The greatness of redeeming love,
  The love of Christ to me.

2 God only knows the love of God;
O that it now were shed abroad
  In this poor stony heart!
For this I sigh; for Thee I pine;
This only portion, Lord, be mine,
  Be mine the better part?

3 O that I could forever sit,
With Mary at the Master's feet!
  Be this my happy choice,
My only care, delight, and bliss,
My joy, my heaven on earth be this,
  To hear the Bridegroom's voice!

690

To Father, Son, and Holy Ghost,
Be praise amid the heavenly host,
  And in the church below;
From whom all creatures draw their breath,
By whom redemption blessed the earth,
  From whom all comforts flow.

The Lord in - to His gar - den comes, The spi - ces yield a

rich perfume, The lil - ies grow and thrive, The lil - ies grow and thrive;

Re - fresh - ing show'rs of grace di - vine, From Je - sus flow to

ev - 'ry vine, And make the dead re - vive, And make the dead re - vive.

691

2 This makes the dry and barren ground
In springs of water to abound,
And fruitful soil become;
The desert blossoms like the rose,
When Jesus conquers all His foes,
And makes His people one.

3 Soon we shall reign, and shout, and sing,
And make the upper regions ring,
When all the saints get home.
Come on, come on, my brethren dear,
Soon we shall meet together there;—
Our Jesus bids us come.

692

Lo, on a narrow neck of land,
'Twixt two unbounded seas I stand,
Secure, insensible:
A point of time, a moment's space,
Removes me to that heavenly place,
Or shuts me up in hell.

2 O God, my inmost soul convert,
And deeply on my thoughtless heart
Eternal things impress:
Give me to feel their solemn weight,
And tremble on the brink of fate,
And wake to righteousness.

ARIEL. C. P. M.

DR. LOWELL MASON.

MODERATO.

Oh, could I speak the match-less worth, Oh, could I sound the glo-ries forth, Which in my Saviour shine! I'd soar, and touch the heav'nly strings, And vie with Ga-briel while he sings In notes al-most di-vine, In notes al-most di-vine.

693

2 I'd sing the precious blood He spilt,
My ransom from the dreadful guilt
Of sin and wrath divine;
I'd sing His glorious righteousness,
In which all perfect, heavenly dress,
My soul shall ever shine.

3 I'd sing the characters He bears,
And all the forms of love He wears,
Exalted on His throne:
In loftiest songs of sweetest praise,
I would to everlasting days
Make all His glories known.

4 Well, the delightful day will come
When my dear Lord will bring me home,
And I shall see His face;
Then with my Saviour, Brother, Friend,
A blest eternity I'll spend,
Triumphant in His grace.

694

1 BEGIN, my soul, the exalted lay;
Let each enraptured thought obey,
And praise the Almighty's name;

Lo, heaven and earth, and seas and skies,
In one melodious concert rise,
To swell the inspiring theme.

2 Ye angels, catch the thrilling sound,
While all the adoring thrones around
His boundless mercy sing;
Let every listening saint above
Wake all the tuneful soul of love,
And touch the sweetest string.

3 Let every element rejoice;
Ye thunders, burst with awful voice
To Him who bids you roll;
His praise in softer notes declare,
Each whispering breeze of yielding air,
And breathe it to the soul.

4 Wake, all ye mounting tribes, and sing;
Ye plumy warblers of the spring,
Harmonious anthems raise
To Him who shaped your finer mould,
Who tipped your glittering wings with gold,
And tuned your voice to praise.

A. WILLIAMS.

How pleas - ant 'tis to see · Kin - dred and friends a - gree,

Each in his proper sta - tion move, And each ful - fil his part,

With sym - pa - thiz - ing heart, In all the cares of life and love!

695

2 Like fruitful showers of rain,
That water all the plain,
Descending from the neighboring hills,
Such streams of pleasure roll
Through every friendly soul,
Where love, like heavenly dew, distils.

696

1 THE Lord Jehovah reigns,
And royal state maintains,
His head with awful glories crowned;
Arrayed in robes of light,
Begirt with sovereign might,
And rays of majesty around.

2 Upheld by Thy commands,
The world securely stands;
And skies and stars obey Thy word;
Thy throne was fixed on high
Before the starry sky;
Eternal is Thy kingdom, Lord.

3 In vain the noisy crowd,
Like billows fierce and loud,
Against Thine empire rage and roar;

In vain, with angry spite,
The surly nations fight,
And dash like waves against the shore.

4 Let floods and nations rage,
And all their powers engage;
Let swelling tides assault the sky;
The terrors of Thy frown
Shall beat their madness down:
Thy throne forever stands on high.

5 Thy promises are true;
Thy grace is ever new:
There fixed, Thy church shall ne'er remove;
Thy saints, with holy fear,
Shall in Thy courts appear,
And sing Thine everlasting love.

697

To Father, Son, and Holy Ghost,
The God, whom heaven's triumphant host
And saints on earth adore,
Be glory as in ages past,
As now it is, and so shall last,
When time shall be no more.

PETERS. S. P. M.

ALLEGRO.   Dr. Lowell Mason.

How pleased and blessed was I To hear the peo - ple cry,

"Come, let us seek our God to - day!" Yes, with a cheerful zeal,

We haste to Zi - on's hill, And there our vows and hon - ors pay.

698

2 Zion, thrice happy place!
    Adorned with wondrous grace,
And walls of strength embrace thee round;
    In thee our tribes appear,
    To pray, and praise, and hear
The sacred gospel's joyful sound.

3 Here David's greater Son
    Has fixed His royal throne;
He sits for grace and judgment here:
    He bids the saints be glad,
    He makes the sinner sad,
And humble souls rejoice with fear.

4 May peace attend thy gate,
    And joy within thee wait,
To bless the soul of every guest;
    The man who seeks thy peace,
    And wishes thine increase,
A thousand blessings on him rest.

5 My tongue repeats her vows,
    " Peace to this sacred house!"
For here my friends and kindred dwell;
    And since my glorious God
    Makes thee his blest abode,
My soul shall ever love thee well.

699

1 To your Creator, God,
    Your great Preserver, raise,
Ye creatures of His hand,
    Your highest notes of praise :
Let every voice proclaim His power,
His name adore, and loud rejoice.

2 Let every creature join
    To celebrate His name,
And all their various powers
    Assist th' exalted theme :
Let nature raise, from every tongue,
A general song of grateful praise.

3 But oh ! from human tongues
    Should nobler praises flow;
And every thankful heart
    With warm devotion glow;
Your voices raise above the rest;
Ye highly blest ! declare His praise.

4 Assist me, gracious God !
    My heart, my voice inspire;
Then shall I grateful join
    The universal choir :
Thy grace can raise my heart, my tongue,
And tune my song to lively praise.

ANIMATO. T. CLARK.

Join all the glo-rious names Of wis-dom, love, and power, That

ev-er mor-tals knew, That an-gels ev-er bore; All are too

mean to speak His worth— Too mean to set my Sa-viour forth.

700

2 Great Prophet of my God,
　My tongue would bless Thy name;
By Thee the joyful news
　Of our salvation came:
The joyful news　| Of hell subdued,
Of sins forgiven, | And Peace with Heaven.

3 Jesus, My great High Priest,
　Offered His blood and died;
My guilty conscience seeks
　No sacrifice beside.
His powerful blood | And now it pleads
Did once atòne, | Before the throne.

4 My dear, almighty Lord,
　My Conqueror and my King,
Thy sceptre and Thy sword,
　Thy reigning grace I sing.
Thine is the power; | In willing bonds
Behold, I sit | Beneath Thy feet.

701

1 Blow ye the trumpet, blow,
　The gladly solemn sound;
Let all the nations know,
　To earth's remotest bound,
The year of jubilee is come;
Return, ye ransomed sinners, home.

2 Jesus, our great High Priest,
　Hath full atonement made;
Ye weary spirits, rest;
　Ye mournful souls, be glad;
The year of jubilee is come;
Return, ye ransomed sinners, home.

3 Extol the Lamb of God,
　The all-atoning Lamb;
Redemption in His blood
　Throughout the world proclaim;
The year of jubilee is come;
Return, ye ransomed sinners, home.

702

1 Shall hymns of grateful love
　Through heaven's high arches ring,
And all the hosts above
　Their songs of triumph sing;
And shall we not take up the strain,
And send the echo back again?

2 Shall they adore the Lord,
　Who bought them with His blood,
And all the love record
　That led them home to God;
And shall not we take up the strain,
And send the echo back again?

DARWELL. H. M.

ALLEGRO.

REV. W. DARWELL.

Gird on Thy conq'ring sword, As-cend Thy shi-ning car, And march, al-migh-ty Lord, To wage Thy ho-ly war. Be-fore His wheels, In glad sur-prise, Ye val-leys, rise, And sink, ye hills.

703

2 Fair Truth, and smiling Love,
  And injured Righteousness,
In Thy retinue move,
  And seek from Thee redress:
Thou in their cause | And far and wide
Shalt prosperous ride, | Dispense Thy laws.

3 Before Thine awful face
  Millions of foes shall fall;
· The captives of Thy grace,
  The grace which conquers all.
The world shall know, | What wondrous things
Great King of Kings, | Thine arm can do.

4 Here to my willing soul
  Bend Thy triumphant way;
Here every foe control,
  And all Thy power display.
My heart, Thy throne, | Bows low to Thee
Blest Jesus, see, | To Thee alone.

704

1 FAR as the isles extend,
  To the vast ocean's bound,
Let Kings to Jesus bend,
  And pour their offerings round;
Arabia raise | And Afric join
The song divine, | To exalt His praise.

2 All princes shall adore,
  And gifts and honors bring,
To hail the Saviour's power,
  To crown Immanuel King:
Remotest lands | And earth obey
Shall homage pay, | His high commands.

705

1 COME, let our voices join
  In one glad song of praise;
To God, the God of love,
  Our thankful hearts we'll raise;
To God alone | Our earliest and
All praise belongs, | Our latest songs.

2 Within these hallowed walls
  Our wandering feet are brought,
Where prayer and praise ascend,
  And heavenly truths are taught;
To God alone | Let young and old
Your offerings bring; | His praises sing.

3 Lord, let this work of love
  Be crowned with full success;
Let thousands yet unborn
  Thy sacred name here bless:
To Thee, O Lord, | Shall rise throughout
All praise to Thee, | Eternity.

MODERATO.

Ye dy - ing sons of men, Immersed in sin and woe,)
The gos - pel calls a - gain, Its mes - sage is to you :)

Ye per - ish - ing and guilt - y, come; In mer - cy's

arms there yet is room, In mer - cy's arms there yet is room.

706

2 No longer now delay,
　Nor vain excuses frame,
Christ bids you come to-day,
　The poor, and blind, and lame:
All things are ready, sinners, come;
In mercy's arms there yet is room.

3 Compelled by bleeding love,
　Ye wandering souls, draw near;
He calls you from above,
　His melting accents hear:
O, whosoever will, may come;
In mercy's arms there yet is room.

707

1 WHERE is my Saviour now,
　Whose smiles I once possessed?
Till He return, I bow,
　By heaviest grief oppressed:
My days of happiness are gone,
And I am left to weep alone.

2 Where can the mourner go,
　And tell his tale of grief?
Ah! who can soothe his woe,
　And give him sweet relief?
Earth cannot heal the wounded breast,
Or give the troubled sinner rest.

3 Jesus ! Thy smiles impart;
　My dearest Lord return,
And ease my wounded heart,
　And bid me cease to mourn:
Then shall this night of sorrow flee,
And peace and heaven be found in Thee.

708

1 SOVEREIGN of worlds above,
　And Lord of all below,
Thy faithfulness and love,
　Thy power and mercy show:
Fulfil Thy word: | Let heathens live
Thy spirit give; | And praise the Lord.

2 On lands that lie beneath
　Foul superstition's sway,
Whose horrid shades of death
　Admit no heavenly ray,
Blest Spirit! shine! | Dispel the gloom
Their hearts illume; | With light divine.

3 Father, who to Thy Son
　Thy steadfast word has given,
That through the earth shall run
　The news of peace with heaven;
Extend His fame; | And let the news
Thy grace diffuse, | The world reclaim.

196   BETHESDA. H. M.

MODERATO.   DR. GREEN.

Hark! what ce-les-tial sounds, What mu-sic fills the air! Soft warbling to the morn, It strikes the ravished ear: Now all is still; Now wild it floats, In tuneful notes, Loud, sweet and clear.

709

2 The angelic hosts descend,
With harmony divine;
See how from heaven they bend,
And in full chorus join:
"Fear not," say they; | Jesus, your King,
"Great joy we bring: | Is born to-day."

3 He comes, your souls to save
From death's eternal gloom;
To realms of bliss and light
He lifts you from the tomb.
Your voices raise, | Your songs unite
With sons of light; | Of endless praise.

4 Glory to God on high;
Ye mortals spread the sound,
And let your raptures fly
To earth's remotest bound;
For peace on earth, | To man is given,
From God in heaven, | At Jesus' birth.

710

1 YES, the Redeemer rose;
The Saviour left the dead;
And o'er our hellish foes
High raised His conquering head.
In wild dismay, | Fell to the ground,
The guards around | And sunk away.

2 Lo, the angelic bands
In full assembly meet,
To wait His high commands,
And worship at His feet;
Joyful they come, | From realms of day
And wing their way | To such a tomb.

3 Then back to heaven they fly,
And the glad tidings bear;
Hark! as they soar on high,
What music fills the air!
Their anthems say, | Hath left the dead
"Jesus, who bled, | He rose to-day."

4 Ye mortals catch the sound,
Redeemed by Him from hell,
And send the echo round
The globe on which you dwell;
Transported cry, | Hath left the dead;
"Jesus, who bled, | No more to die."

5 All hail, triumphant Lord,
Who sav'st us with Thy blood;
Wide be Thy name adored,
Thou rising, reigning God.
With Thee we rise, | And empires gain
With Thee we reign, | Beyond the skies.

A brok-en heart, O Lord, Thou nev-er wilt de-spise;
'Tis writ-ten in Thy word, This is the sa-cri-fice:
The sa-cri-fice that Thou wilt own— It is the brok-en
heart a-lone, It is the brok-en heart a-lone.

711

2 Break Thou my heart, O Lord;
  The rock within me break:
To tremble at Thy word,
  And at Thine anger quake:
Let me in deep contrition lie,
And heave the penitential sigh.

3 For mercy dwells with Thee;
  Compassion, all divine;
That mercy show to me;
  Be that compassion mine:
For sinners did not Jesus bleed ?
And Jesus' blood alone I plead.

712

1 Rise, gracious God! and shine
  In all Thy saving might,
And prosper each design
  To spread Thy glorious light:
Let healing streams of mercy flow,
That all the earth Thy truth may know.

2 Put forth Thy glorious power!
  The nations then will see,
And earth present her store,
  In converts born of Thee:
God, our own God, His church will bless,
And earth shall yield her full increase.

HADDAM. H. M.

ALLEGRO.

Dr. LOWELL MASON.

Rise, Sun of Glo - ry, rise! And chase those shades of night Which now obscure the skies And hide Thy sacred light. O! chase those dis - mal shades a - way, And bring the bright mil - len - nial day.

713

2 Why, Saviour! why conceal
    Thy beams of grace and love?
Those heavenly rays reveal,
    Which cheer the saints above!
Those rays shall chase the night away,
And bring the bright millennial day.

3 Yet Jesus, should Thy will
    Defer that sacred morn,
Hear our petition still,
    Nor leave the world forlorn:
Jesus! till that resplendent day,
Shine on our souls with powerful ray.

714

1 O Zion, tune thy voice,
    And raise thy hands on high;
Tell all the earth thy joys,
    And boast salvation nigh;
Cheerful in God | While rays divine
Arise and shine | Stream far abroad.

2 He gilds thy mourning face
    With beams that cannot fade;
His all-resplendent grace
    He pours around thy head:
The nations round | With lustre new
Thy form shall view, | Divinely crowned.

3 In honor to His name,
    Reflect that sacred light,
And loud that grace proclaim
    Which makes thy darkness bright;
Pursue his praise, | In worlds above
Till sovereign love | The glory raise.

4 There, on His holy hill
    A brighter sun shall rise,
And with his radiance fill•
    Those fairer, purer skies:
While, round His throne, | In nobler spheres
Ten thousand stars | His influence own.

715

1 JESUS, at Thy command,
    I launch into the deep,
And leave my native land,
    Where sin lulls all asleep.
For Thee I would the world resign,
And sail to heaven with Thee and Thine

2 Thou art my pilot—wise,
    My compass is Thy word:
My soul each storm defies,
    While I have such a Lord;
I'll trust Thy faithfulness and power,
To save me in the trying hour.

LENOX. H. M.

CON SPIRITO.

EDSON.

A - rise, my soul, a - rise; Shake off thy guil - ty fears; The bleed-ing sa - cri-

fice In my be - half ap - pears; Be - fore the throne my

Be - fore the throne my sure - ty stands, Be-

surety stands, Be - fore the throne my surety stands, My name is writ - ten on His hands.

fore the throne my surety stands, My name........ is writ - - - ten on His hands.

716

2 He ever lives above,
For me to intercede;
His all-redeeming love,
His precious blood to plead;
His blood atoned for all our race,
And sprinkles now the throne of grace.

3 Five bleeding wounds He bears,
Received on Calvary;
They pour effectual prayers,
They strongly speak for me.
Forgive him, O, forgive, they cry,
Nor let that ransomed sinner die.

4 The Father hears Him pray,
His dear anointed One;
He cannot turn away
The presence of His Son;
His Spirit answers to the blood,
And tells me I am born of God.

5 My God is reconciled;
His pardoning voice I hear;
He owns me for His child;
I can no longer fear;
With confidence I now draw nigh,
And Father! Abba, Father! cry.

717

1 YE tribes of Adam, join
With heaven, and earth, and seas,
And offer notes divine
To your Creator's praise.
Ye holy throng | In worlds of light,
Of angels bright, | Begin the song.

2 Thou sun with dazzling rays,
And moon that rul'st the night,
Shine to your Maker's praise,
With stars of twinkling light.
His power declare, | And clouds that fly
Ye floods on high, | In empty air.

3 The shining worlds above
In glorious order stand;
Or in swift courses move,
By His supreme command.
He spake the word, | From nothing came
And all their frame | To praise the Lord.

4 Let all the nations fear
The God that rules above;
He brings His people near,
And makes them taste His love.
While earth and sky | His saints shall raise
Attempt His praise, | His honors high.

LISCHER. H. M.

CONSPIRITO

From a German Tune,
by DR. LOWELL MASON.

Re-joice! the Lord is King; Your Lord and King a-dore;
Mor-tals, give thanks and sing, And tri-umph e-vermore;

Lift up your hearts, Lift up your voice, Re-joice, a-gain I

say, re-joice, Re-joice, a-gain I say, re-joice.

718

2 Jesus, the Saviour reigns.
 The God of truth and love:
When He had purged our stains,
 He took His seat above;
Lift up your hearts, | Rejoice again
Lift up your voice; | I say, rejoice.

3 His kingdom cannot fail;
 He rules o'er earth and heaven;
The keys of death and hell
 Are to our Jesus given;
Lift up your hearts, | Rejoice, again
Lift up your voice; | I say, rejoice.

4 He sits at God's right hand,
 Till all His foes submit,
And bow to His command,
 And fall beneath His feet;
Lift up your hearts, | Rejoice, again
Lift up your voice; | I say, rejoice.

5 He all His foes shall quell,
 Shall all our sins destroy,.
And every bosom swell
 With pure, seraphic joy;
Lift up your hearts, | Rejoice, again
Lift up your voice; | I say, rejoice.

719

1 WELCOME, delightful morn;
 Thou day of sacred rest,
I hail thy kind return :
 Lord, make these moments blessed :
From the low train | I soar to reach
Of mortal toys, | Immortal joys.

2 Now may the King descend,
 And fill His throne of grace;
Thy sceptre, Lord, extend,
 While saints address Thy face:
Let sinners feel | And learn to know
Thy quickened word, | And fear the Lord.

3 Descend, celestial Dove,
 With all Thy quickening powers;
Display the Saviour's love,
 And bless the sacred hours :
Then shall my soul | Nor Sabbath days
New life obtain, | Be spent in vain.

720

To God the Father's throne
 Your highest honors raise;
Glory to God the Son;
 To God the Spirit praise;
With all our powers, eternal King,
Thy name we sing, while faith adores.

MODERATO.

Friend af-ter friend de-parts; Who hath not lost a friend? There is no

u-nion here of hearts That finds not here an end: Were this frail

world our on-ly rest, Liv-ing or dy-ing, none were blest.

721

2 Beyond the flight of time,
Beyond this vail of death,
There surely is some blessed clime
Where life is not a breath,
Nor life's affections transient fire,
Whose sparks fly upward to expire.

3 There is a world above,
Where parting is unknown;
A whole eternity of love,
Formed for the good alone;
And faith beholds the dying here
Translated to that happier sphere.

722

1 FAITH is the polar star
That guides the Christian's way,
Directs his wanderings from afar
To realms of endless day;
It points the course | And safely leads
Where'er he roam, | The pilgrim home.

2 Faith is the rainbow's form
Hung on the brow of heaven,
The glory of the passing storm,
The pledge of mercy given;
It is the bright | Thro' which the saints
Triumphal arch | To glory march.

3 The faith that works by love,
And purifies the heart,
A foretaste of the joys above
To mortals can impart;
It bears us through | And triumphs in
This earthly strife, | Immortal life.

723

1 LORD of the worlds above,
How pleasant and how fair
The dwellings of Thy love,
Thy earthly temples are!
To thine abode | With warm desires,
My heart aspires | To see my God.

2 The sparrow for her young
With pleasure seeks a nest,
And wandering swallows long
To find their wonted rest;
My spirit faints, | To rise and dwell
With equal zeal, | Among Thy saints.

3 O happy souls that pray
Where God appoints to hear,
O happy men that pay
Their constant service there:
They praise Thee still | That love the way
And happy they | To Zion's hill.

VIGOROSO.

Christ, the Lord, is risen to - day,   Sons of men and an - gels say;

Raise your joys and triumphs high!   Sing, ye heav'ns, and earth reply.

724

2 Love's redeeming work is done,
Fought the fight, the battle won;
Lo, the sun's eclipse is o'er;
Lo, he sets in blood no more.

3 Vain the stone, the watch, the seal;
Christ has burst the gates of hell;
Death in vain forbids His rise;
Christ hath opened paradise.

4 Lives again our glorious King;
"Where, O Death, is now thy sting?"
Once He died our souls to save;
"Where's thy victory, boasting Grave?"

5 Soar we now where Christ has led,
Following our exalted Head;
Made like Him, like Him we rise;
Ours the cross, the grave, the skies.

725

1 HARK! the song of Jubilee,
Loud as mighty thunders roar,
Or the fulness of the sea
. When it breaks upon the shore.

2 Hallelujah! for the Lord
God omnipotent shall reign;
Hallelujah! let the word
Echo round the earth and main.

3 Hallelujah! hark, the sound
From the centre to the skies,
Wakes above, beneath, around,
All creation's harmonies.

4 See! Jehovah's banner furled,
Sheath'd His sword—He speaks, 'tis done,
And the kingdoms of this world
Are the kingdom of His Son.

5 He shall reign from pole to pole,
With illimitable sway,
He shall reign, when, like a scroll,
Yonder heavens have passed away:

6 Then the end;—beneath His rod
Man's last enemy shall fall:
Hallelujah! Christ in God,
God in Christ, is all in all.

726

1 WAKE the song of jubilee;
Let it echo o'er the sea;
Now is come the promised hour;
Jesus reigns with sovereign power.

2 All ye nations, join and sing,
"Christ of lords and kings is King;"
Let it sound from shore to shore,
"Jesus reigns forevermore."

3 Now the desert lands rejoice,
And the islands join their voice;
. Yea, the whole creation sings,
"Jesus is the King of kings."

727

FATHER, Son and Holy Ghost,
One in Three, and Three in One,
As by the celestial host,
Let Thy will on earth be done:
Praise by all to Thee be given,
Glorious Lord of earth and heaven.

DOLCE.

Come, said Je - sus' sa - cred voice, Come, and make my paths your choice;

I will guide you to your home; Wea - ry pilgrim, hith - er come!

728

2 Thou, who, homeless and forlorn,
Long hast borne the proud world's scorn,
Long hast roamed the barren waste,
Weary wanderer, hither haste.

3 Ye who, tossed on beds of pain,
Seek for ease, but seek in vain;
Ye, by fiercer anguish torn,
In remorse for guilt who mourn :—

4 Hither come! for here is found
Balm that flows for every wound;
Peace that ever shall endure,
Rest eternal, sacred, sure.

729

1 HOLY Ghost, with light divine,
Shine upon this heart of mine;
Chase the shades of night away;
Turn the darkness into day.

2 Holy Ghost, with power divine,
Cleanse this guilty heart of mine;
Long has sin, without control,
Held dominion o'er my soul.

3 Holy Ghost, with joy divine,
Cheer this saddened heart of mine;
Bid my many woes depart;
Heal my wounded, bleeding heart.

4 Holy Spirit, all divine,
Dwell within this heart of mine;
Cast down every idol throne;
Reign supreme, and reign alone.

730

1 To Thy pastures fair and large,
Heavenly Shepherd, lead Thy charge,
And my couch with tenderest care,
'Mid the springing grass prepare.

2 When I faint with summer's heat,
Thou shalt guide my weary feet
To the streams that, still and slow,
Through the verdant meadows flow.

3 Safe the dreary vale I tread,
By the shades of death o'erspread,
With Thy rod and staff supplied,
This my guard—and that my guide.

4 Constant to my latest end,
Thou my footsteps shalt attend;
And shalt bid Thy hallowed dome
Yield me an eternal home.

731

1 CAST thy burden on the Lord;
Lean thou only on His word;
Ever will He be thy stay,
Though the heavens shall melt away.

2 Ever in the raging storm,
Thou shalt see His cheering form,
Hear His pledge of coming aid :
" It is I, be not afraid."

3 Cast thy burden at His feet;
Linger near His mercy-seat:
He will lead thee by the hand
Gently to the better land.

4 He will gird thee by His power,
In thy weary, fainting hour;
Lean, then, loving, on His word;
Cast thy burden on the Lord.

MARTYN. 7s.

DIVOTO.

S. B. MARSH

Ma - ry . to her Saviour's tomb   Hast - ed   at   the   ear - ly
Spice she bro't, and   sweet perfume,   But the Lord she loved was
D. C. Shedding tears, a   plenteous flood,   For her heart sup - plied her

FINE.

D. C.

dawn; }   { For   a   while she   weep - ing   stood, }
gone : }   { Struck with sor - row   and   sur - prise, }
eyes.

732

2 Grief and sighing quickly fled,
   When she heard His welcome voice;
Just before she thought Him dead,
   Now He bids her heart rejoice;
What a change His word can make,
Turning darkness into day !
You who weep for Jesus' sake
He will wipe your tears away.

3 He who came to comfort her,
   When she thought her all was lost,
Will for your relief appear,
   Though you now are tempest-tossed,
On His word your burden cast,
   On His love your thoughts employ;
Weeping for awhile may last,
But the morning brings the joy.

733

1 Who are these arrayed in white,
   Brighter than the noon-day sun?
Foremost of the sons of light:
   Nearest the eternal throne ?
These are they that bore the cross;
Nobly for their Master stood;
Sufferers in His righteous cause;
Followers of the dying God.

2 Out of great distress they came:
   Washed their robes, by faith, below,
In the blood of yonder Lamb—
   Blood that washes white as snow;
Therefore are they next the throne;
Serve their Maker day and night;
God resides among his own,
God doth in his saints delight.

734

1 LORD, what offering shall we bring,
   At Thine altars when we bow ?
Hearts, the pure, unsullied spring,
   Whence the kind affections flow;
Soft compassion's feeling soul,
   By the melting eye expressed;
Sympathy, at whose control
Sorrow leaves the wounded breast;

2 Willing hands to lead the blind,
   Bind the wounded, feed the poor;
Love, embracing all our kind;
   Charity, with liberal store :—
Teach us, O Thou heavenly King,
Thus to show our grateful mind,
Thus th' accepted offering bring,
Love to Thee and all mankind.

735

1 'Tis a point I long to know;
   Oft it causes anxious thought :
Do I love the Lord, or no ?
   Am I His, or am I not?
Could my heart so hard remain,
Prayer a task a burden prove,
Every trifle give me pain,
   If I knew a Saviour's love?

2 Lord, decide the doubtful case,
   Thou who art Thy people's Sun;
Shine upon Thy work of grace,
   If it be indeed begun.
Let me love Thee more and more,
   If I love at all, I pray;
If I have not loved before,
   Help me to begin to-day.

Soft - ly glides the stream of life   Oft a - long the flow'ry vale;

Or im - petuous down the cliff   Rushing roars when storms assail.

736

2 'Tis an ever-varied flood,
  Always rolling to its sea,
Slow, or quick, or mild, or rude,
  Tending to Eternity.

737

1 Shepherd of Thy little flock,
  Lead me to the shadowing rock,
Where the richest pasture grows, .
  Where the living water flows.

2 By that pure and silent stream,
  Sheltered from the scorching beam,
Shepherd, Saviour, Guardian, Guide,
  Keep me ever near Thy side.

738

1 When, my Saviour, shall I be
  Perfectly resigned to Thee?
Poor and vile in my own eyes,
  Only in Thy wisdom wise?

2 Only Thee content to know,
  Ignorant of all below?
Only guided by Thy light?
  Only mighty in Thy might?

3 Fully in my life express
  All the heights of holiness;
Sweetly let my spirit prove
  All the depths of humble love.

739

1 Sweet the time, exceeding sweet,
When the saints together meet,
When the Saviour is the theme,
When they join to sing of Him.

2 Sing we then eternal love,
  Such as did the Father move;
He beheld the world undone,
Loved the world, and gave His Son.

3 Sing the Son's amazing love;
  How He left the realms above,
Took our nature, and our place,
Lived and died to save our race.

4 Sing we too the Spirit's love;
  With our wretched hearts He strove,
Filled our minds with grief and fear, ·
Brought the precious Saviour near.

5 Sweet the place, exceeding sweet,
  Where the saints in glory meet,
Where the Saviour's still the theme,
  Where they see and sing of Him.

740

1 Softly fades the twilight ray
  Of the holy Sabbath-day;
Gently as life's setting sun
  When the Christian's course is run.

2 Night her solemn mantle spreads
  O'er the earth, as daylight fades;
All things tell of calm repose
  At the holy Sabbath's close.

3 Still the Spirit lingers near
  Where the evening worshipper
Seeks communion with the skies,
  Pressing onward to the prize.

4 Saviour, may our Sabbaths be
  Days of peace and joy in Thee,
Till in heaven our souls repose,
  Where the Sabbath ne'er shall close.

GERMAN.

Ho - ly, ho - ly, ho - ly Lord!   Be Thy glorious name adored;

Lord! Thy mercies nev - er fail;   Hail, ce - les - tial goodness, hail!

741

2 Though unworthy, Lord, Thine ear,
Deign our humble songs to hear;
Purer praise we hope to bring,
When around Thy throne we sing.

3 While on earth ordained to stay,
Guide our footsteps in Thy way;
Then on high we'll joyful raise
Songs of everlasting praise.

4 Lord! Thy mercies never fail;
Hail, celestial goodness, hail!
Be Thy glorious name adored,
Holy, holy, holy Lord!

742

1 FAINT not, Christian! though the road
Leading to thy blest abode
Darksome be, and dangerous too,
Christ, thy Guide, will bring thee through.

2 Faint not, Christian! though the world
Has its hostile flag unfurled,
Hold the cross of Jesus fast;
Thou shalt overcome at last.

3 Faint not, Christian! though within
There's a heart so prone to sin,
Christ the Lord is over all;
He'll not suffer thee to fall.

4 Faint not, Christian! look on high;
See the harpers in the sky,
Patient wait, and thou wilt join
Chant with them of love divine.

743

1 FATHER of the human race,
Sanction with Thy heavenly grace
What on earth hath now been done,
That these twain be truly one.

2 One in sickness and in health,
One in poverty and wealth,
And as year rolls after year,
Each to other still more dear.

3 One in purpose, one in heart,
Till the mortal stroke shall part;
One in cheerful piety,
One forever, Lord, with Thee.

744

1 PEACE! the welcome sound proclaim
Dwell with rapture on the theme;
Loud, still louder swell the strain,
Peace on earth, good will to men.

2 Breezes, whispering soft and low,
Gently murmur as ye blow;
Breathe the sweet, celestial strain,
Peace on earth, good will to men.

3 Ocean's billows, far and wide
Rolling in majestic pride,
Loud, still louder swell the strain,
Peace on earth, good will to men.

4 Christians, who these blessings feel,
And in adoration kneel,
Loud, still louder swell the strain,
Praise to God, good will to men.

A. DOTT.

Lord, we come be - fore Thee now; At Thy feet we hum - bly bow;

O,. do not our suit dis - dain; Shall we seek Thee, Lord, in vain?

745

2 Lord, on Thee our souls depend;
In compassion now descend;
Fill our hearts with Thy rich grace;
Tune our lips to sing Thy praise.

3 In Thine own appointed way,
Now we seek Thee, here we stay;
Lord, we know not how to go,
Till a blessing Thou bestow.

4 Send some message from Thy word
That may joy and peace afford;
Let Thy Spirit now impart
Full salvation to each heart.

5 Comfort those who weep and mourn;
Let the time of joy return;
Those who are cast down lift up,
Make them strong in faith and hope.

6 Grant that all may seek, and find
Thee a gracious God and kind;
Heal the sick, the captive free;
Let us all rejoice in Thee.

746

1 Lord of hosts, to Thee we raise
Here a house of prayer and praise;
Thou Thy people's hearts prepare
Here to meet for praise and prayer.

2 Let the living here be fed
With Thy word, the heavenly bread;
Here in hope of glory blessed,
May the dead be laid to rest.

3 Here to Thee a temple stand,
While the sea shall gird the land;
Here reveal Thy mercy sure,
While the sun and moon endure.

4 Hallelujah! earth and sky
To the joyful sound reply;
Hallelujah! hence ascend
Prayer and praise till time shall end.

747

1 When thy mortal life is fled,
When the death-shades o'er thee spread,
When is finished thy career,
Sinner, where wilt thou appear?

2 When the world has passed away,
When draws near the judgment day,
When the awful trump shall sound,
Say, O, where wilt thou be found?

3 When the Judge descends in light,
Clothed in majesty and might,
When the wicked quail with fear,
Where, O, where wilt thou appear?

4 What shall soothe thy bursting heart,
When the saints and thou must part?
When the good with joy are crowned,
Sinner, where wilt thou be found?

5 While the Holy Ghost is nigh,
Quickly to the Saviour fly;
Then shall peace thy spirit cheer;
Then in heaven shalt thou appear.

748

Sing we to our God above
Praise eternal as His love:
Praise Him, all ye heavenly host —
Father, Son, and Holy Ghost.

208

LAMARTINE. 7s.

CHORAL.   NASON.

Je - sus, Shepherd of the sheep, Pow'rful is Thine arm to keep

All Thy flocks with saf - est care, Fed in pastures large and fair.

749

2 Thee their guide and guard they own;
Thee they love, and Thee alone:
Thee they follow day by day,
Fearful lest their feet should stray.

3 Lord, Thy helpless sheep behold;
Gather all unto Thy fold;
Gently lead the wanderers home;
Watch them, lest again they roam.

4 Bring Thy sheep, now far astray,
Lost in Satan's evil way;
Then, the fold and shepherd one,
We shall praise Thee round the throne.

750

1 HOLY Bible, book divine,
Precious treasure, thou art mine!
Mine, to tell me whence I came;
Mine, to teach me what I am;

2 Mine, to chide me when I rove;
Mine, to show a Saviour's love;
Mine art thou, to guide my feet;
Mine, to judge, condemn, acquit;

3 Mine, to comfort in distress;
If the Holy Spirit bless;
Mine, to show, by living faith,
How to triumph over death;

4 Mine, to tell of joys to come,
And the rebel sinner's doom;
O, thou precious book divine,
Precious treasure, thou art mine!

751

1 THEY who seek the throne of grace
Find that throne in every place;
If we live a life of prayer,
God is present every where.

2 In our sickness and our health,
In our want or in our wealth,
If we look to God in prayer,
God is present every where.

3 When our earthly comforts fail,
When the woes of life prevail,
'T is the time for earnest prayer;
God is present every where.

4 Then, my soul, in every strait,
To thy Father come and wait;
He will answer every prayer:
God is present every where.

752

1 "GIVE us room that we may dwell,"
Zion's children cry aloud:
See their numbers—how they swell!
How they gather like a cloud!

2 Oh, how bright the morning seems!
Brighter from so dark a night:
Zion is like one that dreams,
Filled with wonder and delight.

753

1 SHEPHERD of the ransomed flock,
Lead us to the shadowing rock,
Where the cooling waters flow,
Where the freshening pastures grow.

2 Grant, O Lord, that we may be
Ever glad to follow Thee;
And with thankful hearts rejoice,
When we hear Thy gracious voice.

ROCK OF AGES. 7s.

ROCK OF AGES. 7s.

ROCK OF AGES. 7s.

Dr. T. Hastings.

Rock of A-ges, cleft for me, Let me hide my-self in Thee;

D. C.—Be of sin the dou-ble cure, Cleanse me from its guilt and power.

Let the wa-ter and the blood, From Thy riv-en side which flowed,

754

2 Could my zeal no respite know,
   Could my tears forever flow,
   All for sin could not atone;
   Thou must save, and Thou alone;
   Nothing in my hand I bring;
   Simply to Thy cross I cling.

3 While I draw this fleeting breath,
   When my heart-strings break in death,
   When I soar to worlds unknown,
   See Thee on Thy judgment throne,
   Rock of Ages, cleft for me,
   Let me hide myself in Thee.

755

1 Go to dark Gethsemane,
   Ye that feel the tempter's power,
   Your Redeemer's conflict see,
   Watch with Him one bitter hour;
   Turn not from His griefs away,
   Learn of Jesus Christ to pray.

2 Follow to the judgment-hall;
   View the Lord of life arraigned;
   O the wormwood and the gall!
   O the pangs His soul sustained!
   Shun not suffering, shame, or loss;
   Learn of Him to bear the cross.

3 Calvary's mournful mountain climb;
   There, adoring at His feet,
   Mark that miracle of time,
   God's own sacrifice complete:
   "It is finished"— here Him cry;
   Learn of Jesus Christ to die.

4 Early hasten to the tomb,
   Where they laid His breathless clay;
   All is solitude and gloom,
   Who hath taken Him away?
   Christ is risen; He meets our eyes;
   Saviour, teach us so to rise.

756

1 GALES from heaven, if God so will,
   Sweeter melodies can wake,
   In the lonely mountain rill,
   Than the meeting waters make.
   Who hath the Father and the Son,
   May be left, but not alone.

2 Sick or healthful, slave or free,
   Wealthy, or despised and poor —
   What is that to him or thee,
   So his love to Christ endure?
   When the shore is won at last,
   Who will count the billows past?

757

1 YE, who in His courts are found,
   Listening to the joyful sound,
   Lost and helpless as ye are,
   Sons of sorrow, sin, and care,
   Glorify the King of kings,
   Take the peace the gospel brings.

2 Turn to Christ your longing eyes,
   View this bleeding sacrifice;
   See, in Him, your sins forgiven,
   Pardon, holiness, and heaven:
   Glorify the King of kings,
   Take the peace the gospel brings.

PLEYEL'S HYMN. 7s.

PLEYEL.

Prince of Peace! control my will; Bid this struggling heart be still;

Bid my fears and doubtings cease,— Hush my spi - rit in - to peace.

758

2 Thou hast bought me with Thy blood,
Opened wide the gate to God;
Peace I ask—but peace must be,
Lord, in being one with Thee.

3 May Thy will, not mine, be done;
May Thy will and mine be one:
Chase these doubtings from my heart;
Now Thy perfect peace impart.

4 Saviour! at thy feet I fall;
Thou my Life, my God, my All!
Let Thy happy servant be
One for evermore with Thee.

759

1 TIME by moments steals away,
First the hour and then the day;
Small the daily loss appears,
Yet it soon amounts to years.

2 Thus another year is flown;
Now it is no more our own,
If it brought or promised good,
Than the years before the flood.

3 Favors, from the Lord received,
Sins, that have His Spirit grieved,
Marked by an unerring hand,
In His book recorded stand.

4 Spared to see another year,
Let Thy blessings meet us here;
Sun of Righteousness, arise,
Warm our hearts, and bless our eyes.

760

1 HASTE, O sinner; now be wise;
Stay not for the morrow's sun:
Wisdom if you still despise,
Harder is it to be won.

2 Haste, and mercy now implore;
Stay not for the morrow's sun,
Lest thy season should be o'er,
Ere this evening's stage be run.

3 Haste, O sinner, now return;
Stay not for the morrow's sun,
Lest thy lamp should cease to burn,
Ere salvation's work is done.

4 Haste, O sinner; now be blest;
Stay not for the morrow's sun,
Lest perdition thee arrest,
Ere the morrow is begun.

761

1 FOR a season called to part,
Let us then ourselves commend
To the gracious eye and heart
Of our ever present Friend.

2 Jesus, hear our humble prayer;
Tender Shepherd of Thy sheep,
Let Thy mercy and Thy care
All our souls in safety keep.

3 In Thy strength may we be strong:
Sweeten every cross and pain;
Give us, if we live, ere long
Here to meet in peace again.

762

SING we to our God above
Praise eternal as His love;
Praise Him, all ye heavenly host—
Father, Son, and Holy Ghost.

GERMAN.

On Thy church, O Power di-vine, Cause Thy glo-rious face to shine,

D. C.—Till her sons from zone to zone Make Thy great sal-va-tion known.

Till the na-tions from a-far Hail her as their guid-ing star, D.C.

763

2 Then shall God, with lavish hand,
Scatter blessings o'er the land;
Earth shall yield her rich increase,
Every breeze shall whisper peace,
And the world's remotest bound
With the voice of praise resound.

764

1 Saviour, when in dust to Thee
Low we bow the adoring knee;
When, repentant, to the skies
Scarce we lift our streaming eyes;
O, by all Thy pains and woe,
Suffered once for man below,
Bending from Thy throne on high,
Hear our solemn litany.

2 By Thy helpless infant years;
By Thy life of wants and tears;
By Thy days of sore distress
In the savage wilderness;
By the dread permitted hour
Of the insulting tempter's power,—
Turn, O, turn a pitying eye;
Hear our solemn litany.

3 By Thine hour of dire despair;
By Thine agony of prayer;
By the cross, the nail, the thorn,
Piercing spear and torturing scorn;
By the gloom that veiled the skies
O'er the dreadful sacrifice,—
Listen to our humble cry;
Hear our solemn litany.

4 By Thy deep, expiring groan;
By the sad sepulchral stone;
By the vault whose dark abode
Held in vain the rising God,—
O, from earth to heaven restored,
Mighty, reascended Lord,
Listen, listen to the cry
Of our solemn litany.

765

1 Light of life, seraphic fire,
Love divine, Thyself impart;
Every fainting soul inspire;
Shine in every drooping heart.
Every mournful sinner cheer,
Scatter all our guilty gloom;
Son of God, appear, appear!
To Thy human temples come.

2 Come in this accepted hour;
Bring Thy heavenly kingdom in;
Fill us with Thy glorious power,
Rooting out the seeds of sin.
Nothing more can we require,
We will covet nothing less:
Be Thou all our heart's desire,
All our joy and all our peace.

766

Sing we to our God above,
Father, Son, and Holy Ghost,
Praise eternal as His love;
Praise Him, all ye heavenly host.

GLADNESS. 7s.

ANDANTE.

High in yonder realms of light, Far above these low - er skies,
Fair and ex - quis - ite - ly bright, Heaven's unfading . . .
D. C. Where no anxious care corrodes, Hap - py in Im-

mansions rise. Glad within these blest abodes Dwell the raptur'd saints above,
man uel's love.

767

2 Once indeed, like us below,
  Pilgrims in this vale of tears,
Torturing pain and heavy woe,
  Gloomy doubts, distressing fears,
These, alas! full well they knew,
  Sad companions of their way;
Oft on them the tempest blew,
  Through the long and cheerless day.

3 Oft their vileness they deplored,
  Wills perverse and hearts untrue,
Grieved they had not loved the Lord—
  Loved as they had wished to do;
But these days of weeping o'er,
  Past this scene of toil and pain,
They shall feel distress no more,
  Never, never weep again.

768

1 PALMS of glory, raiment bright,
  Crowns that never fade away,
Gird and deck the saints in light;
  Priests, and kings, and conquerors they
Yet the conquerors bring their palms
  To the Lamb amid the throne,
And proclaim, in joyful psalms,
  Victory through His cross alone.

2 Kings for harps their crowns resign,
  Crying, as they strike the chords,
"Take the kingdom; it is Thine,
  King of kings and Lord of lords;"
Round the altar priests confess,
  If their robes are white as snow,
'Twas the Saviour's righteousness,
  And His blood that made them so.

3 Who are these? On earth they dwelt;
  Sinners, once, of Adam's race;
Guilt, and fear, and suffering felt,
  But were saved by sovereign grace.
They were mortal, too, like us;
  Ah, when we, like them must die,
May our souls, translated thus,
  Triumph, reign, and shine on high.

769

1 SWELL the anthem, raise the song:
  Praises to our God belong:
Saints and angels, join to sing
  Praises to the heavenly King.
Blessings from His liberal hand
Flow around this happy land:
Kept by Him, no foes annoy:
Peace and freedom we enjoy.

2 Here beneath a virtuous sway,
May we cheerfully obey,
Never feel oppression's rod,
Ever own and worship God.
Hark! the voice of nature sings
Praises to the King of kings:
Let us join the choral song,
And the grateful notes prolong.

770

PRAISE the name of God most high
Praise Him, all below the sky,
Praise Him, all ye heavenly host,
Father, Son, and Holy Ghost;
As through countless ages past,
Evermore His praise shall last.

Gro. Hews.

Soft-ly now the light of day Fades up-on my sight a-way;

Free from care, from la-bor free, Lord, I would commune with Thee.

771

2 Soon for me the light of day
Shall forever pass away;
Then, from sin and sorrow free,
Take me Lord to dwell with Thee.

772

1 GENTLY, gently lay Thy rod
On my sinful head, O God!
Stay Thy wrath, in mercy stay,
Lest I sink beneath its sway.

2 Heal me, for my flesh is weak;
Heal me, for Thy grace I seek;
This my only plea I make—
Heal me for Thy mercy's sake.

3 Who, within the silent grave,
Shall proclaim Thy power to save?
Lord! my sinking soul reprieve;
Speak, and I shall rise and live.

4 Lo! He comes—He heeds my plea;
Lo! He comes—the shadows flee;
Glory round me dawns once more;
Rise, my spirit, and adore!

773

1 DEPTH of mercy! can there be
Mercy still reserved for me?
Can my God His wrath forbear,
Me, the chief of sinners, spare!

2 I have long withstood His grace;
Long provoked Him to His face;
Would not hearken to His calls;
Grieved Him by a thousand falls.

3 Kindled His relentings are;
Me, He now delights to spare;
Cries, how shall I give thee up?
Lets the lifted thunder drop.

4 There for me the Saviour stands;
Shows His wounds, and spreads His hands;
God is love! I know, I feel;
Jesus weeps, and loves me still.

5 Now incline me to repent;
Let me now my fall lament:
Now my foul revolt deplore:
Weep, believe, and sin no more.

774

1 HOLY Spirit, from on high,
Bend o'er us a pitying eye;
Now refresh the drooping heart;
Bid the power of sin depart.

2 Light up every dark recess
Of our heart's ungodliness;
Show us every devious way
Where our steps have gone astray.

3 Teach us with repentant grief,
Humbly to implore relief;
Then the Saviour's blood reveal,
And our broken spirits heal.

4 May we daily grow in grace,
And pursue the heavenly race,
Trained in wisdom, led by love,
Till we reach our rest above.

PROPONTIS. 7s. (6 lines.)

Dr. Lowell Mason.

Ho - ly Lord, our hearts prepare For the sol - emn work of prayer;

Grant that while we bend the knee, All our tho'ts may turn to Thee;

Let Thy presence here be found, Breathing peace and joy a - round.

775

2 Lord, when we approach Thy throne,
Make Thy power and glory known:
Thus may we be taught to call
Humbly on the Lord of all,
And with reverence and fear
At Thy footstool to appear.

3 Teach us, as we breathe our woes,
On Thy promise to repose,
All Thy tender love to trace
In the Saviour's work of grace,
And with confidence depend
On a gracious God and Friend.

776

1 As the hart, with eager looks,
Panteth for the water-brooks,
So my soul, athirst for Thee,
Pants the living God to see:
When, O when, with filial fear,
Lord, shall I to Thee draw near?

2 Why art thou cast down, my soul?
God, thy God, shall make thee whole:
Why art thou disquieted?
God shall lift thy fallen head,
And His countenance benign
Be the saving health of thine.

777

1 Blessed are the sons of God:
They are bought with Jesus' blood:
They are ransomed from the grave:
Life eternal they shall have:
With them numbered may we be,
Now and through eternity.

2 God did love them in His Son
Long before the world begun,
They the seal of this receive,
When on Jesus they believe.
With them numbered may we be,
Now and through eternity.

778

1 Blessed Saviour! Thee I love,
All my other joys above;
All my hopes in Thee abide,
Thou my hope, and naught beside:
Ever let my glory be,
Only, only, only Thee.

2 Once again beside the cross,
All my gain I count but loss;
Earthly pleasures fade away,—
Clouds they are that hide my day:
Hence, vain shadows! let me see
Jesus crucified for me.

S. WEBBE.

While with cease - less course the sun Hasted through the for - mer year,

Ma - ny souls their race have run, Nev - er more to meet us here.

Fixed in an e - ter - nal state, They have done with all be - low;

We a lit - tle long - er wait, But how lit - tle, none can know.

779

2 As the winged arrow flies,
  Speedily the mark to find;
As the lightning from the skies,
  Darts and leaves no trace behind—
Swiftly thus our fleeting days
  Bear us down life's rapid stream :
Upward, Lord, our spirits raise,
  All below is but a dream.

3 Thanks for mercies past receive,
  Pardon of our sins renew;
Teach us henceforth how to live,
  With eternity in view.

Bless Thy word to young and old,
  Fill us with a Saviour's love,
And when life's short tale is told,
  May we dwell with Thee above.

780

PRAISE the name of God most high,
Praise Him all below the sky,
Praise Him, all ye heavenly host,
Father, Son, and Holy Ghost;
As through countlsss ages past,
Evermore His praise shall last.

LARGHETTO.

Je-sus, Lov-er of my soul, Let me to Thy bo-som fly, }
While the ra-ging bil-lows roll, And the tempest still is high; }
D. C. Safe in-to the hav-en guide; O, receive my soul at last.

Hide me, O my Sav-iour, hide, Till the storm of life is past;

781

2 Other refuge have 1 none;
  Hangs my helpless soul on Thee;
Leave, ah, leave me not alone;
  Still support and comfort me.
All my trust on Thee is stayed;
  All my help from Thee I bring;
Cover my defenceless head
  With the shadow of Thy wing.

3 Thou, O Christ, art all I want;
  More than all in Thee I find;
Raise the fallen, cheer the faint :
  Heal the sick, and lead the blind.
Just and holy is Thy name :
  I am all unrighteousness :
False, and full of sin, I am :
  Thou art full of truth and grace.

782

1 FATHER, Thy paternal care
  Has my guardian been, my guide ;
Every hallowed wish and prayer
  Has Thy hand of love supplied;
Thine is every thought of bliss
  Left by hours and days gone by;
Every hope Thine offspring is,
  Beaming from futurity.

2 Every sun of splendid ray,
  Every moon that shines serene,
Every morn that welcomes day,
  Every evening's twilight scene,
Every hour which wisdom brings,
  Every incense at Thy shrine,
These, and all life's holiest things,
  And its fairest, all are Thine.

3 And for all my hymns shall rise
  Daily to Thy gracious throne;
Thither let my aching eyes
  Turn, unwearied, righteous One.
Through life's strange vicissitude,
  There reposing all my care,
Trusting still, through ill and good,
  Fixed, and cheered, and counselled there.

783

1 PILGRIM, burdened with thy sin,
  Come the way to Zion's gate:
There, till mercy speaks within,
  Knock, and weep, and watch, and wait .
Knock—He knows the sinner's cry;
  Weep—He loves the mourner's tears;
Watch, for saving grace is nigh;
  Wait, till heavenly grace appears.

2 Hark, it is the Saviour's voice!
  "Welcome, pilgrim, to thy rest !"
Now within the gate rejoice,
  Safe, and owned, and bought and blest :
Safe, from all the lures of vice:
  Owned, by joys the contrite know;
Bought by love, and life the price;
  Blest, the mighty debt we owe.

3 Holy pilgrim ! what for thee
  In a world like this remains ?
From thy guarded breast shall flee
  Fear, and shame, and doubts, and pains;
Fear—the hope of heaven shall fly,
  Shame, from glory's view retire;
Doubt, in full belief shall die,
  Pain, in endless bliss expire.

MILTON. 7s. 217

MOZART.

Let us, with a joyful mind, Praise the Lord, for He is kind;
For His mercies shall endure, Ev - er faithful, . . . Ever sure.

Hal - le - lu - jah! Hal - le - lu - jah! Hal - le - lu - jah! A - men.

784

2 All things living He doth feed,
His full hand supplies their need;
For His mercies shall endure,
Ever faithful, ever sure.

3 He His chosen race did bless,
In the wasteful wilderness;
For His mercies shall endure,
Ever faithful, ever sure.

4 He hath, with a piteous eye,
Looked upon our misery;
For His mercies shall endure,
Ever faithful, ever sure.

5 Let us, then, with joyful mind,
Praise the Lord, for He is kind;
For His mercies shall endure,
Ever faithful, ever sure.

785

1 If 'tis sweet to mingle where
Christians meet for social prayer;
If 'tis sweet with them to raise
Songs of holy joy and praise—
Passing sweet that state must be,
Where they meet eternally.

2 Saviour, may these meetings prove
Antepasts to that above;
While we worship in this place,
May we go from grace to grace,
Till we each, in his degree,
Fit for endless glory be.

786

1 Happy, Saviour, should I be,
If I could but trust in Thee;
Trust Thy wisdom me to guide;
Trust Thy goodness to provide;
Trust Thy saving love and power;
Trust Thee every day and hour;

2 Trust Thee as the only light
In the darkest hour of night;
Trust in sickness, trust in health;
Trust in poverty and wealth;
Trust in joy and trust in grief;
Trust Thy promise for relief;

3 Trust Thy blood to cleanse my soul;
Trust Thy grace to make me whole;
Trust Thee, living, dying too;
Trust Thee all my journey through;
Trust Thee till my feet shall be
Planted on the crystal sea.

787

1 When along life's thorny road,
Faints the soul beneath the load,
By its cares and sins oppressed,
Finds on earth no peace or rest;
When the wily tempter's near,
Filling us with doubts and fear:
Jesus, to Thy feet we flee,
Jesus, we will look to Thee.

2 Thou, our Saviour, from the throne
List'nest to Thy people's moan;
Thou, the living Head, dost share
Every pang Thy members bear:
Full of tenderness Thou art,
Thou wilt heal the broken heart;
Full of power, Thine arm shall quell
All the rage and might of hell.

3 Mighty to redeem and save,
Thou hast overcome the grave;
Thou the bars of death hast riven,
Opened wide the gates of heaven:
Soon in glory Thou shalt come,
Taking Thy poor pilgrims home:
Jesus, then we all shall be,
Ever, ever, Lord, with Thee!

BALCH. 7s. (Double.)

MODERATO.

GEO. KINGSLEY.

Ho - ly Lamb! who Thee receive, Who in Thee be - gin to live, Day and night they cry to Thee, As Thou art so let us be. Je - sus, see my lab'ring breast, See, I pant in Thee to rest; Glad - ly now would I be clean; Cleanse me now from ev - 'ry sin, Cleanse me now from ev - 'ry sin.

788

3 Fix, oh fix our wavering mind!
To Thy cross our spirit bind;
Earthly passions far remove,
Fill my soul with holy love.
Dust and ashes though we be,
Full of sin and misery,
Thine we are, Thou Son of God:
Take the purchase of Thy blood!

789

1 FATHER of eternal grace,
Glorify Thyself in me;
Meekly beaming in my face,
May the world Thine image see.

2 Happy only in Thy love,
Poor, unfriended, or unknown,
Fix my thoughts on things above,
Stay my heart on Thee alone.

3 Humble, holy, all resigned
To Thy will—Thy will be done!
Give me, Lord, the perfect mind
Of Thy well-beloved Son.

4 Counting gain and glory lost,
May I tread the path He trod—
Die with Jesus on the cross,
Rise with Him to Thee, my God.

MILGROVE.

Stealing from the world a - way,   We are come to seek Thy face;

Kind - ly meet us, Lord, we pray, Grant us Thy re - viv - ing grace.

790

2 Yonder stars that gild the sky,
    Shine but with a borrowed light;
We, unless Thy light be nigh,
    Wander, wrapt in gloomy night.

3 Sun of Righteousness ! dispel
    All our darkness, doubts and fears;
May Thy light within us dwell,
    Till eternal day appears.

791

1 PEOPLE of the living God,
    I have sought the world around,
Paths of sin and sorrow trod,
    Peace and comfort no where found.

2 Now to you my spirit turns—
    Turns a fugitive unblest;
Brethren ! where your altar burns,
    Oh, receive me into rest !

3 Lonely I no longer roam,
    Like the cloud, the wind, the wave :
Where you dwell shall be my home,
    Where you die shall be my grave.

4 Mine the God whom you adore,
    Your Redeemer shall be mine;
Earth can fill my soul no more,
    Every idol I resign.

792

1 JESUS, all-atoning Lamb,
    Thine, and only Thine, I am :
Take my body, spirit, soul;
    Only Thou possess the whole.

2 Thou my one thing needful be;
    Let me ever cleave to Thee;
Let me choose the better part :
    Let me give Thee all my heart.

3 Whom have I on earth below?
    Thee, and only Thee, I know:
Whom have I in heaven but Thee?
    Thou art all in all to me.

793

1 Now may He, who from the dead
    Brought the Shepherd of the sheep,
Jesus Christ, our King and Head,
    All our souls in safety keep !

2 May He teach us to fulfil
    What is pleasing in His sight;
Perfect us in all His will,
    And preserve us day and night ;

3 Great Redeemer ! Thee we praise,
    Who the covenant sealed with blood;
While our hearts and voices raise
    Loud thanksgivings unto God.

794

1 LORD, whom winds and seas obey,
    Guide us through the watery way;
In the hollow of Thy hand
    Hide, and bring us safe to land.

2 Keep the souls whom now we leave;
    Bid them to each other cleave;
Bid them walk on life's rough sea;
    Bid them come by faith to Thee.

3 Save, untill these tempests end,
    All who on Thy love depend;
Waft our happy spirits o'er;
    Land us on the heavenly shore.

EDYFIELD. 7s.

MODERATO.   REV. C. J. LATROBE.

Praise on Thee, in Zi - on's gates, Dai - ly, O Je - ho - vah, waits;

Un - to Thee, O God, be - long Grateful words and ho - ly song.

795

2 Thou the hope and refuge art
  Of remotest lands apart;
  Distant isles and tribes unknown,
  'Mid the ocean waste and lone.

3 Thou dost visit earth, and rain
  Blessings on the thirsty plain,
  From the copious founts on high,
  From the rivers of the sky.

4 Thus the clouds Thy power confess,
  And Thy paths drop fruitfulness,
  And the voice of song and mirth
  Rises from the tribes of earth!

796

1 HASTEN, Lord, the glorious time
  When, beneath Messiah's sway,
  Every nation, every clime,
  Shall the gospel call obey.

2 Mightiest kings His power shall own,
  Heathen tribes His name adore;
  Satan and his host, o'erthrown,
  Bound in chains, shall hurt no more.

3 Then shall wars and tumults cease,
  Then be banished grief and pain;
  Righteousness, and joy, and peace,
  Undisturbed, shall ever reign.

4 Bless we, then, our gracious Lord,
  Ever praise His holy name,
  All His mighty acts record,
  All His wondrous love proclaim.

797

1 CHRIST, of all my hopes the ground,
  Christ, the Spring of all my joy,
  Still in Thee let me be found,
  Still for Thee my powers employ.

2 Fountain of o'erflowing grace,
  Freely from Thy fulness give;
  Till I close my earthly race,
  Be it "Christ for me to live."

3 When I touch the blessed shore,
  Back the closing waves shall roll;
  Death's dark stream shall never more
  Part from Thee my ravished soul.

4 Thus, O thus an entrance give
  To the land of cloudless sky;
  Having known it "Christ to live,"
  Let me know it "gain to die."

798

1 BLESS, O Lord, the opening year
  To each soul assembled here;
  Clothe Thy word with power divine;
  Make us willing to be Thine.

2 Where Thou hast Thy work begun,
  Give new strength the race to run;
  Scatter darkness, doubts and fears;
  Wipe away the mourner's tears.

3 Bless us all, both old and young;
  Call forth praise from every tongue:
  Let the whole assembly prove
  All Thy power and all Thy love.

799

1 CHRISTIANS, brethren, ere we part,
  Every voice and every heart
  Join, and to our Father raise
  One last hymn of grateful praise.

2 Though we here should meet no more,
  Yet there is a brighter shore;
  There, released from toil and pain,
  There we all may meet again.

HEROLD.

Come, De - sire of na - tions, come! Has - ten, Lord, the gen' - ral doom!

Hear the Spi - rit and the Bride; Come, and take us to Thy side.

800

2 Thou, who hast our plans prepared,
Make us meet for our reward;
Then with all Thy saints descend :
Then our earthly trials end.

3 Mindful of Thy chosen race, .
Shorten these vindictive days;
Who for full redemption groan;
Hear us now, and save Thine own.

4 Now destroy the man of sin,
Now Thine ancient flock bring in ;
Filled with rightcousness divine,
Claim a ransomed world for Thine.

5 Plant Thy heavenly kingdom here;
Glorious in Thy saints appear :
Speak the sacred number sealed;
Speak the mystery revealed.

801

1 Songs of praise the angels sang,
Heaven with hallelujahs rang,
When Jehovah's work begun,
When He spake, and it was done.

2 Songs of praise awoke the morn, .
When the Prince of Peace was born;
Songs of praise arose, when He
Captive led captivity.

3 Heaven and earth must pass away—
Songs of praise shall crown that day;
God will make new heavens and earth—
Songs of praise shall hail their birth.

4 And shall man alone be dumb,
Till that glorious kingdom come ?
No; the Church delights to raise
Psalms and hymns and songs of praise.

5 Saints below, with heart and voice,
Still in songs of praise rejoice;
Learning here by faith and love,
Songs of praise to sing above.

5 Borne upon the latest breath,
Songs of praise shall conquer death;
Then amidst eternal joy,
Songs of praise their powers employ.

802

1 SAW ye not the cloud arise,
Little as a human hand !
Now it spreads along the skies,
Hangs o'er all the thirsty land.

2 Lo, the promise of a shower
. Drops already from above;
But the Lord will shortly pour
All the blessings of His love.

3 When He first the work begun,
Small and feeble was its day;
Now the word doth swiftly run,
Now it wins its widening way.

4 Sons of God, your Saviour praise;
He the door hath opened wide;
He hath given the word of grace;
Jesus' word is glorified.

MODERATO.   DR. C. MALAN.

Ma-ny cen-tu-ries have fled' Since our Sa-viour
And this sa-cred feast or-dained, Ev-er by His

broke the bread, }
church re-tained: } Those His bo-dy who dis-cern Thus shall

meet till His re-turn, Thus shall meet till His re-turn.

803

2 Through the church's long eclipse,
When, from priest or pastor's lips,
Truth divine was never heard,
'Mid the famine of the word,
Still these symbols witness gave
To His love who died to save.

3 All who bear the Saviour's name,
Here their common faith proclaim;
Though divine in tongue, or rite,
Here one body we unite.
Breaking thus one mystic bread;
Members of one common Head.

804

1 QUIET, Lord, my froward heart,
Make me teachable and mild,
Upright, simple, free from art,
Make me as a weaned child;
From distrust and envy free,
Pleased with all that pleases Thee.

2 What Thou shalt to-day provide,
Let me as a child receive;
What to-morrow may betide,
Calmly to Thy wisdom leave;
'Tis enough that Thou wilt care—
Why should I the burden bear?

3 As a little child relies
On a care beyond its own;
Knows he's neither strong nor wise,
Fears to stir a step alone;
Let me thus with Thee abide,
As my Father, Guard, and Guide.

805

1 HEART of stone, relent, relent!
Break, by Jesus' cross subdued;
See His body mangled, rent,
Covered with His flowing blood:
Sinful soul, what hast thou done!
Crucified th' incarnate Son!

2 Yes: thy sins have done the deed,
Driven the nails that fixed Him there:
Crowned with thorns His sacred Head,
Pierced Him with the cruel spear,
Made His soul a sacrifice,
While for sinful man He dies.

3 Wilt thou let Him bleed in vain?
Still to death thy Lord pursue?
Open all His wounds again,
And the shameful cross renew?
No: with all my sins I'll part;
Break, oh break my bleeding heart!

SPANISH.

Watchman, tell us of the night, What its signs of promise are.
Trav'ler, o'er yon mountain's height See that' glo - ry - beaming star !
D. C. Trav'ler, yes ; it brings the day, Promised day of Is - ra - el.

Watchman, does its beauteous ray Aught of hope or joy fore - tell ?

D. C.

806

2 Watchman, tell us of the night;
 Higher yet that star ascends.
Traveller, blessedness and light,
 Peace and truth, its course portends.
Watchman, will its beams alone
 Gild the spot that gave them birth?
Traveller, ages are its own;
 See ! it bursts o'er all the earth !

3 Watchman, tell us of the night,
 For the morning seems to dawn.
Traveller, darkness takes its flight,
 Doubt and terror are withdrawn.
Watchman, let thy wanderings cease;
 Hie thee to thy quiet home.
Traveller, lo, the Prince of Peace,
 Lo, the Son of God is come !

807

1 LORD of earth ! thy forming hand
Well this beauteous frame hath planned,
Woods that wave, and hills that tower,
Ocean rolling in his power :
Yet, amid this scene so fair,
Should I cease Thy smile to share,
What were all its joys to me ?
Whom have I on earth but Thee ?

2 Lord of heaven ! beyond our sight
Shines a world of purer light :
There, in love's unclouded reign,
Parted hands shall meet again :
Oh, that world is passing fair !
Yet, if Thou wert absent there,
What were all its joys to me ?
Whom have I in heaven but Thee ?

3 Lord of earth and heaven ! my breast
Seeks in Thee its only rest :
I was lost; Thy accents mild
Homeward lured Thy wandering child.
Oh ! should once Thy smile divine
Cease upon my soul to shine,
What were earth or heaven to me
Whom have I in each but Thee ?

808

1 SLEEP not, soldier of the cross !
 Foes are lurking all around;
Look not here to find repose :
 This is but thy battle ground.

2 Up ! and take thy shield and sword;
 Up ! it is the call of Heaven :
Shrink not faithless from thy Lord;
 Nobly strive as he hath striven.

3 Break through all the force of ill;
 Tread the might of passion down,—
Struggling onward, onward still,
 To the conqu'ring Saviour's crown !

4 Through the midst of toil and pain,
 Let this thought ne'er leave thy breast
Every triumph thou dost gain
 Makes more sweet thy coming rest.

809

PRAISE to God on high be given;
Praise Him all in earth and heaven;
Praise Him at the dawn of light,
Praise Him at returning night;
Saints below and saints above,
Praise, O praise the God of love.

Weeping soul, no long-er mourn, Je-sus all thy griefs hath borne; View Him bleed-ing on the tree, Pour-ing out His life for thee; There thy ev'-ry sin He bore, Weeping soul, la-ment no more.

810

2 All thy crimes on Him were laid;
See upon His blameless head
Wrath its utmost vengeance pours,
Due to my offence and yours;
Weary sinner, keep thine eyes
On the atoning sacrifice.

3 Cast thy guilty soul on Him,
Find Him mighty to redeem;
At His feet thy burden lay,
Look thy doubts and fears away;
Now by faith the Son embrace,
Plead His promise, trust His grace.

4 Lord, Thy arm must be revealed,
Ere I can by faith be healed;
Since I scarce can look to Thee,
Cast a gracious eye on me;
At Thy feet myself I lay,
Take, O take my sins away.

811

1 FROM the cross uplifted high,
Where the Saviour deigns to die,
What melodious sounds we hear,
Bursting on the ravished ear !—
" Love's redeeming work is done—
Come and welcome, sinner, come !"

5 Sprinkled now with blood the throne,
Why beneath thy burdens groan ?
On My pierced body laid,
Justice owns the ransom paid—
Bow the knee, embrace the Son—
Come and welcome, sinner, come !

812

1 BY Thy Spirit, Lord, reprove,
All my inmost sins reveal,
Sins against Thy light and love
Let me see, and let me feel;
Sins that crucified my Lord,
Sins against Thy precious blood.

2 Jesus, seek Thy wandering sheep,
Make me restless to return;
Bid me look on Thee, and weep,
Bitterly, as Peter, mourn :—
Till I say, by grace restored,
" Now, Thou know'st I love Thee, Lord."

3 O remember me for good,
Passing through the mortal vale;
Show me the atoning blood,
When my strength and spirit fail;
Give my fainting soul to see
Jesus crucified for me.

MODERATO.   DR. C. MALAN.

Once I tho't my mountain strong, Firmly fixed, no more to move;
Those were happy, golden days, Sweetly spent in prayer and praise.

Then my Saviour was my song, Then my soul was filled with love;

813

2 Little then myself I knew,
  Little thought of Satan's power;
Now I feel my sins anew,
  Now I feel the stormy hour:
Sin has put my joys to flight,
Sin has turned my day to night.

3 Saviour! shine, and cheer my soul;
  Bid my dying hopes revive;
Make my wounded spirit whole;
  Far away the tempter drive:
Speak the word and set me free;
Let me live alone to Thee.

814

1 WHEN this passing world is done,
When has sunk yon glaring sun,
When we stand with Christ in glory,
Looking o'er life's finished story,
Then, Lord, shall I fully know—
Not till then—how much I owe.

2 When I stand before the throne,
Dressed in beauty not my own,
When I see Thee as Thou art,
Love Thee with unsinning heart,
Then, Lord, shall I fully know—
Not till then—how much I owe.

3 When the praise of heaven I hear,
Loud as thunders to the ear,
Loud as many waters' noise,
Sweet as harp's melodious voice,
Then, Lord, shall I fully know—
Not till then—how much I owe.

815

1 CHOSEN not for good in me,
Wakened up from wrath to flee,
Hidden in the Saviour's side,
By the Spirit sanctified,
Teach me, Lord, on earth to show
By my love how much I owe.

2 Oft I walk beneath the cloud,
Dark as midnight's gloomy shroud;
But when fear is at the height,
Jesus comes and all is light,
Blessed Jesus! bid me show
Doubting saints how much I owe.

3 Oft the nights of sorrow reign—
Weeping, sickness, sighing, pain;
But a night Thine anger burns—
Morning comes, and joy returns:
God of comforts! bid me show
To Thy poor how much I owe.

4 When in flowery paths I tread,
Oft by sin I'm captive led,
Oft I fall, but still arise—
Jesus comes—the tempter flies:
Blessed Jesus! bid me show
Weary sinners all I owe.

816

PRAISE the name of God most high,
Praise Him all below the sky,
Praise Him, all ye heavenly host,
Father, Son, and Holy Ghost;
As through countless ages past,
Evermore His praise shall last.

ALLEGRO.

DR. LOWELL MASON.

Hark! the her-ald ang-els sing, "Glo-ry to the new-born King;

Peace on earth and mer-cy mild; God and sinners re-conciled."

817

2 Joyful, all ye nations, rise;
Join the triumphs of the skies;
With the angelic hosts proclaim
" Christ is born in Bethlehem."

3 Veiled in flesh, the Godhead see;
Hail, the incarnate Deity;
Pleased as man with men to appear,
Jesus, our Immanuel, here.

4 Mild He lays His glory by;
Born that man no more may die;
Born to raise the sons of earth;
Born to give them second birth.

5 Hail, the heaven-born Prince of Peace!
Hail, the Sun of Righteousness!
Light and life to all He brings,
Risen with healing in His wings.

818

1 " COME up hither; come away;"
Thus the ransomed spirits sing;
Here is cloudless, endless day;
Here is everlasting spring.

2 Come up hither; come and dwell
With the living hosts above;
Come, and let your bosoms swell
With their burning songs of love.

3 Come up hither; come and share
In the sacred joys that rise,
Like an ocean, every where
Through the myriads of the skies.

4 Come up hither; come and shine
In the robes of spotless white;
Palms and harps and crowns are thine;
Hither, hither wing your flight.

5 Come up hither; hither speed;
Rest is found in heaven alone;
Here is all the wealth you need;
Come and make this wealth your own.

819

1 IN the sun, and moon, and stars,
Signs and wonders there shall be;
Earth shall quake with inward wars,
Nations with perplexity.

2 Soon shall ocean's hoary deep,
Tossed with stronger tempests, rise;
Wilder storms the mountains sweep,
Louder thunder rock the skies.

3 Dread alarms shall shake the proud,
Pale amazement, restless fear;
And amid the thunder cloud
Shall the Judge of man appear.

4 But, though from His awful face,
Heaven shall fade, and earth shall fly;
Fear not ye, His chosen race,
Your redemption draweth nigh.

820

1 SEE the ransomed millions stand,
Palms of conquest in their hand;
This before the throne their strain—
" Hell is vanquished, Death is slain."

2 " Blessing, honor, glory, might,
Are the Conqueror's native right;
Thrones and powers before Him fall;
Lamb of God, and Lord of all."

DOLCE. CHERUBINI.

Lord, if Thou Thy grace impart, Poor in spi - rit, meek in heart,

I shall as my Mas - ter be, Root - ed in hu - mi - li - ty.

821

2 Simple, teachable and mild,
  Changed into a little child;
  Pleased with all the Lord provides,
  Weaned from all the world besides.

3 Father, fix my soul on Thee;
  Every evil let me flee;
  Nothing want beneath, above,
  Happy in Thy precious love.

4 O that all may seek and find
  Every good in Jesus joined !
  Him let Israel still adore,
  Trust Him, praise Him evermore.

822.

1 SINNERS, turn ! why will ye die ?
  God, your Maker, asks you why ?
  God, who did your being give,
  Made you with Himself to live;

2 He the fatal cause demands,
  Asks the work of His own hands;
  Why, ye thankless creatures, why
  Will ye cross His love, and die ?

3 Sinners, turn; why will ye die ?
  God, your Saviour, asks you why ?
  God, who did your souls retrieve,
  Died Himself, that ye might live.

4 Will you let Him die in vain,
  Crucify your Lord again ?
  Why, ye ransomed sinners, why
  Will ye slight His grace and die ?

823

1 HASTEN, Lord, to my release,
  Haste to help me, O my God !
  Foes, like armed bands, increase;
  Turn them back the way they trod.

2 Dark temptations round me press;
  Evil thoughts my soul assail;
  Doubts and fears, in my distress,
  Rise till flesh and spirit fail.

3 Those that seek Thee shall rejoice;
  I am bowed with misery;
  Yet I make Thy law my choice;
  Turn, my God, and look on me.

4 Thou my only Helper art,
  My Redeemer from the grave;
  Strength of my desiring heart,
  Do not tarry—haste to save.

824

1 When on Sinai's top I see
  God descend in majesty
  To proclaim His holy law,
  All my spirit sinks with awe.

2 When in ecstasy sublime,
  Tabor's glorious mount I climb,
  In the too transporting light,
  Darkness rushes o'er my sight.

3 When on Calvary I rest,
  God, in flesh made manifest,
  Shines in my Redeemer's face,
  Full of beauty, truth, and grace,

4 Here I would forever stay,
  Weep and gaze my soul away;
  Thou art heaven on earth to me,
  Lovely, mournful Calvary !

MODERATO.

Come, my soul, thy suit prepare ; Je - sus loves to an - swer prayer ;

He Himself in - vites thee near, Bids thee ask Him, waits to hear.

825

2 With my burden I begin :
Lord, remove this load of sin;
Let Thy blood, for sinners spilt,
Set my conscience free from guilt.

3 Lord, I come to Thee for rest;
Take possession of my breast;
There Thy blood-bought right maintain
And without a rival reign.

826

1 LORD, forever at Thy side
Let my place and portion be;
Strip me of the robe of pride;
Clothe me with humility.

2 Meekly may my soul receive
All Thy Spirit hath revealed;
Thou hast spoken; I believe,
Though the oracle be sealed.

3 Humble as a little child,
Weaned from its mother's breast,
By no subtleness beguiled,
On Thy faithful word I rest.

4 Israel, now and evermore
In the Lord Jehovah trust;
Him in all His ways adore,
Wise, and powerful, and just.

827

1 THEY who on the Lord rely,
Safely dwell, though danger 's nigh;
Lo, His sheltering wings are spread
O'er each faithful servant's head.

2 Vain temptation's wily snare;
Christians are Jehovah's care;
Harmless flies the shaft by day,
Or in darkness wings its way.

3 When they wake, or when they sleep,
Angel guards their vigils keep;
Death and danger may be near;
Faith and love have nought to fear

828

1 CHILDREN, listen to the Lord,
And obey His gracious word;
Seek His face with heart and mind;
Early seek, and you shall find.

2 Sorrowful, your sins confess;
Plead His perfect righteousness;
See the Saviour's bleeding side;
Come, you will not be denied.

3 For His worship now prepare;
Kneel to Him in fervent prayer;
Serve Him with a perfect heart,
Never from His ways depart.

829

1 LORD, assist us by Thy grace
To instruct our infant race;
Grant us wisdom from above,
Fill us with a Saviour's love.

2 May we teach them day by day,
In the house, and by the way,
When they rise, and when they rest,
Till Thy truth shall make them blessed

3 Gracious Saviour, hear our prayer :
We commit them to Thy care;
Be their Shepherd and their Guide;
Bring them to Thy bleeding side.

HALLE. 7s. 61.

Safe - ly through a - noth - er week God has brought us on our way;
Let us now a bless-ing seek, Wait - ing in His courts to - day:

Day of all the week the best, Em - blem of e - ter - nal rest.

830

2 While we seek supplies of grace,
Through the dear Redeemer's name,
Show Thy reconciling face;
Take away our sin and shame:
From our worldly cares set free,
May we rest this day in Thee.

3 Here we come, Thy name to praise,
Let us feel Thy presence near;
May Thy glory meet our eyes,
While we in Thy house appear:
Here afford us, Lord, a taste
Of our everlasting feast.

4 May the Gospel's joyful sound
Conquer sinners, comfort saints;
Make the fruits of grace abound;
Bring relief from all complaints:
Thus let all our Sabbaths prove,
Till we join the church above.

831

1 MANY woes had Christ endured,
Many sore temptations met,
Patient and to pains inured;
But the sorest trial yet
Was to be sustained in thee,
Gloomy, sad Gethsemane.

2 Came at length the dreadful night;
Vengeance, with its iron rod,
Stood, and with collected might,
Bruised the harmless Lamb of God:
See, my soul, my Saviour see,
Prostrate in Gethsemane.

3 There my God bore all my guilt;
This, thro' grace, can be believed;
But the horrors which He felt
Are too vast to be conceived:
None can penetrate through thee,
Doleful, dark Gethsemane.

4 Sins against a holy God,
Sins against His righteous laws,
Sins against His love, His blood,
Sins against His name and cause—
Sins immense as is the sea!
Hide me, O Gethsemane.

5 Here's my claim, and here alone;
None a Saviour more can need;
Deeds of righteousness I've none;
No, not one good work to plead:
Not a glimpse of hope for me,
Only in Gethsemane.

832

1 Now, with angels round the throne,
Cherubim and seraphim,
And the church, which still is one,
Let us swell the solemn hymn;
Glory to the Great I Am!
Glory to the Victim Lamb.

2 Blessing, honor, glory, might,
And dominion infinite,
To the Father of our Lord,
To the Spirit and the Word,
As it was all worlds before,
Is, and shall be evermore.

ALLEGRO CON SPIRITO.

Children of the heavenly King, As ye journey, sweetly sing;

Sing your Saviour's wor-thy praise, Glorious in His works and ways.

833

2 Ye are travelling home to God
In the way the fathers trod;
They are happy now, and ye
Soon their happiness shall see.

3 Shout, ye little flock, and blessed!
You on Jesus' throne shall rest;
There your seat is now prepared;
There your kingdom and reward.

4 Fear not, brethren; joyful stand
On the borders of your land;
Christ, your Father's darling Son,
Bids you undismayed go on.

5 Lord, submissive make us go,
Gladly leaving all below;
Only Thou our Leader be,
And we still will follow Thee.

834

1 Go, ye messengers of God,
Like the beams of morning, fly;
Take the wonder-working rod,
Wave the banner-cross on high.

2 Where the tow'ring minaret
Gleams along the morning skies,
Wave it till the crescent set,
And the "Star of Jacob" rise.

3 Go, to many a tropic isle,
In the bosom of the deep,
Where the skies forever smile,
And the oppressed forever weep.

4 O'er the negro's night of care,
Pour the living light of heaven;
Chase away the fiend despair,
Bid him hope to be forgiven.

5 Where the golden gates of day
Open on the palmy East,
Wide the bleeding cross display,
Spread the gospel's richest feast.

6 Circumnavigate the ball,
Visit every soil and sea,
Preach the cross of Christ to all;
Jesus' love is full and free.

835

1 HARK! a voice divides the sky!
Happy are the faithful dead,
In the Lord who sweetly die!
They from all their toils are freed.

2 Ready for their glorious crown—
Sorrows past and sins forgiven—
Here they lay their burden down,
Hallowed, and made meet for heaven.

3 When from flesh the spirit, freed,
Hastens homeward to return,
Mortals cry—"A man is dead!"
Angels sing—"A child is born!"

4 Born into the world above,
They our happy brother greet;
Bear him to the throne of love,
Place him at the Saviour's feet!

5 Jesus smiles, and says—"Well done!
Good and faithful servant thou!
Enter and receive thy crown;
Reign with me triumphant now."

Tell me not, in mournful numbers, Life is but an emp-ty dream;
For the soul is dead that slumbers, And things are not what they seem.

D. C. Dust thou art, to dust re-turn-est, Was not spoken of the soul!

Life is 're-al! Life is earnest! And the grave is not its goal;

836

3 Not enjoyment, and not sorrow,
  Is our destined end and way;
But to act, that each to-morrow
  Find us further than to-day.

4 Lives of true men all remind us
  We can make our lives sublime,
And, departing, leave behind us
  Footprints on the sands of time;

5 Footprints which perhaps another,
  Sailing o'er life's solemn main,
A forlorn and shipwrecked brother
  Seeing, shall take heart again.

6 Let us, then, be up and doing,
  With a heart for any fate;
Still achieving, still pursuing,
  Learn to labor and to wait.

837

1 Love divine, all love excelling,
  Joy of heaven, to earth come down;
Fix in us Thy humble dwelling,
  All Thy faithful mercies crown : .
Jesus, Thou art all compassion;
  Pure unbounded love Thou art;
Visit us with Thy salvation,
  Enter every trembling heart.

2 Breathe, O breathe Thy loving Spirit
  Into every troubled breast;
Let us all in Thee inherit,
  Let us find that second rest;
Come, almighty to deliver,
  Let us all Thy life receive;
Suddenly return, and never,
  Never more Thy temples leave.

3 Finish then Thy new creation;
  Pure and spotless let us be;
Let us see Thy great salvation
  Perfectly restored in Thee;
Changed from glory into glory,
  Till in heaven we take our place,
Till we cast our crowns before Thee,
  Lost in wonder, love, and praise.

838

1 Worship, honor, glory, blessing,
  Lord, we offer to Thy name;
Young and old, their thanks expressing,
  Join Thy goodness to proclaim;
As the hosts of heaven adore Thee,
  We too bow before Thy throne;
As the angels serve before Thee,
  So on earth Thy will be done.

839

1 Sing, my tongue, the Saviour's glory;
  Tell His triumph far and wide;
Tell aloud the famous story
  Of His body crucified;
How upon the cross a victim
  Vanquishing in death, He died.

2 Eating of the tree forbidden,
  Man had sunk in Satan's snare,
When our pitying Creator
  Did this second tree prepare;
Destined, many ages later,
  That first evil to repair.

3 Blessing, honor everlasting,
  To the immortal Deity;
To the Father, Son, and Spirit,
  Equal praises ever be;
Glory through the earth and heaven
  To our God in Trinity.

WILMOT. 8s & 7s.

CON SPIRITO.   WEBER.

Je - sus on - ly; when the morning Beams up - on the path I tread:

Je - sus on - ly; when the darkness Gathers round my weary head.

840

2 Jesus only; when the billows
   Cold and sullen o'er me roll;
   Jesus only; when the trumpet
 . Rends the tomb and wakes the soul.

3 Jesus only; when in judgment
   Boding fears my heart appal;
   Jesus only; when the wretched
   On the rocks and mountains call.

4 Jesus only; when, adoring,
   Saints their crowns before Him bring;
   Jesus only, I will joyous,
   Through eternal ages sing.

841

1 DREAD Jehovah, God of nations,
   From Thy temple in the skies,
   Hear Thy people's supplications:
   Now for their deliverance rise.

2 Though our sins, our hearts confounding,
   Long and loud for vengeance call,
   Thou hast mercy more abounding;
   Jesus' blood can cleanse them all.

3 Let that love veil our transgression;
   Let that blood our guilt efface;
   Save Thy people from oppression,
   Save from spoil Thy holy place.

4 Lo, with deep contrition turning,
   Humbly at Thy feet we bend;
   Hear us, fasting, praying, mourning;
   Hear us, spare us, and defend.

842

1 IN the cross of Christ I glory,
   Towering o'er the wrecks of time;
   All the light of sacred story
   Gathers round its head sublime.

2 When the woes of life o'ertake me,
   Hopes deceive, and fears annoy,
   Never shall the cross forsake me;
   Lo, it glows with peace and joy.

3 When the sun of bliss is beaming
   Light and love upon my way,
   From the cross the radiance streaming
   Adds new lustre to the day.

4 Bane and blessing, pain and pleasure,
   By the cross are sanctified;
   Peace is there that knows no measure,
   Joys that through all time abide.

5 In the cross of Christ I glory,
   Towering o'er the wrecks of time;
   All the light of sacred story
   Gathers round its head sublime.

843

1 PRAISE the Saviour all ye nations;
   Praise Him, all ye hosts above:
   Shout, with joyful acclamations,
   His divine, victorious love.

2 With my substance I will honor
   My Redeemer and my Lord;
   Were ten thousand worlds my manor,
   All were nothing to His word.

3 While the heralds of salvation
   His abounding grace proclaim,
   Let His friends, of every station,
   Gladly join to spread His fame.

GEO. F. ROOT.

My days are gliding swift - ly by, And I, a pilgrim stranger,

Would not de - tain them as they fly,—Those hours of toil and dan - ger.

CHORUS.

For now we stand on Jordan's strand, Our friends are passing o - ver;

And just be - fore the shining shore We may al - most dis - cov - er.

844

2 Our absent King the watchword gave,—
"Let every lamp be burning;"
We look afar, across the wave,
Our distant home discerning:
For now we stand on Jordan's strand,
Our friends are passing over;
And just before, the shining shore
We may almost discover.

3 Should coming days be dark and cold,
We will not yield to sorrow,
For hope will sing, with courage bold,
"There's glory on the morrow:"
For now we stand, &c.

4 Let storms of woe in whirlwinds rise,
Each cord on earth to sever,—
There—bright and joyous in the skies—
There—is our home forever,
'For now we stand, &c.

845

1 JESUS our King, in mercy bring
Thine aid for every duty;
And soon a nobler song we'll sing
And see Thee in Thy beauty.
There sorrow's tear shall flow no more;
But eyes with love be gleaming;
For over all the "shining shore,"
Thy radiant smile is beaming.

234   STOCKWELL. 8s & 7s.

DOLCE.   D. E. JONES.

Si - lent - ly the shades of eve - ning Gather round my lone - ly door;

Si - lent - ly they bring be - fore me Fa - ces I shall see no more.

846

2 Oh! the lost, the unforgotten,
   Though the world be oft forgot;
Oh! the shrouded and the lonely!
   In our hearts they perish not.

3 Living in the silent hours
   Where our spirits only blend;
They, unlinked with earthly troubles;
   We, still hoping for its end.

4 How such holy memories cluster
   Like the stars when storms are past;
Pointing up to that far heaven
   We may hope to gain at last.

847

1 CEASE, ye mourners, cease to languish,
   O'er the grave of those you love;
Pain, and death, and night and anguish,
   Enter not the world above.

2 While our silent steps are straying
   Lonely through night's deepening shade,
Glory's brightest beams are playing
   Round the happy Christian's head.

3 Light and peace at once deriving
   From the hand of God most high,
In His glorious presence living,
   They shall never, never die.

4 Endless pleasure, pain excluding,
   Sickness, there, no more can come;
There, no fear of woe intruding,
   Sheds o'er heaven a moment's gloom.

848

1 LIGHT of those whose dreary dwelling
   Borders on the shades of death,
Come, and thy dear self revealing,
   Dissipate the clouds beneath.

2 Still we wait for Thine appearing;
   Life and joy Thy beams impart,
Chasing all our fears and cheering
   Every poor, benighted heart.

3 Save us in Thy great compassion,
   O Thou mild, pacific Prince:
Give the knowledge of salvation,
   Give the pardon of our sins.

4 By Thine all-sufficient merit,
   Every burdened soul release;
By the influence of Thy spirit,
   Guide us into perfect peace.

849

1 SAVIOUR, breathe an evening blessing,
   Ere repose our spirits seal;
Sin and want we come confessing,
   Thou canst save, and Thou canst heal.

2 Though destruction walk around us,
   Though the arrows past us fly,
Angel-guards from Thee surround us;
   We are safe, if Thou art nigh.

3 Though the night be dark and dreary,
   Darkness cannot hide from Thee;
Thou art He, who never weary,
   Watchest where Thy people be.

4 Should swift death this night o'ertake us,
   And our couch become our tomb,
May the last loud trump awake us,
   Clad in bright and deathless bloom.

Hark! an aw-ful voice is sounding: "Christ is nigh!" it seeme to say;
"Cast a-way the dreams of darkness, O ye children of the day."

850

2 Startled at the solemn warning,
Let the earth-bound soul arise;
Christ, her Sun, all sloth dispelling,
Shines upon the morning skies.

3 Lo, the Lamb, so long expected,
Comes with pardon down from heaven;
Let us haste with tears of sorrow,
One and all to be forgiven.

4 So, when next He comes in glory,
Wrapping all the earth in fear,
May He then as our Defender
On the clouds of heaven appear.

851

1 WE are living, we are dwelling,
In a grand and awful time,
In an age on ages telling,
To be living is sublime.

2 Hark! the waking up of nations,
Gog and Magog to the fray,
Hark! what soundeth? is creation
Groaning for its latter day?

3 Will ye play, then, will ye dally,
With your music and your wine?
Up! it is Jehovah's rally!
God's own arm hath need of thine.

4 Hark! the onset! will ye fold your
Faith-clad arms in lazy lock?
Up, O up, thou drowsy soldier;
Worlds are charging to the shock.

5 Worlds are charging—heaven beholding;
Thou hast but an hour to fight;
Now the blazoned cross unfolding,
On—right onward, for the right.

6 On! let all the soul within you
For the truth's sake go abroad!
Strike! let every nerve and sinew
Tell on ages—tell for God!

852

1 CROWN His head with endless blessing,
Who, in God the Father's name,
With compassion never ceasing,
Comes, salvation to proclaim.

2 Lo, Jehovah, we adore Thee—
Thee, our Saviour—Thee, our God;
From Thy throne let beams of glory
Shine through all the world abroad.

3 Jesus! Thee our Saviour hailing,
Thee our God in praise we own;
Highest honors, never failing,
Rise eternal round Thy throne.

4 Now, ye saints, His power confessing,
In your grateful strains adore;
For His mercy, never ceasing,
Flows, and flows for evermore.

853

1 HOLY GHOST, dispel our sadness;
Pierce the clouds of sinful night;
Come, Thou source of sweetest gladness,
Breathe Thy life, and spread Thy light.

2 Author of our new creation,
Bid us all Thine influence prove;
Make our souls Thy habitation;
Shed abroad the Saviour's love.

"Mercy, O, Thou Son of David!" Thus blind Bar-ti-me-us pray'd:

"Others by Thy word are sav-ed, Now to me af-ford Thine aid."

854

2 Many for his crying chid him,
 But he called the louder still;
Till the gracious Saviour bid him—
 " Come, and ask Me what you will."

3 Money was not what he wanted,
 Though by begging used to live;
But he asked, and Jesus granted
 Alms which none but He could give.

4 " Lord, remove this grievous blindness,
 Let my eyes behold the day ? "
Straight he saw, and, won by kindness,
 Followed Jesus in the way.

5 Oh! methinks I hear him praising,
 Publishing to all around:
" Friends, is not my case amazing?
 What a Saviour I have found!

6 " Oh! that all the blind but knew Him,
 And would be advised by me!
Surely they would hasten to Him,
 He would cause them all to see."

855

1 TAKE my heart, O Father, take it!
 Make and keep it all Thine own;
Let Thy Spirit melt and break it—
 This proud heart of sin and stone.

2 Father, make it pure and lowly,
 Fond of peace and far from strife;
Turning from the paths unholy
 Of this vain and sinful life.

3 Ever let Thy grace surround it;
 Strengthen it with power divine,
Till Thy cords of love have bound it:
 Make it to be wholly Thine.

4 May the blood of Jesus heal it,
 And its sins be all forgiven;
Holy Spirit, take and seal it,
 Guide it in the path to heaven.

856

1 From the table now retiring,
 Which for us the Lord hath spread,
May our souls, refreshment finding,
 Grow in all things like our Head.

2 His example by beholding,
 May our lives His image bear;
Him our Lord and Master calling,
 His commands may we revere.

3 Love to God and man displaying,
 Walking steadfast in His way,
Joy attend us in believing,
 Peace from God, through endless day.

857

1 COME to Calvary's holy mountain,
 Sinners ruined by the fall;
Here a pure and healing fountain
 Flows to you, to me, to all.

2 He that drinks shall live for ever;
 'Tis a soul-renewing flood,
God is faithful;—God will never
 Break his covenant in blood.

Come, Thou Fount of ev'ry blessing! Tune my heart to sing Thy grace; }
Streams of mercy, nev - er ceasing, Call for songs of loudest praise. }
D. C. Praise the mount—I'm fixed upon it—Mount of Thy redeeming love.

Teach me some me - lodious son - net Sung by flaming tongues a - bove;

858

2 Here I'll raise mine Ebenezer;
  Hither by Thy help I'm come;
And I hope by Thy good pleasure,
  Safely to arrive at home.
Jesus sought me when a stranger,
  Wandering from the fold of God;
He, to rescue me from danger,
  Interposed His precious blood.

3 O, to grace how great a debtor
  Daily I'm constrained to be!
Let Thy goodness, like a fetter,
  Bind my wandering heart to Thee;
Prone to wander, Lord, I feel it;
  Prone to leave the God I love;
Here's my heart; O, take and seal it;
  Seal it for Thy courts above.

859

1 Jesus, I my cross have taken,
  All to leave and follow Thee;
Naked, poor, despised, forsaken,
  Thou, from hence, my All shalt be.
Perish every fond ambition,
  All I've sought, or hoped or known
Yet how rich is my condition!
  God and heaven are still my own.

2 Let the world despise and leave me;
  They have left my Saviour, too;
Human hearts and looks deceive me;
  Thou art not, like them, untrue;
And while Thou shalt smile upon me,
  God of wisdom, love, and might,
Foes may hate and friends may scorn me;
  Show Thy face and all is bright.

3 Soul, then know thy full salvation;
  Rise o'er sin, and fear, and care;
Joy to find in every station
  Something still to do or bear.
Think what Spirit dwells within thee;
  Think what Father's smiles are thine;
Think that Jesus died to win thee;
  Child of heaven canst thou repine?

4 Haste thee on from grace to glory,
  Armed by faith, and winged by prayer;
Heaven's eternal day's before thee;
  God's own hand shall guide thee there.
Soon shall close thy earthly mission,
  Soon shall pass thy pilgrim days;
Hope shall change to glad fruition,
  Faith to sight, and prayer to praise.

860

1 Suff'ring Son of Man, be near me,
  All my suff'rings to sustain,
By Thy sorer griefs to cheer me,
  By Thy more than mortal pain,
By Thy fainting in the garden,
  By Thy bloody sweat, I pray,
Write upon my heart the pardon;
  Take my sins and fears away.

2 By the travail of Thy spirit,
  By Thine outcry on the tree,
By Thine agonizing merit,
  In my pangs, remember me!
By Thy death I now implore Thee,
  Lord! my dying soul befriend;
Make me lovingly adore Thee,
  Make me faithful to the end.

WORTHING. 8s & 7s. (Or 8s without the tie.)

GERMAN.

Shepherds! hail the wondrous stranger, Now to Bethl'em speed your way;

Lo! in yon-der hum-ble manger, Christ, the Lord, is born to-day.

861

2 Christ, by prophets long predicted,
  Joy of Israel's chosen race;
Light to Gentiles long-afflicted,
  Lost in error's darkest maze.

3 Bright the star of your salvation,
  Pointing to, His rude abode!
Rapturous news for every nation:
  Mortals! now behold your God!

4 Glad, we trace th' amazing story,
  Angels leave their bliss to tell;
Theme sublime, replete with glory:
  Sinners saved from death and hell

5 Love eternal moved the Saviour,
  Thus to lay His radiance by;
Blessings on the Lamb forever:
  Glory be to God on high!

862

1 Praise the Lord; ye heavens, adore Him;
  Praise Him, angels in the height;
Sun and moon, rejoice before Him;
  Praise Him, all ye stars of light.

2 Praise the Lord, for He hath spoken;
  Worlds His mighty voice obeyed;
Laws, which never can be broken,
  For their guidance He hath made.

3 Praise the Lord, for He is glorious;
  Never shall His promise fail;
God hath made His saints victorious;
  Sin and death shall not prevail.

4 Praise the God of our salvation;
  Hosts on High, his power proclaim;
Heaven and earth, and all creation,
  Praise and magnify His name.

863

1 Lauded be Thy name forever,
  Thou of life the guard and giver;
Thou canst guard Thy creatures sleeping,
  Heal the heart long broke with weeping:
God of stillness and of motion,
  Of the rainbow and the ocean,
Of the mountain, rock and river,
  Blessed be Thy name forever!

2 Thou who slumberest not, nor sleepest,
  Blest are they Thou kindly keepest,
God of evening's yellow ray,
  God of yonder dawning day,
That rises from the distant sea,
  Like breathings of eternity:
God of life, that fade shall never,
  Glory to Thy name forever!

864

1 Jesus, hail! enthroned in glory,
  There forever to abide;
All the heavenly hosts adore Thee,
  Seated at Thy Father's side.

2 Then for sinners Thou art pleading,
  Then Thou dost our place prepare,
Ever for us interceding,
  Till in glory we appear.

3 Worship, honor, power and blessing,
  When unworthy to receive ;
Loudest praises without ceasing,
  Meet it is for us to give.

4 Help, ye bright, angelic spirits;
  Bring your sweetest noblest lays;
Help to sing our Saviour's merit;
  Help to chant Immanuel's praise.

Whith - er goest thou, pil - grim stran - ger, Wandering through this
Know'st thou not 'tis full of dan - ger, And will not thy

gloo - my vale?
cou - rage fail? "No! I'm bound for the king - dom; Will you

go to glo - ry with me? Hal - le - lu - jah! Praise ye the Lord!"

865

2 " Pilgrim thou dost justly call me,
    Travelling through this lonely void;
  But no ill shall e'er befall me
    While I 'm blest with such a guide.
      Oh, I'm bound, &c."

3 Such a Guide! no guide attends thee,
    Hence for thee my fears arise;
  If some guardian power defend thee,
    'Tis unseen by mortal eyes.
      " Oh, I 'm bound, &c."

4 " Yes, unseen; but still believe me,
    Such a guide my steps attend;
  He'll in every strait relieve me,
    He will guide me to the end;
      For I am bound, &c."

5 Pilgrim, see that stream before thee,
    Darkly rolling through the vale;
  Should its boisterous waves roll o'er thee,
    Would not then thy courage fail!
      " No! I'm bound, &c."

6 " No; that stream has nothing frightful,
    To its brink my steps I 'll bend;
  Thence to plunge 'twill be delightful;
    There my pilgrimage will end.
      For I'm bound, &c."

7 While I gazed, with speed surprising,
    Down the vale she plunged from sight;
  Gazing still, I saw her rising,
    Like an angel clothed in light!
  Oh, she's gone to the kingdom,—
    Will you follow her to glory ?
  Hallelujah! Praise ye the Lord.

866

1 ONWARD, onward, toiling pilgrim,
    Up the rugged steeps of life,
  Falter not, though weak and weary,
    In the agony of strife !

2 Full of hope, and full of courage.
    Giving not a thought to fear,
  Bravely struggle, onward, upward,
    Singing songs of heavenly cheer !

3 Clouds above may gather blackness,
    Angry lightnings rend the sky,
  Sudden tempests full of danger,
    Sweep in maddened fury by !

4 Yet with soul alive to duty,
    Still press on thy toilsome way,
  Good shall come from every trial,
    Strength divine shall win the day.

Far from mor - tal cares retreat - ing Sor - did hopes and vain de - sires,
Here our willing footsteps meeting, Eve - ry heart to heaven aspires.

From the fount of glo - ry beaming, Light ce - les - tial cheers our eyes,

Mer - cy from a - bove proclaiming Peace and pardon from the skies.

867

2 Who may share this great salvation?
  Every pure and humble mind;
Every kindred, tongue and nation,
  From the dross of guilt refined;
Blessings all around bestowing,
  God withholds His care from none;
Grace and mercy ever flowing
  From the fountain of His throne.

3 Every stain of guilt abhorring,
  Firm and bold in virtue's cause,
Still Thy providence adoring,
  Faithful subjects to Thy laws;
Lord, with favor still attend us,
  Bless us with Thy wondrous love;
Thou, our Sun and Shield defend us;
  All our hope is from above.

868

1 SAVIOUR, visit Thy plantation;
  Grant us, Lord, a gracious rain:
All will come to desolation,
  Unless Thou return again.

Keep no longer at a distance,
  Shine upon us from on high,
Lest for want of Thine assistance,
  Every plant should droop and die,

2 Surely once Thy garden flourished;
  Every part looked gay and green;
Then Thy word our spirits nourished:
  Happy seasons we have seen.
But a drought has since succeeded,
  And a sad decline we see;
Lord, Thy help is greatly needed:
  Help can only come from Thee.

3 Let our mutual love be fervent;
  Make us prevalent in prayers;
Let each one esteemed Thy servant
  Shun the world's bewitching snares.
Break the tempter's fatal power,
  Turn the stony heart to flesh,
And begin from this good hour
  To revive Thy work afresh.

869

PRAISE and honor to the Father,
  Praise and honor to the Son,
Praise and honor to the Spirit,
  Ever Three and ever One.

N. BROUGHTON, JR.

1. Am I com - ing, *tru - ly* com - ing Near - er to my Father's Home?
2. Am I lean - ing, *tru - ly* lean - ing On my Sa - viour as I go?

As, so wea - ry, struggling, straying, Thro' the world's dark paths I roam?
Am I of - ten sigh - ing, praying, That of Him I more may know?

870

3 Am I willing—*truly* willing,
   Having Him, all else to leave?
   In this heart, while He's abiding,
   Do I love, obey, believe?

4 Am I growing—*truly* growing
   In that grace He freely gives,
   To His child, who *all* forsaking
   In Him breathes, and in him lives?

5 Thou art *mine*, my Saviour, take me;
   Drive all unbelief away;
   Save me from all sin and make me
   Do Thy will, and in Thee stay.

871

1 SEE the leaves around us falling,
   Dry and withered to the ground;
   Thus to thoughtless mortals calling
   In a sad and solemn sound,

2 " Sons of Adam, once in Eden,
   Blighted when like us he fell,
   Hear the lecture we are reading;
   'Tis, alas! the truth we tell.

3 " Youths, though yet no losses grieve you,
   Gay in health and manly grace,
   Let not cloudless skies deceive you;
   Summer gives to autumn place,

4 " Yearly in our course returning,
   Messengers of shortest stay,
   Thus we preach, this truth concerning,
   Heaven and earth shall pass away.

5 " On the tree of life eternal,
   Man, let all thy hope be stayed,
   Which alone, forever vernal,
   Bears a leaf that shall not fade."

872

1 COME, Thou long expected Jesus,
   Born to set Thy people free;
   From our fears and sins release us,
   Let us find our rest in Thee.

2 Israel's Strength and Consolation,
   Hope of all the saints Thou art;
   Dear Desire of every nation,
   Joy of every longing heart.

3 Born, Thy people to deliver;
   Born a child—and yet a King;
   Born to reign in us forever,
   Now Thy precious kingdom bring.

4 By Thine own eternal Spirit,
   Rule in all our hearts alone;
   By Thine all-sufficient merit,
   Raise us to Thy glorious throne.

873

1 LORD of heaven, and earth, and ocean,
   Hear us from Thy bright abode,
   While our hearts, with true devotion,
   Own their great and gracious God.

2 Now with joy we come before Thee,
   Seek Thy face, Thy mercies sing;
   Lord of life, of light and glory,
   Guard Thy church, Thou heavenly King.

3 Health and every needful blessing
   Are Thy bounteous gifts alone;
   Comforts undeserved possessing,
   Here we bend before Thy throne.

4 Thee, with humble adoration,
   Lord, we praise for mercies past;
   Still to this most favored nation
   May those mercies ever last.

SICILY. 8s & 7s.

May' the grace of Christ, our Saviour, And the Father's boundless love,

With the Ho-ly Spi-rit's fa-vor, Rest up-on us from a-bove.

874

2 Thus may we abide in union
With each other and the Lord,
And possess, in sweet communion,
Joys which earth cannot afford.

875

1 GENTLY, Lord! O gently lead us, ·
Through this lonely vale of tears;
Through the changes Thou'st decreed us,
Till our last great change appears:

2 When temptation's darts assail us,
When in devious paths we stray,
Let Thy goodness never fail us,
Lead us in Thy perfect way.

3 In the hour of pain and anguish,
In the hour when death draws near,
Suffer not our hearts to languish,
Suffer not our souls to fear:

4 And, when mortal life is ended,
Bid us on Thy bosom rest,
Till, by angel bands attended,
We awake among the blest.

876

1 MEEK and lowly, pure and holy,
Chief among the blessed three,
Turning sadness into gladness,
Heaven-born art thou, Charity!

2 Pity dwelleth in thy bosom,
Kindness reigneth o'er thy heart;
Gentle thoughts alone can sway thee—
Judgment hath in thee no part.

3 Hoping ever, failing never,
Though deceived, believing still;
Long abiding, all confiding
To thy heavenly Father's will;

4 Never weary of well-doing,
Never fearful of the end;
Claiming all mankind as brothers,
Thou dost all alike befriend.

5 Meek and lowly, pure and holy,
Chief among the blessed three,
Turning sadness into gladness,
Heaven-born art thou, Charity!

877

1 HARK! what mean those holy voices,
Sweetly sounding thro' the skies?
Lo! th' angelic host rejoices;
Heavenly hallelujahs rise.

2 Hear them tell the wondrous story,
Hear them chant in hymns of joy:
" Glory in the highest, glory!
Glory be to God Most High!

3 " Peace on earth, good will from heaven,
Reaching far as man is found;
Souls redeemed, and sins forgiven!
Loud our golden harps shall sound.

4 " Christ is born, the great Anointed:
Heaven and earth His praises sing!
Oh, receive whom God appointed
For your Prophet, Priest, and King!

5 " Haste, ye mortals, to adore Him;
Learn His name, and taste His joy:
Till in heaven ye sing before Him,
' Glory be to God Most High!' "

BAVARIA. 8s & 7s.

Je - sus, full of all compassion, Hear Thy humble suppliant's cry;
Let me know Thy great salvation— See, I languish, faint, and die.
D. C. Prostrate at Thy feet repenting, Send, O, send me quick re - lief.

Guilty, but with heart re - lent - ing Overwhelmed with helpless grief,

878

2 Whither should a wretch be flying,
But to Him who comfort gives!
Whither, from the dread of dying,
But to Him who ever lives?
While I view Thee, wounded, grieving,
Breathless, on the cursed tree,
Fain I'd feel my heart believing
That Thou sufferedst thus for me.

3 In the world of endless ruin,
Let it never, Lord, be said,
"Here's a soul that perished suing
For the boasted Saviour's aid!"
Saved! the deed shall spread new glory
Through the shining realms above;
Angels sing the pleasing story
All enraptured with Thy love.

879

1 Yes, for me, for me He careth
With a brother's tender care;
Yes, with me, with me He shareth
Every burden, every fear.
Yes, o'er me, o'er me He watcheth,
Ceaseless watcheth, night and day;
Yes, e'en me, e'en me He snatcheth
From the perils of the way.

2 Yes, for me He standeth pleading,
At the mercy-seat above;
Ever for me interceding,
Constant in untiring love.
Yes, in me abroad He sheddeth
Joys unearthly, love and light;
And to cover me He spreadeth
His paternal wing of might.

3 Yes, in me, in me He dwelleth;
I in Him, and He in me!
And my empty soul He filleth,
Here and through eternity.
Thus I wait for His returning,
Singing all the way to heaven:
Such the joyful song of morning,
Such the tranquil song of even.

880

1 Praise to Thee thou great Creator!
Praise to Thee from every tongue:
Join, my soul, with every creature,
Join the universal song.

2 Father, Source of all compassion,
Pure, unbounded grace is Thine:
Hail the God of our salvation!
Praise Him for His love divine.

3 For ten thousand blessings given,
For the hope of future joy,
Sound His praise thro' earth and heaven,
Sound Jehovah's praise on high.

4 Joyfully on earth adore Him,
Till in heaven our song we raise;
There, enraptured, fall before Him,
Lost in wonder, love, and praise.

881

Praise the God of all creation;
Praise the Father's boundless love;
Praise the Lamb, our Expiation;
Praise the Spirit from above:
Praise the Fountain of salvation,
Him by whom our spirits live;
Undivided adoration
To the one Jehovah give.

MELLEN. 8s & 7s.

Now the Saviour standeth pleading
Now in heaven He's inter - ceding,

At the sinner's bolt - ed heart;
Taking there the sinner's part.

D. C. Once He died for your be - havior, Now He calls you by His charms.

Sin - ner, can you hate the Saviour? Will you thrust Him from your arms?

D. C.

882

3 Sinners, hear your God and Saviour,
    Hear His gracious voice to-day,
  Turn from all your vain behavior;
    O repent, return and pray.

4 O be wise before you languish
    On the bed of dying strife!
  Endless joy or endless anguish,
    Turns upon the events of life.

5 Now He's waiting to be gracious,
    Now He stands and looks on thee;
  See what kindness, love and pity,
    Shine around on you and me.

6 Open now your hearts before Him,
    Bid the Saviour welcome in;
  Now receive, and O, adore Him,
    Take a full discharge from sin.

883

1 LET Thy grace, Lord, make me lowly;
    Humble all my swelling pride:
  Fallen, guilty, and unholy,
    Greatness from my eyes I'll hide.

2 I'll forbid my vain aspiring,
    Nor at earthly honors aim;
  No ambitious heights desiring,
    Far above my humble claim.

3 Weaned from earth's vexatious pleasures,
    In Thy love I'll seek for mine;
  Placed in heaven my nobler treasures,
    Earth I quietly resign.

4 Israel, thus the world despising,
    On the Lord alone rely:
  Then from Him thy joys arising,
    Like Himself, shall never die.

884

1 ALWAYS with us, always with us—
    Words of cheer and words of love·
  Thus the risen Saviour whispers,
    From His dwelling-place above.

2 With us when we toil in sadness,
    Sowing much and reaping none;
  Telling us that in the future
    Golden harvests shall be won.

3 With us when the storm is sweeping
    O'er our pathway dark and drear;
  Waking hope within our bosoms,
    Stilling every anxious fear.

4 With us in the lonely valley,
    When we cross the chilling stream;
  Lighting up the steps to glory
    With salvation's radiant beam.

885

1 THIS is not my place of resting—
    Mine's a city yet to come;
  Onward to it I am hasting—
    On to my eternal home.

2 In it all is light and glory;
    O'er it shines a nightless day:
  Every trace of sin's sad story,
    All the curse, hath passed away.

3 There the Lamb, our Shepherd, leads us
    By the streams of life along,—
  On the freshest pastures feeds us,
    Turns our sighing into song.

4 Soon we pass this desert dreary,
    Soon we bid farewell to pain;
  Never more are sad and weary,
    Never, never sin again.

MOZART.

One there is, a - bove all oth - ers, Well deserves the name of Friend;

His is love be - yond a brother's, Costly, free, and knows no end.
They who once His kindness prove,.... Find it ev - er - last - ing love.

End with second strain.

They who once His kindness prove,.... Find it ev - er - last - ing love.

886

2 Which of all our friends, to save us,
  Could or would have shed His blood?
But our Jesus died to have us
  Reconciled in Him to God.
This was boundless love indeed;
  Jesus is a Friend in need.

3 When He lived on earth abased,
  Friend of sinners was His name;
Now above all glory raised,
  He rejoices in the same.
Still He calls them brethren, friends,
  And to all their wants attends.

4 O for grace our hearts to soften!
  Teach us, Lord, at length to love;
We, alas! forget too often
  What a Friend we have above;
But when home our souls are brought,
  We will love Thee as we ought.

887

1 TOSSED upon life's raging billow,
  Sweet it is, O Lord to know,
Thou didst press a sailor's pillow,
  And canst feel a sailor's woe.
Never slumbering, never sleeping,
  Though the night be dark and drear,

Thou the faithful watch art keeping,
  "All, all's well," Thy constant cheer.

2 And though loud the wind is howling,
  Fierce though flash the lightnings red;
Darkly though the storm-cloud's scowling
  O'er the sailor's anxious head;
Thou canst calm the raging ocean,
  All its noise and tumult still,
Hush the tempest's wild commotion,
  At the bidding of Thy will.

3 Thus my heart the hope will cherish,
  While to Thee I lift mine eye;
Thou wilt save me ere I perish,
  Thou wilt hear the sailor's cry,
And though mast and sail be riven,
  Life's short voyage will soon be o'er;
Safely moored in heaven's wide haven,
  Storm and tempest vex no more.

888

1 MAY our lights be always burning,
  And our loins be girded round,
Waiting for our Lord's returning—
  Longing for the welcome sound!
Thus the Christian life adorning,
  Never will we be afraid;
Should He come at night or morning—
  Early dawn or evening shade.

246 AUTUMN. 8s & 7s. LUDOVICK NICHOLSON,
Of Paisley, Scotland.

Ho - ly Fa - ther, Thou hast taught me I should live to Thee a - lone;

Year by year, Thy hand hath brought me On through dangers oft unknown;

When I wandered, Thou hast found me, When I doubt - ed, sent me light;

Still Thine arm has been a - round me, All my paths were in Thy sight.

889

2 In the world will foes assail me,
  Craftier, stronger far than I;
And the strife may never fail me,
  Well I know, before I die.
Therefore, Lord, I come, believing
  Thou canst give the power I need;
Through the prayer of faith receiving
  Strength—the Spirit's strength, indeed.

3 I would trust in Thy protecting,
  Wholly rest upon Thine arm;
Follow wholly Thy directing,
  Thou, mine only guard from harm!
Keep me from mine own undoing,
  Help me turn to Thee when tried,
Still my footsteps, Father, viewing,
  Keep me ever at Thy side.

890

1 HEAR what God, the Lord, hath spoken:
  "O my people, faint and few,
Comfortless, afflicted, broken,
  Fair abodes I build for you;
Scenes of heartfelt tribulation
  Shall no more perplex your ways;
You shall name your walls 'Salvation,'
  And your gates shall all be 'Praise.'"

2 There, like streams that feed the garden,
  Pleasures without end shall flow;
For the Lord, your faith rewarding,
  All His bounty shall bestow.
Still in undisturbed possession
  Peace and righteousness shall reign;
Never shall you feel oppression,
  Hear the voice of war again.

DR. LOWELL MASON.

Hark! ten thousand harps and voices Sound the notes of praise a - bove;
Je - sus reigns and heav'n rejoices; Je - sus reigns the God of love:
See, He sits on yonder throne; Je - sus rules the world a - lone.
Hal - le - lu - jah, Hal - le - lu - jah, Hal - le - lu - jah, A - - men.

891

2 Jesus, hail! whose glories brightens
All above, and gives it worth;
Lord of life! Thy smile enlightens,
Cheers and charms Thy saints on earth;
When we think of love like Thine,
Lord! we own it love divine.
Hallelujah, &c.

3 Saviour! hasten Thine appearing,
Bring—oh bring the glorious day,
When the awful summons hearing,
Heaven and earth shall pass away;
Then with golden harps we'll sing—
"Glory, glory to our King."
Hallelujah, &c.

892

1 GLORIOUS things of thee are spoken,
Zion, city of our God:
He whose word cannot be broken
Formed thee for His own abode;
On the Rock of Ages founded,
What can shake thy sure repose?
With salvation's walls surrounded,
Thou mayst smile at all thy foes.

2 See, the streams of living waters,
Springing from eternal love,
Well supply thy sons and daughters,
And all fear of want remove!
Who can faint, while such a river
Ever flows their thirst to assuage?
Grace, which, like the Lord, the Giver,
Never fails from age to age.

3 Round each habitation hovering,
See the cloud and fire appear,
For a glory and a covering,
Showing that the Lord is near;
Thus deriving from their banner
Light by night and shade by day:
Safe they feed upon the manna
Which He gives them when they pray.

ZELL. 8s & 7s.

Bost.

He that go - eth forth with weeping, Bearing precious seed in love,

Nev - er tir - ing, nev - er sleeping, Findeth mer - cy from a - bove.

893

2 Soft descend the dews of heaven,
Bright the rays celestial shine ;
Precious fruits will thus be given,
Through the influence all divine.

3 Sow thy seed; be never weary:
Let no fears thy soul annoy;
Be the prospect ne'er so dreary
Thou shalt reap the fruits of joy.

4 Lo! the scene of verdure brightening!
In the rising grain appear;
Look again, the fields are whitening,
For the harvest time is near.

894

1 Hark! the gospel trumpets sounding;
Sinners, hear the joyful call:
Christ, in pardoning love abounding,
Offers liberty to all.

2 Though your crimes have reached to heaven,
And of deepest dye appear,
Ask, and they shall be forgiven;
Seek, and you shall find him near.

3 Cast your load of guilt behind you;
To the Lord for mercy flee;
Though the strongest fetters bind you,
His salvation makes you free.

4 Now He's waiting to be gracious,
Now He stands and looks on thee:
See what kindness, love, and pity,
Shine around on you and me.

5 Come, for all things now are ready,
Yet there's room for many more :
O ye blind, ye lame and needy,
Come to wisdom's boundless store!

895

1 God is love; His mercy brightens
All the path in which we rove;
Bliss He wakes, and woe He lightens;
God is wisdom, God is love.

2 Chance and change are busy ever;
Man decays, and ages move;
But His mercy waneth never;
God is wisdom, God is love.

3 E'en the hour that darkest seemeth
Will His changeless goodness prove;
From the gloom His brightness streameth;
God is wisdom, God is love.

4 He with earthly cares entwineth
Hope and comfort from above;
Everywhere His glory shineth;
God is wisdom, God is love.

896

1 Where the wilderness is lying,—
And the trees of ages nod,
Westward in the desert crying,
Make a highway for our God,—

2 Westward till the Church be kneeling
In the forest aisles so dim,
And the wildwood's arches pealing
With the people's holy hymn.

3 Westward still, O Lord, in glory
Be Thy bannered cross unfurled,
Till from vale and mountain hoary
Rolls the anthem round the world.

4 Reign, O, reign o'er every nation,
Reign, Redeemer, Father King;
And with songs of Thy salvation,
Let the wide creation ring.

Tell us, wan-derer! wild-ly rov-ing From the path that'
*/: When will thy de-

leads to peace, Plea-sure's false en-chant-ment lov-ing—
lu-sion cease?—FINE.

897

2 Once, like thee by joys surrounded,
We could kneel at pleasure's shrine;
Then our brightest hopes were bounded
By delights as false as thine.

3 But those visions never blessed us—
Soon their fleeting day was o'er;
Then the world that had caressed us,
Charmed us with its smiles no more.

4 Such is pleasure's transient story;
Lasting happiness is known
Only in the path to glory,
In the Saviour's love alone.

898

1 LABORING and heavy laden
With my sins, O Lord, I roam;
While I know Thou hast invited
All such wanderers to their home.

2 Make my stubborn spirit willing
To obey Thy gracious voice;
At the cross to leave its burden,
And departing to rejoice.

3 Thy sweet yoke I'd take upon me,
And would learn, O Lord, of Thee;
Thou art meek in heart, and lowly;
Teach me like Thyself to be.

4 Rest my weary soul is seeking
From its sins and all its woes;
In Thy bosom I would place me,
There to find a blest repose.

5 Laboring and heavy laden,
· Lord, no longer will I roam;
Here I fix my habitation
In Thy sheltering love at home.

899

1 JESUS, who on Calvary's mountain
Poured Thy precious blood for me,
Wash me in its flowing fountain,
That my soul may spotless be.

2 I have sinned, but O, restore me;
For unless Thou smile on me,
Dark is all the world before me,
Darker yet eternity!

3 In Thy word I hear Thee saying,
"Come and I will give you rest;"
And the gracious call obeying,
See, I hasten to Thy breast.

4 Grant, O, grant Thy Spirit's teaching,
That I may not go astray,
Till, the gate of heaven reaching,
Earth and sin are passed away.

900

1 SWEET the moments, rich in blessing,
Which before the cross I spend;
Life, and health, and peace possessing,
From the sinner's dying Friend.

2 Truly blessed is this station,
Low before His cross to lie,
While I see divine compassion,
Beaming in His gracious eye.

3 Love and grief my heart dividing,
With my tears His feet I'll bathe;
Constant still, in faith abiding,
Life deriving from His death.

4 May I still enjoy this feeling,
Still to my Redeemer go,
Prove His wounds each day more healing,
And Himself more truly know.

BELLENDEN. 8s & 7s.

O Thou Sun of glorious splendor, Shine with healing in Thy wing;
Chase a-way these shades of darkness; Ho-ly light and comfort bring.

D. C. 'Death and hell are spoiled and vanquish'd Thro' the great Immanuel's name.'

Let the her-alds of sal-va-tion Round the earth with joy proclaim:

901

2 Take Thy power, Almighty Saviour,
  Claim the nations for Thine own;
Reign, Thou Lord of life and glory,
  Till each heart becomes Thy throne.
Then the earth, o'erspread with glory,
  Decked with heavenly splendor bright,
Shall be made, Jehovah's dwelling—
  As at first, the Lord's delight.

902

1 PEACE be to this sacred dwelling,
  Peace to every soul therein;
Peace, of heavenly joy foretelling,
  Peace, the fruit of conquered sin;
Peace, that speaks its heavenly Giver;
  Peace to worldly minds unknown;
Peace divine, that flows forever
  From its source, the Lord alone.

2 Prince of Peace! forever near us,
  Fix in all our hearts Thy home;
With Thy bright appearing cheer us;
  Let Thy blessed kingdom come!
Come with sweeter consolation,
  Come, and give our souls to prove
All the joys of Thy salvation,
  All the joys that spring from love!

903

1 MIGHTY GOD! while angels bless Thee,
  May a mortal lisp Thy name?
Lord of men as well as angels!
  Thou art every creatures theme:
Lord of every land and nation!
  Ancient of eternal days!
Sounded through the wide creation,
  Be Thy just and lawful praise.

2 For the grandeur of Thy nature—
  Grand beyond a seraph's thought;
For the wonders of creation,
  Works with skill and kindness wrought;
For Thy providence that governs
  Through thine empire's wide domain,
Wings an angel, guides a sparrow;
  Blessed be Thy gentle reign.

3 For Thy rich, Thy free redemption,
  Bright though veiled in darkness long;
Thought is pure, and poor expression,
  Who can sing that wondrous song?
Brightness of the Father's glory!
  Shall Thy praise unuttered lie?
Break, my tongue! such guilty silence,
  Sing the Lord who came to die:

4 From the highest throne of glory
  To the cross of deepest woe,
All to ransom guilty captives!
  Flow, my praise! forever flow:
Reascend, immortal Saviour!
  Leave Thy footstool, take Thy throne;
Thence return and reign forever;
  Be the kingdom all Thine own!

904

1 Praise to Thee, thou great Creator!
  Praise to Thee from every tongue:
Join my soul, with every creature,
  Join the universal throng.

2 Father! Source of all compassion!
  Pure, unbounded grace is Thine:
Hail the God of our salvation!
  Praise Him for His love divine.

(By permission.) J. W. DADMUN.

In the Christian's home in glo-ry, There re-mains a land of rest;

There my Saviour's gone be-fore me, To ful-fil my soul's re-quest.

CHORUS.

There is rest.... for the wea-ry, There is rest for the wea-ry,
On the oth-er side of Jor-dan, In the sweet fields of E-den,

There is rest.... for the wea-ry, There is rest for you.
Where the tree of life is bloom-ing, There is rest for you.

905

2 He is fitting up my mansion,
Which eternally shall stand;
For my stay shall not be transient
In that holy, happy land.

3 Pain nor sickness ne'er shall enter,
Grief nor woe my lot shall share;
But in that celestial centre,
I a crown of life shall wear.

4 Death itself shall then be vanquished,
And his sting shall be withdrawn;
Shout for gladness, O ye ransomed!
Hail with joy the rising morn.

5 Sing, O sing, ye heirs of glory;
Shout your triumph as you go;
Zion's gates will open for you,
You shall find an entrance through.

MAESTOSO. DR. LOWELL MASON.

Call Je - ho - vah thy sal - va - tion, Rest beneath th'Almighty's shade ;
In His se - cret ha - bi - ta - tion Dwell and nev - er be dismayed;

D. C. Guile nor vi - o - lence can harm thee; In e - ter - nal si - lence there.

There no tumult shall a - larm thee; Thou shalt dread no hidden snare;

906

2 He shall charge His angel legions,
  Watch and ward o'er thee to keep;
Though thou walk thro' hostile regions,
  Though in desert wilds thou sleep:
On the lion vainly roaring,
  On her young, thy foot shall tread,
And the dragon's den exploring,
  Thou shalt bruise the serpent's head.

3 Since with pure and firm affection
  Thou on God hast set thy love,
With the wings of His protection
  He will shield thee from above;
Thou shalt call on Him in trouble,
  He will hearken, He will save;
Here for grief reward thee double,
  Crown with life beyond the grave.

907

1 FULL of trembling expectation,
  Feeling much, and fearing more,
Mighty God of my salvation!
  I Thy timely aid implore;
Suffering Son of Man be near me,
  All my sufferings to sustain;
By Thy sorer griefs to cheer me,
  By Thy more than mortal pain.

2 Call to mind that unknown anguish,
  In Thy days of flesh below;
When Thy troubled soul did languish
  Under a whole world of woe;
When Thou didst our curse inherit,
  Groan beneath our guilty load,
Burdened with a wounded spirit,
  Bruised by all the wrath of God.

3 By Thy most severe temptation,
  In that dark, Satanic hour;
By Thy last mysterious passion,
  Screen me from the adverse power.
By Thy fainting in the garden,
  By Thy bloody sweat, I pray,
Write upon my heart the pardon,
  Take my sins and fears away.

4 By the travail of Thy Spirit,
  By Thine outcry on the tree,
By Thine agonizing merit,
  In my pangs remember me!
By Thy death I Thee conjure,
  A weak, dying soul befriend;
Make me patient to endure,
  Make me faithful to the end.

908

1 SONGS of joy Jehovah giveth,
  In the night of toil and pain,
When the eye of faith perceiveth
  All that toil is heavenly gain:
Then the burden groweth lighter,
  And the anguish will remove,
While the thoughts of heaven are brighter,
  And the heart is filled with love.

2 Songs of praise Jehovah giveth,
  When the night of death has come;
When the hand that ne'er reprieveth,
  Leads the pilgrim to the tomb:
Angels then are hovering o'er him,
  And the soul within hath peace;
Heaven is opening wide before him,
  And its joys will never cease.

MAESTOSO.

Men of God, go take your stations; Darkness reigns throughout the earth; }
Go, proclaim among the na - tions Joy - ful news of heav'nly birth: }

Bear the tid - ings, Bear the tid - ings Of the Saviour's matchless worth.

909

2 Of His gospel not ashamed,
   As the power of God to save,
Go where Christ was never named,
   Publish freedom to the slave—
      Blessed freedom !
   Freedom Zion's children have.

3 When exposed to fearful dangers,
   Jesus will His own defend;
Borne afar 'mid foes and strangers,
   Jesus will appear your Friend;
      And His presence
   Shall be with you to the end.

910

1 HALLELUJAH ! best and sweetest
   Of the hymns of praise above;
Hallelujah ! thou repeatest,
   Angel host, these notes of love;
      This ye utter,
   While your golden harps ye move.

2 Hallelujah ! church victorious,
   Join the concert of the sky;
Hallelujah ! bright and glorious,
   Lift, ye saints, this strain on high;
      We, poor exiles,
   Join not yet your melody.

3 Hallelujah ! strains of gladness
   Comfort not the faint and worn;
Hallelujah ! sounds of sadness
   Best become the heart forlorn;
      Our offences
   We with bitter tears must mourn.

4 But our earnest supplication,
   Holy God, we raise to Thee;
Visit us with Thy salvation,
   Make us all Thy peace to see.
      Hallelujah !
   Ours at length this strain shall be.

911

1 ANGELS from the realms of glory,
   Wing your flight o'er all the earth;
Ye who sang creation's story,
   Now proclaim Messiah's birth;
      Come and worship,
   Worship Christ, the new-born King.

2 Shepherds, in the field abiding,
   Watching o'er your flocks by night,
God with man is now residing;
   Yonder shines the infant light;
      Come and worship,
   Worship Christ, the new-born King.

3 Saints before the altar bending,
   Watching long in hope and fear,
Suddenly the Lord, descending,
   In His temple shall appear;
      Come and worship,
   Worship Christ, the new-born King.

4 Sinners, bowed in true repentance,
   Doomed for guilt to endless pains,
Justice now revokes the sentence,
   Mercy calls you—break your chains :
      Come and worship,
   Worship Christ, the new-born King.

ZION. 8s 7s & 4.

DR. T. HASTINGS.

On the mountain's top appearing,
Welcome news to Zi - on bearing,
Lo! the sacred herald stands!
Zi - on long in hostile lands. }
Mourning captive!

God Himself shall loose thy bands: Mourning captive! God Himself shall loose thy bands.

912

2 God, thy God, will now restore thee;
    He Himself appears thy Friend:
All thy foes shall flee before thee;
Here their boasts and triumphs end;
    Great deliverance
Zion's King vouchsafes to send.

3 Enemies no more shall trouble;
    All thy wrongs shall be redressed;
" For thy shame thou shalt have double;"
In thy Maker's favor blessed;
    All thy conflicts
End in everlasting rest.

913

1 O'ER the realms of pagan darkness,
    Let the eye of pity gaze;
See the kindreds of the people
Lost in sin's bewildering maze;
    Darkness brooding
On the face of all the earth.

2 Light of them that sit in darkness,
    Rise and shine, Thy blessings bring;
Light to lighten all the Gentiles,
Rise with healing in Thy wing;
    To Thy brightness
Let all kings and nations come.

3 May the heathen, now adoring
    Idol gods of wood and stone,
Come, and worshipping before Thee,
Serve the living God alone;
    Let Thy glory
Fill the earth as floods the sea.

4 Thou to whom all power is given!
    Speak the word; at Thy command,
Let the company of preachers
Spread Thy name from land to land;
    Lord, be with them
Alway, to the end of time.

914

1 SINNERS, will you scorn the message
    Sent in mercy from above?
Every sentence, O, how tender!
Every line is full of love.
    Listen to it;
Every line is full of love.

2 Hear the heralds of the gospel
    News from Zion's King proclaim,
To each rebel sinner pardon,
Free forgiveness in His name.
    How important!
Free forgiveness in His name.

3 Who hath our report believed?
    Who received the joyful word?
Who embraced the news of pardon
Offered to you by the Lord?
    Can you slight it?
Offered to you by the Lord.

4 O, ye angels, hovering round us,
    Waiting spirits, speed your way;
Hasten to the court of heaven,
Tidings bear without delay:
    Rebel sinners
Glad the message will obey.

Come, ye sin-ners, poor and needy, Weak and wounded, sick and sore, }
Je-sus rea-dy stands to save you, Full of pi-ty, love and power. }
D. C. He is a-ble, He is a-ble, He is willing, doubt no more.

He is a-ble, He is a-ble, He is will-ing, doubt no more.

915

2 Come ye thirsty, come and welcome;
  God's free bounty glorify :
True belief and true repentance,
Every grace that brings us nigh—
  Without money,
Come to Jesus Christ and buy.

3 Come, ye weary, heavy laden,
  Lost and ruined by the fall;
If you tarry till you're better,
You will never come at all :
  Not the righteous—
Sinners, Jesus came to call.

4 Let not conscience make you linger,
  Nor of fitness fondly dream;
All the fitness He requireth,
Is to feel your need of Him :
  This He gives you—
'Tis the Spirit's rising beam.

5 Agonizing in the garden,
  Lo ! your Maker prostrate lies !
On the bloody tree behold Him;
Hear Him cry before He dies,
   " It is finished :"
Sinners, will not this suffice ?

916

1 CHRISTIAN, see ! the orient morning
  Breaks along the heathen sky;
Lo, the expected day is dawning,
  Glorious day-spring from on high;
   Hallelujah !
Hail the day-spring from on high !

2 Heathens at the sight are singing;
  Morning wakes the tuneful lays;
Precious offerings they are bringing,
  First fruits of more perfect praise;
   Hallelujah !
Hail the day-spring from on high !

3 Zion's Sun, salvation beaming,
  Gilding now the radiant hills,
Rise and shine, till brighter gleaming,
  All the world Thy glory fills;
   Hallelujah !
Hail the day-spring from on high !

4 Lord of every tribe and nation,
  Spread Thy truth from pole to pole;
Spread the light of Thy salvation,
  Till it shine on every soul;
   Hallelujah !
Hail the day-spring from on high !

917

1 WELCOME, welcome, dear Redeemer;
  Welcome to this heart of mine;
Lord, I make a full surrender,
  Every power and thought be Thine,
   Thine entirely,
Through eternal ages Thine.

2 Known to all to be Thy mansion,
  Earth and hell will disappear;
Or in vain attempt possession,
  When they find the Lord is near;
   Shout, O Zion !
Shout, ye saints ! the Lord is here.

TAMWORTH. 8s 7s & 4.

MAESTOSO.   LOCKHART.

Guide me, O Thou great Je - ho - vah, Pilgrim thro' this bar - ren land ; }
I am weak, but Thou art mighty ; Hold me with Thy powerful hand ; }

Bread of heaven, Bread of heaven, Feed me till I want no more.

918 .

2 Open Thou the crystal fountain
  Whence the healing streams do flow;
Let the fiery, cloudy pillar
  Lead me all my journey through;
    Strong Deliverer,
  Be thou still my Strength and Shield.

3 When I tread the verge of Jordan,
  Bid my anxious fears subside;
Death of death, and hell's destruction,
  Land me safe on Canaan's side;
    Songs of praises
  I will ever give to Thee.

919

1 HARK ! a voice from heaven proclaiming
  Comfort to the mourning slave;
God has heard him long complaining,
  And extends His arm to save;
    Proud oppression
  Soon shall find a shameful grave.

2 See, the light of truth is breaking
  Full and clear on every hand,
And the voice of mercy speaking,
  Now is heard through all the land:
    Firm and fearless
  See the friends of freedom stand.

3 Lo, the nation is arousing
  From its slumber, long and deep,
And the friends of God are waking,
  Never, never more to sleep
    While a bondman
  In his chains remains to weep.

4 Long, too long have we been dreaming
  O'er our country's sin and shame;
Let us now, the time redeeming
  Press the helpless captive's claim
    Till, exulting
  He shall cast aside his chain.

920

1 YES, we trust the day is breaking;
  Joyful times are near at hand;
God, the mighty God, is speaking,
  By His word, in every land.
    Mark His progress—
  Darkness flies at His command.

2 While the foe becomes more daring,
  While he "enters like a flood,"
God the Saviour is preparing
  Means to spread His truth abroad.
    Every language
  Soon shall tell the love of God.

3 O, 'tis pleasant, 'tis reviving
  To our hearts, to hear, each day,
Joyful news, from far arriving,
  How the gospel wins its way,
    Those enlightening
  Who in death and darkness lay.

4 God of Jacob, high and glorious,
  Let Thy people see Thy hand;
Let the gospel be victorious
  Through the world, in every land;
    Let the idols .
  Perish, Lord, at Thy command.

TRALEE. 8s 7s & 4. 257

FINE.

Lead us, heav'nly Father, lead us O'er the world's tempestuous sea;
D. C. Yet pos - sess - ing Ev - 'ry blessing, If our God our Fa - ther be.

Guard us, guide us, keep us, feed, us For we have no help but Thee;

D. C.

921

2 Saviour, breathe forgiveness o'er us;
All our weakness Thou dost know;
Thou didst tread this earth before us;
Thou didst feel its keenest woe;
Lone and dreary
Faint and weary,
Through the desert Thou didst go.

3 Spirit of our God, descending,
Fill our hearts with heavenly joy;
Love with every passion blending,
Pleasure that can never cloy;
Thus provided,
Pardoned, guided,
Nothing can our peace destroy.

922

1 At Thy footstool, humbly blending
Faith and hope with fervent prayer,
On Thy promised help depending,
May our toils Thy blessing share;
Great Jehovah,
Hear us; make us still Thy care.

2 Here reveal Thy power and glory;
Grant each teacher great success;
May those whom we teach adore Thee,
And their Saviour now confess;
Holy Spirit,
Bless us with Thy quickening grace.

3 For Thy love accept this token;
We the young with truth would feed;
'Twas for such Thy heart was broken;
Thou dost for them intercede;
Mighty Saviour,
Help us; 'tis Thy cause we plead.

923

1 Hallowed cross, my God revealing,
Hail thou strange, mysterious tree!
Hallowed fount of love unsealling—
Love of infinite degree—
Love amazing;
God incarnate dies for me.

2 Where the sword of justice gleaming,
Waited for the sinner's blood,
Shines the cross, with mercy beaming,
Mercy from the throne of God—
Bleeding mercy
Pours the sin-atoning flood.

3 Precious cross! my soul subduing,
'Neath thy shadow let me hide;
Mind, and will, and heart renewing,—
Banish all my sinful pride;
All my glory
Be my Saviour crucified.

924

1 Lord of glory, who didst honor
David's humble sling and stone,
Ancient Israel to deliver,
Now as weak an effort own;
Bless the labor
Which our feeble hands have done.

2 And when the great harvest's ended,
When the Master counts our sheaves,
O, let those by us attended
Be as numerous as the leaves
Which we scatter,
And a dying world receives.

OLIPHANT. 8s 7s & 4.

Dr. Lowell Mason.

Zi - on stands with hills sur - round - ed— Zi - on kept by

pow'r di - vine; All her foes shall be con - found - ed,

Tho' the world in arms combine; Hap - py Zi - on, Hap - py Zi - on,

What a favored lot is thine! What a favored lot is thine!

925

2 Every human tie may perish;
   Friend to friend unfaithful prove;
   Mothers cease their own to cherish;
   Heaven and earth at last remove;
       But no changes
   Can attend Jehovah's love.

3 In the furnace God may prove thee,
   Thence to bring thee forth more bright,
   But can never cease to love thee;
   Thou art precious in His sight;
       God is with Thee—
   God, thine everlasting light.

926

1 Hark! the voice of love and mercy
   Sounds aloud from Calvary;

See! it rends the rocks asunder,
   Shakes the earth, and veils the sky:
       "It is finished!"
   Hear the dying Saviour cry.

2 "It is finished!" Oh, what pleasure
   Do these charming words afford!
   Heavenly blessings, without measure,
   Flow to us from Christ the Lord:
       "It is finished!"
   Saints, the dying words record.

3 Tune your harps anew, ye seraphs;
   Join to sing the pleasing theme:
   All on earth and all in heaven,
   Join to praise Immanuel's name:
       Hallelujah!
   Glory to the bleeding Lamb!

God the Lord a King re - maineth, Robed in His own glorious light. God hath

robed Him, and He reigneth, He hath girded Him with might : Hallelujah ! God is

King in depth and height. Hal - le - lu- jah ! God is King in depth and height.

927

2 Lord ! the water-floods have lifted,
  Ocean-floods have raised their roar,
Now they pause where they have drifted,
Now they burst upon the shore :
    Hallelujah !
From the ocean's sounding store.

3 With all tones of waters blending
  Glorious is the breaking deep:
Glorious, beauteous without ending,
God who reigns on heaven's high steep.
    Hallelujah !
Songs of ocean never sleep.

4 Lord ! the words Thy lips are telling
  Are the perfect verity:
Of Thine high, eternal dwelling
Holiness shall inmate be :
    Hallelujah !
Pure is all that lives with Thee.

928

1 Look, ye saints;—the sight is glorious;—
  See the Man of Sorrows now;
From the fight returned victorious,
Every knee to Him shall bow;
    Crown Him, crown Him;
  Crowns before the Victor's brow.

2 Crown the Saviour, angels, crown Him;
  Rich the trophies Jesus brings;
In the seat of power enthrone Him,
While the heavenly concert rings :
    Crown Him, crown Him;
Crown the Saviour King of kings.

3 Sinners in derision crowned Him,
  Mocking thus the Saviour's claim;
Saints and angels crowd around Him,
Own His title, praise His name ·
    Crown Him, crown Him;
Spread abroad the Victor's fame. ·

FENWICK. 8s 7s &4.

Dr. Lowell Mason.

Tossed no more on life's rough billow, All the storms of sorrow fled,
Death hath found a qui - et pil - low For the ag - ed Christian's head,

Peace - ful slumbers Guard - ing now his low - ly bed.

929

2 O may we be reunited
To the spirits of the just,
Leaving all that sin hath blighted
With corruption, in the dust :
Hear us, Jesus,
Thou our Lord, our Life, our Trust.

930

1 WELCOME, days of solemn meeting;
Welcome, days of praise and prayer;
Far from earthly scenes retreating,
In your blessings we would share;
Sacred seasons,
In your blessings we would share.

2 Be Thou near us, blessed Saviour,
Still at morn and eve the same;
Give us faith that cannot waver;
Kindle in us heaven's own flame;
Blessed Saviour,
Kindle in us heaven's own flame.

3 When the fervent heart is glowing,
Holy Spirit, hear that prayer :
When the song of praise is flowing
Let that song Thine impress bear;
Holy Spirit,
Let that song Thine impress bear.

931

1 FATHER, by Thy heavenly blessing,
Now confirm this new-born tie;
To Thine ear our prayers addressing,
We beseech Thee to be nigh.
Seal this union;
Hallow it in courts on high.

2 Now the sacred trust is given;
Now the solemn charge is made;
Help Thy son in strength from heaven,
Keep these vows upon him laid.
Thou art ready
Ever thus to grant Thine aid.

3 And when earth's few years have fleeted,
Grant that, in Thy home of light,
Past the joys and griefs now meted,
Pastor, people, may unite,
Ever dwelling
In the glory of Thy sight.

932

1 WHILE we lowly bow before Thee,
Wilt Thou, gracious Saviour, hear?
We are poor and needy sinners,
Full of doubt and full of fear;
Gracious Saviour,
Make us humble and sincere.

2 Fill us with Thy holy Spirit;
Sanctify us by Thy grace;
And incline us more to love Thee,
And in dust our souls abase.
Hear us, Saviour,
And unveil Thy glorious face.

3 None in vain did ever ask Thee
For the Spirit of Thy love;
Hear us then, dear Saviour, hear us;
Grant an answer from above;
Blessed Saviour,
Hear and answer from above.

J. J. ROUSSEAU.

Gently, Lord, O, gently lead us Thro' this lowly vale of tears,

D. C. O, re-fresh us, O, re-fresh us, O, re-fresh us with Thy grace.

FINE.

And, O Lord, in mer-cy give us Thy rich grace in all our fears.

D. C.

933

2 Though ten thousand ills beset us,
  From without and from within,
Jesus says He'll ne'er forget us,
  But will save from every sin.
    Therefore praise Him—
  Praise the great Redeemer's name.

3 O that I could now adore Him,
  Like the heavenly host above,
Who forever bow before Him,
  And unceasing sing His love !
    Happy songsters !
  When shall I your chorus join ?

934

1 Come, Thou soul-transforming Spirit,
  Bless the sower and the seed;
Let each heart Thy grace inherit;
  Raise the weak, the hungry feed;
    From the gospel
  Now supply Thy people's need.

2 O, may all enjoy the blessing
  Which Thy word 's designed to give;
Let us all, Thy love possessing,
  Joyfully the truth receive;
    And forever
  To Thy praise and glory live.

935

1 Thanks we give, and adoration,
  For Thy gospel's joyful sound;
May the fruits of Thy salvation
  In our hearts and lives abound;
    May Thy presence
  With us evermore be found.

2 Then, whene'er the signal 's given
  Us from earth to call away,
Borne on angel's wings to heaven,
  Glad the summons to obey,
    May we ever
  Reign with Christ in endless day.

936

1 In Thy name, O Lord, assembling,
  We, Thy people, now draw near;
Teach us to rejoice with trembling;
  Speak, and let Thy servants hear—
    Hear with meekness,
  Hear Thy word with godly fear.

2 While our days on earth are lengthened,
  May we give them, Lord, to Thee;
Cheered by hope, and daily strengthened,
  May we run, nor weary be,
    Till Thy glory,
  Without clouds, in heaven we see.

3 There, in worship purer, sweeter,
  Thee Thy people shall adore,
Tasting of enjoyment greater
  Far than thought conceived before—
    Full enjoyment,
  Full, unmixed, and evermore.

937

Great Jehovah, we adore Thee,
  God the Father, God the Son,
God the Spirit joined in glory
  On the same eternal throne;
    Endless praises
  To Jehovah, Three in One.

1. Saviour, like a shepherd lead us, Much we need Thy tend'rest care;
   In Thy pleasant pastures feed us, For our use Thy folds prepare.
2. We are Thine, do Thou befriend us, Be the Guardian of our way;
   Keep Thy flock, from sin defend us, Seek us when we go a - stray.

Bless-ed Je - sus, Bless - ed Je - sus, Thou hast bought us, Thine we are,
Bless - ed Je - sus, Bless - ed Je - sus, Hear young children when they pray,

Bless - ed Je - sus, Bless - ed Je - sus, Thou hast bought us, Thine we are.
Bless - ed Je - sus, Bless - ed Je - sus, Hear young children when they pray.

938

3 Thou hast promised to receive us,
　　Poor and sinful though we be;
　Thou hast mercy to relieve us,
　　Grace to cleanse, and power to free.
　　　Blessed Jesus,
　　Let us early turn to Thee.

4 Early let us seek Thy favor,
　　Early let us do Thy will;
　Blessed Lord and only Saviour,
　　With Thy love our bosoms fill.
　　　Blessed Jesus,
　　Thou hast loved us, love us still.

939

1 Yes—my native land ! I love thee;
　　All thy scenes I love them well;
　Friends, connections, happy country,
　　Can I bid you all farewell ?
　　　Can I leave you,
　　Far in heathen lands to dwell ?

2 Home ! thy joys are passing lovely—.
　　Joys no stranger-heart can tell;
　Happy home !—'t is sure I love thee !
　　Can I—can I say—Farewell ?
　　　Can I leave thee,
　　Far in heathen lands to dwell ?

3 Scenes of sacred peace and pleasure,
　　Holy days, and Sabbath bell,
　Richest, brightest, sweetest treasure !
　　Can I say a last farewell ?
　　　Can I leave you,
　　Far in heathen lands to dwell ?

4 Yes ! I hasten from you gladly,
　　From the scenes I love so well;
　Far away, ye billows ! bear me;
　　Lovely native land ! farewell ;
　　　Pleased I leave thee,
　　Far in heathen lands to dwell.

5 In the deserts let me labor,
　　On the mountains let me tell
　How He died—the blessed Saviour—
　　To redeem a world from hell !
　　　Let me hasten,
　　Far in heathen lands to dwell.

940

Praise the Father, Son, and Spirit
　For election, sovereign, free;
　For redeeming love and merit;
　For renewing such as we;
　　For all blessings
　Praise the glorious One in Three.

ANDANTE. MAZZINGHI.

Lis-ten, sin-ner! Mercy hails you! With her sweet-est voice she calls;
Bids you has-ten to the Sa-viour, ...

Ere the hand of Justice falls; Listen, sinner! 'Tis the voice of Mercy calls.

941

2 See the storm of vengeance gathering
O'er the path you dare to tread;
Hark! the awful thunders rolling
Loud and louder o'er your head;
Tarry, sinner!
Lest the lightnings strike you dead.

3 Haste, ah, hasten to the Saviour!
Sue His mercy while you may;
Soon the day of grace is over,
Soon your life will pass away;
Hasten, sinner!
You must perish if you stay.

942

1 O my soul, what means this sadness?
Wherefore art thou thus cast down?
Let thy griefs be turned to gladness;
Bid thy restless fears be gone:
Look to Jesus,
And rejoice in His dear name.

2 What though Satan's strong temptations
Vex and tease thee day by day,
And thy sinful inclinations
Often fill thee with dismay;
Thou shalt conquer
Through the Lamb's redeeming blood.

3 Though ten thousand ills beset thee,
From without and from within,
Jesus saith, He'll ne'er forget thee,
But will save from hell and sin;
He is faithful
To perform His gracious word.

4 O that I could now adore Him,
Like the heavenly host above,
Who forever bow before Him,
And unceasing sing His love!
Happy songsters!
When shall I your chorus join?

943

1 Day of judgment, day of wonders!
Hark! the trumpet's awful sound,
Louder than a thousand thunders,
Shakes the vast creation round;
How the summons
Will the sinner's heart confound!

2 See the Judge, our nature wearing,
Clothed in majesty divine;
You, who long for His appearing,
Then shall say, "This God is mine!"
Gracious Saviour,
Own me in that day of Thine.

3 At His call the dead awaken,
Rise to life from earth and sea;
All the powers of nature shaken
By His looks, prepare to flee:
Careless sinner,
What will then become of thee?

4 But to those who have confessed,
Loved and served the Lord below,
He will say, "Come near, ye blessed,
See the kingdom I bestow;
You forever
Shall My love and glory know."

MODERATO.

No war nor battle's sound Was heard the earth around, No hos - tile

chiefs to furious com - bat ran: But peaceful was the night In

which the Prince of light His reign of peace up - on the earth be - gan.

944

2 No conqueror's sword He bore,
Nor warlike armor wore,
Nor haughty passions roused to contest wild.
In peace and love He came,
And gentle was the reign, [mild.
Which o'er the earth He spread by influence

3 Unwilling kings obeyed,
And sheathed the battle blade,
And called their bloody legions from the field.
In silent awe they wait,
And close the warrior's gate, [yield.
Nor know to whom their homage thus they

4 The peaceful conqueror goes,
And triumphs o'er His foes,
His weapons drawn from armories above.
Behold the vanquished sit,
Submissive at His feet, [love.
And strife and hate are changed to peace and

945

1 THE morning had not risen,
When to th' entombing prison
Where Christ the crucified, was laid to sleep,
Came Mary Magdalene
With sad and tearful mien,
Her watch beside her buried Lord to keep.

2 But lo! what miracle!
The stone that sealed the cell
By unknown hands had erst been rolled away:
And lone the sepulchre,
Save for two angels fair,
Who sat within, in shining white array.

3 But came another form
All sudden in the dawn,
Where Mary wept without the open door:
With tearful eloquence
She prayed—" Oh sir, if hence
Thou'st borne Him, tell me whither, I im-
plore ! "

4 Divinest accents came
From lips that called her name,
And glad surprise her raptured heart did stir:
" Rabboni ! Master ! here ! "
Fell on the listening air,
For Christ, the Risen, it was who stood with
her.

GEO. F. ROOT.

Come, let us sing of Je - sus, While hearts and ac - cents blend;

Come, let us sing of Je - sus, The sin - ner's on - ly friend;

His · ho - ly soul re - joic - es, A - mid the choirs a - bove,

To hear our youth - ful voi - ces Ex - ult - ing in his love.

946

2 We love to sing of Jesus,
 Who wept our path along;
We love to sing of Jesus,
 The tempted and the strong;
None who besought his healing,
 He passed unheeded by:
And still retains his feeling
 For us above the sky.

3 We love to sing of Jesus,
 Who died our souls to save;
We love to sing of Jesus,
 Triumphant o'er the grave;
And in our hour of danger,
 We'll trust His love alone,
Who once slept in a manger,
 And now sits on the throne.

4 Then let us sing of Jesus,
 While yet on earth we stay,
And hope to sing of Jesus,
 Throughout eternal day;
For those, who here confess Him,
 He will in Heaven confess;
And faithful hearts that bless Him,
 He will forever bless.

947

1 Before Thy cross lamenting,
 My Saviour, I would lie,
Of all my sins repenting,
 That caused my Lord to die.
My soul with tears of anguish,
 My follies would confess ;
While yet in pain I languish,
 Restore me by Thy grace.

MISSIONARY HYMN. 7s & 6s.

DR. LOWELL MASON.

From Greenland's i - cy mountains, From In - dia's cor - al strand,

Where A - fric's sun - ny fountains Roll down their gold - en sand,

From many an an - cient riv - er, From many a palm ₁ y plain,

They call us to de - liv - er Their land from er - ror's chain.

948

What though the spicy breezes
  Blow soft o'er Ceylon's isle,
Though every prospect pleases,
  And only man is vile?
In vain, with lavish kindness,
  The gifts of God are strown:
The heathen, in his blindness,
  Bows down to wood and stone.

3 Can we, whose souls are lighted
  With wisdom from on high,
Can we to man benighted
  The lamp of life deny?
Salvation! O, salvation!
  The joyful sound proclaim,
Till earth's remotest nation
  Has learned Messiah's name.

4 Waft, waft, ye winds, His story,
  And you, ye waters, roll,
Till, like a sea of glory,
  It spreads from pole to pole;
Till o'er our ransomed nature,
  The Lamb, for sinners slain,
Redeemer, King, Creator,
  In bliss returns to reign.

949

To Father, Son, and Spirit
  Eternal praise be given,
By all that earth inherit,
  And all that dwell in heaven.
Thou triune God! before Thee
  Our inmost souls adore:
For Thou alone art worthy,
  And shalt be evermore.

Stand up! stand up for Je - sus! Ye sol - diers of the cross;

FINE.

Lift high His roy - al ban - ner, It must not suf - fer loss:
Till ev' - ry foe is vanquish'd, And Christ is Lord in - deed.

Close with 2d strain.

From vic - t'ry un - to vic - t'ry His ar - my shall be led,

950

2 Stand up!—stand up for Jesus!
The trumpet call obey;
Forth to the mighty conflict,
In this His glorious day:
" Ye that are men, now serve him,"
Against unnumbered foes;
Your courage rise with danger,
And strength to strength oppose.

3 Stand up!—stand up for Jesus!
Stand in his strength alone;
The arm of flesh will fail you—
Ye dare not trust your own:
Put on the Gospel armor,
And, watching unto prayer,
Where duty calls or danger,
Be never wanting there.

4 Stand up!—stand up for Jesus!
The strife will not be long;
This day the noise of battle,
The next the victor's song:
To him that overcometh,
A crown of life shall be;
He with the King of Glory
Shall reign eternally!

951

1 On Thibet's snow-capt mountains,
O'er Afric's burning sand,
Where roll the fiery fountains
Adown Hawaii's strand—
In every distant nation,
The mighty globe around,
The heralds of salvation
The gospel trumpet sound.

2 In golden armor blazing
They press their onward way,
And high in air upraising,
The glorious cross display:
Away their weapons hurling,
The warring nations cease,
And hail with joy, unfurling
The banneret of peace.

3 Where sin hath fixed her dwelling,
Where Death the tyrant reigns,
The heavenly notes are swelling
In loudest, sweetest strains;
They breathe—the bones are shaken,
And clothed with flesh arise,—
They bid the dead awaken
To glory in the skies.

AURA. 7s & 6s.

Now be the gos-pel ban-ner In ev-'ry land unfurled;

FINE.

And be the shout Ho-san-na, Re-ech-oed thro' the world;
Re-ceive the great sal-va-tion, 'And join the hap-py throng.

Close with second strain.

Till ev-'ry isle and na-tion, Till ev-'ry tribe and tongue,

952

2 What though the embattled legions
Of earth and hell combine,—
His arm, throughout their regions,
Shall soon resplendent shine:
Ride on, 'O Lord, victorious!
Immanuel, Prince of Peace!
Thy triumph shall be glorious;
Thy empire still increase.

3 Yes, Thou shalt reign forever,
O Jesus, King of kings!
Thy light, Thy love, Thy favor,
Each ransomed captive sings:
The isles for Thee are waiting,
The deserts learn Thy praise,
The hills and valleys, greeting,
The song responsive raise.

953

1 Roll on, thou mighty ocean!
And, as thy billows flow,
Bear messengers of mercy
To every land below:
Arise, ye gales! and waft them
Safe to the destined shore;
That man may sit in darkness
And death's black shade no more.

2 O Thou eternal Ruler!
Who holdest in Thine arm
The tempests of the ocean,
Protect them from all harm!
Thy presence still be with them,
Wherever they may be;
Though far from us who love them
Still let them be with Thee!

954

1 To Thee, O blessed Saviour,
Our grateful songs we raise;
O, tune our hearts and voices
Thy holy name to praise;
'Tis by Thy sovereign mercy
We're now allowed to meet,
And join with friends and teachers,
Thy blessing to entreat.

2 O, may Thy precious gospel
Be published all abroad,
Till the benighted heathen
Shall know and serve the Lord;
Till o'er the wide creation
The rays of truth shall shine,
And nations now in darkness
Arise to light divine.

G. J. WEBB.

The morn - ing light is break - ing; The dark - ness dis - ap - pears;

FINE.

The sons of earth are wak - ing To pen - i - ten - tial tears;
Of na - tions in com - mo - tion, Pre - pared for Zi - on's war.

Each breeze that sweeps the o - cean Brings tid - ings from a - far—

955

2 Rich dews of grace come o'er us,
   In many a gentle shower,
And brighter scenes before us
   Are opening every hour;
Each cry to heaven going,
   Abundant answers brings,
And heavenly gales are blowing,
   With peace upon their wings.

3 See heathen nations bending
   Before the God we love,
And thousand hearts ascending
   In gratitude above;
While sinners, now confessing,
   The gospel call obey,
And seek the Saviour's blessing,
   A nation in a day.

4 Blest river of salvation,
   Pursue thy onward way;
Flow thou to every nation,
   Nor in thy richness stay;
Stay not till all the lowly
   Triumphant reach their home;
Stay not till all the holy
   Proclaim, "the Lord is come."

956

1 RISE up all ye believers,
   And let your lights appear;
The shades of eve are thickening,
   And darker night is near.
The Bridegroom is advancing;
   Each hour His chariot spy;
Up! watch and pray, nor slumber;
   At midnight comes the cry.

2 See that your lamps are burning,
   Your vessels filled with oil;
Wait calmly your deliverance
   From earthly pain and toil.
The watchers on the mountains
   E'en now His chariot spy;
O, go ye forth to meet Him,
   And raise hosannahs high.

3 The saints, who here in patience
   Their cross and sufferings bore,
With Him shall reign forever,
   When sorrow is no more.
Around the throne of glory
   The Lamb shall they behold,
Adoring cast before Him
   Their diadems of gold.

HARMONY. 7s & 6s.

Arr. by B. F. Edmands.

From ev - 'ry earthly pleasure, From ev - 'ry transient joy, }
From ev - 'ry mor - tal treasure That soon will fade and die; } No

longer these de - sir - ing, Upward our wishes tend, To nobler bliss as-

pir - ing, The joys that nev - er end, The joys that nev - er end.

957

2 From every piercing sorrow,
   That heaves our breast to-day,
Or threatens us to-morrow,
   Hope turns our eyes away :
On wings of faith ascending,
   We see the land of light,
And feel our sorrows ending
   In infinite delight.

3 'Tis true we are but strangers,
   We sojourn here below;
And countless snares and dangers
   Surround the path we go;
Though painful and distressing,
   Yet there's a rest above;
And onward still we're pressing,
   To reach that land of love.

958

1 To Thee, my God, my Saviour,
   My soul, exulting, sings,
Rejoicing in Thy favor,
   Almighty King of kings !
I'll celebrate Thy glory,
   With all the saints above,
And tell the joyful story
   Of Thy redeeming love.

2 Soon as the morn with roses
   Bedecks the dewy east,
And when the sun reposes
   Upon the ocean's breast,
My voice in supplication,
   My Saviour, Thou shalt hear:
Oh, grant me Thy salvation,
   And to my soul draw near !

3 By Thee through life supported,
   I pass the dangerous road,
With heavenly hosts escorted
   Up to their bright abode :
There cast my crown before Thee,
   And, all my conflicts o'er,
Unceasingly adore Thee;
   What would an angel more ?

959

1 I LAY my sins on Jesus,
   The spotless Lamb of God;
He bears them all and frees us
   From the accursed load :
I bring my guilt to Jesus,
   To wash my crimson stains
White in His blood most precious,
   Till not a stain remains.

Rise, my soul, and stretch thy wings: Thy bet-ter por-tion trace;
Rise, from tran-si-to-ry things, Tow'rd heav'n, thy native place;

Sun and moon and. stars de-cay; Time shall soon this earth re-move;

Rise, my soul. and haste a-way To seats pre-pared a-bove.

960

2 Rivers to the ocean run,
  Nor stay in all their course;
Fire ascending seeks the sun;
  Both speed them to their source;
Thus a soul, new born of God,
  Pants to view His glorious face,
Upward tends to His abode,
  To rest in His embrace.

3 Cease, ye pilgrims, cease to mourn;
  Press onward to the prize;
Soon the Saviour will return
  Triumphant in the skies:
Yet a season, and you know
  Happy entrance will be given,
All your sorrows left below,
  And earth exchanged for heaven.

961

1 TIME is winging us away
  To our eternal home;
Life is but a winter's day,
  A journey to the tomb.
Youth and vigor soon will flee,
  Blooming beauty lose its charms;
All that's mortal soon shall be
  Enclosed in death's cold arms.

2 Time is winging us away
  To our eternal home;
Life is but a winter's day,
  A journey to the tomb.
But the Christian shall enjoy
  Health and beauty soon above,
Far beyond the world's alloy,
  Secure in Jesus' love.

962

1 LAMB of God, whose dying love
  We now recall to mind,
Send the answer from above,
  And let us mercy find:
Think on us who think on Thee,
  And every struggling soul release;
O, remember Calvary,
  And bid us go in peace.

2 By Thine agonizing pain,
  And bloody sweat, we pray,—
By Thy dying love to man,—
  Take all our sins away:
Burst our bonds and set us free;
  From all iniquity release;
O, remember Calvary,
  And bid us go in peace.

UTICA. 7s & 6s.

DR. LOWELL MASON.

Drooping souls, no long - er mourn, Je - sus still is precious; . . . .
D. C.—Drooping souls, ye need not die, Go to Him and . . . . hear Him.

FINE.

If to Him you now re - turn, Heaven will be pro - pi - tious;

D. C.

Je - sus now is pass - ing by, Call - ing wan - d'rers near Him;

963

2 He has pardons, full and free,
Drooping souls to gladden;
Still He cries—" Come unto me,
Weary, heavy laden.''
Though your sins like mountains high,
Rise, and reach to heaven,
Soon as you on Him rely,
All shall be forgiven.

3 Precious is the Saviour's name,
Dear to all that love Him;
He to save the dying came;
Go to Him and prove Him,
Wandering sinners, now return;
Contrite souls, believe Him !
Jesus calls you, cease to mourn;
Worship Him; receive Him;

964

1 DYING souls, fast bound in sin,
Trembling and repining,
With no ray of light divine
On your pathway shining;

Why in darkness wander on
Filled with condemnation ?
Jesus lives; in Him alone
Can you find salvation,

2 Prostrate bow; confess your guilt;
Vengeance is pursuing
'Mid the dying and the slain,
Save your souls from ruin;
Flee to Him who can atone;
Flee from condemnation:
Jesus lives; in Him alone
Can you find salvation.

3 Linger not in all the plain;
Vengeance is pursuing;
'Mid the dying and the slain,
Save your souls from ruin.
Flee to Him who can atone;
Flee from condemnation;
Jesus lives; in Him alone
Can you find salvation.

The leaves a-round me fall-ing, Are preaching of de-cay; \
The hol-low winds are call-ing, "Come, pilgrim, come a-way."/

The day, in night de-clin-ing, Says I must, too, de-cline;

The year, its life re-sign-ing— Its lot fore-sha-dows mine.

965

2 The light my path surrounding,
  The loves to which I cling,
The hopes within me bounding,
  The joys that round me wing—
All melt, like stars of even,
  Before the morning's ray—
Pass upward unto heaven,
  And chide at my delay.

3 The friends, gone there before me,
  Are calling from on high;
And joyous angels o'er me,
  Tempt sweetly to the sky.
" Why wait," they say, "and wither
  'Mid scenes of death and sin?
. O, rise to glory, hither,
  And find true life begin."

4 I hear the invitation,
  And fain would rise and come—
A sinner to salvation;
  An exile to his home:
But, while I here must linger,
  Thus, thus let all I see
Point on, with faithful finger,
  To heaven, O Lord, and Thee.

966

1 THERE is a holy city,
  A happy world above,
Beyond the starry regions,
  Built by the God of love;
An everlasting temple,
  And saints arrayed in white,
There serve their great Redeemer,
  And dwell with Him in light.

2 The meanest child of glory
  Outshines the radiant sun;
But who can speak the splendor
  Of that eternal throne
Where Jesus sits exalted,
  In Godlike majesty ?
The elders fall before Him,
  The angels bend the knee.

3 Is this the Man of sorrows,
  Who stood at Pilate's bar,
Condemned by haughty Herod,
  And by his men of war ?
He seems a mighty conqueror,
  Who spoiled the powers below,
And ransomed many captives
  From everlasting woe!

FIDELITY. 7s & 6s.

Vestry Harp.

O, when shall I see Jesus, And reign with Him above,

And from that flowing fountain Drink everlasting love?

When shall I be delivered From this vain world of sin,

And with my blessed Jesus Drink endless pleasures in.

967

2 But now I am a soldier;
My captain's gone before;
He's given me my orders,
And bid me not give o'er;
If I continue faithful
A righteous crown He'll give;
And all his valiant soldiers
Eternal life shall have.

3 Through grace I am determined
To conquer, though I die,
And then away to Jesus
On wings of love I'll fly,
Farewell to sin and sorrow—
I bid you all adieu;
And O, my friends prove faithful,
And on your way pursue.

4 And if you meet with troubles
And trials in your way,
Then cast your care on Jesus,
And don't forget to pray.
Gird on the heavenly armor
Of faith, and hope and love;
Then, when the combat's ended,
He'll carry you above.

968

To Thee be praise forever,
Thou glorious King of kings.
Thy wondrous love and favor
Each ransomed spirit sings;
We'll celebrate Thy glory,
With all Thy saints above,
And shout the joyful story
Of Thy redeeming love.

My faith looks up to Thee, Thou Lamb of Cal-va-ry,

Sa-viour di-vine; Now hear me while I pray: Take all my

guilt a-way; O, let me from this day Be whol-ly Thine.

969

2 May Thy rich grace impart
Strength to my fainting heart,
  My zeal inspire;
As Thou hast died for me,
O, may my love to Thee
Pure, warm, and changeless be—
  A living fire.

3 While life's dark maze I tread,
And griefs around me spread,
  Be Thou my Guide;
Bid darkness turn to day,
Wipe sorrow's tears away,
Nor let me ever stray
  From Thee aside.

4 When ends life's transient dream,
When death's cold, sullen stream
  Shall o'er me roll,
Blest Saviour, then, in love,
Fear and distrust remove;
O! bear me safe above—
  A ransomed soul.

970

1 AUSPICIOUS morning, hail!
Voices from hill and vale
  Thy welcome sing:
Joy on thy dawning breaks;
Each heart with joy partakes
While cheerful music wakes,
  Its praise to bring.

2 When on the tyrants rod
Our patriot fathers trod,
  And dared be free,
'Twas not in burning zeal,
Firm nerves and hearts of steel,
Our country's joy to seal,
  But, Lord, in Thee.

3 Thou, as a shield of power,
In battle's awful hour,
  Didst round us stand;
Our hopes were in Thy throne;
Strong in Thy might alone,
By Thee our banners shone,
  God of our land.

ITALIAN HYMN. 6s & 4s.

CON SPIRITO. GIARDINI.

Come, Thou al - mighty King, Help us Thy name to sing, Help us to praise;

{ Fa - ther all glo - ri - ous, }
{ O'er all vic - to - ri - ous, } Come and reign o - ver us, Ancient of days.

971

2 Jesus, our Lord, arise,
Scatter our enemies,
And make them fall;
Let Thine almighty aid
Our sure defence be made;
Our souls on Thee be stayed;
Lord, hear our call.

3 Come, holy Comforter,
Thy sacred witness bear,
In this glad hour.
Thou, who almighty art,
Now rule in every heart,
And ne'er from us depart,
Spirit of power.

4 To the great One in Three,
The highest praises be,
Hence evermore;
His sovereign majesty
May we in glory see,
And to eternity
Love and adore.

972

1 THE God of harvest praise;
In loud thanksgiving raise
Hand, heart, and voice;
The valleys smile and sing;
Forests and mountains ring;
The plains their tribute bring;
The streams rejoice.

2 Yea, bless His holy name,
And purest thanks proclaim
Through all the earth;

To glory in your lot
Is duty; but be not
God's benefits forgot,
Amid your mirth.

3 The God of harvest praise;
Hands, hearts, and voices raise,
With sweet accord;
From field to garner throng,
Bearing your sheaves along,
And in your harvest song
Bless ye the Lord.

973

1 COME, all ye saints of God,
Wide through the earth abroad,
Spread Jesus' fame:
Tell what His love hath done;
Trust in His name alone;
Shout to His lofty throne,
" Worthy the Lamb!"

2 Hence, gloomy doubts and fears !
Dry up your mournful tears;
Swell the glad theme:
To Christ, our gracious King,
Strike each melodious string;
Join heart and voice to sing,
" Worthy the Lamb !"

3 Hark ! how the choirs above,
Filled with the Saviour's love,
Dwell on His name !
There, too, may we be found,
With light and glory crowned;
While all the heavens resound,
" Worthy the Lamb !"

MAESTOSO.

My coun - try, 'tis of thee, Sweet land of lib - er - ty,

Of thee I sing: Land, where my fa - thers died, Land of the

pil - grims' pride, From ev - 'ry moun - tain side, Let free - dom ring!

974

2 My native country, thee—
  Land of the noble free—
    Thy name I love :
  I love thy rocks and rills,
  Thy woods and templed hills;
  My heart with rapture thrills
    Like that above.

3 Let music swell the breeze,
  And ring from all the trees
    Sweet freedom's song !
  Let mortal tongues awake;
  Let all that breathe partake;
  Let rocks their silence break,—
    The sound prolong !

4 Our fathers' God ! to Thee,
  Author of liberty,
    To Thee we sing :
  Long may our land be bright
  With freedom's holy light;
  Protect us by Thy might,
    Great God, our King !

975

1 LET us awake our joys;
  Strike up with cheerful voice;
    Each creature, sing :
  Angels ! begin the song,
  Mortals ! the strain prolong,
  In accents sweet and strong,
    "Jesus is King ! "

2 Proclaim abroad His name;
  Tell of His matchless fame;
    What wonders done !
  Above, beneath, around,
  Let all the earth resound,
  Till heaven's high arch rebound,
    "Victory is won ! "

3 He vanquished sin and hell,
  And our last foe will quell :
    Mourners, rejoice !
  His dying love adore;
  Praise Him, now raised in power :
  Praise Him for evermore,
    With joyful voice.

HEMANS. 6s & 4s.

STACCATO.

HASTINGS.

What sweet angelic strains Roll o'er Ju - de - a's plains, Waking the morn;

Lo! swift on golden wing } Tidings of Zion's King, "Jesus is born."
Ce - les - tial harpers bring }

976

2 Rising o'er mountains far,
Behold! an orient star
Points to His bed.
Sages with incense sweet
Hasten their Lord to greet,
And low before His feet
Rich offerings spread.

3 Daughters of sorrow, see
Love, light, and liberty,
In Jesus shine.
He hears the ravens cry,
Wipes tears from sorrow's eye,
And brings His people nigh,
By grace divine.

4 He speaks: wild surges sleep;
High o'er the peaceful deep
The rainbow bends.
Bands from the dead are riven,
Sins of the world forgiven,
Flung wide the gates of heaven,
The Dove descends.

5 Beneath His regal sway,
Gross darkness flies away;
The morning glows.
Red roses deck the vale,
Rich perfume scents the gale,
Peace and good will prevail,
And sweet repose.

6 Old ocean, in its roar,
Or murmuring by the shore,
Repeats His name.

Orbs on the brow of night,
Rolling in courses bright;
Angels in robes of light
Spread wide His fame.

7 Then let our tongues express
His lofty deeds, and bless
This King of kings.
He rules the world in love,
And by the sacred Dove
To mansions bright above
His people brings.

977

1 LOWLY and solemn be
Thy childrens cry to Thee,
Father divine;
A hymn of suppliant breath,
Owning that life and death
Alike are Thine.

2 By Him who bowed to take
The death-cup for our sake,
The thorn, the rod,—
From whom the last dismay
Was not to pass away—
Aid us, O God.

3 Tremblers beside the grave,
We call on Thee to save,
Father divine;
Hear, hear our suppliant breath;
Keep us, in life and death,
Thine, only Thine.

DOLCE.

S. HUBBARD.

FINE.

D. C.

978

1 CHILD of sin and sorrow, filled with dismay,
Wait not for to-morrow, yieldthee to-day;
Heaven bids thee come,
While yet there 's room;
Child of sin and sorrow,
Hear and obey.

2 Child of sin and sorrow, why wilt thou die?
Come, while thou canst borrow hope from
Grieve not that love,   [on high;

Which from above—
Child of sin and sorrow—
Would bring thee nigh.

3 Child of sin and sorrow, thy moments glide
Like the flitting arrow, or the rushing tide;
Ere the time is o'er,
Heaven's grace implore,
Child of sin and sorrow,
In Christ confide.

TO-DAY. 6s & 4s.

DOLCE.

To - day   the   Sa - viour   calls!   Ye   wand - 'rers   come;

O,   ye   be - night - ed   souls,   Why   lon - ger   roam?

979

2 To-day the Saviour calls !
O, listen now;
Within these sacred walls
To Jesus bow.

3 To-day the Saviour calls !
For refuge fly;
The storm of vengeance falls;
Ruin is nigh.

¶ The Spirit calls to-day !
Yield to His power;
O, grieve Him not away;
'Tis mercy's hour.

980

1 To Thee my God I come,
In Jesus' name;
No more, no more to roam
In sin and shame.

2 For mercy at Thy throne,
My God, I cry;
O lead me by Thy Son
To realms on high.

3 Thy praises will I sing,
While life is given;
And holier incense bring
To Thee in heaven.

DORT. 6s & 4s.

Maestoso.   Dr. Lowell Mason.

Sound, sound the truth abroad! Bear ye the word of God Thro' the wide world:

{ Tell what our Lord has done, } And from his lof-ty throne Sa-tan is hurled.
{ Tell how the day was won, }

981

2 Far o'er the sea and land,
'Tis our Lord's own command,
Bear ye His name:
Bear it to every shore;
Regions unknown explore;
Enter at every door—
Silence is shame.

982

1 Rise, glorious Conqueror, rise
Into thy native skies—
Assume Thy right:
And where in many a fold,
The clouds are backward rolled—
Pass through those gates of gold,
And reign in light!

2 Victor o'er death and hell!
Cherubic legions swell
The radiant train:
Praises all heaven inspire;
Each angel sweeps his lyre,
And waves his wings of fire,—
Thou Lamb, once slain!

3 Enter, incarnate God!
No feet but Thine have trod
The serpent down:
Blow the full trumpets, blow!
Wider yon portals throw!
Saviour, triumphant, go
And take Thy crown!

4 Lion of Judah—Hail!—
And let Thy name prevail
From age to age:
Lord of the rolling years—
Claim for Thine own the spheres,
For Thou hast bought with tears
Thy heritage.

983

1 Shepherd of tender youth,
Guiding in love and truth
Through devious ways,
Christ, our triumphant King,
We come Thy name to sing,
And here our children bring,
To shout Thy praise.

2 Ever be Thou our Guide,
Our Shepherd and our Pride,
Our Staff and Song.
Jesus, Thou Christ of God,
By Thy perennial word,
Lead us where thou hast trod;
Make our faith strong.

3 So now, and till we die,
Sound we Thy praises high,
And joyful sing.
Infants, and the glad throng
Who to the church belong,
Unite, and swell the song
To Christ our King.

984

1 Gone are those great and good
Who here, in peril stood
And raised their hymn.
Peace to the reverend dead !
The light, that on their head
Two hundred years have shed,
Shall ne'er grow dim.

2 Ye temples, that to God
Rise where our fathers trod,
Guard well your trust—
The faith that dared the sea,
The truth that made them free,
Their cherished purity,
Their garnered dust.

To Je - sus, the crown of my hope, My soul is in haste to be gone;

O, bear me, ye cher - u - bim, up, And waft me a - way to His throne.

985

My Saviour, whom absent I love;
  Whom, not having seen, I adore;
Whose name is exalted above
  All glory, dominion, and power,—

3 Dissolve Thou these bands that detain
  My soul from her portion in Thee,
O strike off this adamant chain,
  And make me eternally free.

4 When that happy era begins,
  When arrayed in Thy glories I shine,
Nor grieve any more, by my sins,
  The bosom on which I recline,—

5 O then shall the vail be removed!
  And round me Thy brightness be poured;
I shall meet Him, whom absent I loved,
  I shall see, whom unseen I adored.

6 And then, never more shall the fears,
  The trials, temptations, and woes,
Which darken this valley of tears,
  Intrude on my blissful repose.

986

1 O WHEN shall we sweetly remove,
  O when shall we enter our rest—
Return to the Zion above,
  The mother of spirits distressed;
The city of God, the great King,
  Where sorrow and death are no more,
Where saints our Immanuel sing,
  And cherub and seraph adore?

2 But angels themselves can not tell
  The joys of that holiest place,
Where Jesus is pleased to reveal
  The light of His heavenly face;

When, caught in the rapturous flame,
  The sight beatific they prove;
And walk in the light of the Lamb,
  Enjoying the beams of His love.

3 Thou know'st in the spirit of prayer
  We long Thy appearing to see,
Resigned to the burden we bear,
  But longing to triumph with Thee;
'Tis good at Thy word to be here;
  'Tis better in Thee to be gone,
And see Thee in glory appear,
  And rise to a share in Thy throne.

987

1 A DEBTOR to mercy alone,—
  Of covenant mercy I sing;
Nor fear, with Thy righteousness on,
  My person and offerings to bring:

2 The terrors of law and of God
  With me can have nothing to do;
My Saviour's obedience and blood
  Hide all my transgressions from view.

3 The work which His goodness began,
  The arm of His strength will complete;
His promise is yea and amen,
  And never was forfeited yet:

4 My name from the palms of His hands
  Eternity will not erase;
Impressed on His heart it remains
  In marks of indellible grace:

5 Yes! I to the end shall endure,
  As sure as the earnest is given:
More happy, but not more secure,
  The glorified spirits in heaven.

HEAVEN. 8s.

MODERATO.

We speak of the realms of the blessed, That country so bright and so fair,

And oft are its glo-ries con-fessed; But what must it be to be there!

988

2 We speak of its pathways of gold,
  Its walls decked with jewels so rare,
  Its wonders and pleasures untold;
  But what must it be to be there?

3 We speak of its freedom from sin,
  From sorrow, temptation, and care,
  From trials without and within;
  But what must it be to be there!

4 We speak of its service of love,
  The robes which the glorified wear,
  The church of the first-born above;
  But what must it be to be there!

5 Do Thou, Lord, 'mid sorrow and woe,
  Still for heaven my spirit prepare,
  And shortly I also shall know,
  And feel what it is to be there!

989

1 My gracious Redeemer I love;
  His praises aloud I'll proclaim,
  And join with the armies above
  To shout His adorable name.

2 To gaze on His glories divine,
  Shall be my eternal employ;
  And feel them incessantly shine,
  My boundless, ineffable joy.

3 Ye palaces, sceptres, and crowns,
  Your pride with disdain I survey;
  Your pomps are but shadows and sounds,
  And pass in a moment away.

4 The crown that my Saviour bestows
  Yon permanent sun shall outshine;
  My joy everlastingly flows;
  My God, my Redeemer, is mine.

990

1 Ye angels, who stand round the throne,
  And view my Immanuel's face,
  In rapturous songs make Him known;
  O, tune your soft harps to His praise.

2 Ye saints, who stand nearer than they,
  And cast your bright crowns at His feet,
  His grace and His glory display,
  And all His rich mercy repeat.

3 O, when will the moment appear
  When I shall unite in your song!
  I'm weary of lingering here,
  For I to your Saviour belong.

4 I'm fettered and chained here in clay;
  I struggle and pant to be free;
  I long to be soaring away,
  My God and my Saviour to see.

991

1 O Thou, who hast spread out the skies,
  And measured the depths of the sea,
  'Twixt heavens and ocean shall rise
  Our incense of praises to Thee.

2 We know that Thy presence is near,
  While heaves our bark far from the land:
  We ride o'er the deep without fear—
  The waters are held in Thy hand.

3 Eternity comes in the sound
  Of billows that never can sleep!
  There's Deity circling us round—
  Omnipotence walks o'er the deep!

4 O Father! our eye is to Thee,
  As on for the haven we roll;
  And faith in our Pilot shall be
  An anchor to steady the soul.

ALLEGRO.   S. A. N.

The win-ter is o-ver and gone, The thrush whistles sweet on the spray,

The turtle breathes forth her soft moan, The lark mounts and warbles away.

992

2 Shall every creature around
Their voices in concert unite,
And I, the most favored, be found
In praising to take less delight?

3 Awake, then, my harp and my lute;
Sweet organs, your notes softly swell;
No longer my lips shall be mute,
The Saviour's high praises to tell.

4 His love in my heart shed abroad,
My graces shall bloom as the spring; *
This temple, His spirit's abode,
My joy, as my duty, to sing.

993

1 How tedious and tasteless the hours,
When Jesus no longer I see! [flowers,
Sweet prospects, sweet birds, and sweet
Have lost all their sweetness with me.

2 The mid-summer sun shines but dim,
The fields strive in vain to look gay;
But when I am happy in Him,
December's as pleasant as May.

3 His name yields the richest perfume,
And sweeter than music His voice;
His presence disperses my gloom,
And makes all within rejoice.

4 I should, were He always thus nigh,
Have nothing to wish or to fear;
No mortal so happy as I—
My summer would last all the year.

5 Dear Lord, if indeed I am Thine,
If Thou art my sun and my song,
Say, why do I languish and pine,
And why are my winters so long?

6 O drive these dark clouds from my sky,
Thy soul-cheering presence restore;
Or take me unto Thee on high,
Where winter and clouds are no more.

994

1 This God is the God we adore,
Our faithful, unchangeable Friend,
Whose love is as large as His power,
And neither knows measure nor end.

2 'Tis Jesus, the First and the Last,
Whose Spirit shall guide us safe home,
We'll praise Him for all that is past,
And trust Him for all that's to come.

995

1 I long to behold Him arrayed,
With glory and light from above;
The King in His beauty displayed,
His beauty of holiest love.

2 With Him I, in Zion shall stand,
For Jesus hath spoken the word;
The breadth of Immanuel's land
Survey in the light of the Lord.

3 But when on Thy bosom reclined,
Thy face I am strengthened to see,
My fulness of rapture I find,
My heaven of heavens in Thee.

996

All praise to the Father, the Son,
And Spirit, thrice holy and blessed,
The Eternal, Supreme, Three in One,
Was, is, and shall still be addressed.

BETHANY. 6s & 4s.

DR. LOWELL MASON.

Near - er, my God, to Thee, Near - er to Thee, E'en tho' it

be a cross That rais - eth me, Still all my song shall be,

Nearer, my God, to Thee, Nearer, my God, to Thee, Nearer to Thee.

997

2 Though like a wanderer,
Daylight all gone,
Darkness be over me,
My rest a stone,
Yet in my dreams, I'd be
Nearer, my God to Thee:
Nearer to Thee.

3 There let the way appear
Steps up to heaven;
All that Thou sendest me
In mercy given,
Angels to beckon me
Nearer, my God, to Thee,
Nearer to Thee.

4 Then with my waking thoughts,
Bright with Thy praise,
Out of my stony griefs,
Bethel I'll raise ;
So by my woes to be
Nearer, my God to Thee,
Nearer to Thee.

5 Or if on joyful wing,
Cleaving the sky,
Sun, moon, and stars forgot,
Upward I fly,
Still all my song shall be,
Nearer, my God, to Thee,
Nearer to Thee.

998

1 I'M but a stranger here,
Heaven is my home;
Earth is a desert drear,
Heaven is my home ;
Danger and sorrow stand
Round me on every hand;
Heaven is my fatherland—
Heaven is my home.

2 What though the tempest rage,
Heaven is my home;
Short is my pilgrimage,
Heaven is my home :
Time's cold and wintry blast
Soon will be overpast;
I shall reach home at last—
Heaven is my home.

MODERATO.   C ZEUNER.

There is a calm for those who weep, A rest for wea-ry pilgrims found: They soft-ly lie and sweet-ly sleep Low in the ground.

999

2 The storm that racks the wintry sky
    No more disturbs their deep repose
  Than summer evening's latest sigh,
    That shuts the rose.

3 I long to lay this painful head
    And aching heart beneath the soil;
  To slumber, in that dreamless bed,
    From all my toil.

4 The soul, of origin divine,
    God's glorious image, freed from clay,
  In heaven's eternal sphere shall shine,
    A star of day.

5 The sun is but a spark of fire,
    A transent meteor in the sky:
  The soul, immortal as its Sire,
    Shall never die.

1000

1 I CAN not always trace the way
    Where Thou, almighty One, dost move;
  But I can always, always say
    That God is love.

2 When fear her chilling mantle flings
    O'er earth, my soul to heaven above,
  As to her native home, upsprings;
    For God is love.

3 When mystery clouds my darkened path,
    I'll check my dread, my doubts reprove;
  In this my soul sweet comfort hath,
    That God is love.

4 Oh may this truth my heart employ,
    Bid every gloomy thought remove,
  And turn all tears, all woes to joy,—
    Thou, God, art Love.

1001

1 My God, my Father; while I stray,
    Far from my home, on life's rough way,
  Oh, teach me from my heart to say,
    "Thy will be done!"

2 What though in lonely grief I sigh
    For friends beloved no longer nigh;
  Submissive still would I reply,
    "Thy will be done!"

3 If Thou shouldst call me to resign
    What most I prize,—it ne'er was mine;
  I only yield Thee what was Thine:
    "Thy will be done!"

4 If but my fainting heart be blest
    With Thy sweet Spirit for its guest,
  My God, to Thee I leave the rest:
    "Thy will be done!"

1002

1 My God, I bring my heart to Thee,
    Though poor and vile the offering be,
  For Christ's dear sake, make it Thy throne;
    Reign there alone!

3 Whene'er temptation's darts assail;
    When all things mortal fade and fail;
  O God, keep my poor heart Thine own;
    Reign there alone!

3 When the last trumpet's peal shall break
    The slumber of the dead—O take
  My trembling heart to be Thine own;
    Reign there alone!

4 And as the immortal ages roll,
    And heavenly anthems feast the soul;
  Still be my raptured heart Thy throne;
    Reign there alone!

CAROLUS. 8s & 6.

MODERATO.

O Thou, the contrite sinner's Friend! Who, loving, lov'st them to the end,

On this a - lone my hopes de - pend, That Thou wilt plead for me.

1003

2 When weary in the Christian race,
Far off appears my resting place,
And, fainting, I mistrust Thy grace,
Then, Saviour, plead for me.

2 When I have erred and gone astray,
Afar from thine and wisdom's way,
And see no glimmering, guiding ray,
Still, Saviour, plead for me.

3 When Satan, by my sins made bold,
Strives from Thy cross to loose my hold,
Then with Thy pitying arms enfold,
And plead, oh, plead for me!

4 And when my dying hour draws near,
Darkened with anguish, guilt and fear,
Then to my fainting sight appear,
Pleading in heaven for me!

5 When the full light of heavenly day,
Reveals my sins in dread array,
Say Thou hast washed them all away;
O, say thou plead'st for me!

1004

1 FROM foes that would the land devour;
From guilty pride, and lust of power;
From wild sedition's lawless hour;
From yoke of slavery;

2 From blinded zeal, by faction led;
From giddy change, by fancy bred;
From poisonous error's serpent head,
Good, Lord, preserve us free.

3 Defend, O God, with guardian hand,
The laws and ruler of our land:
And grant our church Thy grace to stand
In faith and unity.

4 The Spirit's help of Thee we crave,
That Thou, whose blood we shed to save,
Mayst at Thy second coming have
A flock to welcome Thee.

1005

1 O HOLY Saviour! Friend unseen!
Since on Thy arm Thou bid'st us lean,
Help us throughout life's changing scene
By faith to cling to Thee.

2 Blest with this fellowship divine,
Take what Thou wilt, we'll not repine
For, as the branches to the vine,
We only cling to Thee.

3 Though far from home, fatigued, opprest,
Here we have found a place of rest;
As exiles still, yet not unblest,
Because we cling to Thee.

4 What though the world deceitful prove,
And earthly friends and hopes remove,
With patient, uncomplaining love,
Still can we cling to Thee.

5 Though oft we seem to tread alone
Life's dreary waste with thorns o'ergrown
Thy voice of love, in gentlest tone,
Whispers, "Still cling to Me!"

6 Though faith and hope are often tried,
We ask not, need not aught beside,
So safe, so calm, so satisfied
The souls that cling to Thee.

There's a Friend a - bove all oth - ers, O, how He loves!
His is love be - yond a broth - er's, O, how He loves!
D. C.—But this Friend will ne'er de - ceive us— O, how He loves!

Earth - ly friends may fail and leave us, This day kind, the next be - reave us,

1006

2 Blessed Jesus!—would'st thou know Him?
　O how He loves !
Give thyself e'en this day to Him,
　O how He loves!
Is it sin that pains and grieves thee?
Doubts and trials do they tease thee ? .
Jesus can from all release thee?
　O how He loves!

3 All thy sins shall be forgiven,
　O how He loves!
Backward all thy foes be driven,
　O how He loves!
Best of blessings He'll provide thee,
Nought but good shall e'er betide thee,
Safe to glory He will guide thee—
　O how He loves!

4 Let us still this love be viewing,
　O how He loves!
And though faint, keep on pursuing,
　O how He loves!
He will strengthen each endeavor,
And when passed o'er Jordan's river,
This shall be our song forever,
　O how He loves.

1007

1 HARK, those bell-tones sweetly pealing,
　Come, wanderer, come;
Far and wide melodious stealing—
　Come, wanderer, come;
Though each heart the voice is thrilling,
Storms of grief and passion stilling—
Storms of grief and passion stilling—
　Come, wanderer, come.

2 Hark ! the bell to prayer is calling;
　Come, wanderer, come.
In God's house with reverent feeling—
　Seek here thy home.
There 's a mansion far above thee,
For the Spirit's pure and lowly—
For the Spirit 's pure and lowly,
　Come, wanderer, come.

3 Still the echoed voice is ringing;
　Come, wanderer, come.
Every heart pure incense bringing;
　Come, wanderer, come.
Father, round the altar bending,
May our songs to heaven ascending,
Join the anthems never ending—
　Come, wanderer, come.

1008

1 HARK ! the clarion now is breaking
　Come, brothers, come.
Nations from their sleep are waking; —
　Come, brothers, come.
See salvation's banner flying;—
Join the ranks—on God relying;
" Victory !" we shall soon be crying :—
　Come, brothers, come.

2 Christ, the Lord, shall have the glory—
　Come, brothers, come.
As ages roll we'll chant this story
　Come, brothers, come.
Honor to the Father giving;
To Son and Spirit ever living—
To Son and Spirit ever living—
　Come, brothers, come.

G. KINGSLEY.

I would not live al - way—I ask not to stay, Where storm af - ter

storm ris - es dark o'er the way; The few lu - rid morn - ings that

dawn on us here, Are e - nough for life's woes, full enough for its cheer.

1009

I would not live alway thus fettered by sin—
Temptation without and corruption within:
E'en the rapture of pardon is mingled with fears,
And the cup of thanksgiving with penitent tears.

I would not live alway; no, welcome the tomb;
Since Jesus hath lain there, I dread not its gloom;
There sweet be my rest, till He bid me arise
To hail Him in triumph descending the skies.

Who, who would live alway, away from his God,
Away from yon heaven, that blissful abode,
Where the rivers of pleasure flow o'er the bright plains,
And the noontide of glory eternally reigns?

Where the saints of all ages in harmony meet,
Their Saviour and brethren transported to greet;
While the anthems of rapture unceasingly roll,
And the smile of the Lord is the life of the soul.

1010

Rise daughter of Zion, thy mourning is o'er,
The night that hath veiled thee shall veil thee no more;
Wear the robes of the morning, arise thou and shine,
For the beauty and light of Jehovah are thine.

Oh, lift up thine eyes, look around thee and see;
How thy children are gathering together to thee;
Like doves on the wing, flying home to be blest
At thine altar with peace, in thy bosom with rest.

In thy kingdom of love shall all violence cease,
Thine exactors be justice, thine officers peace,
Thy people all righteous, and truth all thy ways,
Thy walls called salvation, thine open gates praise.

Jehovah, Thy beauty, Thy brightness, Thy crown,
Thy moon shall not wane, and Thy sun ne'er go down,
And the tide of Thy glory no ebbing to know,
Shall an ocean of light round the universe flow.

Acquaint thee, O mor - tal, acquaint thee with God, And joy, like the sunshine, shall beam on thy road; And peace, like the dew - drop, shall fall on thy head, And sleep, like an an - gel, shall vis - it thy bed.

1011

2 Acquaint thee, O mortal, acquaint thee with God,
And He shall be with thee when fears are abroad;
Thy Safeguard in danger that threatens thy path;
Thy Joy in the valley and shadow of death.

1012

1 My home is in heaven, my rest is not here,
Then why should I murmur when trials appear?
Be hushed, my dark spirit, the worst that can come,
But shortens my journey, and hastens thee home.

2 It is not for thee to be seeking thy bliss,
And building thy hopes in a region like this;
I look for a city which hands have not piled,
I pant for a country by sin undefiled.

3 The thorn and the thistle around me may grow,
I would not recline upon roses below;
I ask not my portion, I seek not my rest,
Till I find them forever on Jesus' breast.

1013

1 Thou soft-flowing Cedron, by thy silver stream
Our Saviour by midnight, when moonlight's pale beam
Shone bright on thy waters, would frequently stray,
And lose in thy murmurs the toils of the day.

2 How damp were the vapors that fell on His Head!
How hard was His pillow, how humble His bed!
The angels astonished grew sad at the sight,
And followed their Master with solemn delight.

3 O garden of Olivet, dear, honored spot,
Thy name and thy wonders shall ne'er be forgot;
The theme most transporting to seraphs above,
The triumph of sorrow, the triumph of love.

4 Come saints, and adore Him; come bow at His feet; [meet;
O, give Him the glory, the praise that is Let joyful hosannahs unceasing arise,
And join the grand chorus that gladdens the skies.

How firm a founda-tion, ye saints of the Lord, Is laid for your faith in His ex-cel-lent word; What more can He say than to you He hath said—Who un-to the Sa-viour, Who un-to the Sa-viour, Who un-to the Sa-viour for re-fuge have fled.

1014

2 Fear not, I am with thee, Oh ! be not dismayed;
For I am thy God, and will still give thee
   aid;
* I'll strengthen thee, help thee, and cause
   thee to stand,
Upheld by My righteous, omnipotent hand.

1015

1 THE Lord is my Shepherd, nor want shall
   I know;
I feed in green pastures; safe folded I rest;
He leadeth my soul where the still waters
   flow;
Restores me when wandering, redeems
   when oppressed.

2 Through the valley of the shadow of death
   though I stray,
Since Thou art my Guardian, no evil I
   fear;
Thy rod shall defend me, Thy staff be my
   stay;
No harm can befall with my Comforter
   near.

3 In the midst of affliction my table is spread;
   With blessings unmeasured my cup run-
   neth o'er;
With perfume and oil Thou anointest my
   head;
   O, what shall I ask of Thy providence
   more?

O turn ye, O turn ye, for why will ye die, When God in great mer-cy is com-ing so nigh? Now Je-sus 'in-vites you, the Spi-rit says, Come, And an-gels are wait-ing to wel-come you home.

1016

2 How vain the delusion, that while you de-lay,
Your hearts may grow better by staying away;
Come wretched, come starving, come just as you be,
While streams of salvation are flowing so free.

3 And now Christ is ready your souls to re-ceive,
O how can you question if you will believe?
If sin is your burden, why will you not come?
'Tis you He bids welcome; He bids you come home.

4 Come, give us your hand, and the Saviour your heart,
And trusting in heaven, we never shall part;
O how can we leave you! why will you not come!
We'll journey together, and soon be at home.

1017

1 DELAY not, delay not; O sinner, draw near;
The waters of life are now flowing for thee:
No price is demanded; the Saviour is here;
Redemption is purchased, salvation is free.

2 Delay not, delay not; why longer abuse
The love and compassion of Jesus, thy God?
A fountain is opened; how canst thou re-fuse
To wash and be cleansed in his pardon-ing blood?

3 Delay not, delay not, O sinner, to come!
For mercy still lingers and calls thee to-day:
Her voice is not heard in the shade of the tomb:
Her message, unheeded, will soon pass away.

O fly, mourning sinner, saith Je-sus to me, Thy guilt I will pardon, thy
And thy stains I will wash, and thy

FINE. D. S.

soul I will free ; From the chains that have bound thee, my grace shall release,
sorrows shall cease.

1018

2 Too long, guilty wanderer, too long hast
thou been
In the broad road of ruin, in bondage to
sin;
Thee the world has allured, and enslaved,
and deceived, /
While my counsel thou'st spurned, and my
Spirit hast grieved.

3 Though countless thy sins, and though
crimson thy guilt,
Yet for crimes such as thine was my blood
freely spilt:
Come sinner, and prove me; come, mourner, and see
The wounds that I bore, when I suffered
for thee.

4 Thou doubt'st not my power — deny not
my will;
Come, needy, come helpless, thy soul I
will fill;
My mercy is boundless ; no sinner shall
say,
That he sued at my feet — but was driven
away.

1019

1 Lo! Jesus the Saviour, in mercy draws
near,
Salvation he brings, O repent and believe;
The voice of his mercy the doubting shall
hear,
And sinners redemption with gladness
receive.

2 The day-star of promise illumines the sky,
And souls long benighted now welcome
the dawn;
Improve the glad season, or soon you may
cry—
" The harvest is past, and the summer is
gone!"

3 The spirit is striving with sinners to-day,
He graciously knocks at the door of your
heart,
He comes the compassion of God to display,
Your sins to remove and his love to impart.

4 O! welcome the Spirit, and grieve him no
more,
Nor wait till his offers of life are withdrawn;
Lest then you may cry, as your doom you
deplore,
" The harvest is past, and the summer is
gone!"

1020

1 Though faint, yet pursuing, we go on our
way;
The Lord is our Leader, His word is our
stay;
Though suffering, and sorrow, and trial be
near,
The Lord is our refuge, and whom can we
fear?

2 He raiseth the fallen, He cheereth the faint:
The weak, and oppressed—He will hear their
complaint;
The way may be weary, and thorny the road,
But how can we falter? our help is in God!

1021

2 Sweet bonds that unite all the children of peace !
And thrice precious Jesus, whose love can not cease !
Though oft from Thy presence in sadness I roam,
I long to behold Thee in glory, at home.

3 I sigh from this body of sin to be free,
Which hinders my joy and communion with Thee :
Though now my temptation like billows may foam,
All, all will be peace, when I'm with Thee at home.

4 While here in the valley of conflict I stay,
O give me submission, and strength as my day;
In all my afflictions to Thee would I come,
Rejoicing in hope of my glorious home.

5 Whate'er Thou deniest, O give me Thy grace,
The Spirit's sure witness, and smiles of Thy face;
Endue me with ptaience to wait at Thy throne,
And find, even now, a sweet foretaste of home.

6 I long, dearest Lord, in Thy beauties to shine;
No more as an exile in sorrow to pine;
And in Thy dear image arise from the tomb,
With glorified millions to praise Thee at home.

1022

1 To Thee, O my Saviour, to Thee will I cling,'
For Thou art my Lord, my Redeemer and King;
And feeling Thy blessing, my spirit shall know,
Thy mercy is with me wherever I go.

2 Farewell to the anguish of doubt and despair,
And welcome the rapture of praise and of prayer,
Since, meekly confiding, in faith I rejoice,
To hear the sweet tones of Thy comforting voice.

3 Around me there shineth the heavenly ray
Which scattereth clouds and their shadows away,
And melteth my soul in devotional glow,—
For mercy is with me wherever I go.

4 Farewell to the pleasures which time can afford,
Since Thou art my glory, my Saviour and Lord;
Nor fear I the darkness of death and the tomb,
Since Thou art my Light in the midst of the gloom.

5 Before me there gloweth, around and above,
The pledges of favor, the tokens of love;
And gratitude teacheth my spirit to know,
Thy mercy is with me wherever I go.

LEGATO.   DR. HASTINGS.

How calm and beau - ti - ful the morn That gilds the sa - cred tomb,

Where once the Cru - ci - fied was borne, And veiled in mid - night gloom!

Oh! weep no more the Saviour slain; The Lord is risen—He lives a - gain.

1023

2 Ye mourning saints! dry every tear
   For your departed Lord;
" Behold the place—He is not there,"
   The tomb is all unbarred:
The gates of death were closed in vain:
The Lord is risen—He lives again.

3 Now cheerful to the house of prayer
   Your early footsteps bend,
The Saviour will himself be there,
   Your advocate and friend:
Once by the law your hopes were slain,
But now in Christ ye live again.

4 How tranquil now the rising day!
   'Tis Jesus still appears,
A risen Lord to chase away
   Your unbelieving fears:
Oh! weep no more your comforts slain,
The Lord is risen—He lives again.

5 And when the shades of evening fall,
   When life's last hour draws nigh,
If Jesus shine upon the soul,
   How blissful then to die:
Since He has risen who once was slain,
Ye die in Christ to live again.

1024

1 Since o'er Thy footstool here below
   Such radiant gems are strown,
O, what magnificence must glow,
   Great God, about Thy throne!
So brilliant here these drops of light!
There the full ocean rolls, how bright!

2 If night's blue curtain of the sky,
   With thousand stars inwrought,
Hung, like a royal canopy,
   With glittering diamonds fraught,
Be, Lord, Thy temple's outer veil,
What splendor at the shrine must dwell!

3 The dazzling sun, at noonday hour,
   Forth from his flaming vase,
Flinging o'er earth the golden shower,
   Till vale and mountain blaze,
But shows, O Lord, one beam of Thine:
What, then, the day where Thou dost
   shine!

4 O, how shall these dim eyes endure
   That noon of living rays?
Or how our spirits, so impure,
   Upon Thy glory gaze?
Anoint, O Lord, anoint our sight,
And fit us for that world of light,

Come, wan-d'ring sheep, O come! I'll bind thee to my breast;

I'll bear thee to thy home, And lay thee down to rest.

1025

2 I saw thee stray forlorn,
   And heard thee faintly cry,
   And on the tree of scorn
   For thee I deigned to die—

3 I shield thee from alarms,
   And wilt thou not be blest?
   I bear thee in My arms;
   Thou, bear me in thy breast!

1926

1 I FEEL within a want
   Forever burning there,
   What I so thirst for, grant,
   O Thou who hearest prayer!

2 This is the thing I crave,
   A likeness to Thy Son;
   This would I rather have
   Than call the world my own.

3 Like Him, now in my youth,
   I long, O God, to be,
   In tenderness and truth,
   In sweet humility.

1027

1 JEHOVAH is our strength,
   And He shall be our song;
   We shall o'ercome at length,
   Although our foes be strong.

2 The Lord our refuge is,
   And ever will remain;
   Since he hath made us His,
   He will our cause maintain.

3 The Lord our portion is,
   What can we wish for more?
   As long as we are His,
   We never can be poor.

4 The Lord our Shepherd is,
   He knows our every need;
   And since we now are His,
   His care our souls will feed.

5 Our God our Father is,
   Our names are on His heart;
   We ever shall be His,
   He ne'er from us will part.

1028

1 CLING to the Crucified !
   His eye shall guard thee well—
   For thee, fast from His side,
   The crimson current fell.

2 Cling to the Crucified !
   My weary feet in peace
   His tender hand shall guide
   Till all thy wanderings cease.

3 Cling to the Crucified !
   His love the golden door
   For thee shall open wide,
   And bless thee evermore.

Joy - ful - ly, joy - ful - ly, on - ward I move, Bound to the land of bright
An - gel - ic, chor - is - ters, sing as I come— Joy - ful - ly, joy - ful - ly

spi - rits a - bove;
haste to thy home! Soon with my pil - grim - age end - ed be - low,

Home to the land of bright spi - rits I go ; Pil - grim and stran - ger no

more shall I roam : Joy - ful - ly, joy - ful - ly rest - ing at home.

1029

2 Friends, fondly cherished, but passed on
    before;
Waiting, they watch me approaching the
    shore;
Singing to cheer me through death's chill-
    ing gloom:
Joyfully, joyfully haste to thy home.
Sounds of sweet melody fall on my ear;
Harps of the blessed, your voices I hear !
Rings with the harmony heaven's high
    dome—
Joyfully, joyfully haste to thy home.

3 Death, with thy weapons of war lay me low,
Strike, king of terrors ! I fear not the blow;
Jesus hath broken the bars of the tomb!
Joyfully, joyfully will I go home.
Bright will the morn of eternity dawn,
Death shall be banished, his sceptre be gone!

Joyfully, then shall I witness his doom,
Joyfully, joyfully, safely at home.

1030

I'm weary of sighing, O fain would I rest,
In the far distant land of the pure and the blest,
Where sin can no longer her blandishments
    spread;
And tears and temptations forever are fled.

I'm weary of loving what passes away,
The sweetest, the dearest, alas, do not stay;
I long for that land where those partings are
    o'er,
And death and the tomb can divide hearts no
    more.

I'm weary, my Saviour, of grieving thy love;
O, when shall I rest in Thy presence above,
I'm weary, but O, never let me repine,
While Thy changeless love, and Thy promise
    are mine.

MAESTOSO.   F. J. HAYDN. 1732—1810.

O praise ye the Lord; His great-ness pro-claim; Je-ho-vah our

God, how aw-ful Thy name! How vast is Thy pow-er! Thy

glo-ry how great! Lo, my-riads of spi-rits Thy·man-date a-wait. .

1031

2 Thy canopy's heaven, in splendor so
    bright;
Thy chariot the clouds, Thy garment the
    light;
The works of creation Thy bidding per-
    form;
Thou ridest the whirlwind, directest the
    storm.

3 What wisdom is shown, what power dis-
    played,
In all that Thy hand hath fashioned and
    made!
The earth full of riches, in beauty com-
    plete;
The fathomless ocean, with wonders re-
    plete.

1032

1 O worship the King all glorious above,
And gratefully sing His wonderful love—
Our shield and defender, the Ancient of
    days,
Pavilioned in splendor and girded with
    praise.

2 O tell of His might, and sing of His grace,
Whose robe is the light, whose canopy,
    space;
His chariots of wrath the deep thunder-
    clouds form,
And dark is His path on the wings of the
    storm.

3 Thy bountiful care what tongue can re-
    cite?
It breathes in the air, it shines in the light,
It streams from the hills, it descends to the
    plain,
And sweetly distils in the dew and the
    rain.

4 Frail children of dust, and feeble as frail,
In Thee do we trust, nor find Thee to fail,
Thy mercies how tender! how firm to the
    end!
Our Maker, Defender, Redeemer, and
    Friend.

5 Father Almighty, how faithful Thy love!
While angels delight to hymn Thee above,
The humbler creation, though feeble their
    lays,
With true adoration shall lisp to Thy
    praise.

—SOLO

Come, ye dis - con - so - late, where - 'er ye lan - guish:

Come, at the shrine of God, fer - vent - ly kneel;

(1st time, Duet—2d time, Chorus.)

Here bring your wound - ed hearts, here tell your

an - guish; Earth has no sor - row that Heaven can - not heal.

1033

2 Joy of the desolate, light of the straying,
Hope, when all others die, fadeless and pure,
Here speaks the Comforter, in God's name saying,
Earth hath no sorrow that heaven cannot cure.

1034

1 SAVIOUR, whose mercy, severe in its kindness,
Hast chastened my wanderings and guided my way,
Adored be the power which illumined my blindness,
And weaned me from phantoms that smiled to betray.

2 The blossoms blushed bright, but a worm was below;
The moonlight shone fair, there was blight in the beam;
Sweet whispered the breeze, but it whispered of woe;
And bitterness flowed in the soft flowing stream.

3 So, cured of my folly, yet cured but in part,
I turned to the refuge Thy pity displayed;
And still did this eager and credulous heart
Weave visions of promise that bloomed but to fade.

4 I dreamed of celestial rewards and renown;
I grasped at the triumph which blesses the brave;
I asked for the palm-branch, the robe and the crown;
I asked, and Thou showedst me a cross and a grave.

5 Subdued and instructed, at length, to Thy will,
My hopes and my longings I fain would resign;
O, give me the heart that can wait and be still,
Nor know of a wish or a pleasure but Thine.

6 There are mansions exempted from sin and from woe,
But they stand in a region by mortals untrod;
There are rivers of joy, but they roll not below;
There is rest, but it dwells in the presence of God.

O Thou, in whose pre-sence my soul takes de-light, On whom in af-flic-tion I call; My com-fort by day, and my song in the night, My hope, my sal-va-tion, my all!

1035

2 Where dost Thou at noontide resort with
Thy sheep
To feed on the pastures of love?
Say, why in the valley of death should I
weep,
Or alone in the wilderness rove?

3 O, why should I wander an alien from Thee
Or cry in the desert for bread?
Thy foes will rejoice when my sorrows they
see,
And smile at the tears I have shed.

4 Restore, my dear Saviour, the light of Thy
face;
Thy soul-cheering favor impart;
And let Thy sweet tokens of pardoning
grace
Bring joy to my desolate heart.

1036

1 In songs of sublime adoration and praise,
Ye pilgrims, for Zion who press,
Break forth, and extol the great Ancient of
Days,
His rich and distinguishing grace.

2 His love, from eternity, fixed upon you,
Broke forth, and discovered its flame,
When each with the cords of His kindness,
He drew,
And brought you to love His great name.

3 What was there in you that could merit
esteem,
Or give the Creator delight?
'Twas, "Even so, Father," you ever must
sing,
"Because it seemed good in Thy sight."

4 'Twas all of Thy grace we were brought to
obey,
While others were suffered to go
The road which by nature we chose as our
way,
Which leads to the regions of woe.

5 Then give all the glory to His holy name;
To Him all the glory belongs;
Be yours the high joy still to sound forth
His fame,
And crown Him in each of your songs.

I'm a pil-grim, and I'm a stran-ger; I can tar-ry,

I can tar-ry but a night; Do not de-tain me, for I am

go-ing To where the foun-tains are ev-er flow-ing.

1037

2 There the glory is ever shining !
O, my longing heart, my longing heart is there;
Here in this country so dark and dreary,
I long have wandered forlorn and weary.

3 There's the city to which I journey;
My Redeemer, my Redeemer is its light !
There is no sorrow, nor any sighing,
Nor any sinning, nor any dying.

1038

1 FAREWELL, brothers, with tears I've warned you,
I must leave you, I must leave you and be gone;
With this your portion, your heart's desire—
Why will you perish in raging fire.
I'm a pilgrim, and I'm a stranger, &c.

2 Father, mother, and sister, brother !
If you will not journey with me I must go !
Now since your vain hopes you will thus cherish,
Should I too linger and with you perish ?
I'm a pilgrim, and I'm a stranger, &c.

3 Farewell, dreary earth, by sin so blighted,
In immortal beauty soon you'll be arrayed,
He who has formed thee will soon restore thee,
And then thy dread curse shall never more be;
I'm a pilgrim, and I'm a stranger, &c.

1039

1 GIVE me music; oh, give me music
While I linger, while I linger here below.
Let strains of heavenly music cheer me,
For my sinful heart is sad and dreary.

2 Sing of Jesus; oh, sing of Jesus,
His sweet mercy; oh, let me his mercy know.
That for my heart His voice is pleading,
At the great throne for me interceding.

3 Sing of Jesus; oh, sing of Jesus,
His sweet Spirit, oh, let me breathe it.
Let melodies of love unending
Soothe my poor soul in sorrow low bending.

4 Sing of heaven; oh, sing of heaven—
Its clear river; crystal sea and streets of gold.
For that fair land I am ever sighing,
Oh give me music living and dying.

SUPPLEMENT.

CALVIN. L. M.

CHARLES ZEUNER.

E - ter - nal God, e - ter - nal King, Ru - ler of heav'n and earth beneath !

From Thee our hopes, our comforts spring, In Thee we live, and move and breathe.

1

2 Thy word brought forth the flaming sun,
  The changeful moon, the starry host;
In Thine appointed course they run,
  Till in the final ruin lost.

3 At Thy command the storm is dumb:
  And to the sea Thy power hath said,—
No further shalt thou dare to come,
  And here shall thy proud waves be stayed.

4 Thy sway is known below, above,
  And full of majesty Thy voice;
And as it speaks in wrath or love,
  The nations tremble or rejoice.

5 The final, awful hour is near,
  Time paces on with ceaseless tread,
When opening graves Thy voice shall hear,
  And render up the sleeping dead.

6 Oh ! in that great decisive day,
  May we be found in Christ, and stand
While flaming worlds shall melt away,
  Owned and approved at Thy right hand.

2

1 Great God, whose universal sway
  The known and unknown worlds obey,
Now give the kingdom to Thy Son;
  Extend His power, exalt His throne.

2 Thy sceptre well becomes His hands,
  All heaven submits to His commands;
His justice shall avenge the poor,
  And pride and rage prevail no more.

3 With power He vindicates the just,
  And treads th' oppressor in the dust;
His worship and His fear shall last,
  Till hours, and years, and times be past.

4 As rain on meadows newly mown,
  So shall He send His influence down;
His grace, on fainting souls, distils,
  Like heavenly dew on thirsty hills.

5 The heathen lands, that lie beneath
  The shades of overspreading death,
Revive at his first dawning light;
  And deserts blossom at the sight.

HARTFORD. L. M.

CHARLES ZEUNER.

High in the heav'ns, e - ter - nal God! Thy goodness in full glo - ry shines;

Thy truth shall break thro' ev' - ry cloud That veils or dark - ens Thy de - signs.

3

2 For ever firm Thy justice stands,
    As mountains their foundations keep;
Wise are the wonders of Thy hands,
Thy judgments are a mighty deep.

3 My God! how excellent Thy grace,
    Whence all our hope, our comfort springs?
The sons of Adam, in distress,
    Fly to the shadow of Thy wings.

4 From the provisions of Thy house,
    We shall be fed with sweet repast:
There mercy like a river flows,
    And brings salvation to our taste.

5 Life, like a fountain, rich and free,
    Springs from the presence of my Lord;
And, in Thy light our souls shall see
    The glories promised in Thy word.

4

1 Ere the blue heavens were stretch'd abroad,
    From everlasting was the Word:
With God He was; the Word was God,
    And must divinely be adored.

2 By His own power were all things made,
    By Him supported all things stand;
He is the whole creation's Head,
    And angels fly at His command.

3 But lo, He leaves those heavenly forms,
    The Word descends and dwells in clay,
That He may converse hold with worms,
    Dressed in such feeble flesh as they.

4 Mortals with joy behold His face,
    The eternal Father's only Son;
How full of truth, how full of grace,
    When thro' His eyes the Godhead shone.

5 Archangels leave their high abode,
    To learn new mysteries here and tell
The love of our descending God.
    The glories of Immanuel.

5

1 Praise, everlasting praise, be paid
To Him, who earth's foundation laid
Praise to the God, whose strong decrees
Sway the creation, as He please.

2 Praise to the goodness of the Lord,
Who rules His people by His word;
And there as strong as His decrees,
He sets His kindest promises.

3 Whence then should doubts and fears arise?
Why trickling sorrows drown our eyes?
Slowly, alas! our mind receives
The comforts that our Maker gives.

4 Oh! for a strong, a lasting faith,
    To credit what th' Almighty saith;
T' embrace the message of His Son,
    And call the joys of heaven our own.

5 Then, should the earth's old pillars shake,
    And all the wheels of nature break,
Our steady souls would fear no more,
    Than solid rocks when billows roar.

ALLEGRO.

CHARLES ZEUNER.

Sweet is the work, my God, my King! To praise thy name, give thanks and sing;

To show Thy love by morning light, And talk of all Thy truth at night.

6

2 Sweet is the day of sacred rest,
No mortal care shall seize my breast;
Oh! may my heart in tune be found,
Like David's harp of solemn sound.

3 My heart shall triumph in my Lord,
And bless His works, and bless His word;
Thy works of grace—how bright they shine!
How deep Thy counsels—how divine!

4 Lord! I shall share a glorious part,
When grace hath well refined my heart,
And fresh supplies of joy are shed,
Like holy oil, to cheer my head.

5 Then shall I see, and hear, and know
All I desired or wished below;
And every power find sweet employ
In that eternal world of joy.

7

1 Great God, we sing that mighty hand,
By which supported still we stand;
The opening year Thy mercy shows,—
Let mercy crown it till it close.

2 By day, by night—at home, abroad,
Still we are guarded by our God;
By His incessant bounty fed,
By His unerring counsel led.

3 With grateful hearts the past we own;
The future—all to us unknown—
We to Thy guardian care commit,
And peaceful leave before Thy feet.

4 In scenes exalted or depressed,
Be Thou our joy—and Thou our rest;
Thy goodness all our hopes shall raise,
Adored, through all our changing days.

5 When death shall close our earthly songs,
And seal, in silence, mortal tongues,
Our helper, God, in whom we trust,
Shall keep our souls, and guard our dust.

8

1 Now let my soul, eternal King!
To Thee its grateful tribute bring;
My knee with humble homage bring:
My tongue perform its solemn vow.

2 All nature sings Thy boundless love,
In worlds below—and worlds above;
But in Thy blessed word I trace,
Diviner wonders of Thy grace.

3 There what delightful truths I read!
There I behold the Saviour bleed;
His name salutes my listening ear,
Revives my heart, and checks my fear.

4 There Jesus bids my sorrows cease,
And gives my laboring conscience peace;
Raises my grateful passions high,
And points to mansions in the sky.

5 For love like this, oh let my song,
Thro' endless years Thy praise prolong;
Let distant climes Thy name adore,
Till time and nature are no more.

304 WARNER. L. M.

Subject ROSSINI.

Come, blessed Spi-rit! source of light, Whose pow'r and grace are unconfined, Dis-pel the gloomy shades of night,—The thicker darkness of the mind.

9

2 To mine illumined eyes display
  The glorious truth Thy word reveals,
  Cause me to run the heavenly way,
  Thy book unfold and loose the seals.

3 Thine inward teachings make me know
  The mysteries of redeeming love,
  The vanity of things below,
  And excellence of things above.

4 While through this dubious maze I stray,
  Spread like the sun, Thy beams abroad,
  To show the dangers of the way,
  And guide my feeble steps to God.

10

1 Thine earthly Sabbaths, Lord! we love,
  But there's a nobler rest above;
  To that our longing souls aspire,
  With cheerful hope and strong desire.

2 No more fatigue, no more distress,
  Nor sin, nor death shall reach the place;
  No groans shall mingle with the songs
  That warble from immortal tongues.

3 No rude alarms of raging foes,
  No cares to break the long repose,
  No midnight shade, no clouded sun,
  But sacred, high, eternal noon.

4 Soon shall that glorious day begin,
  Beyond this world of death and sin;
  Soon shall our voices join the song
  Of the triumphant, holy throng.

11

1 Sure the blest Comforter is nigh;
  'Tis He sustains my fainting heart;
  Else would my hope for ever die,
  And every cheering ray depart.

2 Whene'er, to call the Saviour mine,
  With ardent wish my heart aspires,—
  Can it be less than power divine,
  That animates these strong desires?

3 And, when my cheerful hope can say,—
  I love my God and taste His grace,
  Lord! is it not Thy blissful ray,
  That brings this dawn of sacred peace?

4 Let Thy good Spirit in my heart
  For ever dwell, O God of love!
  And light and heavenly peace impart—
  Sweet earnest of the joys above.

12

1 The God of love will sure indulge
  The flowing tear, the heaving sigh,
  When righteous persons fall around—
  When tender friends and kindred die.

2 Beneath a numerous train of ills,
  Our feeble flesh and heart may fail;
  Yet shall our hope in Thee, our God,
  O'er every gloomy fear prevail.

3 Our Father-God! to Thee we look,
  Our Rock, our Portion, and our Friend;
  And on Thy covenant love and truth,
  Our sinking souls shall still depend.

GREATOREX.

Why should our tears in sor - row flow When God re - calls his own;

And bids them leave a world of woe· For an im - mor - tal crown.

13

2 Is not e'en death a gain to those
Whose life to God was given?
Gladly to earth their eyes they close
To open them in heaven.

3 Their toils are past—their work is done,
And they are fully blest;
They fought the fight, the vict'ry won,
And entered into rest.

4 Then let our sorrows cease to flow,—
God has recalled His own;
But let our hearts, in every woe,
Still say,—"Thy will be done!"

14

1 In all my vast concerns with Thee,
In vain my soul would try
To shun Thy presence, Lord! or flee
The notice of Thine eye.

2 Thine all-surrounding sight surveys
My rising and my rest,
My public walks, my private ways,
And secrets of my breast.

3 My thoughts lie open to the Lord,
Before they're formed within;
And ere my lips pronounce the word,
He knows the sense I mean.

4 Oh! wondrous knowledge, deep and high,
Where can a creature hide?
Within Thy circling arms I lie,
Enclosed on every side.

5 So let Thy grace surround me still,
And like a bulwark prove,
To guard my soul from every ill,
Secured by sovereign love.

15

1 Oh! for that tenderness of heart,
That bows before the Lord;
That owns how just and good Thou art,
And trembles at Thy word.

2 Oh! for those humble, contrite tears,
Which from repentance flow,
That sense of guilt, which, trembling fears
The long suspended blow!

3 Saviour! to me, in pity give,
For sin, the deep distress;
The pledge Thou wilt, at last, receive,
And bid me die in peace.

4 Oh! fill my soul with faith and love,
And strength to do Thy will;
Raise my desires and hopes above—
Thyself to me reveal.

16

1 And will the Lord thus condescend
To visit sinful worms?
Thus at the door shall mercy stand,
In all her winning forms?

2 Shall Jesus for admittance plead,
His charming voice unheard?
And this vile heart, for which He bled,
Remain for ever barred?

3 'Tis sin, alas! with tyrant power,
The lodging has possessed;
And crowds of traitors bar the door,
Against the heavenly guest.

4 Lord! rise in Thine all-conquering grace,
Thy mighty power display;
One beam of glory from Thy face
Can drive my foes away.

BOARDMAN. C. M. (Double.)

ANDANTINO.

1. Oh! could I find, from day to day, A near-ness to my God,....

Then should my hours glide sweet a-way, Nor sin nor fear in-trude.

2. Lord, I de-sire with Thee to live A-new from day to day;

In joys the world can nev-er give, Nor ev-er take a-way.

17

3 O Jesus! come and rule my heart,
    And make me wholly Thine,
That I may never more depart,
    Nor grieve Thy love divine.

4 Thus, till my last expiring breath,
    Thy goodness I'll adore;
And when my flesh dissolves in death,
    My soul shall love Thee more.

18

1 Oh for a heart to praise my God,
    A heart from sin set free!
A heart that's sprinkled with the blood
    So freely shed for me.

2 Thy temper, gracious Lord, impart;
    Come quickly from above;
Oh write Thy name upon my heart—
    Thy name, O God, is Love!

To - mor - row, Lord, is thine,— Lodg'd in Thy sov'reign hand;

RITARD.

And if its sun a - rise and shine, It shines by Thy command.

19

2 The present moment flies,
And bears our life away;
Oh! make Thy servants truly wise,
That they may live to-day.

3 Since on this fleeting hour,
Eternity is hung,
Awaken by Thy mighty power,
The aged and the young.

4 One thing demands our care;—
Be that one thing pursued;
Lest, slighted once, the season fair
Should never be renewed.

5 To Jesus may we fly,
Swift as the morning light,
Lest life's young golden beams should die,
In sudden, endless night.

20

1 Make haste, O man, to live,
For thou so soon must die:
Time hurries past thee like the breeze,
How swift its moments fly!

2 To breathe, and wake, and sleep,
To smile, to sigh, to grieve,
To move in idleness through earth,
This, this is not to live.

3 Make haste, O man, to do
Whatever must be done;
Thou hast no time to lose in sloth;
Thy day will soon be gone.

4 Up, then, with speed, and work;
Fling ease and self away,
This is no time for thee to sleep,
Up, watch, and work, and pray.

21

1 Behold the throne of grace!
The promise calls us near;
There Jesus shows a smiling face,
And waits to answer prayer.

2 That rich atoning blood,
Which sprinkled round we see,
Provides for those who come to God
An all-prevailing plea.

3 Thine image, Lord! bestow,
Thy presence and Thy love;
We ask to serve Thee here below
And reign with Thee above.

4 Teach us to live by faith,
Conform our will to Thine;
Let us victorious be in death,
And, then, in glory shine.

5 If Thou these blessings give,
And wilt our portion be,
All worldly joys we'll cheerful leave,
And find our heaven in Thee.

22

Ye angels round the throne,
And saints that dwell below,
Worship the Father—love the Son,
And bless the Spirit too.

And must I part with all I have, My dear-est Lord, for Thee?

It is but right, since Thou hast done Much more than this for me.

23

2 Yes, let it go,—one look from Thee
  Will more than make amends,
  For all the losses I sustain
  Of credit, riches, friends.

3 Ten thousand worlds, ten thousand lives,
  How worthless they appear,
  Compared with Thee, supremely good,
  Divinely bright and fair!

4 Saviour of souls, could I from Thee
  A single smile obtain,
  Though destitute of all things else,
  I'd glory in my gain.

24

1 Behold! where, in a mortal form,
  Appears each grace divine;
  The virtues, all in Jesus met,
  With mildest radiance shine.

2 To spread the rays of heavenly light,
  To give the mourner joy,
  To preach glad tidings to the poor,
  Was His divine employ.

3 Mid keen reproach and cruel scorn,
  He, meek and patient, stood;
  His foes, ungrateful, sought His life,
  Who labored for their good.

4 When, in the hour of deep distress,
  Before His Father's throne,
  With soul resigned, he bowed and said,
  "Thy will, not mine, be done!"

5 Be Christ our pattern and our guide,
  His image may we bear;
  Oh! may we tread His holy steps,—
  His joy and glory share.

25

1 My soul! how lovely is the place,
  To which thy God resorts!
  'Tis heaven to see His smiling face,
  Though in His earthly courts.

2 There the great monarch of the skies
  His saving power displays,
  And light breaks in upon our eyes,
  With kind and quickening rays.

3 With His rich gifts, the heavenly Dove
  Descends and fills the place;
  While Christ reveals His wondrous love
  And sheds abroad His grace.

4 There, mighty God! Thy words declare
  The secrets of Thy will;
  And still we seek Thy mercy there,
  And sing Thy praises still.

26

1 Didst Thou, dear Saviour, suffer shame,
  And bear the cross for me?
  And shall I fear to own Thy name,
  Or Thy disciple be?

2 Inspire my soul with life divine,
  And make me truly bold;
  Let knowledge, faith and meekness shine,
  Nor love, nor zeal grow cold.

ALLEGRO ASSAI.

CHARLES ZEUNER.

Awake, ye saints! to praise your King, Your sweetest passions raise;

Your pi - ous pleasure, while you sing, In - creasing with the praise.

27

2 Great is the Lord,—and works unknown
Are His divine employ;
But still His saints are near His throne,
His treasure and His joy.

3 Heaven, earth and sea confess His hand;
He bids the vapors rise;
Lightnings and storms, at His command,
Sweep through the sounding skies.

4 Ye saints! adore the living God,
Serve Him with faith and fear;
He makes the churches His abode,
And claims your honors there.

28

1 Father! how wide Thy glory shines!
How high Thy wonders rise!
Known thro' the earth by thousand signs—
By thousand through the skies.

2 Those mighty orbs proclaim Thy power,
Their motions speak Thy skill;
And on the wings of every hour,
We read Thy patience still.

3 But when we view Thy strange design
To save rebellious worms,
Where vengeance and compassion join,
In their divinest forms,—

4 Here the whole Deity is known;
Nor dares a creature guess,—
Which of the glories brightest shone,
The justice, or the grace.

5 Now the full glories of the Lamb
Adorn the heavenly plains;
Bright seraphs learn Immanuel's name,
And try their choicest strains.

6 Oh! may I bear some humble part,
In that immortal song;
Wonder and joy shall tune my heart,
And love command my tongue.

29

1 Awake ye saints! and raise your eyes,
And raise your voices high;
Awake, and praise that sovereign love
That shows salvation nigh.

2 On all the wings of time it flies,
Each moment brings it near;
Then welcome each declining day,
Welcome each closing year.

3 Not many years their rounds shall run,
Nor many mornings rise,
Ere all its glories stand revealed
To our admiring eyes.

5 Ye wheels of nature! speed your course;
Ye mortal powers! decay:
Fast as ye bring the night of death,
Ye bring eternal day.

30

Ye angels round the throne,
And saints that dwell below,
Worship the Father—love the Son,
And bless the Spirit too.

MOUNT AUBURN. C. M.

Lord, I believe; Thy pow'r I own; Thy word I would o - bey;

I wan - der com - fort - less and lone, When from Thy truth I stray.

31

2 Lord, I believe; but gloomy fears
Sometimes bedim my sight;
I look to Thee with prayers and tears,
And cry for strength and light.

3 Lord, I believe; but oft, I know,
My faith is cold and weak:
My weakness strengthen and bestow
The confidence I seek.

4 Yes! I believe; and only Thou
Canst give my soul relief:
Lord, to Thy truth my spirit bow;
"Help Thou mine unbelief."

32

1 Ye golden lamps of heaven! farewell,
With all your feeble light;
Farewell, thou ever-changing moon!
Pale empress of the night.

2 And thou, refulgent orb of day!
In brighter flames arrayed,—
My soul, that springs beyond thy sphere,
No more demands thy aid.

3 Ye stars are but the shining dust
Of my divine abode;
The pavement of those heavenly courts,
Where I shall see my God.

4 The Father of eternal light
Shall there his beams display;
Nor shall one moment's darkness mix
With that unvaried day.

5 No more the drops of piercing grief
Shall swell into mine eyes;
Nor the meridian sun decline
Amid those brighter skies.

6 There all the millions of His saints
Shall in one song unite;
And each the bliss of all shall view,
With infinite delight.

33

1 Hear what the voice from heaven proclaims,
For all the pious dead;—
"Sweet is the savor of their names,
And soft their sleeping bed.

2 "They die in Jesus, and are blessed,—
How kind their slumbers are!
From sufferings and from sin released,
And freed from every snare.

3 "Far from this world of toil and strife,
They're present with the Lord;
The labors of their mortal life
End in a large reward."

34

1 Unshaken as the sacred hill,
And firm as mountains be;
Firm as a rock the soul shall rest,
That leans, O Lord, on Thee.

2 Not walls nor hills could guard so well
Old Salem's happy ground,
As those eternal arms of love
That every saint surround.

GEO. KINGSLEY.

CON SPIRITO.

Come, ye that love the Saviour's name, And joy to make it known! The Sov'reign

of your hearts proclaim, And bow before the throne, And bow before the throne.

35

2 Behold your King, your Saviour crowned,
With glories all divine;
And tell the wondering nations round,
How bright these glories shine.

3 Infinite power and boundless grace,
In Him unite their rays;
Ye that have e'er beheld His face!
Can ye forbear His praise?

4 When in His earthly courts we view
The beauties of our King,
We long to love as angels do,
And wish like them to sing.

5 And shall we long and wish in vain?
Lord! teach our songs to rise,
Thy love can animate the strain,
And bid it reach the skies.

36

1 Angels rejoiced and sweetly sung,
At our Redeemer's birth:
Mortals! awake; let every tongue
Proclaim His matchless worth.

2 Glory to God who dwells on high,
And sent His only Son
To take a servant's form, and die,
For evils we had done!

3 Good will to men :— ye fallen race!
Arise and shout for joy;
He comes with rich abounding, grace
To save, and not destroy.

4 Lord! send the gracious tidings forth,
And fill the world with light,
That Jew and Gentile, thro' the earth,
May know Thy saving might.

5 Ye poor! who tremble at the word,
Distressed, and helpless too,—
Oh! come and welcome to the Lord,
For He was born for you.

37

1 Let songs of praises fill the sky!
Christ, our ascended Lord,
Sends down His Spirit from on high,
According to His word.

2 The Spirit, by His heavenly breath,
New life creates within:
He quickens sinners, from the death
Of trespasses and sin.

3 The things of Christ, the Spirit takes,
And to our heart reveals:
Our bodies He his temple makes,
And our redemption seals.

4 Come, Holy Spirit! from above,
With Thy celestial fire;
Come, and with flames of zeal and love,
Our hearts and tongues inspire.

38

1 The earth, the ocean, and the sky,
To form one world agree:
Where all that walk, or swim, or fly,
Compose one family.

2 In one fraternal bond of love,
One fellowship of mind,
The saints below and saints above,
Their bliss and glory find.

3 Here, in their house of pilgrimage,
Thy statutes are their song;
There, through one bright eternal age,
Thy praises they prolong.

312 FULTON. 7s. W. B. B.

SLOW.

Who, O Lord, when life is o'er, Shall to heav'n's blest mansions soar?

Who, an ev - er wel - come guest, In Thy ho - ly place shall rest?

39

2 He whose heart Thy love has warmed;
He, whose will to Thine conformed,
Bids his life unsullied run;
He, whose words and thoughts are one:—

3 He, who shuns the sinner's road,
Loving those who love their God;
Who, with hope and faith unfeigned,
Treads the path by Thee ordained:—

4 He, who trusts in Christ alone,
Not in aught himself hath done,—
He, great God! shall be Thy care,
And Thy choicest blessings share.

40

1 Hark—that shout of rapturous joy,
Bursting forth from yonder cloud!
Jesus comes—and, through the sky,
Angels tell their joy aloud.

2 Hark! the trumpet's awful voice
Sounds abroad thro' sea and land;
Let His people now rejoice,
Their redemption is at hand.

3 See! the Lord appears in view;
Heaven and earth before Him fly:
Rise, ye saints! He comes for you,—
Rise, to meet Him in the sky.

4 Go and dwell with Him above,
Where no foe can e'er molest;
Happy in the Saviour's love,
Ever blessing, ever blest.

41

1 Hark! my soul! it is the Lord;
'Tis thy Saviour—hear His word:
Jesus speaks, and speaks to thee,—
"Say, poor sinner! lovest Thou me?

2 "I delivered thee, when bound,
And, when bleeding, healed thy wound;
Sought thee wandering, set thee right,
Turned thy darkness into light.

3 "Can a woman's tender care
Cease towards the child she bare?
Yes, she may forgetful be,
Yet will I remember thee.

4 "Mine is an unchanging love,
Higher than the heights above;
Deeper than the depths beneath—
Free and faithful—strong as death.

5 "Thou shalt see my glory soon,
When the work of grace is done;
Partner of my throne shalt be;—
Say, poor sinner! lovest thou me?"

6 Lord! it is my chief complaint,
That my love is weak and faint;
Yet I love Thee, and adore,—
Oh! for grace to love Thee more.

42

Father, Son and Holy Ghost,
One in Three, and Three in One,
As by the celestial host,
Let Thy will on earth be done:
Praise by all to Thee be given,
Glorious Lord of earth and heaven.

Arranged from HEROLD.

1. Bless - ed fountain, full of grace, Grace for sinners, grace for me,

To this source a - lone I trace What I am and hope to be.

2. What I am as one redeemed, Saved and res - cued by the Lord;

Ha - ting what I once esteemed, Lov - ing what I once abhorred.

43

3 What I hope to be ere long,
When I take my place above;
When I join the heavenly throng;
When I see the God of love.

4 Then I hope like Him to be,
Who redeemed His saints from sin,
Whom I now obscurely see,
Through a veil that stands between.

5 Blessed fountain, full of grace!
Grace for sinners, grace for me;
To this source alone I trace
What I am and hope to be.

44

1 In Thy presence we appear;
Lord! we love to worship here,
When, within the veil, we wait
Thee upon Thy mercy-seat.

2 While Thy glorious name is sung,
Touch our lips, and loose our tongue;
Then our joyful souls shall bless
Thee, the Lord, our righteousness.

3 While to Thee our prayers ascend,
Let Thine ear in love attend;
Hear us, for Thy Spirit pleads;
Hear, for Jesus intercedes.

ANDANTE.   ROSSINI.

Thou who art enthroned a - bove, Thou by whom we live and move!

Oh! how sweet, with joy - ful tongue, To re - sound Thy praise in song!

When the morn - ing paints the skies, When the spark - ling stars a - rise,

All Thy fa - vors to re - hearse, And give thanks in grate - ful verse.

45

2 Sweet is the day of sacred rest,
When devotion fills the breast,
When we dwell within Thy house,
Hear Thy word, and pay our vows;
Notes to heaven's high mansions raise,
Fill its courts with joyful praise;
With repeated hymns proclaim
Great Jehovah's awful name.

3 From Thy works our joys arise,
O Thou only good and wise!
Who Thy wonders can declare?
How profound Thy counsels are!
Warm our hearts with sacred fire;
Grateful fervor still inspire :
All our powers, with all their might,
Ever in Thy praise unite.

46

1 Oh! be joyful in the Lord!
Every land beneath the sun!
In His praise with glad accord,
Let all tongues and hearts be one:
For our God is God alone.
Whose we are, and not our own;
We His people are—the sheep
He will ever rule and keep.

2 Come, and join the joyous throng,
Who Jehovah's praise proclaim;
In His courts, with grateful song,
Speak the honors of His name:
Rich His bounty to our race;
Inexhaustible His grace;
Ready to forgive and bless;
Ever sure His faithfulness .

2 Ye souls that are wounded, Oh flee to the Saviour :
He calls you in mercy—'tis infinite favor ;
Your sins are increasing ; escape to the mountain :
His blood can remove them, it flows from the fountain.
Hallelujah to the Lamb, who hath bought us a pardon !
We'll praise Him again, when we pass over Jordan.

3 When Zion we see, having gained the blest shore,
With harps in our hands, we will praise Him the more ;
We'll range the sweet plains on the banks of the river,
And sing of salvation for ever and ever !
Hallelujah to the Lamb, who hath bought us a pardon ;
We'll praise Him again, when we pass over Jordan.

INDEX OF TUNES.

INDEX OF SUBJECTS.

INDEX OF METERS.

INDEX OF FIRST LINES.

328 INDEX OF FIRST LINES.

Page.

Children of the heavenly King.*Cennick.* 230
Christ leads me through......*Baxter.* 118
Christ, of all my hopes......*Windham.* 220
Christ the Lord is risen to day......... 202
Christians, brethren ere we part. *White.* 220
Christians see! the orient......*Leland.* 255
Chosen not for good in me...*McCheyne.* 225
Come all ye saints of God.*Pratt's Coll.* 276
Come at the morning hour.*Briggs' Coll.* 164
Come children, come to God........... 156
Come, Desire of nations, come......... 221
Come Gracious Spirit...........*Brown.* 22
Come happy souls approach....*Watts.* 125
Come heavenly love........... *Steele.* 80
Come hither all ye weary souls .*Watts.* 44
Come, Holy Spirit, come....*Beddome.* 147
Come, Holy Spirit, come.....*Beddome.* 177
Come holy Spirit, heavenly Dove. *Watts.* 71
Come humble sinner...........*Jones.* 88
Come in thou blessed.....*Montgomery.* 144
Come, let our voices join to raise. *Watts.* 15
Come let our voices join............... 194
Come let us lift our joyful eyes.. *Watts.* 119
Come let us join............... *Watts.* 125
Come let us sing of Jesus ....*Bethune.* 265
Come Lord, in mercy comeagain...... 90
Come my soul, thy suit prepare.*Newton.* 228
Come O my soul...........*Blacklock.* 50
Come O ye saints...............*Steele.* 93
Come said Jesus' sacred voice.*Barbauld.* 203
Come sound his praise abroad... *Watts.* 162
Come Thou Almighty....*Madan Coll.* 276
Come thou desire...........*Steele.* 57
Come, Thou fount...........*Robinson.* 237
Come thou soul...........*Rippon's Coll.* 261
Come Thou long expected.*Madan Coll.* 241
Come to the land of Peace........... 150
Come to Calvary's holy..*Montgomery.* 236
Come up hither, come away....*Nevin.* 223
Come wandering sheep, O come........ 295
Come we who love the Lord.....*Watts.* 151
Come weary soul...............*Steele.* 40
Come ye disconsolate................. 298
Come ye sinners, poor and needy.*Hart.* 255
Come ye that know and fear the Lord.. 116
Crown his head....*Pratt's Collection.* 235

Day of Judgment, day of.....*Newton.* 263
Daughter of Zion! from..*Montgomery.* 89
Dark was the night and cold the ground. 141
Dear Father, to Thy mercy-seat. *Steele.* 93
Dear Lord and shall Thy........*Steele.* 17
Dear refuge of my weary soul... *Steele.* 102
Dear Saviour, ever at.. *Plymouth Coll.* 60
Dear Saviour, if these.. *Plymouth Coll.* 40
Dear Saviour, we are Thine. *Doddridge.* 178
Dearest of all the names above.. *Watts.* 85
Delay not, delay not.........*Hastings.* 291
Delightful work young.....*Strapham.* 136
Depth of mercy can there be.*C. Wesley.* 213
Descend from heaven...........*Watts.* 53
Did Christ o'er sinners weep..*Beddome.* 170

Page.

Dismiss us with Thy blessing......*Hest.* 44
Do not I love Thee.........*Doddridge.* 114
Dread Jehovah, God..*Epis. Collection.* 232
Dread Sovereign, let my........*Watts.* 57
Drooping souls no longer mourn....... 272
Dying souls fast buond in sin.......... 272

Early my God without delay.... *Watts.* 69
Earth has engrossed my love.... *Watts.* 137
Enthroned is Jesus now.......*Judkins.* 181
Eternal Father throned above. 11
Eternal Spirit we confess.......*Watts.* 32
Eternal Father, God of love.*C. Wesley.* 83
Eternal Spirit, God of truth........... 131
Exalted Prince of life......*Doddridge.* 10
Eternal Source of joys divine...*Steele.* 145

Faint not Christian though the road.... 206
Faith is the polar star....*Nason's Coll.* 201
Far as the isles extend ....*Goole.* 194
Far as Thy name is known.......*Watts.* 172
Far from mortal cares......*J. Taylor.* 240
Far from my thoughts vain.... *Watts.* 8
Far from the world O Lord...*Cowper.* 104
Far from these narrow scenes....*Steele.* 64
Far o'er the land the precious...*Smith.* 85
Father by Thy......*Nason's H. Book.* 263
Father of eternal grace...*Montgomery.* 218
Father of mercies in thy word...*Steele.* 87
Father of mercies, God of love.*Raffles.* 11
Father of the human race......*Collyer.* 205
Father, Son and Holy Ghost......... 202
Father, Thy paternal care....*Bowring.* 216
Father, whate'er of earthly bliss.*Steele.* 102
For a season called to part. ..*Newton.* 210
For mercies countless as......*Newton* 90
Forever here my rest shall. *C. Wesley.* 123
Forever with the Lord. ...*Montgomery.* 147
Friend after friend departs.*Montgomery.* 201
From all that dwell below......*Watts.* 54
From busy toil and heavy care......... 135
From deep distress and troubled *Watts.* 15
From every earthly pleasure....*Davis.* 270
From every stormy wind that..*Stowell.* 9
From foes that would the land...*Heber.* 286
From Greenland's icy...........*Heber.* 265
From lowest depths.....*Tate & Brady.* 160
From the cross uplifted high....*Hawes.* 224
From Thee my God...........*Watts.* 130
From the table now......*Exeter Coll.* 236
Full of trembling...........*C. Wesley.* 252

Gales from heaven.....*Plymouth Coll.* 209
Gently, gently lay thy rod........*Lyte.* 213
Gently Lord! O gently lead us......... 242
Gently Lord, O gently lead ...*Hastings.* 251
Gird on thy conquering....*Doddridge.* 194
Give me a sober mind.... .*C. Wesley.* 167
Give me the wings of faith.....*Watts.* 95
Give to the Father praise............. 153
Give to the winds thy fears. .*Gerhard.* 173

330   INDEX OF FIRST LINES.

SUPPLEMENT.

INDEX OF FIRST LINES, TUNES AND METERS.

www.ingramcontent.com/pod-product-compliance
Lightning Source LLC
Chambersburg PA
CBHW021120270326
41929CB00009B/968